Developmental Psychology and You

Developmental Psychology and You

SECOND EDITION

Julia C. Berryman
Pamela K. Smythe   Ann Taylor
Alexandra Lamont   Richard Joiner

BPS Blackwell

© 1991, 2002 by Julia C. Berryman, Pamela K. Smythe, Ann Taylor, Alexandra Lamont and Richard Joiner.

BLACKWELL PUBLISHING
350 Main Street, Malden, MA 02148-5020, USA
9600 Garsington Road, Oxford OX4 2DQ, UK
550 Swanston Street, Carlton, Victoria 3053, Australia

The right of Julia C. Berryman, Pamela K. Smythe, Ann Taylor, Alexandra Lamont and Richard Joiner to be identified as the Authors of this Work has been asserted in accordance with the UK Copyright, Designs and Patents Act 1988.

First edition published 1991 by BPS Books in association with Routledge Ltd
Second edition published 2002 by The British Psychological Society and Blackwell Publishing Ltd

2   2006

Library of Congress Cataloging-in-Publication Data has been applied for

ISBN-13: 978-0-631-23389-3 (hardback)
ISBN-10: 0-631-23389-X (hardback)
ISBN-13: 978-0-631-23390-9 (paperback)
ISBN-10: 0-631-23390-3 (paperback)

A catalogue record for this title is available from the British Library.

Set in 10/12½ pt Sabon
by Graphicraft Ltd, hong Kong

The publisher's policy is to use permanent paper from mills that operate a sustainable forestry policy, and which has been manufactured from pulp processed using acid-free and elementary chlorine-free practices. Furthermore, the publisher ensures that the text paper and cover board used have met acceptable environmental accreditation standards.

For further information on
Blackwell Publishing, visit our website:
www.blackwellpublishing.com

Contents

Start reading this book at the point, chapter or subheading that interests you most. Each chapter is fairly self-contained but refers you to other related chapters as appropriate. A glossary at the end of the book defines all the technical terms. We hope that by dipping in here and there you will soon find that you have read the whole book.

Note: bullet lists at the start of each chapter indicate main topics within each chapter but do not match all chapter subheadings exactly.

Exercises

Figures

Tables

Preface and Acknowledgements

Developmental Psychology and You is written for people with no previous knowledge of this subject. We have assumed that our readers will have only a small acquaintance with psychology – perhaps familiarity with an introductory text such as *Psychology and You*, but no more than this. Our aim is to whet our readers' appetite for the subject and to stimulate interest so that they will want to follow up and extend their knowledge of the topics discussed here. Space does not permit our book to be a comprehensive introduction to developmental psychology; we have had to be selective in the areas that we have chosen, and making such choices is always an invidious task. Our selection of topics has been based on our experience as teachers: we have taken those areas that we have found to be exciting and intriguing to our students and have presented the material in ways that we feel make the topics particularly relevant to everyday life. With this in mind we have included many exercises that we hope will stimulate interest in a very practical way. We have not adopted a uniform 'ages and stages' approach in each chapter, because we have tried to present each topic so that it is most accessible to new students. Psychological research within each area has not produced a uniform picture of development across the life span, and for this reason we have sometimes focused on a particular stage in life – the early years for example – whereas at other times a longer view has been explored or some particularly interesting research studies within a given area have been considered.

The new edition updates all those areas covered in the first edition, and two new chapters have been added. Chapter 11, 'Gender Development and Gender Differences', explores the controversial topic of how and why males and females differ. In the first edition only one chapter examined adult life and growing older. The new edition expands this topic into two chapters: chapter 14, 'Growing Older: Young and Middle Adulthood', and chapter 15, 'Growing Old'. These chapters explore development in later life, and the expansion of this section reflects the change in psychological thinking about human development; today there is a recognition that development and change occurs throughout life and not just in the early years. The new edition also includes more on cross-cultural perspectives, indicating that psychology needs to recognize the impact of culture on us all. Naturally we have not been able to cover everything, but we trust that what we have included will open mental doors and windows. If this is achieved then our aims have been fulfilled. The rest is up to you. The recommended reading and references are annotated to enable you to pursue your interest in what we hope will be a life-long enthusiasm for this subject.

Many people played a vital part in the preparation of this book. In particular we should like to mention Philip Drew, Eric Berryman, Ken Smythe and Roy Davies, who have given much support and made many helpful comments on drafts of the manuscript; Tom Drew and Mark, Adam and Ben Smythe for their good nature, help and patience during the writing phase; also the Davies and Harrill families and John Mack Bennett for allowing us to use the photographs in chapters 14 and 15. We should like to thank Isabel Woodliffe, Joan Garrity and Damla Aras for help in preparing the final manuscript, and last but not least the many students whose queries and comments have been a major stimulus for producing this book. Our grateful thanks to them all.

JULIA C. BERRYMAN

The authors and publishers gratefully acknowledge the sources in the captions for permission to reproduce copyright material. We apologize for any errors or omissions and would be grateful to be notified of any corrections that should be incorporated in the next edition or reprint of this book.

1

What is Developmental Psychology?

- What is normal development?
- Methods in the study of development
- Experiments in psychology
- Asking questions and forming hypotheses
- Ethical issues

Psychology is about people: their thoughts, feelings and behaviour; developmental psychology is concerned with exploring development and change in thoughts, feelings and behaviour across the lifespan. Most books on developmental psychology focus on the early years of life, because we expect children to change, and there is wide acceptance that what happens in the early part of life is crucially influential for later development, as the following sayings indicate.

> And the first step, as you know, is always what matters most, particularly when
> we are dealing with those who are young and tender.
> *Plato, 428–348 BC*

> Train up a child in the way he should go: and when he is old,
> he will not depart from it.
> *Bible, Proverbs 26:22*

> Give me a child for the first seven years and you may do what you like
> with him afterwards.
> *Attributed to the Jesuits; see Lean, 1903*

> The Child is father of the Man.
> *William Wordsworth, 1770–1850*

The essence of all these sayings is that the early years not only lay the foundations of the person; they also shape every aspect of that person, making him or her what he or she will become. There is a sense in which this is irrevocable, that it may be difficult or impossible to alter someone once he or she has been formed in a particular way:

> But once a child's character has been spoiled by bad handling, which can be done in a few days, who can say that the damage is ever repaired?
>
> *John B. Watson, 1878–1958*

> As the twig is bent the tree's inclined.
>
> *Alexander Pope, 1688–1744*

> You cannot teach an old dog new tricks.
>
> *Old proverb*

However, in recent years books on adult or lifespan development have burgeoned. While there may be continuity across the lifespan, change can occur at any point in life as a result of a variety of different influences.

Biology is perhaps the most obvious agent of change, because we know we are programmed to mature at a particular rate: puberty is a period of great change which is timed by our *biological clock*, but even this event is shaped by environmental factors. Poor diet or excessive exercise, such as is seen in gymnasts, may delay puberty.

Our lives are also shaped by *social clocks* – expectations about when things should to occur in our own particular culture. Events such as when we start or leave school, marry and have children, engage in paid work or retire are all culturally defined. In fact, the influence of culture shapes our lives in a multitude of ways, from our ideologies and beliefs down to what may seem trivial day-to-day matters such as our body language – do we shake hands, hug or rub noses with a new acquaintance?

Finally, we all feel unique and we all have unique, non-shared experiences in life which change us in ways that are hard to predict. The death of a loved one, surviving a disaster or meeting a specific person at a particular point in time may all act as personal turning points that can, at any stage in life, make us different people. The task of the developmental psychologist is to try to understand how all these different influences may shape human development.

Studying development

Studying psychological development is a rather recent phenomenon, and the bulk of this work has been carried out since the beginning of the twentieth century. Before this period there was some recognition of the importance of the early years. The historian Philippe Aries (1962) claimed that the idea that childhood is an important and valuable period is probably only a couple of hundred years old.

Charles Darwin was one of the first to keep a detailed baby biography, a diary of one of his sons, Doddy, from birth, which he published in 'A biographical sketch of an infant'. This was more than just notes on his son's behaviour. He also reflected on the possible reasons for what had occurred. In 1891 Stanley Hall published his 'Notes on the study of infants', and he recorded 'the contents of children's minds' by asking children numerous questions. Thus began the systematic study of infancy and childhood.

One of the advantages of studying psychological development is that it enables us to find out what is normal. Most of us like to consider that we are normal, average or fairly typical of people in general, and we can be surprised to discover that someone thinks or feels very differently from us.

Development psychology has provided data which show the range of behaviour, thoughts and feelings typical for any particular population, at any particular time. Thus it may show that thumb sucking, temper tantrums, nightmares and nail biting are all fairly normal at a certain age, because a high proportion of children show these patterns. So what might be viewed as problematic by new parents encountering these in their first child is seen quite differently when put in the context of children's behaviour in general.

Once we have established norms for development within a particular culture, we can then see how particular events may change or shape the individual. For example, we can compare different family structures (the nuclear family, the single parent family, the extended family and so on) to see how they may influence child development.

Development psychology enables us to assess the truth about a range of common assertions about people.

Leave her to cry – if you pick her up you'll only spoil her.

Children need their mothers more than anyone; a father can never provide the special care that a mother can.

There is no substitute for stable family life; children from broken homes are bound to suffer.

Boys are more boisterous and aggressive than girls: it's in their nature.

There is no harm in the occasional smack if a child has been naughty.

He's always been bad-tempered, you'll never change him.

Second children are always more competitive.

Children grow up too quickly these days; it's not good for them.

Childhood is the happiest time of life. Children don't have problems.

Developmental psychologists have devised methods which enable us to investigate the truth of these statements. This also means that we have a much better idea today of the conditions which foster optimum psychological growth and well-being, and if these are not present we also know what to do to compensate.

Developmental psychology has a key role to play if we are to understand ourselves and others better. Understanding the course of human life and the factors which shape the developing person is a cornerstone of psychology, but studying human development is not quite as straightforward as it may, at first, appear to be.

What is normal development?

We all have our own ideas about what people are like at different ages. Two-year-olds have a reputation for being 'terrible', young teenagers troublesome, and students in their late teens idealistic, politically active and so on. If one observes people at different ages it is easy to begin to link physical growth to various types of psychological change. Thus one can derive a picture of *age-related norms*, of what is normal for a given age. However, it has become apparent from research over the last century that the 'normal' course of growth has changed dramatically in a matter of decades.

The age at which puberty is reached is a good example. As boys and girls reach *puberty* (physical maturity), we generally expect psychological changes to accompany the physical changes that take place over some years: the period of adolescence. A growing interest in the opposite sex is the one obvious change, but we also expect a greater maturity of outlook to be linked to this stage. In the 1860s girls in the UK were on average aged 16 or more at menarche (the start of menstruation). For anyone studying development the natural conclusion might be that girls take about 16 years to reach physical maturity, the age when they can become mothers. However, during the past 140 years the age at menarche has dropped, and today it occurs on average at about $12\frac{1}{2}$ years. So what has happened? How can a biological timetable speed up so rapidly in such a short period? After all, if this rate continued for just a few more centuries the ludicrous outcome would be menstruating newborns! It is not just the age of puberty that has changed: growth rates in two- to five-year-olds are markedly faster today, and full adult height is achieved much earlier than in previous decades and centuries.

The explanation put forward has been that greatly improved nutrition, general health and living conditions have accelerated the rate of growth. James Tanner argues that there is always a biological limit for accelerated development, and he believes that we are unlikely to see a continued decline in the age at menarche. Perhaps the social conditions of today are so much better than those of a century ago that it may be easier to explain by saying that poor diet and health impede and slow down growth, and that much of the Western world now has optimum conditions for children's growth and development.

But what are the implications of this for developmental psychologists? If physical and psychological development are linked then our picture of the 12-year-old girl of today is quite different from that of only a century ago. The same applies to boys. In medieval Europe then the adult male was the size of the average 10- to 12-year-old American boy of today – we know this from the size of knights' armour (see Muuss). Yet although our notion of the age of adulthood has altered, it has certainly not kept pace with the accelerated growth rates discussed here. We may be shocked at the idea of a 12-year-old girl marrying and having a child, yet it is likely that a 16-year-old who did so a hundred years ago did not differ so greatly either physically or psychologically from a 12-year-old today.

To return to one of the functions of developmental psychology – to define age-related norms – we can see that age *per se* may not necessarily be a helpful guide. In underdeveloped countries of today menarche occurs much later than in developed countries, so we need to take social conditions into account if we are to explain human development. Let us now briefly explore how psychological research into development is carried out.

Methods in the Study of Development

Longitudinal and cross-sectional studies

The quickest way of answering the question 'how do people change as they get older?' is to do a *cross-sectional study*. To investigate how learning ability changes with age, for example, we might devise a series of learning tests and, in a controlled setting, invite groups of 10-, 20-, 30-, 40-, 50-, 60- and 70-year-olds to take the tests, allowing a specified time only. Our participants would be selected so that education, socioeconomic status and health would be matched across the age groups. The result of this study would be quite likely to show that people in their twenties have the greatest learning ability, and that as age increases a slight decline occurs initially and then more markedly in the upper age groups. So could we conclude from this that learning abilities decline after the age of 20? Let us leave this question unanswered while we contrast the cross-sectional study with the longitudinal study.

A *longitudinal study* is designed so that individuals are tested or assessed in some way at regular intervals over a period of their lives. In order to study learning ability a sample of individuals would be tested at, for instance, age 20, then tested again 10 years later at 30, and then again after a further 10 years in the final test at 40 years. Thus each participant would be tested three times over 20 years. In this study the three tests given to the participant would have to be similar, but they should not be identical or the experimenter might be accused of simply observing the practice effect (an improvement due merely to repeating the same task).

What results might be recorded after 20 years? Would they be the same as those found for the cross-sectional study? It might reveal a decline in the two last tests, but it is more likely to show little change with age, or even an increase in ability. So two procedures, apparently designed to answer the same question, give us quite different answers. Which one is right?

To put it simply: neither test is measuring age alone, and thus each has quite specific problems. Historical events affecting some or all the participants, as well as the individual life experiences unique to each participant, may have a greater impact on the characteristic being measured by the psychologist than age itself. Resolving these and other problems is complex, and the final chapter of this book considers Warner Schaie's solution.

Although developmental psychology is concerned with people throughout their lives, many of the research studies discussed in this book concentrate on explaining behaviour within a relatively limited time period. For example, chapter 2 on perception describes work that has looked at changes in olfactory or visual perception over a matter of days, weeks or months within the first year of life. Often when studying one such age group in detail psychologists use the experimental method.

Experiments in psychology

The essence of the experimental method is that the psychologists can investigate how some aspect of behaviour is changed by a given factor which is thought to influence it. To take an example, in 1960 Orvis Irwin investigated what effect reading to children had on their language development. He devised a simple experiment in which 24 children aged 13 months were read to by their mothers for 15–20 minutes a day until the age of 30 months. The mothers of a second group of 10 children, matched on the basis of their fathers' occupational status, received no instructions about special reading, but were treated otherwise exactly as the experimental group. It was common for a family's socioeconomic status to be defined by the husband's occupation; hence a woman's status was taken as that of her husband.

The first group, the *experimental group*, is the group exposed to the variable which the psychologist believes may influence language development. This variable is 'being read to', and the psychologist thus varies the amount of 'being read to' in the two groups. We call the variable that is being manipulated by the psychologists the *independent variable*, and the behaviour which it is thought to affect is the *dependent variable* – in this case language development. Language development was measured by recording the children's spontaneous speech (the types of sound made and their frequency) assessed at two-monthly intervals throughout the study. The children who were not exposed to the independent variable (being read to) formed what is called the *control group*. They provided a baseline with which the experimental group's language development could be compared.

Experiments allow us to infer a cause and effect relationship. Thus in Irwin's study we can see the effect of 'being read to' on language development; he found that being read to did accelerate language development, because the experimental group were soon ahead of the controls when measures of language development were compared. Consistent differences became evident from about 17 months. (See chapter 6 for further discussion of language development.)

Asking questions and forming hypotheses

Before embarking on a rigorously controlled experiment it is necessary to make sure that the questions asked are sensible ones not wildly at odds with common-sense views. It would be unwise not to make preliminary observations of the behaviour you are interested in or to observe children or adults in situations relevant to the type of question posed. For instance, in the above example young children would need to be observed in their first months and years, and some knowledge of how much exposure they had to books and being read to would have to be gleaned, before an experiment was devised. However, common sense varies. For instance:

> Rushing to pick up baby when she cries just encourages her to fuss more.

> Responding quickly to your baby's cries makes for a happier baby who cries less.

At different points in the last four decades both these views have been forcefully propounded, to the confusion of new parents. Psychologists interested in investigating the role of picking up in encouraging or discouraging crying would start by *observing* parents and infants to see whether clues could be found to the truth of either statement. From these observations a hypothesis would be generated:

> Responding quickly to infants' cries by picking them up reduces the total number of crying bouts in a given period, compared with infants who are left for some moments before being picked up.

Lynn Johnston, from *David We're Pregnant*, Cressrelles Publishing Co. Ltd, Malvern

This hypothesis is a prediction of what the psychologist thinks may happen.

The psychologist is now in a position to plan a controlled experiment in which babies, matched on a variety of variables such as age, socioeconomic factors and so on, are exposed to different treatment regimes varying in the interval between the onset of crying and being picked up.

If the research shows that babies picked up quickly over a given period start crying less often, then our hypothesis could be accepted. But if the babies picked up after a longer period start crying less overall then the hypothesis would have to be rejected. However, if there is no consistent pattern of results, or if some babies cried more often and some cried less often, the psychologist might conclude that the approach had been too simplistic. A different sort of hypothesis might be required, which could, for instance, take into account temperamental factors in the infants, or the parents' style of picking up.

Reading about this hypothetical experiment you may find yourself thinking 'I wouldn't dream of leaving a baby of mine to cry for ten minutes just for the sake of a psychological experiment.' This raises the important and very difficult question of ethics in research.

Ethical issues in research

Just because a psychologist comes up with an interesting hypothesis does not mean he or she is entitled to test it. There are many areas of human development which, for ethical reasons, we could not investigate experimentally. The British Psychological Society has detailed guidelines for researchers to help them plan their investigations which recognize that the rights of the human participants, and their welfare, are paramount. Although the degree of distress, pain or inconvenience might be considered minimal in relation to the benefits that would accrue if a given experiment were carried out, the people who volunteer to participate in it must always be free to drop out if they wish to, even if the ethical guidelines permit a particular area of study.

A number of topics that are not investigated in humans on ethical grounds have been explored in non-human animals. The importance of parents, and in particular of mothers, has been a question continually probed by psychologists, yet no experiment would be contemplated which involved taking a child from its mother for a prolonged period solely for experimental purposes. We have to rely for our data on this from naturally occurring situations in which children and parents are parted.

Nevertheless, among non-human animals Harry Harlow did investigate empirically how baby rhesus monkeys coped without their mothers (see chapter 3). Guidelines for animal experimentation are also available: the Society for the Study of Animal Behaviour issues guidelines for researchers, and the Home Office is the ultimate control for research in this area in the UK. Regulations are being tightened up continually, and many psychologists of today feel revulsion at some of the studies carried out in the past.

Thus in some important areas in human life we may never be able to be truly 'scientific' in our methods of investigation.

Other research methods

The experimental method is not always appropriate as a means of answering questions about behaviour. We cannot always manipulate the independent variable so that two groups of participants differ only in the presence or absence of this variable (or the amount of this variable).

The study of sex and gender is a case in point. Suppose we think that maleness is associated with certain characteristics and femaleness with others, and we believe that 'sex' hormones may be responsible for the differences observed, we cannot run an experiment in which male or female sex hormones are used as the independent variable on two otherwise identical groups. We all have a biological sex of one sort or the other – no one is neutral – so hormones have, from before birth, influenced our development. All that is possible is to correlate behaviour patterns with each sex (i.e. show an association between them), but this tells us nothing about *causal* differences. An example may explain this better. In Britain males are traditionally encouraged not to cry when they are hurt, upset or distressed. Observers, ignorant of this British characteristic, might thus correlate crying with femaleness and not crying with maleness. If they believed that biological sex played a causal role in this difference they might suggest that the adult human male is unable to cry – his hormones make crying impossible!

Used and interpreted correctly, *correlational studies* have an important place among the methods available to psychologists, and there are many other methods and techniques, which are explained in the final chapter. Methodology is often described by those new to psychology as uninteresting, and, although its place is fundamental in exploring developmental psychology, we propose to postpone further discussion until later and start by examples. Each chapter describes one particular area of interest and concern to developmental psychologists. Just how questions about behaviour, thoughts and feelings have been investigated will become clear. The importance of the methods available is often lost until we try to answer a particular question within psychology, so we shall now turn to some of those questions.

What next?

Let us start at the beginning. Our earlier years are widely viewed as laying the foundations of who and what we are, and experiences in the first few years may have long-lasting influence. So how do the foetus and newborn experience the world through their senses? Can they hear, see and smell as we adults can? If not, what sense can they make of the world? How soon does a baby recognize its mother? Do babies prefer some sorts of visual, olfactory and auditory stimulations over others? Psychologists are beginning to find some of the answers.

Recommended Reading

Berryman, J. C., Hargreaves, D. J., Howells, K. and Ockleford, E. (1997) *Psychology and You: An Informal Introduction*. Leicester: BPS Books. [See the introduction and chapter 12 for a discussion of 'what is psychology?' and methodology.]

Colman, A. M. (1999) *What is Psychology? The Inside Story*. London: Routledge. [Excellent book explaining what psychology is through numerous examples.]

Messer, D. and Dockrell, J. (eds) (1998) *Developmental Psychology: A Reader*. London: Arnold. [Most interesting collection of core articles, useful for the person who wants to delve more deeply into the topics covered in the chapters in this book.]

References

Aries, P. (1962) *Centuries of Childhood*. London: Jonathan Cape. [Historical attitudes to children.]

ASAB/ABS (1997) *Guidelines for the Treatment of Animals in Behavioural Research and Teaching*. London: ASAB. [Guidelines for animal research.]

Darwin, C. R. (1877) A biographical sketch of an infant. *Mind*, 2, 28–294. [Description of Doddy's behaviour.]

Code of Conduct, Ethical Principles and Guidelines (2000) Leicester: British Psychological Society. [Guidelines for research in psychology.]

Hall, G. S. (1891) Notes on the study of infants. *The Pedagogical Seminary*, 1, 127–38. [One of the first systematic studies of children.]

Harlow, H. F. (1958) The nature of love. *American Psychologist*, 13, 673–85. [Infant monkeys reared without their mothers.]

Irwin, O. C. (1960) Infant speech: effect of systematic reading of stories. *Journal of Speech and Hearing Research*, 3(2), 187–90. [Experiments on reading to babies.]

Lean, V. S. (1903) *Lean's Collectanea*, vol. 3. Bristol: J. W. Arrowsmith. [Quotation attributed to the Jesuits.]

Muuss, R. E. (1970) Adolescence development and the secular trend. *Adolescence*, 5, 267–86. [Medieval knights' armour fits boys of 10–12 today.]

Schaie, K. W. (1975) Age changes in adult intelligence. In D. S. Woodruff and J. E. Birren (eds), *Aging: Scientific Perspects and Social Issues*. New York: Van Nostrand. [Longitudinal and cross-sectional studies compared.]

Tanner, J. M. (1978) *Foetus into Man*. London: Open Books. [Age at menarche.]

2

First Views of the World

- When does perception start?
- Vision in infants
- Research studies on infant perception
- Critical periods in perceptual development

One great blooming, buzzing confusion
The infant's world according to William James (1890)

New parents may wonder to what extent their baby can make sense of the world – is everything as confusing as William James thought, or is the baby born with rather more competence in perception than his view suggests?

This chapter focuses on perception rather than sensation, but first we must make clear the nature of these two. Being able to sense the environment means that the infant can respond to sensations – the sensory receptors detect and transmit information to the brain. Perception is more than this, because it is the interpretation of sensory input by the brain, recognizing what the stimulation is – the mother's voice, her face and so on.

It is often said by those who care for a new baby – usually the mother, in our society – that a baby knows its own mother very early on, can distinguish her from others and prefers her. Indeed, many mothers comment that their babies can distinguish between different sounds even before birth, and anecdotes about the noises, or tunes, that babies like in the womb are common.

All of us know that the premature (or pre-term) baby born just three or four weeks early is not a creature totally different from the full-term baby. The baby's eyes are open, and in terms of its awareness of the world it does not seem much less mature than one born on time. Does this mean that the foetus can experience sensations inside the womb, and, if so, in what way can it make sense of that dark and watery world before birth? Studies of pre-term babies and babies *in utero* have provided some of the answers, as we shall see.

Philosophers and psychologists have long been intrigued by the question 'Are babies born with some built-in abilities to organize or make sense of the stimuli impinging on their sense organs, or must they learn to make sense of their world by trial and error?' The two opposing views come from the nativists and the empiricists. Nativists argue that the baby's senses work like the adult's, and once the baby opens its eyes it can see much as we adults do – perceiving objects, space, distance and so on. Empiricists would argue that only through experience of the world can the baby really perceive it as adults do, and that at birth the notion that a baby can distinguish an object from the background, or recognize the object as close by rather than at a distance, is meaningless. As we shall see, research has thrown considerable light on this debate, and like so many situations in which views are polarized, both views are in fact right to some extent. The baby is programmed to a degree, but experience also plays a vital role in perception.

Before we consider the research findings on infant perception let us consider how we carry out this type of research.

Studying Visual Perception

Babies have few well-coordinated movements, so carrying out research on infant perception has particular problems; but psychologists have devised some intriguing ways to get round this difficulty. For example, we know that infants look at some parts of their environment for longer periods than other parts, and researchers have realized that by recording patterns of attention this might reveal more about the way in which the infant sees the world.

The preference method

By recording what an infant looks at, and the time spent looking at a given stimulus, researchers can show whether or not the infant can discriminate between stimuli. Typically in this sort of research the experimenter presents two different visual stimuli side by side and observes whether these two measures vary in relation to each stimulus. If the baby looks at one target much more than the other it is argued that it can distinguish them, and prefers one to the other. The stimuli need not be visual ones – the baby's head turning towards an odour can reveal a preference equally well.

The habituation–dishabituation method

Researchers have found that by varying the degree of novelty or familiarity of a stimulus, they can learn about an infant's ability to discriminate. One way of doing this is to give a baby many repeated exposures to a single visual stimulus until a decline in looking is observed. The infant seems to have become bored with looking at the same old thing: it is said to have habituated to the stimulus. If at this point a new stimulus is presented, one that the infant can perceive as different, the baby then perks up, and the attention score goes up. This procedure, called the habituation–dishabituation method, enables psychologists to compare a variety of stimuli, differing in various ways, and through recording a baby's attention we can gain some insight into the degree of difference that a given baby can perceive.

The use of reinforcement

In this method a particular response of the infant, such as head turning, is rewarded by the researcher. Tom Bower used as a reward, or reinforcer, an adult playing peek-a-boo every time the infant turned its head in one particular direction. Once the infant has learned this head turning response the experimenter can then go on to reward head turning only when one particular stimulus is present. Subsequently the stimulus can be changed slightly, and it is then possible to find out whether the baby can distinguish the two stimuli. Does the baby's head turn equally for both stimuli and hence behave as if both are the same, or does the baby discriminate between the two stimuli and head turn only for the original?

A variation on this method uses the sucking response of the infant. A newborn baby spends a lot of time sucking, and the rate of sucking may vary. The researcher can reward the faster sucking rate by the presentation of the stimulus. Infants can exert control over their sucking rate, and if a particular stimulus is always associated with this rate of sucking an infant will learn that this rate of sucking will produce this particular stimulus. Thus the infant can control the amount of time the stimulus is presented. If fast sucking occurs more often in relation to stimulus A than in relation to stimulus B we can infer that the baby can discriminate between the two stimuli. This method has been used by Anthony DeCasper and William Fifer with auditory stimuli.

The methods described above enable psychologists to learn a great deal about the way the infant perceives its environment and the preferences shown for particular stimuli.

Perception *In Utero* and in the Neonate

Auditory perception

The auditory system of the human foetus is functional at about 30 weeks conceptual age, or ten weeks before the birth of the full-term baby, but sound may be experienced by the foetus (in the womb) or the pre-term baby earlier than 30 weeks in the form of vibrations.

Studies by Elizabeth Ockleford show that a full-term baby is pacified by a metronome beat like its own heart beat (144 beats per minute), but not by one at the rate of its mother's heart beat (72 beats per minute). Research shows that babies born at least ten weeks *before* term are not similarly pacified, suggesting that the full-term baby's ten weeks of experience of its own heart rate may account for this. The maternal heart beat is not always audible to infants, as was thought by Lee Salk and others. Ockleford also showed that newborns can discriminate their own mother's voice from other voices when under 24 hours old. She found that newborns showed an 'orienting' response (heart rate deceleration) to the mother's voice which was not shown to other voices, and she also linked this response to auditory experience *in utero*.

Anthony DeCasper and William Fifer also showed that a newborn (under three days of age) could distinguish between its own mother's voice and the voice of a stranger. Infants could control which voice they heard by non-nutritive sucking on a teat. The sucking rate of the infant (fast or slow) determined which of two auditory stimuli was played during sucking; these stimuli were the mother's voice and a stranger's voice. Half the infants' mothers' voices were linked to the fast sucking rate and half to the slow rate, and the reverse for the strange mother. Over a 20-minute test infants learned to produce the sucking rate that was associated with their mothers' voice, in preference to the strange mothers' voice. Since the babies were less than a day old this study showed either very rapid learning or, a more likely explanation, that the mother's voice was familiar to the infant from the experience of it in the womb. DeCasper and Melanie Spence subsequently showed that infants sucked more to hear a story that they had been exposed to before birth (their mothers had been asked to read a story out loud, twice a day for six weeks before they gave birth), than to hear an unfamiliar story. This preference occurred even when the familiar story was read by a stranger. This study provides good evidence for prenatal learning.

Olfactory perception

Adam Macfarlane in 1975 was the first to demonstrate that babies recognize their own mothers' breast odours. In this research odourized and unscented cotton pads were presented to each baby in the study by suspending the pads on either the side of the baby's face while the baby was lying faces upwards. One pad had been worn over the baby's mother's breast and the other pad was a clean control pad. Significantly more breastfed babies aged 2–7 days spent a long time with their faces turned in the direction of the breast odour. Subsequently experiments of a similar type showed that breast odours from lactating women elicit preferential orientation when paired with a variety of alternative scents. In general it seems that chemical odours from the breast region are particularly salient for infants.

Michael Russell explored babies' responses more fully, testing babies at two days, two weeks and six weeks after birth. In this study Russell looked at the baby's sucking movements in response to a milky smell. Babies show this response even when asleep, which is quite convenient for the researcher. In this study pads of different olfactory characteristics, such as the 'mother's' pad (placed inside her bra for three hours), the 'strange mother's' pad (treated in the same way as the mother's) and a 'control' clean but moist pad, were used.

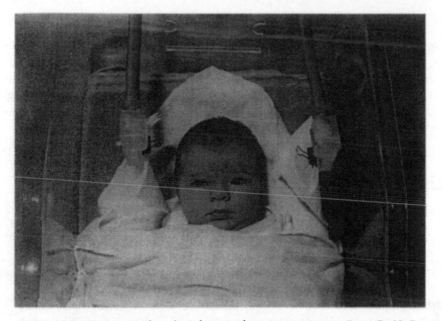

Figure 2.1   *A baby being tested in the odour preference experiment. From R. H. Porter, Advances in Infantry Research, Ablex Publishing Corp., 1988. Courtesy of Richard Porter and colleagues*

The sucking reflex was shown in response to both mothers' pads in babies at all ages tested, but by six weeks all the babies showed a more marked sucking response to their own mothers' pads – indicating a preference for the familiar odour. Using a procedure similar to Macfarlane's, Richard Porter and Jan Winberg tested babies' responses to a range of other odours associated with the mother – such as underarm (or axillary) odours and artificial scents worn by the mother. In the latter case it was shown that infants in tests conducted one or two weeks after birth showed a preference for the familiar maternal scent rather than a novel one (see figure 2.1).

Richard Porter and Jan Winberg believe that babies' responsiveness to maternal breast odours may reflect exposure to similar substances prior to birth, because it is known that the odour of amniotic fluid resembles that of breast secretions. Indeed, in tests beginning only a few minutes after birth newborn babies have been shown to spontaneously select (suck from) a breast treated with a small amount of their own amniotic fluid applied to the breast area. The attraction to the nipple/areola was likely to be based more on olfactory cues than on taste, since the babies oriented to the breast first before sucking occurred. However, the attraction to amniotic fluid is transient, because at 2–5 days postpartum babies no longer displayed a reliable preference for the breast treated with amniotic fluid. Porter and Winberg argue that this attraction to the odour of the amniotic fluid suggests that foetal learning occurs which influences responsiveness after birth. It has been demonstrated that young rats and rabbits whose mothers had eaten strongly flavoured food in pregnancy responded more positively to these dietary odours postnatally than control pups, because it is known that aromatic substances in the mother's diet can taint the amniotic fluid. Pilot research on humans has shown that mothers who change their diet abruptly after delivery – thereby lessening the degree of prenatal–postnatal olfactory continuity – experienced increased difficulty in establishing breast-feeding. Thus foetal learning can play an important role in facilitating breastfeeding after birth.

Exercise 2.1

Can You Smell the Difference?

Research studies show that our sense of smell is quite acute and that, as we saw earlier, babies can identify odours associated with their own mothers (milk smells and axillary odours) very soon after birth. Since you are unlikely to have access to newborn babies this test uses adult participants, ideally no older than about 40 years and non-smokers (because researchers find that older adults and smokers are less sensitive to odours – see the chapter by Schiffman in Gregory and Colman, 1995, in the recommended reading).

PROCEDURE

For this exercise you will need a small group of males and females, a blindfold (a scarf will do) and a pack of disposable rubber gloves (one per person) or some clean polythene bags. Before this exercise all participants should be asked to wash their hands in the same, non-scented soap, and they should then place one hand in the glove (or bag tied round the wrist) for 15 minutes, both before the exercise and in between trials, so that the hand is perspiring on presentation.

The purpose of the trial is to see whether the participant can distinguish between pairs of hands that are randomly male–male, female–female and female–male. Once blindfolded each participant should stand about one arm's length from the person presenting the 'stimulus hand'. In the first trial the participant should be presented with each person's hand, in turn, placed 1 cm beneath the nose and palm upwards. Thus a participant may be told that hand A is male, hand B is female, hand C is female, hand D is male (do not identify individuals). When each hand has been sniffed once, the trial can begin. The participant should be presented with two hands, one following the other, and, having sniffed both, asked to say whether the hands are from the same sex or from opposite sexes, and if possible whether they belong to males or females. Pairs of hands should be presented in varying combinations, over 15 trials, allowing five presentations of each of male–male, female–female and female–male combinations (using only one male and one female for this latter task). The participants can be informed after each trial whether they are correct in saying 'same' or 'different', and their responses should be recorded. The participants who achieve 11 successful trials or more out of 15 are deemed to be able to discriminate.

Repeat the exercise with a new blindfolded participant and a new combination of hands. When you have tested as many people as you can, compare the female and male success rates. Generally females perform better than males.

COMMENT

This exercise is based loosely on an experiment by Patricia Wallace (1977) and lacks many of the features of her very carefully controlled study. Consider how you could improve the design of this exercise. For example, Wallace had the stimulus hands placed through a slot in a box into which the participant placed his or her head. In our study participants must be silent; this ensures that no other clues reveal the person to which the hand belongs, so that the olfactory clues are the salient ones.

Vision in Infants

No parents would doubt that their newborn infant can see something of the world, but exactly how well he or she sees has been a matter of debate for many decades. William James's views of the infant's world given at the start of this chapter are far from the reality. Babies do not see just as adults do, but psychologists are continually being surprised as evidence accumulates about the newborn's and young infant's abilities, and this has led to the notion of the 'competent infant' in relation to perceptual abilities.

The baby's eye is, of course, smaller than the adult's, and the immaturity of the whole nervous system affects the optic nerve and hence the efficiency with which visual information is transmitted. The retina, and the rods and cones, are fairly well developed at birth, so there is no obvious area where we might expect major deficits. The newborn's natural focal length is about 17 cm so we should expect that stimuli close to the baby are likely to be seen more easily than those at some distance.

Lynn Johnston, from *David We're Pregnant*, Cressrelles Publishing Co. Ltd, Malvern

Alan Slater has compared the newborn's visual acuity to that of the adult cat – it is between 10 and 30 times poorer than that of adult humans, which means that fine lines are much harder for babies to perceive and appear as a blurred grey. The infant's field of view is also more restricted. Objects are most likely to be looked at by a baby of 0–5 months if they fall within the range 25–30° to the left or right of centre, 10° above or below the line of sight, and within 90 cm of the baby. Babies also require stimuli of high contrast if their attention is to be gained. If this sounds as if the baby is likely to be rather unresponsive, this is not the case, as every mother knows. Babies seem particularly interested in faces, as we shall see, and it is argued that they may have an in-built predisposition to respond to them.

Seeing colour

Adults see in colour, so it is likely that most of us assume that babies also can. Is this true? Russell Adams tells us that newborns are able to distinguish some colour and thus are using cone receptors (the receptors on which colour vision depends), although it is not certain whether infants are using all three cone types. There is a suggestion that information from the cone type sensitive to blue may be lacking in babies earlier on. Research by Angela Brown reveals that infants can distinguish all the basic colours when they are 2 months old.

Pattern perception

Using a 'looking chamber', Robert Fantz carried out a series of now famous studies, which were published in 1961. Fantz recorded the amount of time babies spent looking at various stimuli (he was able to see what was reflected in a baby's eye and hence know exactly what was being observed – today more sophisticated methods of recording the infants' gaze are available, using video film, for example).

Fantz tested infants aged 1–15 weeks on a series of paired stimuli differing in complexity. These were two identical triangles, a cross and a circle, a chequer board, two sizes of a plain square, horizontal stripes and a bull's eye design. Babies spent longer looking at parts of the more complex stimuli, and within each pair the more patterned stimulus of the two was fixated for longer. He also studied the perception of stripes and showed that infants under one month of age could perceive 3 mm stripes (at 25 cm distance from the baby) and that by 6 months stripes of less than 0.5 mm could be distinguished.

In a further series of experiments Fantz included face-like stimuli and, as we shall see, found that babies were very interested in these.

Face perception and recognition

The duration of fixation was also recorded when a further selection of stimuli were used by Fantz. He compared three plain coloured discs (red, yellow and white), a bull's-eye pattern, a disc of newsprint and a stylized face in black and white and again found a preference for patterns over plain, and the face was preferred most. In another study three face-like stimuli were used (see figure 2.2); these were a stylized 'real' face, a 'scrambled' face (i.e. an equally complex pattern but lacking the resemblance to a face) and a control pattern in which the same amount of black was used as was present in the other two stimuli. All the stimuli were black on a pink background. As can be seen in the figure, babies aged from 4 days to 6 months all preferred the more complex patterns, the real and scrambled faces, the real face being fixated slightly, but not significantly, longer. Fantz suggested that children may have an innate preference for faces, but could the symmetry of the stylized face have given rise to the slight preference shown for it over the scrambled face?

Daphne Maurer and Maria Barrera developed Fantz's ideas by using a symmetrical scrambled face and a non-symmetrical scrambled face, as well as the stylized real face. Babies of one month did not show a preference, but at two months the real face was preferred; thus symmetry alone did not explain Fantz's findings. Exercise 2.2 is based on Maurer and Barrera's research – if you have a baby in the family why not try it out?

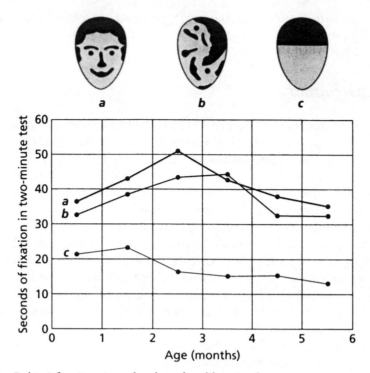

Figure 2.2   *Babies' fixation times for three face-like stimuli*

Exercise 2.2

Visual Preferences in Infants

This experiment is a simplified version of that run by Daphne Maurer and Maria Barrera described above. The participants are babies aged 0–6 months.

PROCEDURE

Photocopy and enlarge to 10 cm diameter the three stimuli (a), (b) and (c) in figure 2.3 or draw three circles with a 10 cm diameter on a piece of white card and follow the instructions below.

- On the first circle draw in black a simple stylized face such as that shown in *figure* 2.3(a).
- On the second circle draw a scrambled version of this face as shown in (b).

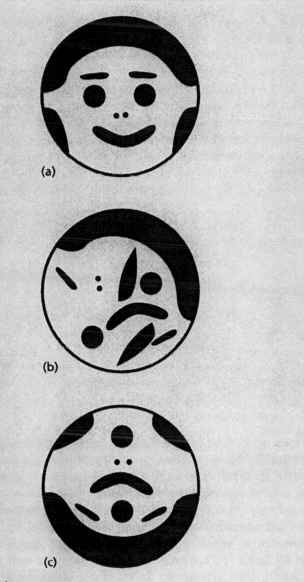

(a)

(b)

(c)

Figure 2.3   *Stimuli for exercise 2.2*

- On the third circle draw a second scrambled version of the face as in (c), but this time rearrange the features symmetrically, as shown.

Cut the stimulus circles out.

Test as many infants as you can, giving each infant three tests, (for example ab, ac, bc), randomly pairing the stimuli in all combinations.

Each pair of stimuli should be presented to the baby simultaneously for 60 seconds. The stimuli may be attached to each end of a 30 cm ruler and the ruler should be held about 30 cm from the baby's face, so that its centre is directly in front of the baby's eyes. For infants under about one month the stimuli may need to be held slightly closer to the head (18 cm away). Record the amount of time the baby fixates each stimulus over a 60-second test; it may be helpful to ask the baby's carer to hold the stimuli while you record the fixation times on two cumulative stopwatches. If you do not have access to stopwatches, simply record the stimulus which appears to be preferred most. Repeat this procedure with each combination of stimuli, allowing a rest period between tests.

Record the fixation times (or preference scores) for each stimulus in its pair. Repeat the whole procedure with the other infants.

COMMENT

Do your results correspond with those of Maurer and Barrera? What problems did you find when testing the babies? You can extend this study by preparing other types of stimuli – for example a chequerboard pattern, plain black, plain white, plain colours, stripes, a bull's-eye pattern, newsprint – and repeat the procedure.

The notion of an inborn preference for faces is given support by the work of Mark Johnson and his team. These researchers used a 'geodesic net' (see Figure 2.4) placed gently on a baby's head (it is entirely painless). This net contains a large number of passive sensors (electrodes), which pick up the natural electrical changes on the scalp caused by neurons activated in the brain. Johnson found that newborns 'will look more towards faces than at any other objects' and that this elicits widespread brain activity which is much greater than that in adults.

Smiling by babies in response to various face-like and true face stimuli has been studied by other researchers. Infants from about six weeks of age (when the social smile first becomes evident) were studied, and it was found that such infants would smile at two eyes on a black background. The contours of the face become more important as babies get older, and by six months of age smiling is elicited by the whole face. Smiling at a face is not the same as showing recognition of it. Recognition requires that the elements within the face are related to each other in a particular manner. Smiling at mother, therefore, does not tell us that mother's features are recognized and distinguished from those of other women. Several studies have suggested that facial recognition occurs between the sixth and the ninth week of life (for example those by Robert Haaf and Cheryl Brown, and Daphne

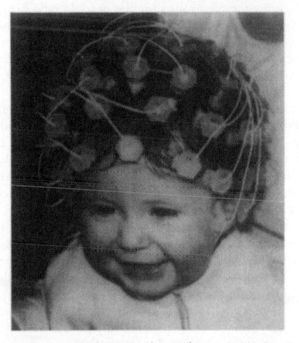

Figure 2.4   *A baby wearing a 'geodesic net' (from Johnson, 2000). Reprinted by permission*

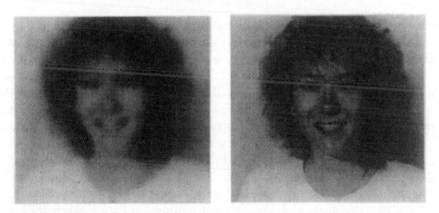

Figure 2.5   *The face as it might appear to the newborn, and to us. Courtesy of Dr Alan Slater*

Maurer and Philip Salapatek), but a study by Ian Bushnell and others reported in 1989 claims to have shown that neonates can recognize and show a preference for their mothers 'on the basis of visual clues alone'. Figure 2.5 shows what the human face may look like to the newborn and us.

Bushnell and his colleagues recorded the fixation times shown by alert newborns placed in a upright position in front of two faces that were behind a screen. These were the faces of the mother and a strange mother, matched for hair colour and complexion. The procedure controlled for the possible influences of a directional bias in looking by the baby, the influence of olfactory cues from the mother and actions by the mothers which might make them try to gain the attention of their infants (since they could see them during the procedure). The authors concluded that infants can rapidly learn the visual features of their mother's face, within a few hours of birth.

Clearly visual experience of the mother cannot be acquired prenatally, so this research inevitably poses problems for those who believe recognition takes some time to develop. While some researchers have argued that it is possible that the 'infant's nervous system is especially equipped to respond to face-like configurations' – and that this may produce the preferential responding noted by Bushnell – this is not the same as saying that a baby knows the 'meaning' of the face and recognizes that it belongs to the person from whom it receives love and care.

Bushnell's work has been confirmed by a study by Gail Walton and colleagues in 1992. These researchers videotaped mothers and paired them with other similar looking women, and found that 1–4-day-old infants distinguished their mothers from the unfamiliar females. Presumably the baby learns the mother's face rapidly after birth, just as he or she learns the olfactory and auditory characteristics of the mother.

The perception of depth and distance

Picnicking at the Grand Canyon, Eleanor Gibson pondered whether babies can judge distances and perceive depth? To find out she devised the 'visual cliff', a step-shaped apparatus in which the top step, the cliff, was covered with glass extending horizontally over a steep drop of about a metre. The whole apparatus was covered with a chequerboard pattern. Eleanor Gibson and Richard Walk tested babies individually as soon as they could crawl – from about 6 months of age – by placing them on the top of the cliff and getting their mothers to encourage them to cross the steep drop and come towards them. In spite of the glass preventing a fall off the cliff (the top step) the babies showed apprehension at the cliff edge, and very few crawled onto the glass over the drop. The researchers concluded that infants could probably perceive the drop because they could see the change in size of the chequered pattern over the one metre drop, and also through motion parallax – when they moved their head the distant side of the cliff would be seen to move more than the near or shallow side of the cliff.

The essential problem with the cliff experiment is that all infants will have had considerable experience of the environment before the test, so the study tells us little about the extent to which depth perception may be in-built. A number of other researchers have devised experiments for younger infants, and, in particular, infants' responses to approaching objects have been explored. Tom Bower and his colleagues designed an experiment using a real object moving towards the infant. Two-week-old babies were placed in an upright position, and their behaviour was recorded.

Bower noted three types of defensive behaviour in this situation: eye widening, head retraction and moving the hands up between the face and the approaching object (blinking was not observed and indeed does not occur in this situation until about eight weeks).

A variety of cues could play a part in eliciting this behaviour: the object is perceived as expanding (increasing in size on the retina) as it approaches, and it would also produce a rush or displacement of air, which might also indicate movement to the baby. Bower was able to show that air movement alone did not produce the head and hand movements described above, and that responses to the optical expansion pattern alone were less intense than in the natural situation.

Bower argued, however, that one-week-old infants can perceive distance as specified by the optical expansion pattern and probably therefore have a built-in capacity to do so.

Object perception and size constancy

The size, shape and brightness of an object all change when it moves, but we *perceive* it to be the same regardless of how these three elements change in relation to us. We refer to these effects as perceptual 'constancies'. As your friend walks away from you, you do not perceive her to shrink, even though on your retina she is rapidly occupying less and less space (size constancy). Similarly, you still recognize her as your friend, whether she is in profile or at a variety of different angles in relation to you (shape constancy), and she is still the person you know as having a particular skin and hair colour, whatever the level of light (brightness constancy).

Size constancy in infants was first demonstrated by Tom Bower in the 1960s, using 2-month-old infants. However, his research could not reveal whether learning was involved. More recently Alan Slater and colleagues have been able to do this. They familiarized newborn babies with a single cube which was presented at different distances from their eyes. When, subsequently, a different-sized cube was paired with the familiar one, but placed at a different distance in order that the retinal sizes of both objects were the same, it was found that the babies looked more at the novel cube.

Alan Slater and Victoria Morison also looked at shape constancy in newborns. In this experiment babies were given a period of familiarization with either a square or a trapezium (see Figure 2.6), the stimulus being shown at different slants from one trial to the next. After this the square and the trapezium were shown for two, paired test trials (i.e. two stimuli per trial). In these trials only one stimulus was familiar to each infant, and this was shown at a slant different from any of the slants used during familiarization. All the babies spent more time looking at the novel shape in the test trials – showing that they display shape constancy, because, even when the familiar object is displayed at a novel slant, it is evidently recognized as more familiar than a truly novel (but similarly shaped) stimulus.

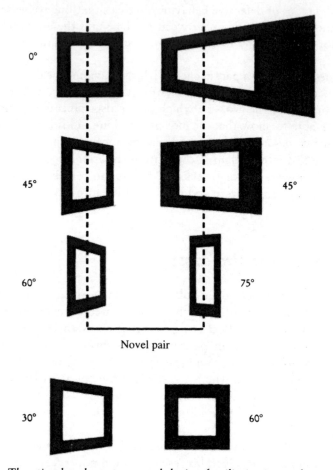

Figure 2.6   *The stimulus slants presented during familiarization and post-familiarization (test) trials by Slater and Morison (1985). The familiarization stimulus (for half the infants the square, for half the trapezium) was shown in six slants, the ones shown here and their mirror images*

The perception of partly hidden objects

Jean Piaget has been influential in shaping our ideas about the infant's knowledge of the world. Indeed his work persuaded us that up to around 9 months of age the baby behaves as if what is out of sight is also out of mind.

More recently his idea has been questioned and has led to research on hidden objects, or partly hidden objects. In a series of studies Philip Kellman and others tested 4-month-old babies who were habituated to a rod, partly hidden by a block, moving back and forth behind the block (see Figure 2.7). Later, the babies were shown test displays as shown, of either a complete rod or two small rods exactly as they might have appeared without the block. If they had perceived the rod in the

Habituation display

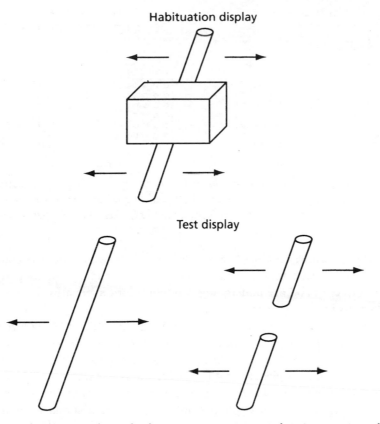

Test display

Figure 2.7 *Habituation and test displays in experiments on infants' perception of partly occluded objects (from Slater, 1997). Reprinted by permission*

habituation display as two rods, then the whole rod would be the novel stimulus; but if they had seen the rod as a single object, then the two rods would be novel. In their research the babies spent more time looking at the two-rod pieces, indicating that their initial perception was of one rod.

Alan Slater and his colleagues repeated this study and were able to replicate the finding with another group of 4-month-old infants, but when they tested newborn babies they found a preference for the complete rod, indicating that the babies saw the original display as two rods. Why might this be?

What information do we need to decide whether or not something is a single object if we can only see part of it? Slater tells us this includes:

- common motion
- the perceptual similarity of the two pieces (of the rod in this case)
- the clear depth relationship between the two rod pieces
- the fact that the two separate pieces are seen, never one piece.

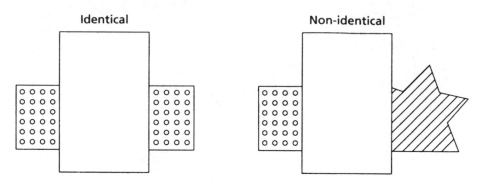

Figure 2.8   *When two objects are seen behind an occluder, 4¹/₂ -month-olds assume that there is one object if the parts are identical (left), and two if the parts are not identical (right) (from Slater, 1997, derived from Needham, 1994). Reprinted by permission*

So at what stage do new babies begin to behave as if the two objects could be just one? Research suggests that at 2 months old babies behave as if they are unsure. But if two pieces of rod are undergoing common motion, then by 4 months babies expect them to be a single object behind the block.

What happens with stationary objects that are partly hidden? Amy Needham and Renee Baillargeon found that perceptual similarity becomes the crucial element that links the stimuli. As we can see in figure 2.8, when the two elements appearing to the left and right of the object appear the same, adults expect them to be one object, but if the display is changed and one of the two elements is moved while the other remains unchanged, this upsets the notion that perceptual similarity is the clue to the presence of a single object which is partly hidden. Intriguingly, 4¹/₂-month-old babies respond as adults do when they observe the 'moving apart' condition; but 4-month-olds look equally at 'moving together' and 'moving apart' conditions, suggesting that they are unsure whether there are two objects or just one. Needham argues that babies at about 4-months-old begin accurate visually directed reaching, and it may be that the experience gained from reaching for objects in their environment enables them to come to the same view as adults when deciding whether one or two objects are obscured.

Finally, what happens when an object is completely hidden? When can an infant imagine or represent its existence? Renee Baillargeon and others found that a 5-month-old infant shows an awareness of its continued existence. Thus Piaget's belief that an infant can represent this only at 9 months is mistaken; clearly it can occur several months earlier according to these findings.

Critical Periods in Perceptual Development

It is easy to assume that our eyes and brain are programmed in such a way that they respond automatically to visual stimuli. Although the infant does not see as adults do at birth, many people probably assume that maturation sorts out any deficiencies and that what we see makes no difference to this process. In fact, there is now evidence that certain sorts of visual experience, or the lack of it, may be crucial in shaping the development of vision and visual perception.

Binocular vision

Research on kittens by Torsten Weisel and David Hubel has shown that the development of binocular vision (the ability to perceive an object with both eyes simultaneously so that the two images fuse) is shaped by early visual experience. Many cells in the part of our brain dealing with visual input (the visual cortex) will respond to a visual stimulus shown to either eye, but if one eye is covered early on it is subsequently found that the cortical cells will respond only to a stimulus presented to the other eye.

Martin Banks and his colleagues noted that children who are born with a squint may be affected in a similar way. If the eyes look in different directions this is bound to affect the degree to which the cortical cells, which respond binocularly, receive input from both eyes simultaneously. If such children are operated on before they are three then subsequently their binocular vision is very like that of normal children; however, if surgery is delayed binocular vision is adversely affected. The first three years are the critical period for the development of binocular vision in humans.

Seeing horizontals and verticals

Another area in which early visual experience appears to be important and possibly crucial for the development of visual perception is the ability to recognize horizontal and vertical stimuli. Colin Blakemore and Grahame Cooper reported an experiment in 1970 which explored the effect of limited early visual experience on kittens.

Some kittens were raised in the dark from birth, and at about two weeks of age they were placed in a special apparatus for five hours a day. Each kitten was exposed to either a totally horizontal world or a vertical world, where the walls were totally striped. The kittens were placed in large Elizabethan-like collars so that they could not even see their own bodies. After five months of this experience, tests showed that when the kittens were placed in a normal environment they were effectively blind to the type of stimulus (either vertical or horizontal) that they had not experienced. Evidence suggested that the kittens lacked cells in the visual cortex which could respond to the stimuli they had been reared without. Again, it seems that there is a critical period for the development of appropriately responding cortical cells, and these kittens had missed the period during which their brains could develop a response to either the vertical or the horizontal stimuli which had been denied them. The findings of this experiment have not been fully replicated, but the result is generally accepted as revealing the crucial role of early experience in the development of normal visual perception.

Cultural Influences

In the previous section we saw that early visual experience may influence perception, because the brain requires certain types of input during development for optimal functioning later.

Another example of the way in which experience can influence perception is seen in auditory perception. As babies we can make fine distinctions between sounds, but as our auditory environment is influenced by the language we speak as adults we may lose our ability to make those distinctions not required in our language. Thus adult Chinese speaking English cannot easily distinguish r and l in the way that all infants can – they have lost what they have not used. Thus our culture, or the world we live in, may shape our perceptions, and some things that have had the potential for development in infancy decline or disappear if they are not required in our particular environment.

In conclusion

In this chapter we have been able to consider only a few aspects of early perceptual development. To some extent the topics covered reflect the areas that have been well researched. This is certainly true of visual perception, but little has been said about hearing, and it would be wrong to conclude that we are quite ignorant of this area, although it is less widely discussed in most developmental textbooks. Our main aim has been to show, in selected areas only, that the human infant, even before full-term, is amazingly sensitive to its environment, and that researchers are being continually surprised by its abilities.

Recommended Reading

Bremner, G., Slater, A. and Butterworth, G. (1997) *Infant Development: Recent Advances.* Hove: Psychology Press. [Some excellent chapters; see in particular Slater's on visual perception.]

Gregory, R. L. and Colman, A. M. (1995) *Sensation and Perception.* London: Longman. [Covers some key areas in an accessible way.]

Kellman, P. J. and Arterberry, M. E. (1998) *The Cradle of Knowledge.* London: MIT Press. [A very informative text on perception.]

References

Adams, R. J. (1989) Newborns' discrimination among mid- and long-wave length stimuli. *Journal of Experimental Child Psychology*, 47, 130–41. [Colour vision in newborns.]

Baillargeon, R., Spelke, E. S. and Wasserman, S. (1985) Object permanence in 5-month-old infants. *Cognition*, 20, 191–208. [Babies' responses to hidden objects.]

Banks, M. S., Aslin, R. N. and Letson, R. D. (1975) Sensitive period for the development of human binocular vision. *Science*, 190, 675–7. [Children with squints and the development of binocular vision.]

Blakemore, C. and Cooper, G. R. (1970) Development of the brain depends on the visual environment. *Nature*, 228, 477–8. [Research on the perception of horizontals and verticals.]

Bosher, S. K. (1975) Morphological and functional changes in the cochlea associated with the inception of hearing. *Symposium of the Zoological Society of London*, 37, 11–22. [Function of the foetal auditory system.]

Bower, T. G. R. (1966) The visual world of infants. *Scientific American*, 215, 80–92. [Size constancy in infants.]

Bower, T. G. R. (1982) *Development in Infancy*. San Francisco: W. H. Freeman. [Babies and their ability to judge distances.]

Bower, T. G. R., Broughton, U. M. and Moore, M. K. (1970) Infant responses to approaching objects: an indicator of response to distil variables. *Perception and Psychophysics, 9*, 193–6. [Infants' perception of distance.]

Bremner, G., Slater, A. and Butterworth, G. (1997) *Infant Development: Recent Advances*. Hove: Psychology Press. [Excellent reviews of the research on visual perception.]

Brown, A. M. (1990) Development of visual sensitivity to light and colour vision in human infants: a critical review, *Vision Research*, 30, 1158–88. [Colour vision.]

Bushnell, I. W. R., Sal, F. and Mullin, J. T. (1989) Neonatal recognition of the mother's face. *British Journal of Developmental Psychology, 7*, 3–15. [Neonatal recognition of the mother's face.]

DeCasper, A. J. and Fifer, W. P. (1980) Of human bonding: newborns prefer their mothers' voices. *Science*, 208, 1174–6. [Studies of newborns' preferences for their mothers' voices.]

DeCasper, A. J. and Spence, M. J. (1986) Prenatal speech influences newborns' perception of speech sounds. *Infant Behaviour and Development*, 9, 133–50. [Newborns' preferences for the stories heard before birth.]

Fantz, R. L. (1961) The origin of form perception. *Scientific American*, 204, 1097–104. [Perception of various patterned stimuli.]

Gibson, E. J. and Walk, R. D. (1960) The visual cliff. *Scientific American*, 202, 64–71. [The visual cliff experiment.]

Haaf, R. A. and Brown, C. J. (1976) Infants' responses to face-like patterns: developmental changes between 10 and 15 weeks of age. *Journal of Experimental Child Psychology*, 22, 155–60. [Facial recognition in infants.]

James, W. (1890) *The Principles of Psychology*. New York: Holt, Rinehart and Winston. [Quotation on infant perception.]

Johnson, M. H. (2000) State of the art: how babies' brains work. *The Psychologist*, 13(6), 298–301. [Research using the 'geodesic net'.]

Macfarlane, A. (1975) Olfaction in the development of social preferences in the human neonate. In *Parent–Infant Interaction Ciba Foundation Symposium*, 33. New York: Elsevier. [Studies of smell recognition.]

Maurer, D. and Barrera, M. (1981) Infants' perception of natural and distorted arrangements of a schematic face. *Child Development*, 52, 196–202. [Study using scrambled symmetrical and non-symmetrical faces.]

Maurer, D. and Salapatek, P. (1976) Developmental changes in the scanning of faces by young infants. *Child Development*, 47, 523–7. [Facial recognition in infants.]

Needham, A. (1994) Infants' use of perceptional similarity when segregating partly occluded objects during the fourth month of life. Paper presented at the 9th international conference on Infant Studies (ICIS), 2–5 June, Paris; cited in Slater, 1997. [Various research studies on partly occluded objects.]

Ockleford, E. (1984) Response to rhythmical sound in pre-term infants and full-term neonates. *Journal of Reproductive and Infant Psychology*, 2, 92–6. [Pre-term and full-term babies' responses to rhythmic sounds.]

Ockleford, E. M., Vince, M. A., Layton, C. and Reader, M. R. (1988) Responses of neonates to parents' and others' voices. *Early Human Development*, 18, 27–36. [Newborns' responses to mothers' and others' voices.]

Porter, R. H. and Winberg, J. (1999) Unique salience of maternal breast odours for new born infants. *Neuorscience and Biobehavioural Reviews*, 23, 439–49. [Newborns' olfactory preferences.]

Russell, M. J. (1976) Human olfactory communication. *Nature*, 260, 520–2. [Olfactory recognition of mother's milk.]

Salk, L. (1960) The effects of the maternal heartbeat sound on the behaviour of the newborn infant: implications for mental health. *World Mental Health*, 12, 168–75. [Mother's heartbeat and its effects on baby.]

Slater, A. (1989) Visual memory and perception in early infancy. In A. Slater and G. Bremner (eds), *Infant Development*. Hove and London: Lawrence Erlbaum. [Newborns' visual acuity.]

Slater, A. (1990) Infant development: the origins of competence. *The Psychologist*, 3, 109–13. [The face as it might appear to the newborn.]

Slater, A. (1997) Visual perception and its organisation in early infancy. In G. Bremner, A. Slater and G. Butterworth (1997), *Infant Development: Recent Advances*. Hove: Psychology Press. [Visual perception in infancy.]

Slater, A. M. and Morison, V. (1985) Shape constancy and slant perception at birth. *Perception*, 14, 337–44. [Shape constancy in newborns.]

Wallace, P. (1977) Individual discrimination of humans by odour. *Physiology and Behaviour*, 19, 577–9.

Weisel, T. N. and Hubel, D. H. (1963) Single cell responses to striate cortex of kittens deprived of vision in one eye. *Journal of Neurophysiology*, 26, 1003–17. [Binocular vision in kittens.]

3

First Relationships

- The growth of love
- Mothers and fathers
- Short-term separations
- Long-term separations and substitute care
- Recovery from early deprivation

What makes a baby love its parents? Is it a natural and inevitable process, just as night follows day, or are special conditions required before the growth of love can occur? Are loving parents a necessary prerequisite, or will any parents, loving or cruel, elicit love from their offspring? This chapter explores the development of the first relationships in the infant's life. We consider the importance of mother and father and look at the development of the infant whose biological parents are not its carers. We consider children who have lost their parents and those who have never had an opportunity to form a close relationship early in life – how do such children fare compared with their peers living within their natural biological families?

Before reading further, why not find out just how much you know about the development of attachments by completing *Exercise 3.1*.

Exercise 3.1

Exploring Infant Social Relationships

Explore your knowledge of infant social relationships by answering the following questions:

1 Does a mother bond with her baby shortly after birth?
   Yes/No
2 Does a woman have a maternal instinct to care for a baby, unlike a man?
   Yes/No

3   At what age does an infant smile in response to other people?
    (a) 3 weeks   (c) 12 weeks
    (b) 6 weeks   (d) 20 weeks

4   What is the likely response of babies at the following ages to a
    'peek-a-boo' from a stranger?
    (a) at 4 months   (c) at 9 months
    (b) at 7 months

5   How would you expect an infant to behave at the following ages if
    left with a stranger?
    (a) at 5 months
    (b) at 15 months

6   At what age do infants show the first signs of a preference for
    their caregiver(s)?
    (a) at 0–3 months   (c) at 7–9 months
    (b) at 4–6 months   (d) at 10–12 months

7   At what age do children show specific attachments to particular
    individuals?

8   If your 18-month-old was ill and had to go into hospital without
    you, how do you think he or she would react?

9   A child *always* loves one person more than any other?
    Yes/No

10 Do you think that a father can look after a baby (excluding breast-
    feeding) just as well as a mother can?
    Yes/No

11 A child that is securely attached to its mother will be equally secure
    in its other relationships?
    Yes/No

12 Do you think that adopted children are likely to have identity
    problems at any stage?
    Yes/No

13 Can children who have experienced extreme adversity and almost
    no personal care in the first months of life (such as many Romanian
    orphans) ever recover even if adopted into loving families?
    Yes/No

14   If children lose their parents and are orphaned at the age of two (or thereabouts) can they ever make up for their loss and learn to love others?
Yes/No

Chapter 3 provides all the answers to these questions in so far as they are answerable with our present psychological knowledge.

Mother love

The crucial role played by the mother in childcare has rarely been questioned until recent decades. Early psychologists wrote about a maternal instinct; it was assumed that mothers were born with an in-built capacity to love and care for their offspring. The notion that a father might have a similar capacity was not considered. Indeed, it was simply assumed that mother must be the primary caregiver – children without their mothers were believed to be deprived and at risk of long-term damage.

John Bowlby was a psychiatrist who contributed to this debate. He worked with 'separated' children and adolescents living in hospitals and orphanages. He was greatly influenced by Sigmund Freud's views on the importance of the mother as the primary attachment figure and the research on non-human animals by Konrad Lorenz and Harry Harlow. Lorenz studied *imprinting* in various bird species. He showed that ducklings and goslings become strongly attached to one specific individual soon after hatching. This rapidly formed bond was termed imprinting, and Lorenz believed that it had major and long-term effects on the young animal's later social and sexual behaviour.

Harlow's research on rhesus monkeys reared without their mothers, but given a choice between a wire surrogate mother providing milk and a towelling-covered surrogate mother not providing milk, showed that infants preferred the 'contact comfort' of the latter to the wire surrogate who was just a source of food. This work was evidence, until then not recognized, that mother love is not just cupboard love (based on the association of food and mother), but something more. Infants are, it seems, biologically designed to become attached to a mother figure – independently of the satisfaction of basic physiological needs, such as hunger (see figure 3.1).

Bowlby argued that, to an infant, becoming attached to the individual who can attend to its needs is adaptive – without this the vulnerable infant would die. Thus the infant is biologically prepared to elicit caregiving and to become attached to its caregiver. Bowlby described attachment behaviour as 'any form of behaviour that results in a person attaining or retaining proximity', and attachment as a bond that is developed with 'some other differentiated and preferred individual, who is usually . . . stronger and/or wiser'.

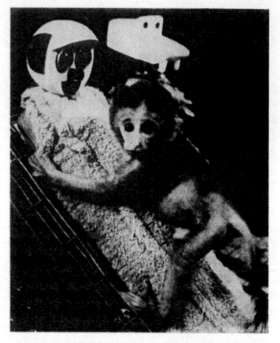

Figure 3.1   *The cloth and wire surrogate monkeys in Harlow's research. Courtesy of Harlow Primate Laboratory, University of Wisconsin-Madison*

The absence of attachment by the infant towards the mother shortly after birth was not viewed as essential because, unlike Lorenz's goslings, it cannot crawl and get away. However, once crawling is established, in the latter half of the first year, an exclusive relationship with mother (or other major caregiver) is formed. Now the baby can keep close to the mother and continue to elicit her caregiving behaviour.

For Bowlby, the mother's place in infant care was crucial. She was considered to be the primary attachment figure, and Bowlby emphasized that the infant needed to have her above all others as the source of care and love, because he believed that initially infants are unable to form attachments to more than one person (this is his concept of 'monotropism'). He recognized that children become attached to others but believed that their mothers usually remain their 'primary' attachment figures.

Maternal bonding

Just as the mother was believed to be of vital importance to her baby, her need to bond with the baby soon after childbirth was stressed by researchers in the 1980s. In their book *Parent-Infant Bonding*, Marshall Klaus and John Kennell described a rapidly appearing mother-to-infant attachment following the birth, which was said not only to have long-lasting effects on the relationship between parent and child, but also to affect the child's subsequent development.

These authors believed that early mother–infant contact was crucial for the development of the mother's bond with her child, and that mothers deprived of early contact with their offspring might have difficulties in developing a relationship with their child. This research had positive benefits and increased the amount of contact permitted in hospitals between premature and full-term babies and their parents, but negatively it alarmed parents who had been deprived of these opportunities – perhaps through illness of either mother or baby. Wladek Sluckin and colleagues investigated this topic by reviewing the literature on the degree of infant contact experienced and its effect on the subsequent mother–child relationship, but found no evidence for the crucial nature of this early contact.

Researchers such as Klaus Minde have concluded that, while early mother–infant contact does seem to increase parental confidence, and helps the establishment of nursing by the mother, in the long term it has no effect on the subsequent relationship established between the mother and her infant. Nevertheless, because parents enjoy such contacts – and gain benefit from them – such contact is now encouraged whenever possible.

Fathers and babies

At the time of Bowlby's early writings in the years following the Second World War, men's and women's roles in the family were generally felt to be quite distinct. The male was the provider and the female was the carer within the traditional nuclear family. In postwar Britain women were removed from the labour force so that men, returning from the war could return to their civilian jobs. Women were put back in the home, and Bowlby's writings encouraged everyone to believe that this was the best thing for their children. In that social climate the father's role in childcare was rarely considered.

Traditionally, fathers had been seen as rather distant figures in their children's lives. Childcare was women's work, and children were often almost ignored until they reached 'the age of reason' (in their teens according to Lord Dacre).

A child whose mother had died was typically cared for by another woman rather than the father; thus he or she might be looked after by an aunt, a grandmother, a stepmother or a paid female carer. A man was not considered to have the qualities – the maternal instinct – needed for the task. However, the central role of the mother in her children's lives, as the person whom they would naturally love most, was not borne out by the research of Rudolf Schaffer and Peggy Emerson. In their research in and around Glasgow in the 1960s they found that a considerable number of children did not love their mothers most. In one study nearly one-third of 18-month-old children were most strongly attached to their fathers; some were equally attached to both parents or to three or more figures; and about half were most strongly attached to their mothers. Infants direct their love to those who

are sensitive to their needs and attend to them quickly. It is the quality of care given that is important in eliciting love.

Maternal instinct as a concept is now questionable. Harry and Margaret Harlow's work on female rhesus monkeys reared with surrogate mothers revealed that such females made very poor mothers. They did not know what to do with their babies. If they had possessed some inbuilt package enabling them to provide appropriate care for their babies, surely this would have been evident. While no one denies that mothers carry babies for nine months, give birth and lactate – and thus can do things males cannot – all other aspects of infant care can be provided by others just as effectively. In the traditional family – where mother has the role of primary caregiver – father interacts with his offspring in a more physical way than the mother. However, fathers who are primary carers relate to their children much more like traditional mothers, according to Tiffany Field.

The Growth of Love

When do babies begin to show love, and what types of love are there? Parents soon learn that their offspring go through different phases; in the early months of life small babies can be very sociable and are often happy to be passed around from one person to another, but as the months pass they are not so willing to be held by anyone; in fact they may be very clingy indeed and resist all attempts to be held by others or to be talked to by strangers.

The signs of attachment

As we have seen, even before birth there is evidence that infants are familiar with certain features of their environment, and after birth babies will show preferences for the salient features of those who care for them. But, although some preferential responding is evident in general, infants go through an indiscriminate *attachment* phase in the first six months. They are highly sociable creatures, enjoying the smiles and coos of anyone who interacts with them. Rudolf Schaffer and Peggy Emerson are the researchers who have clearly identified the changes that take place at about six to seven months. Studies of the effects on infants of both brief and longer-term separations show that the period between six and eight or nine months is the time when attachments become focused. By their behaviour, babies show clearly who they want to be with, and who by their absence cause distress. This change marks the beginning of the specific attachment phase.

Under six months, separation from the caregiver typically produces only a temporary upset; the baby can be comforted by others. After this time, separation distress is much harder to relieve – indeed, comforting from strangers may cause even more distress.

In 1967 Mary Ainsworth described 16 types of behaviour that reveal evidence of an infant's love or attachment for another person; these include differential smiling, differential crying and differential vocalization. Infants display each of these patterns at different frequencies in the presence and absence of the attachment figure – thus they might smile and vocalize more towards their mothers than towards others, and cry in their absence. Other patterns include greeting responses, following, clinging, embracing, hugging and kissing, and flight to the caregiver as a haven of safety.

Becoming attached to a person or persons has always been recognized – certainly since Freud – as vital for the normal development of the human baby. Freud believed that later psychological problems could be attributed to problems in the first and, for him, the primary relationship – that with the mother. Bowlby followed in this tradition, and, whether or not psychologists agree about who should be the attachment figure, or whether several people will do equally well, all agree that children suffer if deprived of the opportunity to form attachments. Measuring attachments has thus become important for those assessing infant development.

Measuring attachment

Mary Ainsworth devised a standard procedure for assessing 12–24-month-old infants' relationships to their mothers or other caregivers, called the 'strange situation'. This has been widely used in the USA and in parts of Europe, Israel and Japan. She described it in 1982 as follows:

> An infant and mother are brought into a comfortable laboratory room; a stranger enters and sits talking to the mother and then to the infant; the mother leaves the room

unobtrusively; the mother returns and the stranger leaves them together; the mother leaves the infant alone in the room; the stranger returns; the mother returns once more. Each of these seven episodes lasts three minutes unless the infant is more than mildly distressed.

Each stage in the procedure is increasingly more stressful for the infant (and, as we shall see later, perhaps too stressful for babies from some cultures), and, by video-taping the session, attachment in the infant is assessed. Measures of proximity and contact seeking, contact maintaining, resistance, avoidance, search and interaction at a distance are all made, and the infant's responses when reunited with its mother (or caregiver) are regarded as particularly important indicators of the relationship.

Ainsworth classified infants in three ways as types A, B and C, shown below; later the category D was added by other researchers.

Type A   Anxious/avoidant infants showed avoidance of their mothers.
Type B   Secure infants actively sought their mothers and were described as securely attached.
Type C   Anxious/resistant infants were resistant to or ambivalent towards their mothers.
Type D   Disorganized/disorientated behaviour by children during the strange situation.

Type D is a less common category, and in general infants are described simply as securely attached or anxiously attached (type B or types A and C).

Although measured only in the second year, the behaviour shown has been found to be a stable indicator of the relationship studied (see Randolph Paterson and Grey Moran) and is felt to be primarily an indicator of the interaction between mother (or caregiver) and baby, rather than of the infant's temperament alone. Attachment status refers only to a specific relationship, so a secure attachment to the mother does not predict the nature of the attachment to others. If family life is relatively stable, then so is attachment status – but in more stressful environments secure infants may become insecure or anxiously attached. In recent years, the 'strange situation' has been used very extensively in research on attachment, yet it does have problems.

The situation is contrived and artificial, and it does not take into account the mother's or caregiver's behaviour. It is always limited by the time during which such an assessment can be made, as for infants over two years it becomes inappropriate as a measure of attachment. However, one of the main criticisms is of the assumption it makes about who cares for the child and the nature of the relationship, which can differ greatly across cultures.

Cultural differences

The 'strange situation' has been used primarily in the USA and in general research shows that 70 per cent of infants are securely attached to their mothers (Type B) with 20 and 10 per cent of infants in the anxious categories Types A and C respectively. In some cultures infants have much greater physical contact with their mothers and minimal or no separation from them during the day or night, e.g. Ganda infants in Uganda and Japanese infants. For these infants the physical separation required in the 'strange situation' is extremely distressing. Over one-third of Japanese babies are likely to be identified as anxious/resistant type C infants, which may be misleading if it is interpreted as showing that such infants are less securely attached to their mothers.

In Israel, children reared in kibbutzim spend most of their days with metapelets, trained carers. Again a higher proportion of infants are type C in relation to their mothers, yet research shows that they form strong attachments with their mothers. Thus we need to be aware of the difficulties of transferring this measure to other cultures, where childrearing practices may be very different from those typical in the UK and the USA.

Attachment to siblings

A modified version of the 'strange situation' has also been used with siblings, and it was found that babies, when left by their mothers, were calmed if their older siblings were present and went to reassure them. Similarly, if a stranger entered the room, the baby moved towards the older sibling – treating it as a 'secure base'.

Judy Dunn notes that by the end of their first year, many babies are attached to their older siblings, and that this has a great impact on their behaviour. Much imitation takes place, and this is greater when the older sibling is of the same sex. Of course, not all siblings love each other, and the arrival of a new sibling always heralds a period of emotional adjustment for an older child. Even when an attachment is evident between children, interactions may be aggressive and hostile at times, or show a mismatch, one child being friendly while the other is indifferent or hostile.

Short-term Separations

Once a relationship is established, short-term separations – even for a few minutes – will in many cases lead to great distress in an infant. Ainsworth's 'strange situation' is, as we have seen, one way in which reactions to such separations can be measured. If a mother (or other caregiver) leaves her baby, the separation anxiety exhibited commonly takes the form of screaming, shouting, crying and searching behaviour.

The following paragraphs will discuss separation anxiety in relation to separation from the mother, but it should be noted that the attachment figure could be the father, or any other caregiver to whom the baby has formed a strong attachment.

Protest and despair

The distress of a separated infant is evident to anyone hearing this response, and there can be few parents who do not feel the searing feelings that such responses evoke. This first reaction to separation is known as the phase of protest, and it is clear that the infant is trying desperately to get its mother back. If the separation continues, perhaps because it is caused through illness or death, the child then moves into the phase of despair. This phase resembles the response of a bereaved person who feels sad, hopeless and apathetic. The despair phase also includes anger directed towards the lost loved one; should the mother return, or any sign of her be found, the infant may well fly into a rage. Anger may seem to be an unexpected aspect of despair, but the angry cry 'How could you leave me?' is a natural reaction to loss and is also common in adults who mourn a loved one. The similarity to the situation of the bereaved can be explained because the young infant cannot comprehend the notion that mother will return. After the age of six months, the infant knows that objects out of sight are still there; it is this knowledge that adds to the pain – mother is there somewhere but not with me. A mother cannot explain to her nine- or twelve-month-old child that she will only be gone for a short time; nor can the child hold in mind an image of the absent mother. Unless the child can be left with someone to whom it is also attached, the separation will be exactly like a loss through death.

Detachment

If the separation continues for weeks or months, the child moves into the phase of detachment. Now the child seems to be coping well, has recovered its vitality and is getting on with life, but in fact this phase is really the sign that all hope has gone. The child is friendly with everyone but may not risk forming a relationship with anyone for fear of losing them too. Should the mother now return, she will be hardly noticed; indeed, the child may seem almost not to know her.

Because Bowlby stressed the tendency of a child to attach to *one* figure, typically the mother, from this it naturally follows that she is indispensable to it. Separation from her, even for short periods, was viewed as damaging and leading to long-term ill effects on the child. The full-time employment of the mother was thought to cause suffering to the family, and Bowlby stressed that it 'must be regarded as a potential source of a deprived child'. This view of Bowlby's was, and continues to be, a source of great controversy. Nowadays it is expected that women will form a significant part of the paid workforce, yet many, perhaps most, mothers are dogged by the view that they, and only they, can care for their children adequately. Despite the work of Rudolf Schaffer and others, who have shown that mother is not necessarily the most loved person in a child's life, and also that the notion of a primary attachment figure is not upheld, the effect of Bowlby's opinion is not lightly shaken off. Women's place is still considered by many to be in the home, and if mother is not there, dire consequences for her children are predicted.

Maternal employment

In recent years there has been much discussion about the thorny issue of working or employed mothers and their effects of this on their children. Bowlby, as we have seen, believed that working mothers were potentially a problem, but research produces a rather more complex picture.

In her review of research on the effects of daycare on children Alison Clarke-Stewart finds that there are no simple answers. In some respects children who are in daycare rather than being reared in the home may be more socially skilled and independent than home-reared infants. One-year-olds of full-time employed mothers may be less compliant with their mothers, and slightly more daycare children will be classed as more insecurely attached to their mothers than the children of mothers who have part-time or no employment. However, the effects of daycare depend in great part on its quality, the stability of the care and a child's particular characteristics. If children are moved from one arrangement to another this has an adverse effect on child outcomes. Research by Wendy Goldberg and colleagues on 5–7-year-old children whose mothers were employed either full-time, part-time or not at all reveals a range of outcomes. In general it was found that the higher the mothers' working hours the lower the children's grades were in school, the poorer their work habits were and the less they displayed resilience, resourcefulness and adaptability in the classroom. Within the sample of employed mothers boys were more vulnerable when their mothers had more time-consuming jobs, whereas for girls increased working hours by their mothers were associated with higher grades. Thus maternal employment may be more disadvantageous for sons than for daughters.

Today the employment of mothers is a fact of life, and research is needed to find out how to help families and 'working' parents ensure the best possible outcomes for their children.

Long-term Separations and Substitute Care

For most people the ideal family is the one in which children are loved and cared for by their biological parents. However, there are a variety of circumstances, such as the death, divorce or separation of the parents, that may make this impossible. If children are reared by carers other than their natural parents, how do they fare? Is biology crucial, or can substitute care such as fostering or adoption provide an equally successful alternative to the natural situation?

In the past unwanted children were often reared in foundling homes and orphanages. Typically these were places lacking in stimulation, with few staff and numerous children. Research by Spitz and Goldfarb highlighted the damaging effects of such places. In fact, in the cases they described the opportunities for children to become attached to a substitute carer were very limited, and their experience was not so much maternal deprivation as privation, as we shall see later. Today in Britain it is generally recognized that children thrive best in a family setting, and the orphanage is less widely used; the alternative that a real family can offer through fostering or adoption is more widely sought for children who are unable to live with their parents.

Adoption

Let us look at the success of adoption. Can this ever be as good as rearing by the biological parents? The answer is undoubtedly yes.

Barbara Tizard is widely known for her work in this field. In general, children adopted early in life, preferably before six months (i.e. the age when infants first form specific attachments to their carers), progress as well as children reared with their natural parents. Even those adopted between the ages of two and four showed, according to Tizard and others, on average, no more problems than were found in home-reared controls, although they were more likely to be described as overfriendly and more attention seeking in their behaviour.

Tizard has also demonstrated that children given an opportunity to return to their biological families after a period in care fared less well than those who went on to be adopted. In her study the children were taken into care early in life and remained in institutions for between two and seven years; some were then returned to their natural mothers, while others were adopted.

Tizard found that although the biological parent might seem preferable the return to the family was less than satisfactory. Parents often favoured siblings over the 'restored' child and on a wide range of measures: intellectually, scholastically and emotionally, the adoptees fared better.

Genealogical anxiety

The worry of adoptees about their biological origins has been much discussed, and this genealogical anxiety is felt to be a particular issue at puberty, when identity becomes more important for all. A study of white, mainly middle-class young people, all of whom were adopted before the age of two, found no evidence of more identity problems than in a carefully matched control group. A similar concern about transracial adoption has been discussed by Kwame Owusu-Bempah and Dennis Howitt. However, the importance of 'sociogenealogical connectedness' is not universally recognized. A Swedish study of foreign-born adoptees, when in their teens, did not indicate more problems than those of a non-adopted Swedish sample, and the adoptees coped well with their 'special outsider situation'. Attitudes to adoption, whether transracial or not may be important to its success. This issue will be discussed further in chapter 13.

The Failure to Form Bonds

The failure of an infant to form bonds with the mother (or other caregiver) is termed maternal *privation*, and it must be distinguished from maternal deprivation, in which the bond with the mother has been disrupted or broken. Bowlby suggested that the 'affectionless' character (affectionless psychopath) may be the result of a child's failure to form bonds. Such a person is without feelings for others and is unable to form relationships.

Isolated monkeys

If we consider research into non-human animals, the work of Harlow and others on rhesus monkeys reared in total isolation for six months showed dramatic and damaging effects on their later social and sexual behaviour. These monkeys, reared alone with a cloth-covered mother surrogate, were either aggressive or indifferent when they were eventually placed with other monkeys. Their sexual behaviour was so disrupted that normal reproduction was impossible. These infants had missed the sensitive period for the development of attachments, and their rehabilitation seemed unlikely.

However, Melinda Novak and Harlow found that if they gradually introduced the isolated monkeys to a 'therapist monkey' – a younger normally reared monkey – it was possible for them to recover and go on to become adequate parents later on. This recovery is impressive, but can we hope to effect the same kind of rehabilitation in humans?

Isolated humans

Fortunately very few humans experience the extreme isolation imposed on Harlow's monkeys. None the less, there are some reported cases of 'wild' children or 'isolated' children that seem to be analogous to the isolated monkeys.

In 1801 Jean-Marc Itard reported on the capture of a 'wild boy', who ran on all fours, grunted and had been sighted over many years in the woods around Aveyron, France. Despite five years of intensive care little progress was made, and Victor never learned to speak. Lack of knowledge about his origins means that we can never know if his disabilities were present at birth or the result of isolation.

Kingsley Davis (in 1947) described the case of Isabelle, a child kept hidden in an attic, with her deaf mute mother, until the age of six. She was without speech and severely subnormal, but after two years of intensive care she achieved the normal educational level and was described as a 'very bright, cheerful, energetic little girl'. A rather similar case of twin boys in Czechoslovakia was reported by Jarmila Koluchová in the 1970s. They too had years of virtual isolation until discovery at seven years of age, but after good care achieved normal intelligence and enjoyed warm relationships with others. These miraculous recovery stories suggest that even extreme adversity may be offset by some degree of human contact.

Recovery from Early Deprivation or Privation

It has long been thought that early experiences are crucial in determining the course of subsequent development. Psychoanalysts stress that many problems have their roots in early childhood experience. Bowlby, following in this tradition, has stressed that children should experience a warm, intimate and continuous relationship with their mothers (or permanent mother substitutes), and that without this their mental health will suffer. Today, however, views on this matter are changing.

Romanian orphans

In recent years probably the worst cases of privation documented are the Romanian children whose plight was the result of the terrible Ceauşescu regime; this required women to have at least five children. The result was that poverty led them to abandon their children and place them in orphanages, where they existed in appalling conditions.

In their book *Early Experience and the Life Path*, published in 2000, Ann and Alan Clarke discuss the research carried out by Michael Rutter and the English and Romanian Adoptees (ERA) Study Team. Rutter studied 111 Romanian orphans, adopted under 2 years of age and followed up at age 4 and 6 years. These children were compared with 52 within-country UK adoptees, adopted under the age of 6 months.

On arrival in the UK the Romanian children were found to be severely mentally impaired and severely malnourished. Previously most of these infants had been confined to cots, had no personal caregiving, were fed with gruel from propped up bottles and were washed by being hosed down with cold water. Half had spent their whole lives in institutions; the remainder had spent some period within families but at least half of their lives in institutions.

The Romanian orphans adopted early (under 6 months) made remarkable progress and were very like the within-UK sample, but the later-adopted Romanian children, those adopted under 2 years but over 6 months, made good progress but were a standard below the early adoptees; in particular seven of this sample showed very marked intellectual impairments.

The Clarkes argue that there may be a sensitive period for cognitive ability at around 6 months of age, but there is not a critical period or else the achievements of some of the later-adopted children could not have occurred.

This research leaves us with a revised view of the impact of early experience on later development. The Clarkes sum up by saying that

> the life path is not predetermined by the experiences of the early years alone, but results from the long-term cumulative development of genetic and environmental interactions and transactions. (p. 103)

In other words, later positive interventions can in many cases offset earlier privation. Now go back to exercise 3.1 on page 33 and see whether you know all the answers.

Recommended Reading

Cassidy, J. and Shaver, P. R. (1999) *Handbook of Attachment: Theory, Research and Clinical Application*. London: Guilford Press. [An excellent, advanced text; chapters 1, 4 and 36 are particularly recommended.]

Clarke, A. M. and Clarke, A. D. B. (2000) *Early Experience and the Life Path*. London: Jessica Kingsley Publishers. [Includes research on Romanian adoptees.]

Murray, L. and Andrews, L. (2000) *The Social Baby*. Richmond, Surrey: C P Publishing. [A delightful book, well illustrated with photographs showing the baby's social world.]

Rutter, M. (1990) *Maternal Deprivation Reassessed*. Harmondsworth: Penguin. [A useful review of the topic.]

Schaffer, H. R. (1990) *Making Decisions About Children: Psychological Questions and Answers*. Oxford: Blackwell. [Asks and answers lots of important questions, many about attachments, and summarises the principal research studies.]

References

Ainsworth, M. D. S. (1967) *Infancy in Uganda*. Baltimore, MD: Johns Hopkins University Press. [Patterns of attachment behaviour.]

Ainsworth, M. D. S. (1982) Attachment: retrospective and prospect. In C. M. Parkes and J. Stevenson-Hinds (eds), *The Place of Attachment in Human Behaviour*. New York: Basic Books. [Quotation on the 'strange situation'.]

Aviezer, O., Van IJzendoorm, M. H., Sagi, A. and Schuengel, C. (1994) 'Children of the Dream' revisited: 70 years of collective early child care in Israeli Kibbutzim. *Psychological Bulletin*, 116, 99–116. [Children reared in kibbutzim.]

Bettleheim, B. (1959) Feral children and autistic children. *American Journal of Sociology*, 64, 455–67. ['Wild' children may have been abandoned because of various problems.]

Bowlby, J. (1944) Forty-four juvenile thieves: their characters and homelife. *International Journal of Psychoanalysis*, 24, 19–52, 107–27. [The affectionless character.]

Bowlby, J. (1952) *Maternal Care and Mental Health*. Geneva: World Health Organization. [Includes comment on the nature of the relationship that a child needs from mother.]

Bowlby, J. (1977) The making and breaking of affectional bonds. I. Aetiology and psychopathology in the light of attachment theory. *British Journal of Psychiatry*, 130, 201–10. [Quotation concerning attachment behaviour.]

Cederbald, M., Höök, B., Irhammar, M. and Mercke, A. M. (1999) Mental health in international adoptees as teenagers and young adults: an epidemiological study. *Journal of Psychology and Psychiatry*, 40(8), 1239–48. [The Swedish study of adoptees.]

Clarke, A. M. and Clarke, A. D. B. (eds) (1976) *Early Experience: Myth and evidence*. London: Open Books. [Comment on 'wild children'; review of the effects of early experience.]

Clarke, A. and Clarke, A. (1998) Early experience and the life path. *The Psychologist*. September, 433–6 [Review of many studies, including Tizard's restored adoptees.]

Clarke, A. M. and Clarke, A. D. B. (2000) *Early Experience and the Life Path*. London: Jessica Kingsley. [Includes research on Romanian adoptees.]

Clarke-Stewart, K. A. (1989) Infant day care? Maligned or malignant? Special issue: children and their development: knowledge base, research agenda, and social policy application. *American Psychologist*, 44(2), 266–73. [Review of studies of infants in daycare.]

Dacre, Lord (1989) Relative values. *Sunday Times Magazine*, 21 May, 11–14. [The quotation on fathers.]

Davis, K. (1976) Final note on a case of extreme isolation. In A. M. Clarke and A. D. B. Clarke (eds), *Early Experience*. [The case of Isabelle.]

Dunn, J. (1993) *Young Children's Close Relationships: Beyond Attachment*. London: Sage. [Sibling relationships.]

Field, T. (1978) Interaction behaviours of primary versus secondary caretaker fathers. *Developmental Psychology*, 14, 183–5. [Father's role in childcare.]

Goldfarb, W. (1947) Variations in adolescent adjustment of institutionally reared children. *American Journal of Orthopsychiatry*, 17, 449–57. [Children in institutions.]

Goldberg, W. A., Greenberger, E. and Nagel, S. K. (1996) Employment and achievement: mothers' work involvement in relation to children's achievement behaviour and mothers' parenting behaviours. *Child Development*, 67(4), 1512–27. [Maternal employment effects on children.]

Griffin, G. A. and Harlow, F. (1966) Effects of three months of total social deprivation on social adjustment and learning in the rhesus monkey. *Child Development*, 37(3), 533–47. [Monkeys reared for three months in isolation, then exposed to others.]

Harlow, H. F. (1958) The nature of love. *American Psychologist*, 13, 673–85. [Infant monkeys reared without mothers.]

Harlow, H. F. and Harlow, M. K. (1962) Social deprivation in monkeys. *Scientific American*, November, Reprint no. 473. [The inability of female monkeys reared in isolation to care for their offspring.]

Humphrey, M. and Humphrey, H. (1988) *Families with a Difference: Varieties of Surrogate Parenthood*. London: Routledge. [The dangers of overstressing the handicap of ancestral ignorance in adoptees.]

Humphrey, M. and Ounsted, C. (1963) Adoptive families referred for psychological advice: 1. The children. *British Journal of Psychiatry*, 109, 599–608. [Adoption and psychiatric problems.]

Itard, J. M. G. (1962) *The Wild Boy of Aveyron*. New York: Appleton-Century-Crofts. [The 'civilization' of an isolated boy.]

Klaus, M. H. and Kennel, J. H. (1982) *Parent–Infant Bonding*. St Louis, MO: Mosby. [Maternal bonding.]

Koluchová, J. (1976) A report on the further developmnent of twins after severe and prolonged deprivation. In A. M. Clarke and A. D. B. Clarke (eds), *Early Experience*. [Twin boys and their recovery from early adversity.]

Lorenz, K. (1952) *King Solomon's Ring*. London: Methuen. [Studies of imprinting.]

Main, M., Kaplan, N. and Cassidy, J. (1985) Security in infancy, childhood, and adulthood: a move to the level of representation. *Monographs of the Society for Research in Child Development*, 50, 66–104. [Insecure-disorganized/disorientated attachment.]

Minde, K. (1986) Bonding and attachment: its relevance for the present day clinician. *Developmental Medicine* and *Child Neurology*, 28(6), 803–6. [Early mother–infant contact increases mothers' confidence.]

Novak, M. A. and Harlow, H. F. (1975) Social recovery of monkeys isolated for the first years of life. I. Rehabilitation and therapy. *Developmental Psychology*, 11, 453–65. [Recovery of isolated infant monkeys.]

Owusu-Bempah, J. and Howitt, D. (1997) Socio-genealogical connectedness, attachment theory and childcare practice. *Child and Family Social Work*, 2, 199–207. [Transracial adoption studies.]

Owusu-Bempah, J. and Howitt, D. (2000) *Psychology Beyond Western Perspectives*. Leicester: BPS Books. [Discusses cross-cultural perspectives.]

Paterson, R. J. and Moran, G. (1988) Attachment theory, personality development, and psychotherapy. *Clinical Psychology Review*, 8, 611–36. [Review of attachment.]

Robertson, J. and Bowlby, J. (1952) Responses of young children to separation from their mothers. *Courrier de la Centre Internationale de l'Enfance*, 2, 131–42. [Effects of separation on children.]

Ruppenthal, G. C., Arling, G. L., Harlow, H. G., Sackett, G. P. and Suome, S. J. (1976) A 1-year perspective of motherless-mother monkey-behaviour. *Journal of Abnormal Psychology*, 85, 341–9. [Motherless monkeys can be rehabilitated.]

Rutter, M. (1990) *Maternal Deprivation Reassessed*, 3rd edn. Harmondsworth: Penguin. [Effects on an infant of separation from its caregiver.]

Schaffer, H. R. and Emerson, P. E. (1964) The development of social attachments in infancy. *Monographs of Social Research in Child Development*, 29, Serial no. 94. [Attachment to mothers, fathers and others.]

Sluckin, W., Harbert, M. and Sluckin, A. (1983) *Maternal Bonding*. Oxford: Blackwell. [Reviewed research into degree of contact between infant and mother and its effect on subsequent mother–child relationship.]

Spitz, H. R. (1946) Hospitalism: a follow-up report. *Psychoanalytic Study of the Child*, 2, 113–18. [Long-term separation effects.]

Stein, L. M. and Hoopes, J. L. (1985) *Indentity Formation in the Adopted Adolescent: The Delaware Family Study*. New York: Child Welfare League of America. [Identity problems in adopted children.]

Tizard, B. (1977) *Adoption: A Second Chance*. London: Open Books. [Discusses research on adoption.]

4

Early Influences and Personality

- What is personality?
- Do early influences affect personality?
- Inheritance and environment – an interaction
- Prenatal effects
- The importance of temperament
- Theories of personality
- Childrearing strategies

> From the day your baby is born, you must teach him to do without things.
> Children today love luxury too much. They have execrable manners, flaunt
> authority, have no respect for their elders.
>
> *Socrates, 469–399* BC

> Come listen now to the good old days when children,
>   strange to tell,
> Were seen not heard, led a simple life, in short,
>   were brought up well.
>
> *Aristophanes, 5th century* BC

> Famous men are usually the product of an unhappy childhood.
> *Winston Churchill, 1874–1965*

What do we mean by personality?

If we hear someone say a person has a strong personality or no personality we
usually know what is meant (i.e. the person is either strong-willed or boring).
However, when psychologists consider personality a strong person has no more
personality than a weak person. People do not vary in the *amount* of personality
they have, but they do vary in the *type* of personality they have.

So what do psychologists mean by personality? There is no simple answer to the
question. The study of personality has interested psychologists for a long time, but

no single generally accepted definition has been agreed on. One possible definition is 'Personality is a collection of individual, relatively lasting, patterns of reacting, to others and to situations, which distinguish a child or adult.'

A consistent idea about personality is that each person has a unique, individual and enduring set of psychological tendencies that can be found in the way he or she interacts in social environments (e.g. home, school, work, play). As children grow up, biological and environmental influences are expected to interact so that gradually a characteristic pattern of behaviour develops. These patterns of behaviour are the outer, visible signs of inner moral values, traits, habits, cognitive structures and needs, which become more resistant to change with maturity.

Self-awareness

Self-awareness is a very important human characteristic. It is impossible to be aware of ourselves, and to have a self-image, without being aware of others. How we see ourselves is affected by how others see us and also by how we think others see us. These ideas (of who or what we are) are socially defined, so self-awareness is a social concept. Self-awareness leads to a desire for love and a feeling of relatedness to others, which are strong motivators in shaping personality. Most things that motivate us (e.g. love, security, prestige, power) and many things that cause frustration and conflict are related to needs of the self. They have an influence on how we feel about ourselves and how we judge ourselves. If we value ourselves in terms of what we own, then we shall be motivated by material gain; if we value ourselves in terms of non-material things, then these will motivate us.

Love and early relationships

The self is often the part of the personality that people are most concerned about. Our sense of self leads to a need for love and relationships with others, and these strongly influence our personalities. It is generally agreed that the first human relationships a baby experiences form the foundation stones of the child's developing personality. A baby has basic needs of food and warmth; he or she must be kept clean and given attention, affection and stimulation, which come from loving interactions with adults (usually parents).

In turn children usually try to please their parents, to win their love and approval. Children imitate attitudes and behaviours they see in the home, difficult skills are mastered, and, most of the time, they try to be obedient. Often children will explicitly be told that parental approval depends upon obedience ('I love you when you are good.'), and when they are naughty disapproval is usually clear. However, social training (or socialization) depends on a certain level of compliance from children, and this has important implications for very rebellious children (for example those with conduct disorders: see chapter 12).

One psychologist and psychoanalyst, Erik Erikson, has proposed that a baby learns whether the world is a good, pleasing, predictable, trustworthy place or a miserable, uncertain, frustrating one. He called these opposites 'basic trust' and 'basic mistrust', which are similar to adult attitudes of optimism and pessimism. Erikson proposed eight stages in life, each with a specific conflict (resulting in the development of a particular quality). The quality to be developed in infancy is trust. (You could try exercise 4.1 at this point.)

Neglect

A child who is neglected, abused or treated with indifference is unlikely to develop a warm, friendly impression of the world. An impression of unpredictability will prevent the child from feeling secure enough to seek independence and from seeing his or her own actions as being important and having results. These influences are likely to produce a troubled child who is difficult to bring up.

Martin Seligman describes the relationship between a caregiver and an infant as the beginning of a dance, a complex interaction with the environment that lasts through childhood. The result of this dance establishes the infant's level of helplessness or control. A baby responding (maybe by crying) to an event (perhaps a sudden, loud noise) may bring about a change in the environment (comfort from a caregiver), or there may be no predictable effect (the caregiver may or may not respond, irrespective of the baby's activities). Seligman has proposed that an infant learns to associate his or her behaviour with its consequences, so that helplessness results when there is no association between the two. When the baby's behaviour and its consequences (good or bad) correlate, the infant learns to repeat the action (if the outcome was good) or to avoid it (if it was bad). The baby learns the major lesson, that *responding works*, and that usually actions are connected with outcomes. When there is no connection between actions and outcomes it can lead to the development of helplessness, which can be found in severely neglectful homes. Children stop responding and learn that responding in general does not work or matter. The effects of this can be similar to those found in adults (failure to initiate responses, negative thoughts, anxiety and depression), but they could be more disastrous in infants. Babies are at a sensitive stage when learning about the self and its importance in the world, concepts thought by many to be the foundations of personality and confidence.

Biosocial Aspects

Prenatal influences

If early experiences are important foundations on which personality is built, then do even earlier environmental and biological influences, in the womb, also have an

Exercise 4.1

Erikson's Developmental Tasks and the Influences which may Hinder Children's Progress

STAGES OF DEVELOPMENT TOWARDS MATURITY

This table describes Erikson's ideas of the main developmental tasks for each stage from birth to adolescence. Consider each stage in turn and insert in the right-hand column the main hazards that you think could hinder a child's progress.

Age period	Characteristics to be achieved	Major hazards
Birth to 1 year	Sense of trust or security – gained from affection and gratification of needs	[For example, parental neglect or abuse]
1–4 years	Sense of autonomy – child viewing self as an individual in his or her own right, apart from parents although dependent on them	
4–5 years	Sense of initiative – period of vigorous reality testing, imagination and imitation of adult behaviour	
6–11 years	Sense of duty and accomplishment – laying aside fantasy play and undertaking real tasks, developing academic and social competencies	
12–15 years	Sense of identity – clarification in adolescence of who one is and what one's role in life is	
15 to adulthood	Sense of intimacy – ability to establish close personal relationships with members of both sexes	

Answers are on page 56.

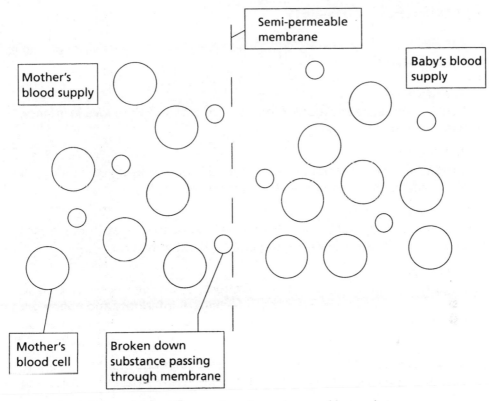

Figure 4.1   *A diagrammatic representation of a semi-permeable membrane*

effect? The foetus is not simply part of the mother's body, but is a different individual growing inside her. The mother and the foetus have different genes and
different nervous systems, with no direct connection between the two. They also
have their own blood streams, which are separated by a semi-permeable barrier (the
placenta). This barrier acts like a loosely woven filter: blood itself cannot pass
through, only nourishment and broken down substances, chemical elements and so
on (see Figure 4.1).

Nutrients pass from the mother, through the placenta, to the developing foetus.
However, in addition to nutrients toxic agents and viruses can also penetrate the
barrier and move from mother to embryo (or foetus). Such active substances may
affect the developing structures of the foetus (for example neural or endocrine
structures). These damaging substances have most effect during the early months
of pregnancy, the first eight weeks after conception when organ systems are first
emerging. Diseases (for example german measles or rubella and syphilis) are most
dangerous, as are drugs (for example alcohol, nicotine, thalidomide and barbitur-
ates), each causing different degrees of damage to the child.

Exercise 4.1 Answers

Major hazards

Birth to 1 year
Neglect, abuse, deprivation of consistent and appropriate love in infancy, harsh or early weaning

1–4 years
Conditions which interfere with the child's achieving a feeling of adequacy or the learning of skills such as talking

4–5 years
Over-strict discipline, internalization of rigid ethical attitudes which interfere with the child's spontaneity and reality testing

6–11 years
Excessive competition, personal limitations, other conditions which lead to experiences of failure, resulting in feelings of inferiority and poor work habits

12–15 years
Failure of society to provide clearly defined roles and standards, formation of cliques which provide clear but not always desirable roles and standards

15 to adulthood
Cultural and personal factors that lead to psychological isolation or to formal rather than warm personal relationships.

Severe distress in pregnancy

Some physical and psychological factors, which upset the mother considerably, can disrupt the embryo/foetus. Severe distress alters the chemical composition of the mother's blood (through stress-related effects on the endocrine system). Studies of non-human pregnant female animals exposed to severe stress have frequently shown that their offspring are smaller than average and prone to other physical and behavioural problems. Similarly, human mothers who report great anxiety during pregnancy are more likely to give birth to premature or low birth weight babies than those who do not. In 1999, Mary Curry and Marie Harvey examined the records of 403 women reporting among other things stress due to abuse or the recent loss of a loved one, and they found that this significantly predicted low birth weight babies.

Depression in women who are pregnant has also been shown to affect babies. Depression is associated with increased levels of cortisol in the blood, and in 1999

Brenda Lundy and colleagues reported that babies of prenatally depressed mothers whose blood cortisol levels were raised also showed raised cortisol levels in their blood. As newborns, these babies also performed less well than controls on tests of infant behaviour. It must be emphasized that the levels of stress discussed here are those caused by extreme and prolonged stress; the mild anxiety common in most pregnancies is not thought to have harmful effects on a developing child.

Long-term effects

It is still debatable what, if any, long-term effects on the unborn child are caused by maternal stress during pregnancy. Recent evidence suggests that severe distress during pregnancy, in the *short term*, results in a fretful, restless baby. However many of the studies investigating relationships between maternal attitudes and emotions suffer from considerable methodological problems, which make firm conclusions difficult. Most evidence in this area is from correlation studies, as it would be unthinkable to investigate the problem experimentally by deliberately stressing a group of pregnant mothers in order to measure any later effects upon their unborn children; consequently it is possible that other factors, rather than purely maternal stress, could be causing the effects on the babies.

Heredity and Environment: An Interaction

Genes plus environment

There are two basic requirements for the satisfactory development of a child's personality and the achievement of useful and adaptable behaviours for coping with life. These basic requirements are a normal set of genes (the basic units of heredity) and a suitable, encouraging environment in which the child can grow. Each child begins with a certain potential for development, which the environment he or she grows in can either limit or enhance. A child who is born with considerable potential for physical growth will not develop fully if nourishing food is severely restricted and if there are no opportunities for exercise. Equally a child who is born with considerable potential for cognitive ability will not fully develop that ability if stimulation or opportunities to learn are limited. Eleanor Maccoby has suggested, in 2000, that we should not underestimate the contribution of either nature or nurture, as they are 'inextricably interwoven all along the pathway from birth to maturity'.

Phenotypes

A person's phenotype is the sum of his or her characteristics that can be observed (seen, heard, touched etc.). Hair colour and personality are phenotypes. A person

Exercise 4.2

Your Family

Describe your family, in a few sentences, taking the viewpoint of three different family members. In what ways do the three 'environments' differ? What effect is this likely to have had upon the three family members?

inherits a particular set of genes (half each from the mother and the father), but the way these genes work depends on environmental influences too. The phenotype is the result of this interaction between all that has been inherited and all the environmental influences that have affected that person. (Environmental influences can include anything from those of the wider world and the family down to the chemical environment of the cells surrounding the person's genes.) You could try exercise 4.2 now.

In this way any personality is the result of an inherited disposition combined with the effects of that person's environments. This type of interaction is thought to influence the development of personality problems. Parents who have developed problems over the years cannot pass them on to their children by inheritance; they can be transmitted only by psychosocial means (e.g. teaching and learning). A fear of spiders cannot be passed from father to son by biological means, but what can be inherited is a *potential* to behave in a particular way if the conditions are right. A daughter who, like her mother, is afraid of leaving the home could have inherited a predisposition from her in the form of an over-reactive *autonomic nervous system* (ANS) and an introverted personality type. (The ANS is concerned with general activation, emergency responses and emotion, affecting such organs as the heart, stomach and bladder.) In these circumstances, if the right conditions are added to an inherited predisposition then neurotic fears are likely to develop, but if the right conditions are not present the fears will not develop. There is evidence that some psychological disorders (including schizophrenia) involve an inherited susceptibility, but this does not mean that the disorder *has* to develop, only that it is likely to if conditions are right.

Characteristics such as temperament (and intelligence) are very complicated, with multiple differences involved. These types of characteristic are too complex to be inherited by the action of one, single gene; they are polygenic (depending on the action of several genes). This *polygenic inheritance* is thought to be more important than abnormalities of a single gene in children with a neurotic personality, behaviour problems, learning difficulties and developmental problems.

Specific responses combine to form habitual responses, which in turn merge to form traits, until finally the dimension is a combination of traits.

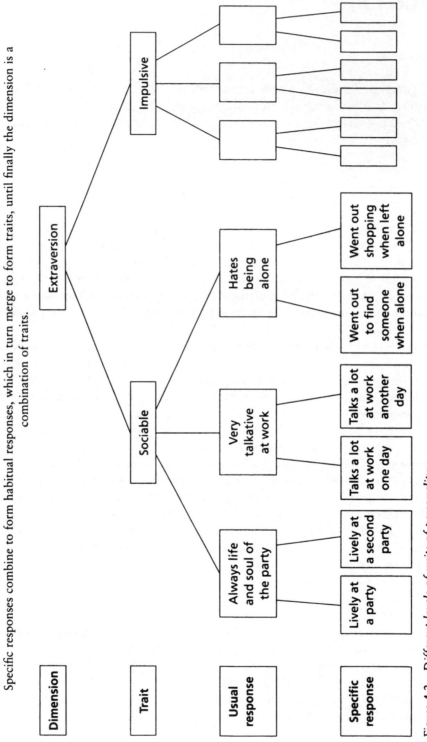

Figure 4.2 *Different levels of units of personality*

Traits

Trait theories of personality

Trait theories of personality suggest that traits are the fundamental building blocks of personality. We often use traits to describe others; saying 'Ranjeev is shy' implies that he behaves consistently in a shy way. If on one occasion he behaves differently it does not mean he is not generally shy. So a trait is a response to a situation that happens regularly, but need not occur every time. If some traits regularly go together, in many situations, they can be used to identify a psychological type. Figure 4.2 illustrates this hierarchical system. Hans Eysenck (and Raymond Cattell) analysed quantities of complex data (using a statistical technique called factor analysis) to identify basic traits which group together into underlying dimensions of personality.

A major idea of trait theorists is that an individual's personality is made up of a combination of traits, and how much of any particular trait we possess varies. In this view different personalities will be composed of varying numbers of traits combined in an assortment of ways. It is suggested that personality characteristics are relatively stable over time and that a person's personality is consistent in different situations.

Personality dimensions

Eysenck proposed two major personality dimensions, extraversion–introversion and stability–neuroticism. Extraverts tend to be sociable, like parties, need people around to talk to and dislike being alone. They are impulsive, easygoing and optimistic, take chances and need excitement, but can be aggressive and lose their tempers quickly. In contrast introverts tend to be shy, quiet, introspective, fond of solitary pursuits and cautious; they avoid excitement and keep their emotions under control. Not usually aggressive or quick-tempered, they are often more reliable than extraverts and more influenced by ethics, but they can be more pessimistic.

On the second dimension those who are strongly neurotic are not necessarily clinically neurotic. They can be well adjusted to work, family and social life, but tend to have mood swings and are easily upset, over-reacting in situations that would not bother a more stable person. Prone to psychosomatic symptoms (e.g. digestive disorders, insomnia) they suffer from anxiety and under severe stress may become neurotic more quickly than those at the stable end of the range. These descriptions are obviously the extremes of the dimensions, most of us coming somewhere in between. Sometimes it is said that a child was born an extravert, but early family life and all its environmental experiences have an effect too.

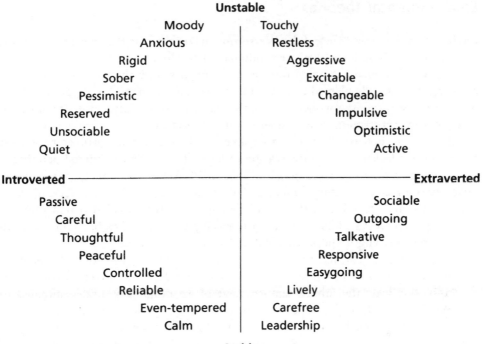

Figure 4.3   *Eysenck's extraversion/introversion and neuroticism/stability dimensions*

Early Environment

Pleasant, encouraging social experiences mean that a child will want to repeat them, while too many miserable social experiences will reinforce negative attitudes towards other people and to life in general. During the first six or seven years a child is more easily influenced than at later times towards being sociable or unsociable, or even antisocial. These very early social experiences at home and within the family are very important in determining lasting patterns of behaviour (extravert or introvert).

In 2000, Penny Roy, Michael Rutter and Andrew Pickles demonstrated marked differences between two groups, each of 19 children, from very similar biological backgrounds, who were reared in very different ways (one group in institutional care, the other in continuous long-term foster family care). Both groups were matched for sex, age and ethnicity; all the children came from extremely troubled families and were removed, on average, by 3 months. At 80 months, much higher levels of hyperactivity, inattention and, possibly, unsociability were found in the institutionally reared children than in those who were fostered. There is considerable evidence that environmental influences are important, but the question remains – how important?

Environmental theories

Environmental theorists (e.g. John Watson) focus on the role the environment plays in behaviour. These ideas were very popular in the first half of the twentieth century, and the emphasis on environment became so strong that parents (especially mothers) were usually blamed when their children had problems. For decades mothers became the scapegoats for their children's problems and 'maternal deprivation' or 'maternal overprotection' was frequently cited as the cause.

Fathers were not usually held responsible for their children's problems, because at that time a father's role in the rearing of his children was considered peripheral. This view has now changed, and in 1997 Henry Biller and Jon Lopez-Kimpton reviewed research connecting the father–child relationship to children's level of social competence and their interactions with their peers. They concluded that effective fathering increases a child's chances of developing a positive body image, self-esteem, moral strength and intellectual and social competence.

Watson's views reflected the extreme environmentalist's idea that the planned training of children's habits and ways of thinking could mould them into any desired result. In this view the inborn temperament of an infant was underestimated or completely ignored. A child does not just react, but also *acts* on the environment. Watson did not consider children's ability to think for themselves, nor did he take into account their capacity to be proactive in changing their environment to their own benefit. Each child processes information and superimposes an individual interpretation on events. In addition, people's sensitivity to their environments varies. These differences mean that any one environment can have different effects on two children, and even the most carefully planned training can have unexpected results. Watson's idea of the 'passive' child ready for training does not appear to reflect reality.

Social learning theorists such as Albert Bandura have proposed that we observe people around us who supply us with models for imitation. In a famous experiment he showed that children were more likely to behave aggressively after witnessing aggressive behaviour. Together with Walter Mischel, he demonstrated that watching adult models could change children's levels of self-control. After observing adult models the children in the experiment imitated the adults' level of self-control (or lack of it). If those around us behave in helpful ways we are likely to imitate their behaviour, and this is especially likely if we see them being rewarded for being helpful. If they say that selfish behaviour is bad, or if we see them being punished for behaving selfishly, we shall be less likely to behave selfishly. However, models often behave inconsistently; few people are always good or always bad, and some psychologists (e.g. Mischel) have proposed that our different behaviours result from the specific situations in which they occur. Social learning theory is discussed further in chapter 10.

Temperament

'Easy' and 'difficult' children

Most mothers will tell you that their children had personalities of their own from the moment of birth. Some seem to be easygoing and happy from the start, while others appear to begin life restless and easily disturbed. Many psychologists believe that these differences in *temperament* are inherited and remain stable throughout life. The word temperament refers to aspects of personality concerning mood, activity and general levels of energy. These general behavioural dispositions are present from infancy, so they influence the way a person reacts to the environment right from the beginning. Differences in temperament can influence the infant's interactions with carers and also may later develop into stable personality traits. When Stella Chess and her colleagues examined the temperaments of many infants over several years they found that some children stood out very early in life as either 'easy' or 'difficult' (see Thomas and colleagues, 1968). Approximately 70 per cent of the difficult children developed quite serious behaviour problems later. In contrast, the easy children made life trouble-free for their carers: the adults were allowed to feel that they were good, effective parents.

A large longitudinal study (the Dunedin Multidisciplinary Health and Development Study) has traced the health and behaviour of about 1,000 children in New Zealand (born in 1972 or 1973) from infancy to adolescence. Medical, psychological and sociological measurements were taken at two-yearly intervals, and in one section of the study Avshalom Caspi and colleagues followed the stability of children's temperament from 3 years of age. Twenty-two behaviours (e.g. fear, self-confidence, impulsivity) were rated and then combined on four dimensions of temperament (irritability, distractibility, sluggishness, and approach or friendliness). The researchers found some consistency, but only a very rough prediction for later childhood could be made from early temperament. A follow-up at 21 years found that inhibition and under-control at 3 years gave clues to adult personality. When Jerome Kagan and Marcel Zentner reviewed 70 longitudinal studies they concluded that the most consistent finding was that an *extreme* degree of impulsivity in preschool children predicted adolescent delinquency.

Early Experience

An impressionable age

It has long been believed that the first five or six years of a child's life are a critical or sensitive period, when there is a particular vulnerability to the effects of the environment. This idea has existed for many centuries, from the writings of the ancient Greeks (for example Plato) to more recent psychoanalytical theories. The belief generally focuses on the importance of character development in the first six years of life, viewing later experience as irrelevant.

The psychodynamic theory of personality

Sigmund Freud suggested a psychoanalytical theory concerning the influence of childhood experiences on personality development, which was based on case studies of adults in his clinical practice. In Freud's view the personality is made up of three aspects, the id, the ego and the superego. He believed the id to be innate (present at birth). It contains all of our instincts and drives, and being ruled by the pleasure principle it needs immediate gratification. In contrast, the ego is guided by the reality principle; it is rational and logical, and its task is to find safe and socially acceptable ways of satisfying the basic desires and demands of the id. The id demands immediate gratification, but the ego advises self-control. Freud suggested that the third part of the personality, the superego, develops at about 4 years of age and is the part of our personality that reminds us of the moral values we learned from our parents. The superego is perfectionist and forces the ego to consider moral judgements in addition to rational ones.

In a healthy individual these three parts are in balance, but Freud believed that we become anxious when the ego is threatened by too much conflict with the id or the superego. To cope with this we use defence mechanisms (for example, we may deny, even to ourselves, something that is unpleasant or embarrassing). He suggested that we all use defence mechanisms to reduce anxiety some of the time, but excessive use leads to psychological problems.

Freud claimed that all children go through five stages as they develop (oral, anal, phallic, latency, genital). At each stage of psychosexual development Freud believed there is a conflict to resolve. Failure to resolve the conflict successfully means the child becomes fixated at that stage, so that characteristics from the stage remain in the personality. (For example, a child who becomes fixated at the first oral stage and gets much pleasure from sucking would be passive; their sense of well-being would depend on those who care for them. If fixation happens later in this stage, when biting is more pleasurable, the person could be aggressive and sarcastic. Smoking, thumb sucking and chewing sweets are all thought to be ways of satisfying these oral needs.)

Despite describing a theory of personality development in childhood, Freud did not actually study any children, using only his account of memories from his adult patients. He did treat one child, 'Little Hans', but only indirectly by sending letters of advice to his father. Freud's theory is also very difficult to test; many of his concepts are difficult to define and measure, and many of his followers have disagreed strongly about interpreting his work. However, his theory has helped us to appreciate that childhood experiences can influence personality development.

So what do we know about the later effects of early experience and learning? Alan Clarke reviewed the available evidence about the effects of early experience and came to the conclusion that there is a shortage of valid scientific studies in the area. He did, however, suggest that there is little evidence that infants learn and remember more easily than adults. In fact, research indicates that adults are superior to infants in some measures of learning. Incidents that are traumatic in the short term seem to have only slight long-term effects on young children, while the specific effects of experiences before 7 months of age appear to be very short-term. However, when early learning is repeated and continually reinforced then long-term effects do appear, but these may well be the result of the later reinforcement rather than of the original learning. Clarke doubted the idea of an unchanging nature that develops during infancy and then remains static; early learning experiences do not seem to set the child on an inevitable pathway in life.

This is reassuring for parents who worry about the 'mistakes' they have made when dealing with their child, or about the disturbing emotional events the child has experienced. The most important thing is to act sensibly, and with sensitivity, when handling trauma, so that the negative experiences are not repeated until their temporary ill effects become deep and persistent.

Traumatic experience

Even studies of children who have experienced post-traumatic stress disorder (PTSD) indicate that most recover within one year. Paul Stallard and his colleagues reported, in 1999, that of 170 children (7 to 18 years) attending hospital after road accidents or sports injuries, 39 were suffering from PTSD. However, eight months later only nine of the children were still affected by the condition. In 2000, William Yule his and colleagues followed up children and adolescents who were involved in a shipping disaster. Approximately half of the 217 survivors developed PTSD at some time following the incident, but even after such a devastating experience about one-third of those recovered within one year, and two-thirds recovered by five to eight years later.

Personal constructs

In contrast to psychoanalytical theory George Kelly proposed a theory of personality in which differences in personality and behaviour are due to the various ways people perceive and process the information around them. Kelly suggested that we all need to make sense of the world about us and that, in attempting to do this, while still feeling in control, we try to predict what is going to happen. If we are unable to make predictions, we experience anxiety. We react consciously to our own interpretations of the world and we then test this view against reality. Consequently we all construct ideas about what is likely to happen, test these ideas out and change them if they don't work. In order to do this we use constructs (which can be imagined as the templates we use to view the world and make our predictions). We all have different constructs, and each reflects a person's individual personality.

Constructs are bipolar (with two opposite extremes, e.g. honest/dishonest or friendly/ unfriendly). Kelly argued that to understand a person's personality we must understand how he or she makes sense of the world and that we can do this by identifying his or her *personal constructs*. The Role Construct Repertory Test was developed to do this. You could try working out a list of your own personal constructs (see exercise 4.3).

Exercise 4.3

An Adaptation of Kelly's Role Construct Repertory Test

This is a very shortened version of Kelly's Repertory Test.

Opposite each item write down the name of the person in your life who fits that role. Each must be a personal acquaintance of yours, and if no one fits the description exactly write down the name of the person in your life who seems closest to the description. (For example, if you have no brother write the name of a person who you feel has been closest to a brother in your life.) You should not use any name more than once.

Role	Name
1 Your mother	....
2 Your father	....
3 Your brother (the closest to your age)	....
4 A teacher you liked	....
5 A teacher you disliked	....
6 The most intelligent person you know	....
7 The most successful person you know	....
8 The person you feel most sorry for	....
9 Someone you would like to know better	....

Now think about the people you have named, in groups of three, as indicated on the following page.

In each group think of some way in which any two of them are similar but the third is different (for example, in (a) numbers 2 and 8 may be friendly while number 4 is unfriendly).

Write the word that describes how two are similar in column 1 and the word describing how the third is different in column 2 (in the example above 'friendly' would go in column 1 and 'unfriendly' in column 2).

Groups of three people	Column 1	Column 2
(a) Nos 2, 4 and 8 (e.g. your father, a teacher you liked, and the person you feel most sorry for).	....	....
(b) Nos 3, 5 and 6	....	....
(c) Nos 4, 7 and 9	....	....
(d) Nos 6, 7 and 9	....	....

You may, of course, select other groups of three yourself and continue the exercise.

Do you feel that the contrasts in the two columns represent qualities that are important to you? If you remember, try the exercise again in a year's time, to see if the constructs have changed.

Are Western models universal?

Kwame Owusu-Bempah and D. Howitt have proposed that although Western models of human development claim to be universal they in fact have their roots in Judaeo-Christian religion and philosophy. They suggest that these models cannot be applied to all human groups, because there are many obvious differences between them, in their culture, religion and political and economic systems. The main psychological traditions were developed in particular cultures (Western) with particular needs at particular times, and in particular political and economic circumstances. Because of this, they cannot provide a complete understanding of the developmental process and needs of different groups, even within Western societies, and applying them to societies outside the Western world is even more inappropriate, leading to portrayals of these societies as not normal.

It has been proposed that Western perspectives are different from those of other world cultures on many dimensions – emotion, personality, health etc. Several psychologists have expressed the view that Western psychology is concerned with the personal growth of the individual, but that Asian and African psychologies are concerned with harmony with other humans, society, nature and the cosmos. Concerns have been expressed about the inadequacy and potential dangers of transporting Western ideas of personality development into these very different cultures. It is suggested that the self-reliant, self-directing ego of Western individualism is irrelevant to Asian and African cultures, but that other kinds of psychological structure and cognitive ability which contrast with Western ones but are appropriate to the different social and cultural contexts in which development occurs are neglected.

Different Styles of Child Rearing

There has been considerable research into how different styles of child rearing could influence a child's developing personality. However, there is still doubt about the answers to this. We do not know whether various methods of child rearing (e.g. late or early weaning, breast or bottle feeding) affect the psychological development of a child, but the evidence available indicates that it does not make much difference. All societies appear to be reasonably successful in turning helpless babies into independent, responsible members of their communities. In fact infants seem to have a basic readiness for training that takes the form of an inbuilt bias towards anything social.

Later parent–child relationships

When we consider the length of the relationship between parents and a child, its intimacy and influence over time, it is difficult not to expect that the quality of the relationship and early experiences must affect the child's developing personality. However again, valid research evidence in the area of human parenting is limited. Only long-term research can provide us with definite answers to these questions, and the studies that have been done have often suffered from several methodological problems. Research designs have been flawed, and samples have often been taken from biased groups. In addition, different questions have been asked and different assumptions made for various social classes and ethnic groups.

However, it is agreed by many researchers that there are two main dimensions underlying the attitudes and behaviour of parents, which seem to affect their children's personalities in predictable ways. These dimensions of warmth-hostility (or love–rejection) and control–autonomy (or restrictive–permissive) are independent, and in combination with each other have different effects on children's behaviour.

Strategies of parenting

The two dimensions have been combined (by Diana Baumrind) into four prototype styles of parenting. These are:

1 *authoritative* (combining a fair degree of control with warmth and responsiveness). These parents explain rules and encourage discussion.
2 *authoritarian* (combining high control with little warmth). These parents lay down rules expecting them to be followed without discussion or argument. Generally they wish to encourage hard work and respect in their children, but there is little give and take in the relationship and their demands are not moderated according to the children's needs.
3 *indulgent-permissive* (combining warmth and caring with little control). These parents tend to accept their children's behaviour without punishment when they misbehave.

4   *indifferent-indulgent* (combining little warmth with little control). These parents provide basic physical and emotional necessities for their children but not much else. They spend the minimum amount of time with their children and avoid emotional involvement.

Authoritative parents try to direct their child's activities rationally, being influenced by any relevant issues. Verbal give-and-take is encouraged, and the reasoning behind decisions is explained to the child. Respect is shown for the child's self-expression, respect for authority and work etc., encouraging a balance between independence and conformity. Firm control is provided when opinions differ, but the child is not suppressed with restrictions. These parents recognize their own rights as adults but also appreciate their child's individuality. (You could try exercise 4.4.)

Exercise 4.4

Parenting Styles

Use the information about styles of parenting given above to decide which style of parenting is represented in each example.

Four 14-year-old girls (Sian, Louise, Asher and Shelley) wanted to go to a midweek disco with their friends. However, it meant their staying out late, and they had school the next day. When they asked their parents for permission to go they got very different responses, as follows:–

Shelley's parents said yes, but they were not interested and did not really want to bother to answer.

Louise's parents said 'Yes, if you want to you can go. What time will you be home?'

Asher's parents said 'No, it goes on too late for a midweek event; perhaps we could come to a compromise.' When Asher asked 'Can I go if I leave early so that I can get to bed at a reasonable time?', they said yes.

Sian's parents said no. When she asked why, they exploded saying 'Because we say so, stop arguing.'

Before reading the answers, you may like to consider what your answer would have been in that situation.

See page 72 for the answers.

Exercise 4.4   Answers

Sian's parents are authoritarian; they felt no obligation to explain why she cannot go and there was little give and take.

Shelley's parents are indifferent-uninvolved; they did not care whether she went to the disco or not.

Asher's parents are authoritative; they explained why they did not want her to go and encouraged her to discuss the issue with them.

Louise's parents are probably indulgent-permissive; they readily agreed to the request, because it was something she wanted to do.

A review of the literature on character development in early childhood by Marvin Berkowitz and John Grych has identified five core strategies in parenting that together encourage character development. These are:

1   the use of induction (or reasoning)
2   nurturance and support
3   reasonable levels of 'demandingness'
4   modelling desirable behaviour
5   democratic family processes.

Research concerning the development of prosocial (socially acceptable) behaviour has also provided useful information about childcare procedures. Prosocial personality attributes are fostered by parental affection and nurturing, parental control (setting limits to behaviour), consistent childcare and training, the use of induction (reasoning) in discipline, modelling, giving children (especially adolescents) responsibility.

Caregivers have developed many strategies to encourage prosocial behaviour. Two that seem to be particularly helpful are explicit modelling (in which adults behave in ways they want the child to imitate) and induction (in which explanations are given that appeal to children's pride, their desire to be grown-up and their concern for others). It is impossible to use strategies intended to increase prosocial behaviour without also using ones to decrease aggressive behaviour. A variety of techniques are likely to be combined, and in the process a variety of socialization patterns are produced.

Personality disturbance

Large variations (extremely permissive or extremely authoritarian parents) from these 'ideal' strategies are usually considered to involve risks to a child's healthy development. However, the most serious consequences for children come from parents with hostile rejecting attitudes who persistently use punitive methods of control.

It has been found that the use by parents of extreme levels of physical punishment, imposed unpredictably, is associated with high levels of aggression in children.

Extreme levels of parental permissiveness toward a child's aggressive acts are also associated with aggression in the child. Psychologists often help parents deal with aggressive children by teaching them to observe what they do and to enforce rules consistently with their children. In this way parents can learn effective but non-punitive ways of controlling their aggressive children. When severe breakdowns in parenting occur, society provides several alternative systems of care (foster care, adoption, residential care), and psychological help and support is often available informally (from family, friends, neighbours etc.). Fortunately most children are remarkably robust, and research is continuing to investigate why some children are more resilient to life's experiences than others.

Recommended Reading

Cloninger, C. R. (1999) *Personality and Psychopathology*. Washington, DC: American Psychiatric Press. [A review of aspects of personality development in childhood and adolescence.]

Derlega, V. J. and Winstead, B. A. (1999) *Personality: Contemporary Theory and Research*, 2nd edn. Chicago: Nelson-Hall. [Major theoretical approaches to personality are discussed.]

Howe, J. A. M. (1990) *Encouraging the Development of Exceptional Skills and Talents*. Leicester: BPS Books. [Challenges the assumption that we have no control over the growth of outstanding ability.]

Kagan, J., Snidman, N., Arcus, D. and Resnick, J. S. (1994) *Galen's Prophecy: Temperament in Human Nature*. New York: Basic Books. [The effects of temperament.]

Lamb, M. E. (1997) *The Role of the Father in Child Development*, 3rd edn. New York: John Wiley. [The role of a father's influence on his children.]

Lewis, M. and Ramsay, D. (1999) *Soothing and Stress*. Mahwah, NJ: Lawrence Erlbaum. [Behavioural and physiological approaches to temperament, emotional expression, emotional regulation and mother–child interaction.]

Messer, D. and Millar, S. (1999) *Exploring Developmental Psychology: From Infancy to Adolescence*. London: Arnold. [An account of childhood to adolescence.]

References

Bandura, A. and Walters, R. (1959) *Social Learning and Personality Development*. New York: Holt. [The role of imitation and modelling in personality development.]

Baumrind, D. (1975) *Early Socialization and the Discipline Controversy*. Morristown, NJ: General Learning Press. [A discussion of discipline and early socialization.]

Baumrind, D. (1991) Parenting styles and adolescent development. In R. M. Learner, A. C. Petersen and J. Brookes-Gunn (eds), *Encyclopaedia of Adolescence*. New York: Garland. [A comparison of various parenting styles.]

Berkowitz, M. W. and Grych, J. H. (2000) Early character development and education. *Early-Education-and-Development*, 11(1), 55–72. [Five core parental strategies to foster character development.]

Biller, H. B. and Lopez-Kimpton, J. (1997) The father and the school-aged child. In M. E. Lamb (ed.), *The Role of the Father in Child Development*, 3rd edn. New York: John Wiley. [A review of research into the father–child relationship.]

Caspi, A. (2000) The child is father of the man: personality continuities from childhood to adulthood. *Journal of Personality and Social Psychology*, 78(1), 158–72. [A study of the stability of temperament.]

Cattell, R. (1990) Advances in Cattellian personality theory. In L. A. Pervin (ed.), *Handbook of Personality*. New York: Guilford Publications. [Trait theory of personality.]

Clarke, A. D. B. (1968) Problems in assessing the later effects of early experience. In E. Miller (ed.), *Foundations of Child Psychiatry*. Oxford: Pergamon. [The impressionable child.]

Connolly, K. and Martler, M. (1999) *Psychologically Speaking: A Book of Quotations*. Leicester: British Psychological Society. [For the sources of the quotations by Socrates and Churchill.]

Curry, M. A. and Harvey, S. M. (1998) Stress related to domestic violence during pregnancy and infant birth weight. In J. C. Campbell (ed.), *Empowering Survivors of Abuse: Health Care for Battered Women and their Children*. Thousand Oaks, USA: Sage. [The effects on newborn babies of severe maternal stress during pregnancy.]

Erikson, E. (1965) *Childhood and Society*. Harmondsworth: Penguin. [Erikson's theory of development.]

Eysenck, H. (1976) *The Measurement of Personality*. Lancaster: M.T.P. [A trait theory of personality.]

Freud, S. (1940/64) An outline of psychoanalysis. In J. Strachey (ed. and trans.), *The Standard Edition of the Complete Psychological Works of Sigmund Freud*. London: Hogarth Press. [A psychodynamic account of personality.]

Kagan, J. and Zentner, M. (1996) Early childhood predictors of adult psychopathology. *Harvard Review of Psychiatry*, 3(6), 341–50. [A review of 70 longitudinal studies concerning predictors of adult personality.]

Kelly, G. (1955) *The Psychology of Personal Construct*. New York: Norton. [A personal construct theory account of personality.]

Lundy, B. L., Jones, N. A., Field, T., Nearing, G., Davalos, M., Pietro, P. A., Schanberg, S. and Kuhn, C. (1999) Prenatal depression effects on neonates. *Infant Behavior and Development*, 22(1), 119–29. [A study of the effects on newborns of maternal prenatal depression.]

Maccoby, E. E. (2000) Parenting and its effects on children: on reading and misreading behaviour genetics. *Annual Review of Psychology*, 51, 1–28. [An account of the contributions to development of both nature and nurture.]

Owusu-Bempah, K. and Howitt, D. (2000) *Psychology Beyond Western Perspectives*. Leicester: BPS Books. [Looks at psychology across cultures.]

Roy, P., Rutter, M. and Pickles, A. (2000) Institutional care: risk from family background or pattern of rearing? *Journal of Psychology and Psychiatry*, 41(2), 139–49.

Seligman, M. E. P. (1975) *Helplessness: On Depression, Development and Death*. San Francisco, CA: Freeman. [Learned helplessness and its relationship to depression.]

Stallard P., Velleman, R. and Baldwin, S. (1999) Psychological screening of children for post-traumatic stress disorder. *Journal of Child Psychology and Psychiatry*, 40(7), 1075–82.

Thomas, A., Chess, S. and Birch, H. G. (1968) *Treatment and Behaviour of Disorders in Children*. London: London University Press. [Discusses work on 'difficult' children.]

Watson, J. B. and Watson, R. R. (1928) *Psychological Care of the Infant and Child*. New York: Norton. [An early behaviourist view of childhood.]

Yule, W., Bolton, D., Orlee, U., Boyle, S., O'Ryan, D. and Nurrish, J. (2000) The long-term psychological effects of a disaster experienced in adolescence, 1: The incidence and course of PTSD. *Journal of Child Psychology and Psychiatry*, 41(4), 503–11. [A study of post-traumatic stress disorder in the schoolchildren survivors of a shipping disaster.]

5
Playing and Learning

- The development of children's play
- Girls and boys at play
- The purpose of play
- The effects of play
- Playing or learning?

A mother hides her face behind her hands and then shouts 'peekaboo' while showing her face to her baby; a 3-year-old boy gives a toy Godzilla dinosaur a drink of water; two 7-year-old girls play hopscotch in the school playground; a 15-year-old boy practises bowling with his friends in the cricket nets at the weekend; two university students spend hours on the computer competing against each other at rally driving. All of these would be widely accepted as examples of playful behaviour.

Exercise 5.1

Play Activities

Consider the following activities:

- a pair of kittens chasing a ping-pong ball;
- a group of young chimpanzees playing with sticks;
- a team of office managers chasing each other in the woods with paintball weapons;
- a space crew carrying out a simulated mission.

What is being achieved in these different instances of 'play'?

Turn to page 76 for the answers.

Exercise 5.1 Answer

The kittens are learning to coordinate their chasing abilities in order to catch prey. The chimpanzees are practising the skills required for catching termites in their nests, using stripped sticks as bait. The office workers are learning team-building and collaborative skills in a different environment, which may involve changing roles and working together in various ways. The space crew are learning important lessons about what might go wrong in a safe and controlled environment. And all these play examples may also be pleasurable – which we can think of as a function in its own right.

Each of the activities in exercise 5.1 can be called play, yet they take place in different situations, are carried out by different people (or even non-human animals) and seem to have very different purposes. These examples remind us that play is not something confined to children, and they also show us that play may have some very serious real-world consequences. You may have been able to think of some of these already – compare your answers with ours.

Returning to the examples of children's play, we see that these are also very different from one another. Play can take place in various situations or contexts. Some kinds of play are solitary and others are social; some are more or less organized or formal; some are spontaneous and others have strict rules; some have clear aims while others are more exploratory; some are practical and others more diversional. It is hard to provide a clear definition of play – this umbrella term covers a wide range of activities, which can take place at many different points in children's and adults' lives. We can also find a range of different theoretical frameworks applied to understanding play in all its contexts. Play is no longer seen as simply children's games but as an important aspect of growing up, and one that can also have an effect on children's social development and their cognitive growth.

In this chapter we shall take a more detailed look at studies of children's play and its relationship to learning. We shall pick various examples of recent research that can help us answer some critical questions, such as why children play, whether play is necessary for healthy social and cognitive development, what can happen to children who have problems playing due to temperamental or physical difficulties, and whether play can be dangerous for children.

The Development of Children's Play

Piaget's theory of play

Jean Piaget, whose well-known theory of child development is outlined in chapter 7, suggested that there are three stages to the development of children's play. As in other areas of development, Piaget believed that play was inextricably linked to children's cognitive abilities. In the first two years of life, babies and young children engage in practice play, involving the simple repetition of actions for 'functional pleasure'. Blowing bubbles, sticking out your tongue, repeatedly kicking or throwing objects such as toys out of a pram or from a high chair, are all examples of this practice play.

As children become able to use symbols, which Piaget believed occurred after the age of two, they express this in *symbolic play*, through pretence, make-believe and fantasy. Piaget noticed that this kind of play involves the identification of one object with another, in the same way that language (which is a very important kind of symbol system) uses words to stand for objects. Piaget's own daughter Jacqueline at the age of two pretended that a pebble was a dog, that a biscuit was a lion, that a brush, held over her head, was an umbrella, and so forth. At about three years, children also start to use parts of their own bodies to identify with other people or things, such as brushing their teeth with a finger to stand for a toothbrush.

More recent studies support this relationship between play and children's other cognitive abilities. Vicky Lewis and her colleagues found that children's symbolic play relates to their verbal abilities, while functional play is more related to non-verbal cognitive abilities. Lewis also shows that children with visual impairments have been found to demonstrate similar levels of symbolic play sophistication to children without impairment, although the levels of functional play are lower for the visually impaired children.

Another important kind of symbolic play, which emerges a little later, is the elaborate sequences of sociodramatic play. These kinds of play are often based on imitating adult activities, such as doctors and patients and mummies and daddies, and conform to 'scripted' episodes, such as going to the shops or cooking a meal. As children become more experienced at their use of language they also engage in specific verbal games, consisting of plays on words, rhymes and jokes.

The final stage of play is an extension of the make-believe play which culminates in games with rules, and which Piaget documented as starting around the age of 6 or 7 years. They can be standardized games such as football or netball, whose rules are public, or they may be made-up games with rules that are spontaneously created, but stuck to rigidly. Piaget studied the game of marbles as played by children, showing that children younger than 10 considered the rules were determined by an authority higher than the players themselves, and thus were unchangeable, but children older than 10 could understand that rules were created to make the game playable by all, and that they could be changed by mutual agreement.

This progression from practice play through symbolic play to games with rules seems to hold for many children in many different contexts. The main problem with this model is that, as you will see in chapter 7, many of the abilities that Piaget ascribes to children have more recently been found in children of earlier ages and in different situations. One of the crucial aspects missing from Piaget's theory is a full consideration of the social nature of development, and play is an area in which social interaction is absolutely vital. Let us now consider how children can be helped in their play by other people.

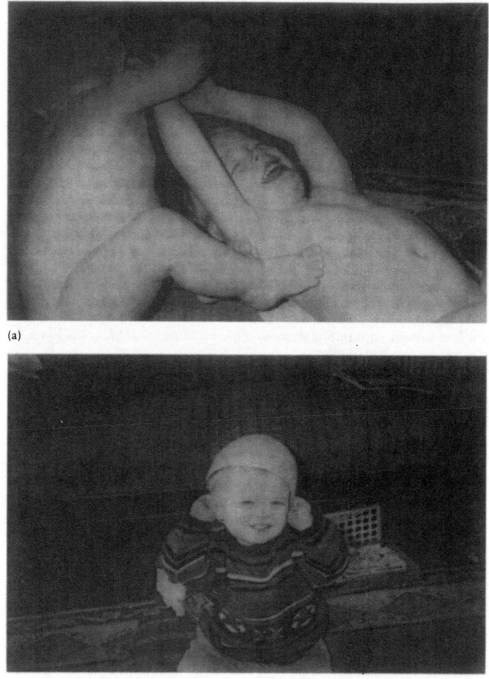

(a)

(b)

Figure 5.1   *Different kinds of play: a) rough and tumble play; b) pretend play.*
Reprinted by permission of Cerian Black

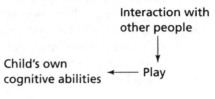

Piaget's approach

Child's own cognitive abilities ⟶ Play

Sociocultural approach

Interaction with
other people

Child's own ⟵ Play
cognitive abilities

Figure 5.2   *Different theories of play*

Sociocultural approaches to play

As illustrated in chapter 7, sociocultural theorists view play in a different light. While Piaget saw play as the expression of children's cognitive abilities, psychologists such as Lev Vygotsky believe play results from interactions with other people, which help children to develop their own cognitive abilities. For example, the game of peekaboo introduces the young baby to the ideas of pretence, early social interaction and turn-taking. The main differences between these two theoretical approaches to play are shown in Figure 5.2.

In infancy, babies tend to be played *to* by adults and older children, and they take a more passive role, such as in the game of peekaboo. As soon as they are able to imitate actions, which we now know can happen as early as 12 months, babies take a more active role in play activities, imitating adult actions that are within their own range of abilities, such as sticking out their tongues or babbling. At this stage babies can be played *with*: they then take an equal part in the activities and even initiate games themselves. Later in development, children become able to play with peers and on their own, making up their own forms of play and games.

Pretend play has been treated as related to a more sophisticated ability to integrate different representations of objects and events. For example, seeing its mother pretending that a banana is a telephone, a child must be able to infer that she is pretending, and that the true identity of the object – a banana – is different from the pretend identity – a telephone. Some important evidence supporting the sociocultural approach comes from a recent study with children aged 3 to 5 years by David Schwebel and his colleagues. The children were observed in free-play sessions at their preschool nursery, which were coded for imagination and for joint versus solitary play. The children were then tested for their ability to distinguish appearance from reality, being asked questions about a set of objects designed to be visually confusing, for example a sponge designed to look like a rock, or rubber fried eggs. Both imagination in pretend play and engagement in joint pretend play were found to relate to success with the appearance/reality task, but solitary pretend play did not lead to greater success.

A study by the English and Romanian Adoptees Study Team (discussed in chapter 3) comparing pretend play among various groups of 4-year-olds found that early deprivation strikingly affected children's play abilities. Children who had been adopted into the UK from Romanian orphanages and other institutions showed far less incidence of pretend play, or enjoyment of play, than children adopted from within the UK. These differences could not be explained by any variations in either cognitive or verbal abilities and suggest that early experiences can lead to deficits in children's socioemotional development, which make them less able to engage in this kind of play. These studies support the sociocultural emphasis on the importance of *other people* in helping children develop, even when playing.

Girls and Boys at Play

Recent work on gender typing (see chapter 11) tells us that children develop a *gender schema*, deciding that other people and they themselves belong to one or other sex, and that this leads to *gender-typed* preferences for people and activities. So do boys and girls play differently, and choose to play with different things? If so, how early do these differences begin, and how do they develop?

Gender-typed preferences

In an interesting study comparing the same infants at 3, 9 and 18 months, Anne Campbell and her colleagues found some very early gender-typed preferences. This study used a preferential looking procedure, in which babies are shown pairs of stimuli, and the time they spend looking at each one is a measure of preference. If a baby looks longer at one particular stimulus, it is assumed it can tell the difference between the two and prefers the one looked at for longer. Campbell's babies were shown pictures of themselves, older boys and girls, sex-typed toys and a video of children carrying out gender-typed activities. Even at 18 months, none of the infants showed a preference for their own photographs. But when they were shown pictures of gender-typed toys there were differences between the two sexes. At 9 months, boys preferred to look at pictures of a ball, a steering wheel, a train, cars and blocks. But there was no preference among the toy pictures for the girls of the same age. At 18 months, however, the girls also showed sex-typed preferences, for the pictures of a doll, an oven, a dustpan and brush, a pram and a toaster. We do not know from this study whether the babies would prefer to play with these toys, but it does suggest that gender-typing can begin very early on.

Is gender typing in play inevitable?

A study with older children by Jackie Marsh has attempted to break down some of this gender typing in sociodramatic play. Marsh's research is based on the assumption that the superheroes in children's popular culture reflect stereotypical gender differences (e.g. Superman compared with Supergirl). She set up an *intervention study* with a role-play area named the Batman and Batwoman HQ and provided resources for both literacy activities and active play. A group of 6- and 7-year-old children first discussed these resources and then spent ten days playing in the HQ 'cave'. Marsh found that girls engaged in role-play just as often as boys, although the female narratives usually placed Batwoman in a supportive role to Batman – and if Batwoman did work alone she was typically rescuing children or old women. However, the boys engaged in twice as much imaginative play (active, physical play involving the creation of imaginative scenarios) as the girls. Interestingly, Marsh describes findings similar to those of many other studies, in that the children preferred to play with same-sex peers: both girls and boys constructed elaborate narratives and same-sex role-play in small groups.

Boys and girls do play differently, but it seems that much of this difference is the result of social learning. From birth, male and female babies are treated differently by adults, and this socialization process continues throughout life. Gender differences show themselves in play just as in many other areas of children's development (see chapter 11).

The Purpose of Play

Piaget largely ignored the social aspects of development, and his theory focuses on how children's play reflects their levels of cognitive ability. Sociocultural theorists suggest that play is a useful way of practising, in a non-threatening environment, abilities that will be used later in real-life situations. 'Giving Godzilla a drink' can be seen as an opportunity to practise coordination skills in a setting where accuracy is less important than if you were trying to give a real person a drink with a real cup and real liquid. The context of play is one where things can be tried out. Sociodramatic play also helps children learn about relationships, roles and conventional patterns of behaviour, and to strengthen the distinction between appearance (or 'let's pretend') and reality, as well as to provide social interaction, which forms the basis for cognitive development.

Freud's view of play

The psychoanalytic approach takes a different view of play, but one in which its function is equally important. Sigmund Freud saw play as a means by which children could compensate for the anxieties and frustrations that they experience in everyday life. For example, their 'desire for mastery', because of which they want to emulate their parents by staying up late, being able to buy things and generally being free from childhood restrictions, can be acted out in a safe, stress-free environment through play. Anxiety about going to the doctor or taking medicine can be released through play with a teddy who has to visit the doctor or be given some imaginary cough mixture. Psychoanalytic approaches also suggest that play is one outlet for children's creativity (the other outlets being creating and dreaming). As children get older, their play and their creative activities (such as drawing or story-telling) become more repetitive, structured and formalized (you can read about these changes in creativity in chapter 9), leaving dreams as the only outlet for creativity in later childhood and adulthood.

These two theoretical approaches set the foundations for the emphasis on play both in a therapeutic setting, such as in play therapy, in which children are encouraged to express their hidden impulses in a harmless therapeutic context, and also in a business setting, in which playing games and game theory are used as tools to predict people's behaviour in given scenarios. At the time of writing, a literature search on play results in almost as many references to economics journals as to sources on child development. Play can be a serious business indeed!

Are friends always real?

Many children have imaginary companions at some stage. Attitudes towards these imaginary playmates have changed: in the 1930s, childcare books often warned of the negative effects of children playing with imaginary playmates, as it was believed this could easily lead to schizophrenia. By the 1960s, imaginary playmates had begun to be seen as positive and even as an expression of children's creativity. However, a recent survey of British children aged between 5 and 12 found that, while nearly half the children reported having past or present imaginary companions, there were no differences in creativity between those children with imaginary friends and those without. Girls were more likely than boys to report having imaginary friends. This study argues that rather than being the exception, having an imaginary friend is a part of mainstream child development. The imaginary friend can provide an opportunity to practise interactive skills, as he or she may be more easily swayed than real people to follow instructions or play according to the child's wishes. As children acquire a broader range of social interaction skills, imaginary friends tend to recede in frequency – by age 12 only 9 per cent of the children reported having a current imaginary friend.

The Effects of Play: Prosocial Behaviour and Aggression

We have seen that play can serve some useful purposes in children's lives, such as providing non-threatening environments for them to try out new skills and helping them to learn about social interaction and express desires. Let us focus in more detail on how these purposes might affect specific aspects of children's behaviour. Does playing 'nicely' result in better-behaved children? Does playing with aggressive toys reinforce children's aggressive tendencies? Much concern has focused on the boundary between play and aggression. There are two areas we can look at: first, the influence of children who do not seem able to play 'properly' and who disrupt other children's play activities, and, second, the influence of external forces, such as television and violent computer games.

Disruptive children and bullies

Studies of children's friendships using a *sociometric approach* have developed various social status categories. Popular children are those with positive, happy dispositions who show high levels of cooperative play, a willingness to share and little aggression. Unpopular children can be categorized into two groups. Rejected children are disruptive and argumentative, are extremely active and talkative, yet show little cooperative play, an unwillingness to share and much solitary behaviour as a consequence. Neglected children are shy, are rarely aggressive or antisocial and will avoid interaction with one other person, preferring to spend more time with groups. Rejected children are far more likely than those in either of the other two groups to be truants, drop out of school, come into contact with the police and reveal other problems of adolescence.

Clearly children's play abilities and friendships can have considerable after-effects. These are particularly marked in children who become bullies. Bullying differs from playful fighting or rough and tumble play, which is very common in school-aged children and is characterised by laughter and smiling and a degree of restraint. The bully, in contrast, engages in repeated and intentional hurt (either physical or psychological) to the victim. Rejected children are most likely to become bullies, and are also most often liable to misread a play fight situation as inviting a real fight. Rejected children are also likely to become victims of bullying. Both sides of the coin seem to be related to a lack of appropriate social skills, which could be lacking either in the children's home environment or in previous unsuccessful play experiences with other children.

Violent games and their effects

The range of toys that children would have had 100 years ago is far more limited than children in Western society have today. As well as the favourite teddy bear or stuffed doll, which can be seen as a substitute *attachment figure*, children now have an enormous range and variety of specially constructed toys which can play music, make sounds, talk to them, and even interact with them. There are also many technological toys, from the dummy mobile telephone to the home computer. These toys can bring potential dangers, and research has studied the negative effects of violent television and computer games on children.

There are two theoretical approaches we can apply to this issue. First, according to social learning theory children will learn the actions they observe or participate in in a virtual reality situation and then transfer them to real-life contexts. Sociocultural approaches also suggest that children may learn important lessons about violence through engaging in violent computer games, these being a more active form of

Exercise 5.2

Children's Behaviour

Think of two different children, one younger than 7 and one older than 11, whom you know from personal experience. How many of the criteria below would apply to their behaviour? If you can, ask the children's parents how they would rate them.

- Often fidgets with hands or feet or squirms in seat.
- Often leaves seat in classroom or when seating is expected.
- Often runs or climbs in situations where this is inappropriate.
- Often has difficulty playing quietly in leisure activities.
- Often is 'on the go' or acts as if 'driven by a motor'.
- Often talks excessively.
- Often blurts out answers to questions before they are completed.
- Often has difficulty awaiting his or her turn.
- Often interrupts or intrudes on others.

Turn to the end of the chapter to see how these types of behaviour have been used by developmental psychologists.

See page 86 for comments

learning than the more passive form of violence experienced on television. The second approach follows psychoanalytic theory and argues that playing aggressive games has a relaxing effect by channelling any latent aggression in a cathartic manner, thus having a positive effect on children's behaviour.

The social learning theory approach to the effects of watching violent behaviour starts from a well-known study by Albert Bandura and his colleagues in 1961, in which some preschool children watched an adult hitting and being aggressive towards a large inflatable 'Bobo' doll, while others watched the adult playing with different toys in the room and ignoring the doll. When the children were later allowed to play in the room, those who had watched the violent adult imitated the aggressive behaviour (figure 5.3). As well as imitating the adult's actions, they also invented new forms of aggression towards the doll, such as pretending to shoot it with a toy gun. Look carefully at the body language and facial expressions on the children and the adult in the photographs. Do you think this is true violent behaviour or simply imitation of a fun activity?

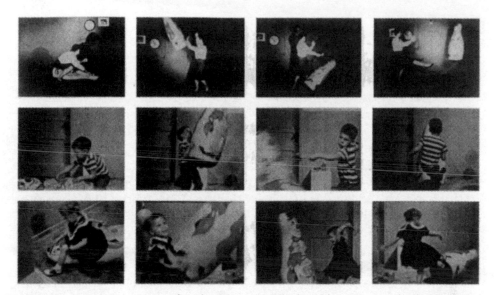

Figure 5.3 *Learning aggression by observation. Reproduced by courtesy of Albert Bandura*

More recent research into the effects of television seems to support Bandura's view of the effects of observing violent behaviour. We can see this from naturalistic studies, such as the one carried out in Canada in the 1980s, in which television was introduced to a small isolated community. During the two years after the introduction of television, the children's behaviour in the playground became more aggressive. But there is plenty of evidence to suggest that children with aggressive tendencies are more likely to watch aggressive television programmes, so the *correlational* nature of this research is important.

Research also shows short-term increases in aggressive behaviour following children's playing of violent computer games (e.g. Space Invaders) or watching violent cartoons (e.g. Road Runner), and that these are more commonly found among boys and among young children. A recent study by John Colwell and Jo Payne of children aged 12–13 in England found that 91.7 per cent played computer games, over half of them reporting that they had been playing for more than two years. They found gender differences too, the boys playing more often and for longer than girls, and the boys seemed to be more affected by their game-playing behaviour: those that played longest and most often had fewer friends and lower self-esteem and tended to prefer more aggressive games. The amount of exposure to games also appeared to relate to some extent to boys' scores on aggression measures. The jury is still out on the effects of violence in computer games on children's aggression, but there are some clear-cut gender differences, many more boys than girls choosing to spend time on such games. One possible reason for this is that the games often depend on complex spatial–temporal coordination, and boys are typically stronger at this kind of cognitive ability (see chapter 11).

Exercise 5.2   Comments

You have just rated the children on a list of symptoms outlined by the American Psychiatric Association's Diagnostic and Statistical Manual of Mental Disorders relating to Attention Deficit Hyperactivity Disorder (ADHD). ADHD is a fairly rare neurological developmental disorder which can be treated with drugs. Children who exhibit six or more of the nine symptoms listed, in at least two different contexts (such as at school and at home), would be classified as ADHD Hyperactive/Impulsive Type. (There is a second kind of ADHD, Inattentive Type, whose symptoms are not included in this list.)

Before worrying about the children you have just scored, it is very important to note that these symptoms can also be normal features of childhood. Researchers working in the field of ADHD argue that these patterns of behaviour can be normal when they apply to younger children, but by the age of about 11 it is clear that they are likely to cause problems. The symptomatic behaviour can also be due to more general features of distress or of children whose needs for attention are not being met.

You probably found that the younger child you thought about was likely to show more symptoms than the older child. (If you are at all concerned about your answers for the child aged 11 or above, consult the child's parents and an expert – ADHD affects less than 5 per cent of the normal child population and should be properly diagnosed only by a clinical child psychologist.)

It is important to remember, as we showed earlier, that even young children are clearly able to distinguish between make-believe and reality. Violence in cartoons is the least likely to be damaging from this perspective. For example, parents are not seriously concerned about the extreme levels of violence and mayhem in *Tom and Jerry* cartoons. Similarly, children in Bandura's original study were less likely to imitate violent behaviour if it was represented by a cartoon than if it was performed by real adults. Playing computer games may be a more dangerous activity, but the 'catharsis' explanation would suggest that children may expend some of their aggression in the game itself. And playing computer games can be just as social an experience as other forms of game playing, particularly with the advent of dual player games and internet gaming.

Playing or Learning?

We have already mentioned the wide range of educational toys marketed for young children. Any children's toy shop will include specifically educational toys which help children learn to spell, count, read and write, and solve mathematical problems, and the growing range of educational computer software and CD-ROMs testify to the appetite of parents and children to learn through less formalized play activities. This is a good place to think about the relationship between play and learning in more formal settings, such as school.

The educational reforms in the United Kingdom in the 1990s have ensured that every 4-year-old can attend school or nursery, and an early years curriculum has been specifically designed as an addition to the national curriculum introduced in 1988, which begins at age 5. Reception classes and preschool have often been seen as playful settings. In an important book, *Just Playing*, Janet Moyles discusses the different types of play that can take place in early education settings, identifying three main types: physical play, intellectual play and social/emotional play. Within each type of play, finer distinctions can be drawn and learning outcomes can be set out. For example, linguistic play (part of intellectual play) can be used to develop communication, word functions, explanations and so on through the medium of hearing, telling or writing stories. Moyles also differentiates between free and directed play, and shows how these two types of play can reinforce each other:

> Through free, exploratory play, children learn something about situations, people, attitudes and responses, materials, properties, textures, structures, visual, auditory and kinesthetic attributes, dependent upon the play activity. Through directed play, they are proposed another dimension and a further range of possibilities extending to a relative mastery within that area or activity. Through subsequent extended free play activities children are likely to be able to enhance, enrich and manifest learning.

Play would seem to be an important component of children's learning, and one well suited to nursery school activities. Yet play does not feature strongly in the activities of the infant school day. Various studies in England indicate that children work on their own for about 60 per cent of the day, 30 per cent of the day is spent on whole class teaching, and the remaining 10 per cent is devoted to child-to-child interaction – as little as 1 per cent is spent on free play activities. The pressures of the curriculum also lead to a reduction in the amount of time available for 'simply playing', despite the clear importance of this activity for other kinds of learning (as we have shown above).

School breaktimes do provide other opportunities for children to play, and surveys show some clear developmental changes: 11-year-old children tend to spend most of their time playing active games, the most popular being ball games and chasing games, while 16-year-olds spend their breaktimes mostly 'hanging around'. We see gender differences in breaktime activities: at age 11 boys are more likely to engage in active games than girls, while at age 16 girls tend not to play any active games at all, while boys' breaktime game-playing becomes dominated by football. We can see bully/victim scenarios unfolding, as well as playful rough-and-tumble games. In short, all the features of children's play that have been reviewed above manifest themselves in the school playground. Not surprisingly, schoolchildren often report breaktimes as their favourite part of the school day – the opportunities to play rather than work remind us that all work and no play makes Jack and Jill very dull indeed.

General Summary

We have looked at many different forms of play that take place at different points in a child's development, and identified some of the causes and effects of different types of play. Piaget's theory of play describes a progression from practice play, through symbolic play, to games with rules, a progression which unfolds with age. Play, for Piaget, reflects cognitive ability. Sociocultural theorists emphasize the outcomes of play – practising abilities in a non-threatening setting – and its interactional nature. The psychoanalytic view considers play to be a means of working out tensions in children's lives. Evidence shows us that girls and boys play in different ways, ways shaped by their gender schemas of gender-appropriate behaviour from an early age. Various behavioural problems that children demonstrate through play, such as bullying or aggression, are linked to disorders in social and emotional development, and can have far-reaching consequences. In short, play is an important part of children's development – one that can tell us about their social and cognitive abilities and which can affect their future lives in many different ways.

Recommended Reading

Barnes, P. (ed.) (1995) *Personal, Social and Emotional Development of Children*. Milton Keynes: Open University Press/Blackwell. [An accessible edited volume on various aspects of children's social development.]

Craig, W. (ed.) (2000) *Childhood Social Development: The Essential Readings*. Oxford: Blackwell. [Includes original articles on children's social relationships, bullying, the social world of the school, and aggression.]

Moyles, J. R. (1989) *Just Playing? The Role and Status of Play in Early Childhood Education*. Milton Keynes: Oxford University Press. [Discusses the relationship between play and learning, focusing mainly on early school contexts.]

Schaffer, H. R. (1996) *Social Development*. Oxford: Blackwell. [A comprehensive review of every aspect of children's social development from infancy to adolescence.]

Wood, D. J. (1998) *How Children Think and Learn: The Social Context of Cognitive Development*. Oxford: Blackwell. [Looks at play in relation to thinking and learning.]

References

American Psychiatric Association (1994) *Diagnostic and Statistical Manual of Mental Disorders*, 4th edn. Washington, DC: American Psychiatric Association. [A classification of psychological disorders.]

Bandura, A., Ross, D. and Ross, A. (1961) Transmission of aggression through imitation of aggressive models. *Journal of Abnormal and Social Psychology*, 63, 575–82. [The original 'Bobo doll' social learning theory study of aggression.]

Blatchford, P. (1998) *Social Life in School: Pupils' Experiences of Breaktime and Recess from 7 to 16 Years*. London: Falmer. [Survey of breaktime activities.]

Campbell, A., Shirley, L., Heywood, C. and Crook, C. (2000) Infants' visual preferences for sex-congruent babies, children, toys and activities: a longitudinal study. *British Journal of Developmental Psychology*, 18, 479–98. [Study showing preferences for same-sex toys in young babies.]

Colwell, J. and Payne, J. (2000) Negative correlates of computer game play in adolescents. *British Journal of Psychology*, 91, 295–310. [Survey of 12–13-year-olds showing the effects of playing computer games by sex on friendship, self-esteem and aggression.]

Comstock, G. and Scharrer, E. (1999) *Television: What's On, Who's Watching, and What Does it Mean?* New York: Academic Press. [Includes correlational studies of television watching and aggression.]

Gimpel, G. A. and Kuhn, B. R. (2000) Maternal report of attention deficit hyperactivity disorder symptoms in preschool children. *Child: Care, Health and Development*, 26(3), 163–79. [A study of ADHD including list of symptoms, suggesting parents may be at risk for over-diagonizing young children.]

Kreppner, J. M., O'Connor, T. G., Dunn, J., Andersen-Wood, L. and the English and Romanian Adoptees Study Team (1999) The pretend and social role play of children exposed to early severe deprivation. *British Journal of Developmental Psychology*, 17, 319–32. [A comparison study of Romanian and UK adoptees on social play abilities.]

Kupersmidt, J. B. and Coie, J. D. (1990) Preadolescent peer status, aggression and school adjustment as predictors of externalizing problems in adolescence. *Child Development*, 61, 1350–62. [A study showing consequences of friendship and social status in childhood.]

Lewis, V., Boucher, J., Lupton, L. and Watson, S. (2000) The relationships between symbolic play, functional play, verbal and non-verbal ability in young children. *International Journal of Language and Communication Disorders*, 35, 117–27. [Links between symbolic play and verbal ability and between functional play and non-verbal cognitive ability.]

Lewis, V., Norgate, S., Collis, G. and Reynolds, R. (2000) The consequences of visual impairment for children's symbolic and functional play. *British Journal of Developmental Psychology*, 18, 449–64. [Children with visual impairments show no differences in sophistication of symbolic play from children without impairments.]

Marsh, J. (2000) 'But I want to fly too!': girls and superhero play in the infant classroom. *Gender and Education*, 12(2), 209–20. [Gender differences in children's role-play – the 'Batman and Batwoman HQ'.]

Parker, J. G. and Gottman, J. M. (1987) Peer relations and later personal adjustment: are low-accepted children at risk? *Psychological Bulletin*, 102, 357–89. [A review article of long-term consequences of children's peer difficulties.]

Pearson, D., Rouse, H., Doswell, S., Ainsworth, C., Dawson, O., Simms, K., Edwards, L. and Faulconbridge, J. (2001) Prevalence of imaginary companions in a normal child population.

Child: Care, Health and Development, 27(1), 13–22. [A study of imaginary friends and creativity in childhood.]

Perlmutter, J. C. and Pellegrini, A. D. (1987) Children's verbal fantasy play with parents and peers. *Educational Psychology*, 7, 269–81. [A study showing links between verbal abilities and pretend play in early childhood.]

Piaget, J. (1951) *Play, Dreams and Imitation in Childhood*. London: Routledge & Kegan Paul. [Piaget's theory of play.]

Schwebel, D. C., Rosen, C. S. and Singer, J. L. (1999) Preschoolers' pretend play and theory of mind: the role of jointly constructed pretence. *British Journal of Developmental Psychology*, 17, 333–48. [A study of 3–5-year-olds showing joint play leading to success at appearance/reality task.]

Silvern, S. B. and Williamson, P. A. (1987) The effects of video game play on young children's aggression, fantasy, and pro-social behaviour. *Journal of Applied Developmental Psychology*, 8, 453–62. [More aggressive and less prosocial behaviour in 4–6-year-olds after watching violent cartoons or playing violent computer games.]

Williams, T. M. (1986) *The Impact of Television: A Natural Experiment in Three Communities*. Orlando, FL: Academic Press. [An introduction of television into isolated community in Canada leading to increased aggression among schoolchildren.]

6

Developing Language

- Is there an innate potential for language?
- The beginnings of language
- Developing sign language
- How do children learn language?
- Baby talk

Human language is a very complex system of communication. People can, and do, communicate by using gestures, postures and facial expression, and when we talk to each other some meaning is conveyed by the pace, tone, pitch and volume of our speech. But we communicate with one another principally by using words and sentences that convey meaning, and our use of words and sentences is highly creative, even in the most ordinary conversations. Language is organized at two levels: the level of sounds, which are meaningless in themselves, and the level of meaning – words, parts of words and combinations of words. There are reckoned to be about 50 or fewer separate speech sounds, but we can combine speech sounds to form large numbers of words, and combine words to form even larger numbers of sentences, including sentences which we have never heard before. This characteristic of language is called productivity, or creativity, and it means that there is no limit to the number of possible sentences in any language.

More complicated still, although some words in our language – such as crash or gurgle – sound rather like their meanings, the vast majority of them are arbitrary. The word dog, for example, does not sound or look more like a dog than like a cat, or a canary, or an easy chair; and cat and cot are very similar words in structure, but quite different in meaning; if you heard a sound halfway between cat and cot, you would understand it as either cat, cot or, perhaps, cut; you would not give it a meaning somehow halfway between a cat and a cot. The very specific meanings of different speech sounds and combinations are referred to as discreteness.

Is there an innate potential for language?

These and other characteristics of language make it so sophisticated that it seems quite a puzzle that any but the most intelligent of us manage to master the system.

Yet virtually all humans acquire language, and young children normally use it fluently and creatively from a very early age. Some psychologists and linguists (for example Noam Chomsky and Eric Lenneberg, and more recently Steven Pinker) have argued that human language is too complex to be learned from scratch, and that since all humans readily acquire language there must be some innate potential, or *language acquisition device* (LAD), which predisposes infants to extract linguistic information and form grammatical hypotheses from the language to which they are exposed, even if that language is poorly developed. Some of Pinker's examples of the creativity with which children acquire language are shown in box 6.1.

Chomsky, Lenneberg and Pinker have also argued that language is species-specific, that is exclusive to humans, since while virtually all humans acquire language, often

---

Box 6.1   Children Creating Language

Steven Pinker has argued that language is an instinct. Its development in a child does of course require exposure to language from others, and exposure is more effective when the learning child is younger. But even when children are exposed to only a bare and poorly structured language sample they usually develop for themselves a more complex and more creative language system. He quotes a number of examples, including the following:

1   children of immigrant workers from many countries in Hawaiian sugar plantations during the early years of the twentieth century, exposed only to a basic pidgin English consisting of borrowed phrases from English and other native languages of the workers, with very little grammatical structure;

2   children in a school for the deaf in Nicaragua, where communication consisted of unsuccessful attempts to teach lipreading and speech, plus the children's use of primitive gestural speech used to their hearing parents and siblings at home;

3   a single case study of a deaf child acquiring American Sign Language from two deaf parents, both of whom had learned the language only in their late teens and had learned, and spoke, it badly.

In all these cases the children growing up in linguistically impoverished environments developed a language system which was richer, and more clearly structured and rule-following, than that from which they had learned. Steven Pinker argues that the same creativity and independence apply to 'normal' language development: 'the same kind of linguistic genius is involved every time a child learns his or her mother tongue'.

in spite of imperfect exposure to it, no non-human appears capable of acquiring it. In many respects human language does seem to be unique and species-specific. Although some non-verbal communication systems do have human features, such as discreteness, the use of symbols and the ability to communicate about things remote in time and space, attempts to teach non-human animals (for example chimpanzees) human language or something like it have had only very limited success. The use of signs to communicate can be sophisticated and creative, but any evidence that animals can combine symbols into grammatical sentences is very doubtful. It seems that this crucial characteristic of human language, at least, may well be a quality not found in the communication systems of other animals.

How Does Language Develop?

Language development does not happen in a vacuum; it depends on, and largely parallels, cognitive and social development. For example, certain cognitive structures, notably representation and object permanence, are generally held to be prerequisite for naming behaviour and therefore language; and language development is mostly concerned with linguistic and non-linguistic interactions between children and caregivers.

Almost from its beginning, language is lawfully patterned. Children do not just learn words and sentences; they learn rules, and the job of the psychologist is essentially to discover the rules which most economically and adequately describe their language behaviour without either underestimating or overestimating their capacity. One important difficulty is that throughout development understanding exceeds, and precedes, production. Children can understand certain words and respond appropriately to them before they use them spontaneously in speech; this is true also for grammatical features of many kinds, and it is also true for phonological development (the development of speech sounds). Studies of spontaneous speech are often in danger of underestimating children's capacity (although they can also overestimate it, for example when children use words and phrases from songs and nursery rhymes without understanding them); they need to be supplemented by studies of comprehension and of speech in response to questions or prompts.

The beginnings of language

Babies vocalize from birth, although we do not normally describe their early crying as language. The first evidence of language is usually assumed to be a child's first recognizable word (although a recognizable word for one adult may not be one for another). 'Normal' children may produce their first word at any age between 7 months and 2 years or later; but even before the first word is produced a great deal of development relevant to language will have occurred. The child will have established a high degree of communicative skill, with the use of gesture and facial expression, and will be having 'conversations' with caregivers. These early conversations consist of talking by the adult, and vocalizations, movements, smiles and funny faces from the child. They are regulated, as adult conversations are, by variations in pitch and intensity and by the establishment and variation of eye contact between the speakers to indicate turn taking. More specifically, over the months before language proper begins, the child's vocalizations and perceptions develop phonologically in ways which have considerable implications for speech. For example, studies using the sucking response, discussed in chapter 2, as a measure of attention have found that as infants grow older they become more aware of phonological differences that are significant in their own spoken language, and less aware of differences that are not.

Babbling

Clearly varied vocalization appears when a child is a month or two old. Over the following months the frequency and variety of sounds – vowels, consonants and combinations and repetitions – increase dramatically until the first words appear; this preverbal vocalizing is known as babbling. It has been suggested that babbling is a phonological preparation for speech. According to this argument, during the babbling stage the sounds which are used in the child's local language are in some way 'reinforced' and become more frequently babbled, while sounds which are not so used tend to drop out – a process that can be described as acculturation.

But the relation between babbling and early speech is not as straightforward as this; for example, the consonants k and g appear early in a child's repertoire and are fairly frequently used in babbling, but in early speech they are almost always replaced by so-called 'front' consonants such as t and d: a child says 'tum and det it' rather than 'come and get it'. There are a number of possible reasons for sound substitutions of this kind, which are very consistent in young children's speech and are also mirrored, as we shall see later, by adults' talk to children, but they do indicate a certain discontinuity between babbling and speech. We should be cautious about accepting too easily that one is an obvious preparation for the other.

Early words

The age at which children produce their first word varies greatly; it depends on a child's sex and social class, on whether he or 'she is a twin or an only child, on whether the home is monolingual or bilingual. The first words produced are usually nouns, at least partly because these are frequently used in the caregivers' speech at this stage, and also adjectives. Verbs tend to come later, and words of other types hardly at all until sentences are produced (and not very early even then). Using words, of course, involves not only knowing the words but also knowing their referents – the things or events that they signify. Children at the one-word stage frequently 'overextend' words – for example referring to all four-legged animals as 'doggie', or all men as 'daddy'. They also sometimes 'underextend', so that 'doggie'

"*Not ŏ, dummy, ōo.*"

Drawing by Modell, New Yorker Magazine, 1983/© Cartoonbank

is reserved for one particular toy or pet but not used for other dogs. So meanings as well as words have to be learned as the vocabulary grows.

One-word utterances may have several functions. Some may be simply labelling, but others refer to absent objects and appear to be orders for the caregiver to provide them; some are self-imperatives, apparently announcing the child's intention to do or get something; and some express emotion. So single-word statements may be semantically complex, and some psychologists have suggested that they are also grammatically complex. According to this view, a single-word statement is a *holophrase* – a sentence with an underlying grammar which, however, is only one word long. Its length is not limited by an absence of grammar, but by the child's limited vocabulary, memory and attention span, and perhaps by a failure to recognize the need to verbalize all its parts. After all, if you mean to tell your mother that you want some milk, why bother to name yourself when you are obviously the speaker and saying 'milk' will do the job? But this interpretation of single-word statements has been challenged by other researchers, who claim that at the one-word stage children's cognitive development is not far enough advanced for them to possess grammar; clear evidence can appear only when sentences are more than one word long.

Early sentences

A sentence can be defined as the occurrence of more than one word in a single utterance, joined together in a pattern. Evidence of 'patterning', or rule following, in early sentences is generally in terms of word ordering. If a child often says 'mummy coat' and never says 'coat mummy', this is evidence that he or she possesses a rule governing the order in which different words (or types of word) should be combined in a sentence.

Early sentences are very short, mostly only two words long with a few longer utterances and probably quite a few one-word utterances as well; so the *mean length of utterance,* or MLU, is less than two. They consist mostly of 'content' words – nouns, verbs and adjectives for the most part – and contain very few 'function' words – such as to, for, and, but, the and a, which essentially bind content words together in a sentence without substantially adding meaning of their own. Also missing are auxiliary bits of verbs, such as is, am, and will, and *inflections* – endings such as -ing, -s (for a plural word or for the present tense) and -d (for the past tense of a verb). The result has been described as telegraphic: sentences like 'Adam coat', 'big car', 'doggie bite'. Telegraphic speech occurs both spontaneously and in imitation: children frequently imitate adults' speech, and when they do they preserve the word order of the original but shorten the utterance, by dropping its function words and keeping the content words (probably largely because those are the words most heavily stressed by the adult model).

Early sentences clearly have a grammatical structure; but children do not necessarily follow quite the same rules as those of adults. To discover and describe a child's rules we need to consider both the patterns in which their words are ordered and the context in which they are used. For example, 'mummy sock' may be used to mean one thing when mummy puts her own sock on in front of her child but another when the child's own sock is being put on by mummy (this real-life example was reported by Lois Bloom). The same phrase in different contexts has not only two meanings but also two underlying grammatical structures. Bloom, Roger Brown and others have suggested that it is important to define the structure of a child's speech with respect to the semantic (or meaning-related) functions of the words in it: agent, action, object, location and so on. By such criteria, too, early speech is lawfully patterned, and order rules are observed in the expression of semantic categories.

Inflections

When young children talk they tend not to use inflections, word endings which convey extra meanings. Where an adult would say 'daddy goes' a young child says 'daddy go', and 'mummy's sock' is 'mummy sock'. Some inflections come into a child's repertoire earlier than others. Plural endings (for example socks rather than sock when there are two of them) begin to be used quite early, while past tense endings (washed instead of wash when the washing has already been done) appear later, and usually at a time when the MLU is longer than two; saying goes instead of go may come later still. One explanation for the difference in timing is the frequency with which the inflections are used in caregivers' speech; plurals are used more often than past tenses, so the child's exposure to plural forms is greater. This is a good explanation of some differences, but not of others, such as the late appearance of goes for go. Other factors are likely to be the complexity of the meaning conveyed by the inflection, and the amount of change to the original word that is required. This is more noticeable in languages more heavily inflected than English, such as German and Russian.

When children do use inflections, it is clear that they very quickly develop rules for using them rather than learn, say, plural words or past-tense verbs piecemeal. Oddly enough, some of the best evidence for this comes from children's mistakes, as box 6.2 illustrates. It seems to be very easy to learn a rule, but it takes time to learn exceptions and irregularities. Gary Marcus described the process as one of 'rule-and-memory', in which a rule is applied unless it is blocked by the memory of an irregular form; retrieving the irregular form from memory is not always efficient, and its efficiency is improved by practice and by the frequency of its occurrence in the speech of parents and others.

Complex sentences

Adults speaking to each other use not only simple sentences of the kind used by youngish children but also sentences which are in some way transformed, for example into a negative form – 'I don't want any supper' – or into an interrogative form – 'Who took my pen? Was it you?' or a passive form – 'The match was stopped by the referee'. These transformations are complex and may involve several rules for producing and ordering the elements within the sentence. Children may take some time to produce sentences of this kind, and they seem to master and apply the different rules one by one. Early negatives and questions, for example, may be like 'No want some supper' and 'Why he's got my car?' because 'transportation', or reordering, rules are not yet learned. Indeed, adult forms in many cases cannot emerge until a child has learned quite complex verb forms employing auxiliaries such as is (followed by a verb ending in -ing), can, may, will and so on. As with the use of inflections, learning to produce complex sentences depends on conceptual difficulty (what do relative clauses and conditional tenses mean?) and also grammatical complexity, as cross-cultural studies have shown. When the grammatical complexity of a sentence type is pretty well the same in two languages, children begin to produce it at much the same age in both languages; when grammatical complexity differs, so does the age of acquisition. For example, well-formed questions appear early in Hebrew, in

Box 6.2   Rules and Mistakes

The English language is full of exceptions and irregularities: we say grew instead of growed, dug instead of digged, feet instead of foots, mice instead of mouses. But young children, by the time they are 3–4 years old, often produce sentences containing regularized forms of irregular words, for example:

'I digged in the garden.'
'The sheeps runned away.'
'Look at the mouses.'
'Peter Pan never growed up.'
'We holded the kittens.'
'My foots gotted wet.'

At the same age children can apply appropriate plural and past-tense endings to nonsense words, as Jean Berko and Roger Brown, among others, showed. Children might be shown a picture of a nonsense animal and told 'This is a wug. Now, (a second picture being added) this is another one. There are two . . .' and children as young as 4 years old have no difficulty in finishing the sentence with wugs.

Or they might be told 'This is a man who wugs. He wugs every days. Yesterday he . . .' and children supply the final word wugged. Incidentally, they also tell you with confidence that a man who glings today glinged yesterday, although adults in the same situation are apt to suggest that he glung, glang – or even glought!

Both mistakes and nonsense-word formations are evidence that children possess rules, apply them rigorously (even when adults seem to be going wrong) and generalize them easily to new instances.

which they are structurally quite simple, and later in English, in which they are quite complex.

Adults can also use 'embedded' sentences, in which one sentence is included within another: 'Here's the book I was reading yesterday'; 'I don't want you to do that'; 'The girl I wanted to marry turned me down.' They produce, and understand, sentences in which the semantic relations among the words do not closely mirror the surface structure of the sentences: for example, in the sentence 'John is easy to please', who is doing the pleasing and who is being pleased? Is your answer the same for the sentence 'John is eager to please'? Adults observe a number of rules which most of them have never heard in so many words, such as the 'minimal distance principle' (MDP) and its exceptions. If John persuades Sarah to read this chapter, who reads it, John or Sarah? If John promises Sarah to read it, which of them does the reading? Ask your friends and see if you all agree on the answers. If you do, you may be surprised to learn that you have all learned the MDP, which is that when a sentence contains a 'complement clause', with an infinitive verb and no subject, the implied subject of that verb is the noun, or noun phrase, immediately before it. You have also all learned that certain verbs, such as promise, consistently violate the MDP.

Children take time to acquire these features of adult speech, and a number of studies have shown imperfections in their understanding. Carol Chomsky, for example, showed children 5–10 years old a blindfolded doll and asked them 'Is the doll hard to see or easy to see?' Young children were apt to answer with confidence that the doll was hard to see, because it was blindfolded; in other words, they interpreted the sentence as though the doll was expected to do the seeing. The adult interpretation, that the doll is to be seen rather than to see, appeared reliably only in children of 7 or 8. It is misleading, then, to think of language development as something which is more or less over by the time a child is about 4 or 5. Important language learning continues throughout much of childhood.

Developing sign language

We have argued that there are general similarities among various languages in the course of development. Does the acquisition of a very different type of language, the manual sign languages of deaf communities, show similar characteristics? There is some evidence that it does. For example, Laura Pettito and Paula Marentette found that 10–14-month-old deaf children learning American Sign Language (SL) 'babble' manually, using hand gestures which will later be significant for their language, as well as others which will not be. Hearing children also show manual babbling, and the range of gestures seems much the same; the difference is in the babbling's frequency, which is greater in the deaf children. For that matter, deaf children also vocalize, but vocal babbling does not seem to develop in the way that it does for hearing children. Nor is there much evidence concerning the development, or possible acculturation, of manual babbling over the early months.

One reason for this may be that the first signs are produced quite early by deaf children – at about 7 or 8 months old – in contrast to the average age of 12 months for the first spoken word. The early beginning of signing occurs in both deaf and hearing children of deaf-and-signing parents, and Philip and Elisabeth Prinz found that a hearing child in a bilingual household produced her first sign at 7 months and her first word at 12 months. Joseph Garcia has suggested that parents in hearing families should communicate with their babies in sign language; communication is established earlier and is more precise, and babies and toddlers are less likely to be frustrated because they cannot make themselves understood. He also reported that hearing babies who used sign language with their parents learned to speak earlier and were more advanced in vocabulary at 2–3 years old than babies who had not signed.

One suggested reason for the earlier production of signs is that they are easier to learn, because more signs than words are iconic: signs such as pointing or raising the hand to the mouth to indicate eating bear an obvious relation to their meanings. But much of SL is not iconic; Michael Orlansky and John Bonvillian studied signing children at 12 and 18 months old, and found that at both ages only about a third of signs were iconic; another third were 'metonymic', bearing only a remote and hardly perceptible relation to their meanings, and the rest were arbitrary, bearing no discernible relation. Another difference of course is modality: SL is visual, spoken language auditory, and there may be maturational differences in the modalities for infants of 8–10 months or so which could explain the difference in onset. It is also likely that the motor control needed for the reasonably accurate production of signs may be achieved at an earlier age than that needed to produce distinct, comprehensible speech sounds.

Whatever the reason for the earlier emergence of signs, the advantage of SL does not seem to persist into later development; children reach the two-sign stage at much the same age as others reach the two-word stage, and show similar features. For example, although SL does have inflections, as spoken language does, young children use sign order, and appear to possess order rules, to convey meaning, while the use of inflections comes later. They also use semantic relations in their multi-sign utterances, as others of the same age do in early spoken sentences, and different relations emerge in pretty well the same order in both types of language. The similarity among languages superficially so different may be partly because factors such as frequency in parental language and semantic and grammatical complexity are likely to be important for every language; some researchers and theorists also feel that it is confirming evidence for the importance of biological predispositions to language.

Two qualifications need to be added. First, about 90 per cent of deaf children are born to hearing parents, so they do not grow up in homes where SL is the native language; if they learn to sign they often do so later, and less fluently, than native speakers. This means that most studies of SL development include *hearing* as well as deaf children of deaf-and-signing parents, and these children are bilingual, and therefore a special group, almost from the start. Secondly, SL is not universal; the sign languages of different communities are scarcely more alike than are different spoken languages. So, as with spoken languages, findings from the study of one language are likely, but can not be automatically assumed, to generalize completely to others.

How Do Children Learn Language?

Language learning seems an immense task, and conventional learning theory has difficulty in explaining it; see, for example, the account suggested by Burrhus Skinner, which is described in box 6.3. As we have seen, many psychologists have explained language development more in terms of innate potential and instinct. But whether or not human babies have a biologically given predisposition to help them

Box 6.3   Learning Language: A Behaviourist Account

In the 1930s and 1940s an eminent American psychologist, Burrhus Skinner, suggested that we learn language as we learn other kinds of behaviour, by *operant conditioning*. He argued that learning is the association of stimuli with behavioural responses through selective reinforcement, shaping and generalization. How can these principles be applied to language learning?

Skinner proposed that when children produce vocalizations – either spontaneously or as an imitation of the sounds produced by parents or others – they may be selectively reinforced, that is they are rewarded and become more likely to occur in certain situations than in others. Reinforcement may take the form of parental approval or attention, or it may mean 'getting what you want'. Some vocalizations may be rewarded when, and only when, they occur in a certain 'stimulus condition': for example, a sound like 'doggie' will be greeted with attention and praise when it is produced in the presence of the family dog, not when it is addressed to the cat. Skinner called a verbal response reinforced in this way a 'tact' (related to touching or pointing to a stimulus object). Other vocalizations are reinforced when they occur in certain motivating conditions: for example, saying milk when you are thirsty is likely to result in getting a drink, while saying doggie will not. Skinner called this kind of 'verbal operant' a 'mand' (related to command or demand).

Once a mand or a tact is learned as an appropriate response in a given situation, it can be 'shaped': parents and others at first reward any vocalization that is remotely like an appropriate one, but as the child grows older they become more fussy, rewarding only the sounds that are a better and better approximation to the 'right' one, from their point of view. The use of speech sounds can also be extended by generalization from one context to a similar one.

What about learning whole sentences, rather than isolated words and simple, short phrases? Skinner suggested that this can be explained, like serial learning of other kinds, by the experience of 'verbal chaining' and the learning of 'sequential probabilities' – the probability that certain words, or parts of speech, may be followed by others. For example, we learn that a definite or indefinite article – the or a – is very likely to be followed, immediately or almost immediately, by a noun, which in turn is likely to be followed by a verb, and then perhaps by another noun as the object of that verb. So from exposure to sentences children may learn sequential rules, which they can then generalize to form, and to understand, new sentences.

Is Skinner's model of language learning a feasible one?

Certainly children do learn to label and to ask for what they want; parents do reinforce the appropriate utterances of their children; and older children and adults do seem to have a good grasp of the sequential probabilities of words, or at least word types, in the language.

But probably most psychologists would argue that the model does not come to terms with the complexity of grammatical structures, which often require deeper and more intricate analysis than the relatively superficial 'left-to-right' description of sentence structure, and that it cannot adequately explain the productivity and creativity of even young children's language.

to acquire language, it is clear that they have a lot to learn. Obviously, they learn the particular language to which they are exposed, and human languages are so different from one another, in vocabulary and structure, that the characteristics of any one language could not possibly be inbuilt. The extremely rare cases which have been reported, of children who have grown up virtually isolated from language, indicate that exposure, probably at a comparatively early age, is essential if language is ever to be adequately mastered (see, for example, the case of Genie reported by Susan Curtiss and described in box 6.4). This has been taken as evidence not only of the need for exposure but also of the existence of a 'critical period' or age of optimal receptivity for language learning.

To a large extent, then, we have to learn language from others; and it is possible to see ways in which this can happen. Young children almost invariably receive an easy introduction to language from their caregivers, and the natural interactions between children and caregivers provide plenty of opportunity for teaching and learning.

Babytalk

When adults talk to young children, their speech is different from that used with other adults; they use what is known as an *adult-child register* or, more colloquially, baby talk or 'motherese'. The characteristics of babytalk have been studied for several different languages, and while naturally details do vary they tend to show common features.

What are the essentials of babytalk? There are probably well over 100 separate features; some of the most notable are listed in box 6.5. Catherine Snow and Charles Ferguson argued that there are essentially three components – simplifying, clarifying and expressive. Babytalk is simplified, in that sentences are shorter and simpler in structure and vocabulary; it is clearer, in that it is slower and more clearly articulated; and it is expressive, in that it uses diminutives, pet names and euphemisms. As

Box 6.4   Genie: Growing up Without Language

Genie, as she is known to us, was reared in extreme social isolation and physical constraint from early infancy until she was about 13½ years old. She was kept virtually immobilized and alone in her room, her only human contact being with her father, who apparently did not speak to her but beat her when she made a sound. When rescued from these conditions, she was severely undernourished and largely unsocialised and had no language skills. She rapidly acquired a large vocabulary of words and became able to express quite sophisticated meanings, but there was little grammatical structure in her 'sentences', which were word strings, if anything rather less patterned than the typical 'telegraphic speech' of young children, for example:

applesauce buy store
Genie have Momma have baby grow up
I like elephant eat peanut

By the time she was 18, in spite of a long-running language training programme, Genie still showed little evidence of syntactic development. She could not use auxiliary verbs to form complex tenses (can go, will go, have gone, do go, is going), could not produce properly formed questions, and found it hard to understand complex sentences. Her difficulty in developing syntax, although she could understand and express complex semantic relations, has been taken as further evidence of a critical period, or at least a sensitive period, for language learning; as with the learning of a second language, if the exposure needed for learning a language does not occur in early childhood, language is much more difficult to master, and if it does not occur until puberty or later, language mastery will almost certainly be poor and incomplete.

we have already mentioned, babytalk is similar in some ways to the speech of young children, both in its simplicity and, for example, in its use of 'consonant substitution': adults talking to little children are apt to say 'tum on' rather than 'come on', just as the children themselves do. You may like to observe some features of babytalk for yourself by trying out exercise 6.1.

As children develop, and as they show more signs of comprehension and produce more elaborate language, caregivers' speech becomes more complex. Several investigators have found that the speech of mothers is finely tuned to that of their children, slightly more advanced in its complexity, and increasing in complexity as the children's production grows. In other words, the developing child is presented,

Box 6.5   Some Characteristics of Babytalk

Utterances are:

- shorter (in MLU or mean preverb length)
- simpler (fewer clauses)
- better formed (fewer dysfluencies, errors, interruptions)
- more limited in vocabulary
- more repetitive

Speech is:

- slower
- more articulated (longer pauses at the ends of clauses, more stress on the separate syllables of long words and phrases)
- higher and more varied in pitch (so-called 'nursery tone')

Phonology is often modified by:

- the substitution of 'front' for 'back' consonants (e.g. tum for come)
- the reduction of consonant clusters (e.g. t instead of st)
- the deletion or weakening of final syllables (e.g. tummy instead of stomach)

Vocabulary and *syntax* are often modified by:

- the replacement of pronouns by proper names or kin terms (e.g. mummy instead of me; Katie instead of you)
- pet names and affixes (dolly, Johnny, Katykins)
- 'let's' and 'shall we . . . ?' (instead of orders)

in the mother's speech, with a well-designed set of language lessons. However, we still do not know exactly what babytalk accomplishes, and how. It is clear that what Snow termed 'conversation with an interested adult' is important for children's language development in general terms, but not so clear whether children learn specific features of language from exposure to their mothers' conversation.

Imitation

Children frequently *imitate* the utterances of their caregivers; by one estimate, about 10 per cent of a child's speech at 2–3 years of age consists of repetition of what an

Exercise 6.1

Talking to Children and Talking to Adults

What differences do people make in their speech when they are talking to children rather than adults? Ask your friends, acquaintances or relations to help you with 'a study of children's stories'. Take one person at a time into a quiet area, with a tape recorder, and ask him or her to make up a story which would be good to tell to a group of 3-year-old children (if your helpers can not think of anything, you can show them a picture from a book or magazine, or suggest a story or nursery rhyme, to get them started). Ask your helper to describe the story to you; then ask him or her to record it as though telling it to the 3-year-old children.

Afterwards, compare the speech of your helpers (a) when they tell you the story and (b) when they tell it to the children. Look for possible differences in complexity, articulation, pitch, rate of speaking; and consult Box 6.5 for other differences you might expect to find.

Some measures of complexity include:

Mean length of utterance   An utterance is usually a sentence, but can also be an incomplete sentence or phrase if it is clearly marked off from the speech around it by a pause or a change of intonation or pitch.
Mean preverb length   the number of words preceding the main verb in a sentence or phrase.
Verbal complexity   the number of verbs in a sentence, or the number of *complex verbs* (such as will do, have done, were doing).

Measures of articulation and pitch may be hard to quantify, but include:

use of pauses between words and sentences.
emphasis on individual syllables in longer words.
variation in pitch.

Obvious measures of rate of speech are:

time taken (in seconds) to produce, say, 50 words or
number of words/syllables produced in, say, 60 seconds.

For either measure, take a number of samples if you can.
You could explore more questions:

If some of your helpers are more experienced with young children than others, does this make a difference?

How does a story told into a tape recorder differ from one told directly to young children?

What happens to your helpers' speech when they are telling a story to older children, or to elderly people in a nursing home, or talking to a pet cat or dog? Do they seem to use special 'registers' different from their normal adult–adult register?

adult (or sometimes an older child) has just said. It has been suggested that imitation may provide powerful opportunities for language learning, but the evidence is not straightforward. One problem is that, as we have already seen, children 'imitate with reduction', so that their imitative speech is remarkably like their non-imitative speech in length and complexity, rather than more advanced. There is also plenty of evidence that children are very resistant to imitating forms that do not obey their current rules. When Jean Berko, for example, showed 4-year-old children pictures of geese, saying 'Here is a goose, and here are two geese; now there are three . . .', the children replied 'gooses'. There is not much evidence that imitation helps a child to understand a given phrase or a grammatical structure. It is more likely that imitation is a way of learning to produce words and structures that the child already understands but has not yet produced in spontaneous speech.

Natural language interactions

It is obvious that, in some sense or other, parents and other caregivers teach their children language. But most observers (including parents themselves) have found that explicit teaching, for example correcting a child's ungrammatical sentences, is not a very successful technique. For one thing, parents do not often do it; they may correct pronunciation, the use of 'naughty' words and, sometimes, the use of regularized irregular forms such as digged and goed, but they do not normally bother to correct syntax and are more likely to approve or disapprove of the truth of their children's utterances than their grammar. For another thing, when parents do try explicitly to correct children's speech the children are usually very resistant to being corrected, and there is some evidence that children whose speech is often corrected may develop language more slowly, rather than faster, than others.

It is much more likely that parents train their children in less direct and less formal ways, through natural, everyday communicative exchanges. For example, mothers frequently imitate their children's utterances (rather more often, in fact, than children imitate theirs!); when they imitate, they expand the children's utterances, filling in function words and elaborating their grammatical and semantic content. They also use new sentences to comment on the children's speech, or on the situations, or on the non-verbal behaviour of the children or themselves, and in this way they 'model' grammatical and semantic forms for the children to observe.

In everyday conversations between children and caregivers, modelling, imitation (on both sides), corrections and comments generally exist side by side, so that it is perhaps an artificial exercise to try to distinguish their effects. Linguistic interactions are also cognitive interactions, in which children learn about the world, about the concepts of time and space and causality, and they are social interactions in which children explore their relationships with others. Language does not develop in isolation. It develops within the context of cognitive and social development and is best studied within that context, where it has a central and crucial part to play.

Recommended Reading

Carroll, D. W. (1999) *Psychology of Language*, 3rd edn. Pacific Grove, CA: Brooks/Cole. [Chapters 10, 11 and 12 give a fairly full and up-to-date account of language development research.]

Pinker, S. (1994) *The Language Instinct*. Harmondsworth: Penguin. [A fascinating discussion of language, with a strong emphasis throughout on its creativity and on its biological basis.]

Sutton-Spence, R. and Woll, B. (1999) *The Linguistics of British Sign Language: An Introduction*. Cambridge: Cambridge University Press. [A comprehensive account of BSL, with comparisons with other sign languages and spoken English.]

References

Berko, J. (1958) The child's learning of English morphology. *Word*, 14, 150–77. [A classic experiment on children's possession of grammatical rules.]

Bloom, L. (1970) *Language Development: Form and Function in Developing Grammars*. Cambridge, MA: MIT Press. [A description of language development which emphasizes the semantic characteristics of children's early speech.]

Brown, R. (1973) *A First Language: The Early Stages*. Cambridge, MA: MIT Press. [A classic, entertaining and beautifully written account of language development.]

Chomsky, C. (1969) *The Acquisition of Syntax in Children from 5 to 10*. Cambridge, MA: MIT Press. [As title indicates, a discussion of language development in older children.]

Curtiss, S. (1977) *Genie: A Psycholinguistic Study of a Modern-day 'Wild Child'*. New York: Academic Press. [The best-known and most fully researched recent case of a child reared virtually without language.]

Garcia, J. (1999) *Sign with Your Baby*. Seattle, WA: Northlight Communication. [A parents' guide to use of manual signs with hearing babies.]

Lenneberg, E. H. (1967) *Biological Foundations of Language*. New York: Wiley. [A famous statement of evidence that language is species-specific to humans; now out of date.]

Lyons, J. (1970) *Chomsky*. London: Fontana. [An assessment of Noam Chomsky's views on language and psycholinguistics.]

Marcus, G. F. (1996) Why do children say 'breaked'? *Current Directions in Psychological Science*, 5, 81–5. [A 'rule-and-memory' explanation of over-regularizations in children's speech.]

Orlansky, M. D. and Bonvillian, J. (1984) The role of iconicity in early sign language acquisition. *Journal of Speech and Hearing Disorders*, 49, 287–92 [A comparison of iconic and more abstract signs in young children's SL.]

Pettito, L. A. and Marentette, P. (1991) Babbling in the manual mode: evidence for the ontogeny of language. *Science*, 251, 1493–6. [An examination of role of manual, compared with vocal, babbling.]

Prinz, P. M. and Prinz, E. A. (1979) Simultaneous acquisition of ASL and spoken English (in a hearing child of a deaf mother and hearing father): Phase 1. Early lexical development. *Sign Language Studies*, 25, 283–96. [A comparison of age of emergence of early signs and early words.]

Rymer, R. (1993) *Genie: An Abused Child's Flight from Silence*. New York: HarperCollins. [A recent update on case of Genie.]

Skinner, B. F. (1957) *Verbal Behavior*. New York: Appleton-Century-Crofts. [Skinner's theory of language learning.]

Snow, C. and Ferguson, C. A. (eds) (1977) *Talking to Children: Language Input and Acquisition*. Cambridge: Cambridge University Press. [The definitive collection of papers on baby talk and its implications at different ages and in different cultures.]

7
Children's Thinking

- Piaget's theory of cognitive development
- Ages and stages
- Vygotsky's theory of development
- The zone of proximal development
- Information processing models of development

This chapter examines children's thinking and how it differs from thinking in adults. It looks at three different explanations or theoretical approaches to the development of children's thinking: Piaget's theory of cognitive development, Vygotsky's theory of cognitive development and the information processing models of cognitive development.

Piaget's Theory of Cognitive Development

Piaget's theory of cognitive development addresses these questions. How does children's thinking develop? What makes it different from adults' thinking?

Piaget was born in 1896 in Neuchatel, Switzerland. From a very early age he was interested in biology and knowing this helps us understand his theory. It is based on the assumption that intelligence is a form of biological adaptation, in which the organism is trying to adapt to more and more aspects of reality. Another assumption is that cognition is organized into systems whose parts are integrated to form a whole, just as the human body has digestive, circulatory and nervous systems. Each system is organized within itself and interacts with other systems. A change in one system will affect all the other systems. Cognitive development is a progression through a series of qualitatively different stages, each stage better adapted to reality than the previous stage. Action is also seen as the means through which development occurs. A child acts on the environment and adapts to the environment, so development occurs.

The following sections will outline Piaget's theory in more detail.

Schemes

The basic mental structure in Piaget's theory is the *scheme*. Schemes (or schemata as they are often called today) are sets of related operations which children use to think, and act on the world. A scheme is a type of template for acting or thinking which is applied to a class of objects or situations. For example, an infant will throw a ball and see it bounce, throw a plate and see it smash; so the 'throw scheme' changes to take into account the fact that some classes of objects smash and others bounce.

Assimilation and accommodation

Piaget believed that schemes, such as the throw scheme, change through a process of adaptation, which consists of two complementary processes. The first is *assimilation*. It refers to the way that people transform incoming information so that it fits their existing ways of thinking. For example, one moonlit night Daniel, a young friend of one of the authors, saw a large, round white light in a neighbour's house and immediately said 'Hey, look! They have a moon in their house.' The light did look remarkably like the moon, indeed it looked almost identical. Daniel had assimilated this light to his moon scheme.

The second process is *accommodation*. It refers to the way in which people will adapt their thinking to new experiences. In the moon example, Daniel's father tried to explain to his son that the round light was in fact a light, and that the earth only had one moon, which was a couple of thousand miles wide and hundreds of thousands of miles away. By doing this, he was trying to help Daniel accommodate his moon scheme to reality.

Equilibration

When assimilation and accommodation are balanced the cognitive system is in a state of equilibrium. The organism is striving for this state of equilibrium, and this drive is the motivating force behind developmental change. This process has three phases and is called equilibration. First, the child is satisfied with his or her cognitive systems, then becomes aware of their shortcomings, and finally adopts a new cognitive system which does not have these shortcomings. For example, children think that heavy objects sink and light objects float. When they see that a small iron nail sinks and a large heavy wooden block floats, they experience a state of disequilibrium. They then have to change their cognitive schemes to reach a new state of equilibrium.

The stages of development

Piaget viewed cognitive development as the progression through four stages of development. All children progress through these stages in the same order. The first is the sensorimotor stage, which lasts from birth to about 2 years. The second, the pre-operational stage, lasts from 2 to about 7. The third is the concrete operational stage, lasting from 7 to about 11. The fourth and final stage is the formal operations stage and lasts from 11 to adulthood.

The sensorimotor stage (0–2 years): thinking through action

Infants at this stage are coordinating their sensory perceptions and motor actions to acquire knowledge (for example reaching for an object or sucking a toy). Knowledge for an infant is recognizing or anticipating regularly occurring events and objects (for example, if the child shakes a rattle it makes a noise). Thinking in this stage is acting towards an object with the hands, eyes and other sensory motor actions. For Piaget, an infant at this stage does not possess even the basic rudiments of symbolic thought.

A major achievement in this stage is the development of *object permanence*. At about 4–8 months infants, if a new and interesting toy is put within reach and then hidden under a cloth, will not reach out for it. Piaget interpreted this behaviour as indicating that the infants had no notion that an object exists when it is out of sight; this is what Piaget called object permanence. Only when infants are between 8 and 12 months old will they search for hidden objects (this is also discussed in chapter 2). The child is beginning to realize that an object exists even when it is out of sight.

Some researchers claim that infants possess object permanence a lot sooner than Piaget's theory predicts, and have employed a technique called habituation–dishabituation to test his theory (for a full description of this technique see chapter 2). Renee Baillargeon and colleagues conducted a series of experiments in which

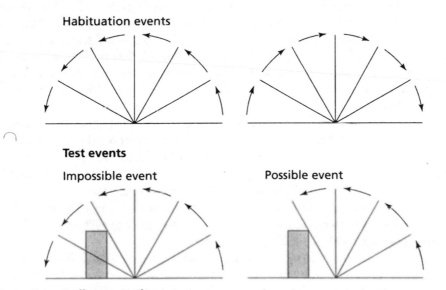

Figure 7.1   *Baillargeon's object permanence experiment*

5-month-old infants were shown a flap rotating 180 degrees and then 180 degrees back to its original position (see figure 7.1). After the infants were habituated to this event, a block was placed in the path of the flap, and the two types of flap rotation occurred: a possible event and an impossible event. In the possible event the flap stopped when it reached the block. In the impossible event, the flap rotated through 180 degrees as if the block no longer existed. An experimenter achieved the illusion by removing the block without the child seeing. The infants looked significantly longer at the impossible event than at the possible event. Baillargeon concluded that the infants understood that the block continued to exist even when out of sight and that the flap could not move through 180 degrees. Other researchers using similar methods have found evidence for object permanence with infants as young as 2½ months old.

The pre-operational stage (2–7 years): the beginning of symbolic thought

At the end of the sensorimotor stage children can begin to think about objects and events when the objects are not present. They have acquired the basic rudiments of symbolic thought. They understand that one thing can stand for another. During the pre-operational stage symbolic thought continues to develop. However, in this stage children often fail to differentiate their points of view from those of others. Piaget referred to this as *egocentrism*, and it is one of the basic characteristics of children's thought in the pre-operational stage.

An example of egocentrism is the failure to realize that others can have thoughts different from one's own and can possess false beliefs. For example, some children are shown a box of Smarties and asked what they think is in the box. All of course say 'Smarties'. They are then shown that in fact the box contains pencils. Next the children are asked what a friend who has not seen the box would think it contains. Most 3-year-old children will say that the friend will think that the box will contain pencils. It is not until about the age 4–5 that children will correctly answer Smarties, showing evidence of thinking about the mental states of others, often referred to as the *theory of mind*.

The 'three mountains task' was devised by Piaget as a test of egocentric thought. He asked 4-year-old children from Geneva to sit in front of a table-top model of three mountains near Geneva (see figure 7.2). The children sitting in position A then had to choose which of ten photographs corresponded to the views of the children who were sitting at position B, C or D. Piaget found that pre-operational children were unable to complete this task and would pick the photograph that corresponded to their own point of view. It is only after the age of 9 that a child can accurately pick out another child's point of view.

Margaret Donaldson criticized this task because it does not make 'human sense'. She argued that children should be tested in situations they understand. She reported a study by Martin Hughes, which tried to make Piaget's three mountains task more

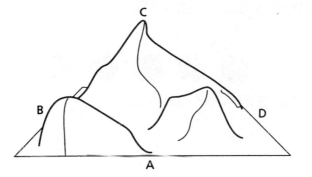

Figure 7.2   *Piaget's three mountains task*

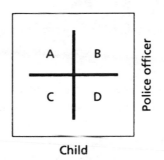

Figure 7.3   *Hiding from the police*

familiar to the child. In their new task the children had to hide a doll from the police officer doll (see figure 7.3). The situation consisted of two walls intersecting each other to give a cross. Children played a game where they had to hide a doll in one of the four quadrants so that the doll could not be seen from the position of the police officer doll. Martin Hughes found that the youngest children were over 90 per cent successful at identifying when the police officer could see the child. Other researchers have reported similar findings.

Concrete operational stage (7–11 years): internalized mental actions

Children's thinking becomes more and more flexible during the concrete operational stage. Piaget believed that the reason for this new flexibility in thinking was the development of concrete operations. Concrete operations are internalized mental actions. Children who have developed concrete operations become capable of combining, separating, ordering and transforming objects in their minds. The operations are termed concrete because children can manipulate objects mentally only if the objects are physically present. According to Piaget, the development of concrete operations transforms all psychological functioning. The world becomes more and

Figure 7.4   *Two rows of counters of equal length*

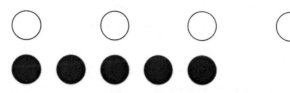

Figure 7.5   *Two rows of counters of unequal length*

more predictable. Children realize that certain properties of objects remain the same even when their appearance has changed. Children's social behaviour also changes. They are more skilled at interpreting other people's intentions, which transforms their social relations.

One of the main achievements of this stage is the ability to conserve. The conservation of number tasks is one of Piaget's classic tests of conservation. Children are first shown two rows of counters (see figure 7.4) and asked if there are more black counters than white counters. Children of all ages correctly answer that there is the same number of counters in each row. The experimenter then transforms the materials by spreading out the white counters as shown in figure 7.5 and asks the children again if there are more black counters than white counters. Pre-operational children generally reply that there are more white than black counters, and if asked will say 'Because the row is longer.'

Only when children have acquired concrete operations can they begin to solve conservation tasks. These operations allow them to understand the logical relations involved. For example, concrete operational children faced with the conservation of number task realize that the length of the line of white counters can be shortened so that it is the same length as the row of black counters (i.e. the principle of reversibility). You could try exercise 7.1 now.

Donaldson also challenged these findings by claiming that the conservation task does not make 'human sense'. In a classic study, James McGarrigle and Donaldson set out to investigate whether this was the case by trying to give the task more 'child sense'. In the child-friendly conservation task, the transformations were made to appear accidentally, by the introduction of a naughty teddy bear who spoilt the game; over 60 per cent of children showed evidence of conservation, compared with only 16 percent in the standard Piagetian conservation task. Other researchers have replicated this finding by using other methods to transform the material which would make more human sense.

Exercise 7.1

Conservation of Area

Prepare two sheets of cardboard, each with 12 blocks positioned as shown in A. Then follow instructions 1 to 3.

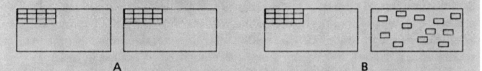

A   B

1 Show the child two sheets of cardboard. Ask the child if each sheet has the same amount of covered area. Record the child's answer either by writing it down or by tape recording it.
2 Scatter the blocks around one of the cardboard sheets, as in B, and repeat the question.
3 Replace the blocks in their original position and ask the child again.

Try this exercise with a 5-year-old, a 7-year-old and a 9-year-old child. Do your results support Piaget's theory of conservation?

Cross-cultural research into children's acquisition of conservation reveals the important influence of the cultural context on their development. Pierre Dasen found that children would perform at a higher level on conservation tasks which were valued by their culture and were useful for their daily activities.

Formal operational stage (11–adulthood): abstract thinking

The fourth and final stage of development Piaget called the formal operational stage. He believed that in this stage of development children can think systematically about all the logical relations within a problem and use hypothesis testing, that adolescents can solve problems by manipulating mental objects, whereas children in the concrete operational stage can solve problems only by manipulating physical objects.

The development of scientific reasoning is a major achievement of the formal operational stage. The chemical combination task is one test of scientific reasoning. In this task, children have five chemicals and a mixer chemical, which are all colourless. They have to find out which chemical or chemicals when combined with the mixer chemical turn the resulting liquid yellow. During the stage of concrete operation children will often try all five chemicals, then a few of the possible combinations of three chemicals or possibly a few combinations of two chemicals. They will often repeat chemical combinations and do not test all the possible chemical combinations. In contrast, formal operational children will *systematically* try all the chemical combinations and will draw the appropriate conclusion. Concrete operational children will often stop when they find the first chemical combination that turns the liquid yellow.

Like concrete operational reasoning, the development of formal operational reasoning appears to be strongly influenced by culture. People in cultures which have very little formal education and which do not value symbolic skills rarely demonstrate formal operations when they are tested using Piagetian methods. Also, it is quite a common finding that reasoning in everyday situations is very different from the reasoning observed in experimental or test situations. People tend to reason at a high level in everyday situations compared to test situations.

Educational implications: the active child and the teacher as facilitator

Piaget's theory of cognitive development has a number of very important implications for education. First, in the theory children progress through four different stages of development and this stage-like development has important consequences for education. The first is the notion of readiness. Children can learn effectively only if their educational experiences match their levels of development. For example, according to Piaget it is not until formal operations that children can think abstractly; it is therefore not until children have acquired formal operations that it would be possible for them to understand abstract concepts, such as density and chemical equilibrium. The second is that teachers should adapt their teaching methods to suit the children: they should not assume that teaching methods that work with one age group would necessarily work with another.

Another important contention of Piaget's theory is that learning and understanding are active processes. The importance of direct activity holds for young infants as much as it does for older adolescents. The child constructs knowledge for himself or herself, and that active exploration leads to deeper understanding. Teachers can foster active learning in their classrooms in a number of different ways. They can set activities which are at the appropriate level for the children. For example, in a nursery school the presence of climbing frames and construction toys allows children to develop spatial understanding. In science classrooms, children can explore the properties of springs and learn about the methods of science. From these active experiences the children begin to develop an understanding of the social and physical world. The teacher's role has changed from the all-knowing expert to the facilitator.

Piaget's theory also has an important influence on curricula, in particular the science and mathematics curricula. In primary schools, the children are helped to make the transition from pre-operational to concrete operational thinking through a series of carefully selected activities. Later, the children are encouraged to participate in practical and experimental work before they engage in more abstract deductive reasoning.

In summary, Piaget proposed that children's thinking develops through a series of stages: sensorimotor, pre-operational, concrete operational and formal operational. His theory has been influential in the fields of developmental psychology and education. His findings on the development of children's thinking have been replicated countless times, by numerous researchers in a wide range of countries. Current research suggests that children's understanding of concepts such as object permanence, the perspectives of others and conservation develops a lot earlier than Piaget thought, and that culture has a stronger influence on development than his theory suggests.

Vygotsky's Theory of Cognitive Development

The influence of the sociocultural context on cognitive development was an area that was missing in Piaget's theory of cognitive development. However, Lev Vygotsky, in his theory of cognitive development, was directly concerned with the role of sociocultural context on cognitive development. Vygotsky was born in Russia in 1896, but died when he was only 37. He proposes that children's cognitive development is a product of their interaction with more skilled members of their culture, such as their parents, teachers, siblings and peers. Through interacting with more able members of a society children can do things that they would not be able to do on their own. Learning and development occurs through the internalization of social processes.

Higher and elementary mental functions

Vygotsky believed that children at birth have a number of innate abilities and called them *elementary mental functions*. They include perception, attention and certain forms of memory. Through interacting with others children develop more complex cognitive abilities, which Vygotsky called *higher mental functions*. They depend on the use of ever more sophisticated psychological tools. Examples of psychological tools are graphs, number systems, mnemonic strategies and language.

The zone of proximal development

Vygotsky introduced the notion of the *zone of proximal development* as a way of understanding how cognitive development occurs through social interaction. He defined it as the difference between a child's actual developmental level as determined by independent problem solving and her or his potential developmental level as determined through problem solving with an adult or more able peer. Cognitive development occurs when children are working in this zone of proximal development.

The amount of assistance provided by the adult is critical for a child working within the zone of proximal development. Too much assistance and it is too easy for the child; too little and it is too difficult. It should be at a level just beyond the child's existing developmental level to provide a challenge for the child. It should also be sensitive to changes in the child's developmental level; as the child progresses the adult should provide less and less assistance, and if the child starts to regress the adult should provide more help.

Scaffolding

Unfortunately, Vygotsky did not suggest any methods of providing assistance in the zone of proximal development. One method that has been used is *scaffolding*. It was a term coined by David Wood, Jerome Bruner and Gail Ross in their observational studies of mothers helping their children to build a wooden tower. It is characterized by six features:

1   encouraging the child's interest in the task;
2   simplifying the task by reducing the number of possible actions that the child could carry out;
3   keeping the child in pursuit of a particular objective;
4   marking the critical features of the task;
5   controlling the child's frustration during problem solving;
6   demonstrating solutions to the child or explaining the solutions that the child has partially completed.

Wood proposes that instructors who are successful at providing scaffolding follow two rules. The first rule states that if the child is failing the instructor should provide more help and guidance, and the second rule states that if the child is successful then the adult should provide less assistance. Wood and his colleagues compared scaffolding with three other methods of instructing children and found that children who were taught using scaffolding could, after instruction, build the wooden tower on their own a lot better than the children who were instructed using other methods. Other researchers have also reported similar findings across a range of tasks and ages.

The role of culture

Vygotsky emphasized the importance of society and culture in cognitive development, and this was clear in a study reported by Terezinah Nunes. She and her colleagues investigated young street vendors in the cities of Brazil. These children had not been to school, yet they were capable of performing mathematical reasoning that was thought possible only through formal schooling. They compared their performance on problems which were either typical of those they came across in their everyday activity of selling or the same problems as they would be presented in school terms. They found that these street children were correct almost all the time on the familiar, street-based examples, but were successful less than half the time on the unfamiliar, school-based problems. Below are two examples which illustrate the different strategies they used in the two situations.

Example 1: street-based example

Adult   I'm going to take four coconuts (each coconut costs 35 cruzados). How much is that ?

Child   Three will be 105, plus 30, that's 135 . . . one coconut is 35 . . . that is 140.

Example 2: school-based example

Adult   How much is 35 × 4?

Child   4 times 5 is 20, carry the 2 plus 3 is 5, times 4 is 20. [Written answer 200.]

In example 1 the children solved the problem using strategies that they had acquired through selling merchandise in the streets. In example 2 they incorrectly applied pencil and paper strategies that they had been taught at school. They confused addition procedures with multiplication procedures. To start, they correctly multiplied 5 by 4, to get 2 10s. Then they incorrectly added 2 10s to 3 10s, equalling 5 10s and then multiplied 5 10s by 4 to reach 200. This study shows clearly the importance of cultural context for understanding cognitive development.

Educational implications

There have been a number of applications of Vygotsky's theories to classroom learning. One recent example comes from the work of Ann Brown and her colleagues. They have developed the idea of a community of learners, in which children and adults work together on a shared activity. Peers learn from each other, and the teacher serves as an expert guide, who facilitates the process by which the children learn from both the teacher and each other.

In summary, in his theory Vygotsky stressed the importance of the sociocultural context in children's cognitive development. He distinguished between elementary and higher mental functions. Elementary functions are present at birth, whereas higher mental functions are acquired through interacting with more able members of society. Vygotsky introduced the notion of the zone of proximal development, which is the difference between what children can do on their own and what they can do with the guidance of an adult. Scaffolding has been employed as a method of providing that assistance, and research indicates that it facilitates children's thinking. Recent research has also shown how the culture dramatically influences children's thinking in the way that Vygotsky suggested.

Information Processing Theories of Cognitive Development

The third and final approach we shall examine is the information processing approach to cognitive development. Information processing is not a theory like Piaget's or Vygotsky's, but more like a framework for characterizing a group of theories. These theories all have in common the view that thinking is information processing and best understood through analogy with a computer. Computers are systems that process information through the application of logical rules. They have a limited capacity, which can be improved through either changes in the hardware or changes in the software. Using this analogy, cognitive development can be seen as the result of either changes in the hardware (i.e. changes in the brain) or changes in the software (i.e. children learning new knowledge and strategies).

The structure of the information processing system

An influential model for cognitive development is Richard Atkinson and Richard Shiffrin's store model of human information processing (see figure 7.6). Information first enters the system through our senses via the sensory registers. There is one register for each of the senses. These registers can store large amounts of sensory information for brief periods of time. Research suggests that this information begins to fade after about one-third of a second and has completely disappeared after a second. Research on children indicates that 5-year-old children's sensory memory is approximately the same size as an adult's sensory memory.

The next phase of the store model is the short-term or working memory. This is where the active thinking occurs. This is where people construct new strategies, solve problems and comprehend reading. Working memory is limited in several different ways. First, the capacity of working memory is limited to between 3 and 7 units. These units correspond to meaningful chunks of information. A word can be a meaningful chunk, even a phrase. Thus it is just as difficult to remember three letters as it is to remember three words. The second limit on working memory is how long information remains. Typically it will lasts for 15–20 seconds. This can be lengthened with the use of rehearsal. Research indicates that older children can maintain more information in their working memories than younger children. Working memory can be split into separate systems for verbal and spatial memory.

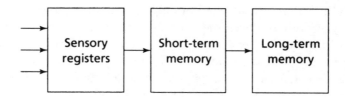

Figure 7.6   *Atkinson's and Shiffrin's three store model of memory*

Research shows that the development of working memory involves increases in the amount of information that can be stored in each of these subsystems and greater differentiation between them.

Information can then be transferred from working memory to long-term memory. There is no limit to the amount of information that can be kept in long-term memory or how long the information can be stored in it. Long-term memory stores a range of information, from the meanings of words to how to play tennis.

The processes of the information processing system

Processes are used to actively manipulate information in sensory, working and long-term memory. Encoding is an important process in cognitive development and refers to the process of transforming information from the environment into a lasting representation. People cannot store every single item of information in the environment. They have to select or encode those aspects of the environment they think are relevant. Children often fail to encode important aspects of the environment, either because they do not know what information to encode or because they are unable to encode it.

Another important process in cognitive development is automatization, which is the process of transforming conscious controlled processes into unconscious and automatic processes. Processes vary in the amount of attention they require. Those processes that require a lot of attention have been termed controlled processes, and those processes that are automatic and do not require much attention have been termed automatic processes. The degree of attention a process requires is dependent on the nature of the task and also how familiar the person is with that task. With practice, processes that require a lot of attention become more and more automatic and thus require less and less attention. Automatization is useful because it frees mental resources for solving other problems.

Children's eye witness testimony: an application of information processing theory

Research on children's memory has become more than just an academic exercise, but is now an important legal issue. More and more children are appearing in the courts, sometimes for crimes they may have committed but more often for crimes committed against them. For a long time children's testimonies were thought to be unreliable, because they were thought to be prone to fantasy and unable to distinguish fact from fiction. The research has examined the accuracy of children's reports. It has found that younger children will recall less information, but not less accurately. Also a considerable amount of research has examined the suggestibility of children's memories, in particular whether preschool children are more suggestible than school children. Maggie Bruck and Stephen Ceci reviewed a series of studies that examined the suggestibility of children's memories. These studies showed that when interviewers

Exercise 7.2

Twenty Questions

This task requires you to find two children one aged 7, the other 12.

Tell the children that you will be thinking of something and that they have to guess what it is by asking questions that can be answered only with yes or no. The children have only 20 questions to try to figure it out. Use an easy example to begin with, and then make it harder.

Write down or tape record all the children's questions. Try to analyse their strategies. Were they constraint questions (trying to work to narrow categories – for example 'Is it an animal?'), specific questions (for example 'Is it this chair?'), or random questions?

When you have carried out this exercise with both children, and using several examples for each, try to identify any differences in the strategies they used.

employ suggestive interview techniques a child's recall of events can be influenced and that preschool children are influenced more than schoolchildren. However, children's recall of events in the absence of these suggestive techniques is very accurate when they are questioned by interviewers employing a neutral tone and very few misleading questions, and when they have no motive to make a false report.

Information processing: in summary

Information processing theories of cognitive development view thinking as information processing similar to the sort that goes on in a computer. The store model of information processing has been used as a model of the structure of the cognitive system. Information enters the cognitive system through the sensory stores, before moving into short-term memory, or working memory, where it is processed. It is then stored in long-term memory. Two important processes for cognitive development are encoding and automatization. Research suggests that development is less to do with changes in the structure of the cognitive system and more to do with changes in information processing. See exercise 7.2.

General Summary

This chapter has presented three different views of cognitive development: Piaget's theory, Vygotsky's theory and information processing models. Piaget considered children active participants in their own development. They move through an invariant series of four general stages of development. Children's thinking in each stage is qualitatively different from that of the previous or the succeeding stage. Vygotsky, unlike Piaget, stressed the importance of social interaction in a child's cognitive development, in particular social interaction with adults or more able members of the child's community. Learning and development occurs through the internalization of social processes. He introduced the concept of the zone of proximal development to help us understand how learning arises through social interaction. It is the distance between what children can do on their own and what they can do with the help of more able members of their communities. The information processing models of cognitive development use the computer either literally or metaphorically to model the development of children's thinking. Research from this tradition tends to view development not as changes to the structure of the cognitive system, but as changes in a child's knowledge and/or mental strategies. Each explanation offers us a very different view of the remarkable process of cognitive development.

Recommended Reading

Baillargeon, R. (1994) How do infants learn about the physical world. *Current Directions in Psychological Science*, 3, 133–40. [A good review of Renee Baillargeon's work with others on children's understanding of the physical world.]

Boden, M. (1977) *Piaget*. Glasgow: Fontana. [A concise account of Piaget's theory.]

Piaget, J. and Inhelder, B. (1967) *The Psychology of the Child*. London: Routledge. [Piaget's introduction to his theory of cognitive development.]

Rogoff, B. (1998) Cognition as a collaborative process. In D. Kuhn and R. S. Siegler (eds), *Handbook of Child Psychology*, 5th edn, vol. 2: *Cognition, Perception and Language*, 679–744. New York: Wiley. [A good review of research inspired by Vygotsky.]

Siegler, R. S. (1997) *Children's Thinking*, 3rd edn. London: Prentice-Hall. [A good introduction to research on information processing models of cognitive development.]

Vygotsky, L. S. (1962) *Thought and Language*. Cambridge, MA: MIT Press. [The first English translation of Vygotsky's theories.]

Vygotsky, L. S. (1978) *Mind in Society*. Cambridge, MA: Harvard University Press. [More of Vygotsky's theory, including zone of proximal development.]

References

Atkinson, R. C. and Shiffrin, R. M. (1968) Human memory: a proposed system and its control processes. In K. W. Spence and Spence, J. T. (eds), *The Psychology of Learning and Motivation: Advances in Research and Theory*, vol. 2. London: Academic Press. [The three store model of cognition.]

Baillargeon, R., Spelke, E. and Wasserman, S. (1985) Object permanence in five month old infants. *Cognition*, 20, 191–208. [Baillargeon's first paper on object permanence in infants.]

Borke, H. (1975) Piaget's mountains revisited: changes in the egocentric landscape. *Developmental Psychology*, 11, 240–3. [Children display less egocentrism on tasks that are familiar to them.]

Brown, A. (1997) Transforming schools into communities of thinking and learning about serious matters. *American Psychologist*, 52(4), 399–413.

Bruck, M. and Ceci, S. J. (1999) The suggestibility of children's memory. *Annual Review of Psychology*, 50, 419–39. [A review of research on accuracy and suggestibility of children's memory.]

Dasen, P. (1972) Cross-cultural Piagetian research: a summary. *Journal of Cross Cultural Psychology*, 3, 29–39. [A paper that describes Dasen's research comparing different cultures' performance on Piagetian tests.]

Donaldson, M. (1978) *Children's Minds*. London: Fontana. [The classic book, in which Donaldson makes her criticisms of Piaget and reports the studies which show that Piaget underestimated children's cognitive abilities.]

Gopknik, A. and Astington, J. W. (1988) Children's understanding of representational change and its relation to the understanding of false belief and the appearance reality distinction. *Child Development*, 62, 83–97. [A study of children's theory of mind using Smarties task.]

Hargreaves, D., Molloy, C. and Pratt, A. (1982) Social factors in conservation. *British Journal of Developmental Psychology*, 73, 231–4. [A replication of McGarrigle and Donaldson's naughty teddy study.]

McGarrigle, J. and Donaldson, M. (1974) Conservation accidents. *Cognition*, 3, 341–50. [McGarrigle and Donaldson's original naughty teddy bear study.]

Nunes, T., Schliemann, A. D. and Carraher, D. W. (1993) *Street Mathematics and School Mathematics*. Cambridge: Cambridge University Press. [A review of Nunes and colleagues' work comparing Brazilian children's mathematics in school and in the streets.]

Spelke, E. S., Breinlinger, K., Macomber, J. and Jacobson, K. (1992) The origins of knowledge. *Psychological Review*, 99, 605–32. [A paper reporting the research which suggests that infants as young as $2^{1}/_{2}$ months show some evidence of object permanence.]

Wood, D., Bruner, J. and Ross, G. (1976) The role of tutoring in problem solving. *Journal of Child Psychology and Psychiatry*, 17, 89–100. [The first paper to introduce the metaphor of scaffolding.]

Wood, D., Wood, H. and Middleton, D. (1978) An experimental evaluation of four face-to-face teaching strategies. *International Journal of Behavioural Development*, 1, 131–47. [David Wood compares scaffolding with three other methods of teaching.]

8

Intelligence and Experience

- What is intelligence?
- Measuring intelligence
- Differences in ethnic, racial and social groupings
- The effectiveness of early intervention programmes
- Performance on intelligence tests
- Intelligence at different ages

While the teacher tried to cultivate intelligence, and the psychologist tried to measure intelligence, nobody seemed to know precisely what intelligence was.

P. B. Ballard, Mental Tests, 1990

What is intelligence? In 1996 a distinguished panel of experts, led by Ulric Neisser, suggested the following definition: 'Intelligence refers to individuals' abilities to understand complex ideas, to adapt effectively to the environment, to learn from experience, to engage in various forms of reasoning, and to overcome obstacles by careful thought.' See box 8.1 for other opinions.

Various people, however, have had quite diverse views about the nature of intelligence. This lack of agreement is probably caused by the idea of intelligence as a general property that people have to different degrees and that is applied to various activities. We may think that one of our friends is very intelligent, another less so; it has sometimes been argued that some racial groups, or national groups, are more intelligent than others; and when describing non-human animals we may suggest that dogs and chimpanzees, for example, are intelligent, while chickens and cows are stupid. But these ideas may not be true, or even sensible. For example, comparing the intelligence of different species of animal is a logical nonsense. An animal species may seem intelligent if its members are capable of acquiring bits of behaviour that humans can acquire – for example learning the path through a maze, or solving other problems set by human researchers, or sitting up to beg for food, or fetching the newspaper, or responding to words and commands. But intelligence can really be judged only within a species, because different species need different types of adaptation (how would you manage, for example, if you had to build a spider's web in a windblown bush?). If we devised an intelligence test for hamsters, and one for

Box 8.1   Some Views about Intelligence

'With about fifty intellectual factors already known, we may say there are about fifty ways of being intelligent.' J. P. Guilford, *American Psychologist*, 1959.

'When new turns in behaviour cease to appear in the life of an individual its behaviour ceases to be intelligent.' G. E. Coghill, *Anatomy and the Problem of Behaviour*, 1929.

'A good sort of man is this Darwin and well meaning, but with little intellect.' Thomas Carlyle (1725–1881), *The Times*, 1877.

'We should take care not to make intellect our God; it has, of course strong muscles, but no personality.' Albert Einstein (1879–1955), *Out of My Later Life*.

'To judge well, to comprehend well, to reason well. These are the essential activities of intelligence.' A. Binet and T. Simon, *The Intelligence of the Feeble-minded*, 1916.

Source: all quotations from Connolly and Martlew, 1999.

goldfish, and one for dogs, they would look very different and would certainly bear very little relation to intelligence tests designed to discriminate between humans.

Assessing whether one racial, social or cultural group is more or less intelligent than another is a lot more complex, and even saying that one person within the same species or group is more intelligent than another is not a straightforward or obvious matter. We have to be able to measure intelligence in a way that is valid and reliable, and we have to justify the assumption that intelligence is a stable individual characteristic rather than an ability which differs according to context and time. But measuring intelligence is not easy, and intelligence may not be a simple characteristic or even a stable one. In real life, people are more 'intelligent' in some activities than others. Many people are good with numbers but not at writing and spelling, or good at practical tasks, such as repairing a car, but not at reading.

One Characteristic or Several?

Is intelligence one characteristic, or does it consist of several distinct parts? In the past there has been considerable disagreement between psychologists on this question. Some, like C. Spearman in 1927, saw intelligence as one general capacity that underlies performance on all cognitive tasks, with individuals varying in their abilities. Spearman was influenced by findings that although tests of intelligence often

Box 8.2 Gardner's Multiple Intelligences
(adapted from Gardner, 1983)

Intelligence type	Meaning
Linguistic	Knowing word meanings and the ability to use words to understand new ideas and communicate them to others.
Logical-mathematical	Understanding the relations between objects, actions and ideas including the performance of mathematical relations.
Spatial	Perceiving objects accurately and imagining the appearance of an object from different angles.
Musical	Comprehending and producing sounds of a variety of pitch, rhythm and emotional tone.
Bodily-kinaesthetic	Using the body in very distinctive ways (e.g. dancers, craftspeople, athletes).
Interpersonal	Identifying other people's feelings, moods, motivations and intentions.
Intrapersonal	Understanding one's own emotions and being aware of personal strengths and weaknesses.

contained various types of task (which were designed specifically to measure different aspects of intelligence) the scores on those tasks were often highly correlated. This led to the conclusion that intelligence was related to one *general* factor ('g'), which could be demonstrated in many different ways.

Other researchers have proposed that intelligence is composed of several separate abilities that are more or less independent. In this view any person can have high levels of one component of intelligence and low levels of another. Thurstone suggested in 1938 that intelligence consisted of seven separate primary mental abilities, including verbal meaning (understanding ideas and word meanings), number (speed and accuracy when using numbers) and space (visualizing objects in three dimensions). In 1983 Howard Gardner added further abilities (e.g. musical, bodily kinaesthetic and inter-personal intelligence (see box 8.2). Most modern theories of intelligence fall between these two opposites, recognizing that intelligence may involve a general ability for a large range of cognitive tasks but also that it is expressed in a variety of ways.

The triarchic theory and practical intelligence

In 1995, Robert Sternberg proposed a triarchic theory of intelligence that included three basic types of human intelligence. These were componential (or analytic), experiential (or creative) and contextual (or practical) intelligence. Componential intelligence is the ability to think critically and analytically, so people who score highly on this usually do well in standard academic tests. Experiential intelligence stresses insight and the ability to create new ideas. High scorers on this aspect can pick out the crucial information in a situation, being able to find a solution to a problem by putting together facts that to others might appear to be unrelated. Many scientific geniuses and inventors (e.g. Isaac Newton, Albert Einstein) have demonstrated this type of intelligence. The third type, contextual intelligence, involves the solving of problems in everyday life (skilful adaptation to the environment) and relies on the use of tacit knowledge. This differs from academic knowledge, which usually involves remembering definitions, formulae etc., as tacit knowledge usually involves action, is generally immediately useful and is often acquired on one's own. The action involved can be knowing how to do something (for example persuading someone to do something rather than knowing about persuasion techniques in theory). The practical aspect is that it helps people achieve their goals and, as it is often picked up in an informal, unspoken way, individuals must recognize the value of tacit knowledge for themselves.

In 1997 Sternberg found that tacit knowledge was an important predictor of success in various aspects of life, including getting on with others and success in a career: the greater a person's tacit knowledge, the higher his or her salary and the greater his or her number of promotions. Tacit knowledge was found to predict career success nearly as well as years in education and years of job experience. The evidence that intelligence is more than just verbal, mathematical and reasoning abilities appears to be growing, and practical intelligence has been found to be very important in its contribution to success in many areas of life.

The importance of emotional intelligence for personal success and a happy, productive life was suggested by David Goleman, in 1995. Emotional intelligence is a cluster of abilities relating to the emotional aspects of life, abilities such as recognizing and managing our own and other people's emotions, motivating ourselves, restraining our impulses and handling relationships effectively. Goleman argues that each component plays an important part in shaping our lives. Increasing evidence suggests that emotional intelligence can play an important role in our success and personal happiness.

The Development of Intelligence Testing

In the early twentieth century Alfred Binet was asked to develop a test so that the French government could identify children in need of extra help with their education. The tests were published in 1905 and involved subtests of comprehension and reasoning, word definition and work with numbers. This first version was quite

Box 8.3 The Meaning of IQ

How can a person's intelligence be quantified? Early intelligence tests were used on children of various ages, so it was possible to establish from this the tasks that most children of those ages could be expected to complete successfully. This gave an indication of the mental age of a child. If a child of 9 had a mental age of 9, that child could solve most of the problems that an average 9-year-old could solve. This meant that it was possible to have a mental age above or below your chronological (actual) age. A bright 7-year-old with a mental age of 8 would be able to solve most of the problems that the average 8-year-old could solve. A 9-year-old who could solve most of the problems that the average 8-year-old could solve, but no more, would have a mental age of 8.

This idea was used to develop the concept of *intelligence quotient* or IQ, which expresses the association between mental age and actual age. To find a child's IQ an examiner would divide mental age by chronological age and then multiply by 100. Numbers above 100 indicate an intellectual age greater than chronological age so that the individual is more intelligent than typical children of that age. Alternatively, numbers below 100 would indicate that the child is less intelligent than others of that age.

$$IQ = \frac{Mental\ age}{Chronological\ age} \times 100$$

Using this method the 7-year-old mentioned above would have an IQ of

$$\frac{8}{7} \times 100 = 114$$

There is a major problem with this type of IQ score. Can you see it? Eventually mental growth is likely to level off, so mental age will remain constant, but chronological age will continue to increase. As a result IQ scores will decline after the early teenage years. Partly because of this, IQ scores are now calculated differently, so that a person's performance is compared with other people of the same age. An IQ of 100 is still average, and if a child solves more problems than others of the same chronological age he or she will have an IQ of more than 100.

successful in identifying the children who needed special help, so Binet and his colleague Simon broadened the range of their test to measure variations in intelligence among all children. These tests were revised and adapted for use in many countries, and Lewis Terman, a psychologist at Stanford University in the USA,

developed the Stanford–Binet test. This test has been revised many times since then. An important quality of the Stanford–Binet test was that it resulted in a single score which was thought to reflect a person's level of intelligence – his or her IQ. Box 8.3 shows how an IQ is calculated.

The Stanford–Binet test was popular for many years, but there was one major difficulty. The subtests were mainly verbal in content, so non-verbal abilities were largely ignored. To remedy this David Wechsler designed a set of tests for children (the Wechsler Intelligence Scale for Children or WISC) and adults (the Wechsler Adult Intelligence Scale-Revised or WAIS-R) that included non-verbal (or performance) as well as verbal tasks. These tests are widely used and have also been updated several times. Scores on the scale are again designed so that the average score for adults is 100, below 70 is subnormal, and above 130 qualifies as genius.

Exercise 8.1

An Extract from a Standard Verbal Processing IQ Test

Can you supply the answers to the verbal reasoning questions below?
Try them out with any children you know well.

Information

1 What are the colours of the British flag?
2 Who wrote Hamlet?

Arithmetic

3 How much is £4 plus £5?
4 How many hours will it take a man to walk 24 miles at the rate of
   3 miles an hour?

Similarities

5 In what way are an orange and a banana alike?
6 In what way are a fly and a tree alike?

Answers are on page 134.

Validity

Many psychologists have been concerned about the validity of IQ tests. The validity of a test is the extent to which it measures the property that it is supposed to measure. Comparing a test's scores with some external measure of that property is commonly used to assess its validity. IQ tests have generally been validated by comparing their scores with educational attainment, such as examination grades and successes or failures. But exam success involves the ability to do well in activities such as IQ tests, so defining intelligence in terms of the abilities that are needed to succeed in academic life is a circular definition. It seems fair to conclude that intelligence tests are reasonably valid for measuring those components of intelligence that are related to achievement in school.

In later decades many other tests of intelligence were developed (e.g. the Lorge–Thorndike tests, the Henmon–Nelson tests, the Scholastic Aptitude Test, the Otis–Lennon School Ability Test, British Ability Scales, Raven's Progressive Matrices, Alice Heim's AH4, AH5 and AH6 tests, the Moray House and NFER tests); all can be easily administered to large numbers of people, and many soon became routinely used in school systems.

Exercise 8.2

An IQ Test from a Different Culture

Try this IQ test, which was designed for people of an Aboriginal culture.

ABORIGINAL IQ TEST

1   As Wallaby is to animal so cigarette is to . . .

2   Three of the following items may be classified with salt-water cro-
    codile. Which are they?

   (a)   Marine turtle
   (b)   Frilled lizard
   (c)   Budgerigar
   (d)   Black snake

3   You are out in the bush with your children and you are hungry. You
    have a loaded rifle. You see three animals, all within range: a young
    emu, a large kangaroo and a small female wallaby. Which should
    you shoot for food?

Turn to page 135 for the answers.

Source: Saunders, Pearce and Amato, 1983. *The Original Australian Test of
Intelligence.*

Culture fairness

During the 1960s, group tests were seriously criticized for showing 'culture bias'.
Because they were developed in one culture, people from other backgrounds are
likely to be at a disadvantage when taking them. Aboriginal Indians, and our own
ancestors, would do badly on one of these tests, but we should not know the
answers to the simplest questions relating to *their* lives or cope 'intelligently' with
their world (see exercise 8.2). Many items in conventional intelligence tests assume
that all children have had the opportunity to acquire particular types of knowledge,
but this may not be so for children from disadvantaged, or just different, backgrounds. Different cultures define intelligence differently, in terms of the specialized
skills necessary for living within them.

Other more subtle forms of cultural bias may also be found in intelligence tests.
It has been suggested that they often include an implicit acceptance of European

Exercise 8.1 Answers

1 Red, white and blue
2 Shakespeare
3 £9
4 8 hours
5 2 points if the answer is 'they are both fruit'.
  1 point if there is no mention of fruit, but mention of 'food', 'to eat', 'have peels', 'same colour', 'grow', 'contain vitamins'.
  0 points for 'round', 'same shape' or 'contain calories'.
6 2 points if the answer is 'they are living things' or 'they have life'.
  1 point if there is no mention of life but mention of 'breathe', 'grow', 'need food', 'created by nature', 'need sunlight to live'.
  0 points for 'up in the air, outdoors', 'fly has wings, tree has leaves', 'fly is small, tree is big', 'useful to man' or 'carry germs'.

The British Supplement to the Manual of The Weschler Adult Intelligence Scale, 1971. Windsor: NFER Publishing.

values and standards. European cultures place a high value on answers being right or wrong, so children from a European cultural background will search for the correct answer when attempting the tests. However, children from other backgrounds (e.g. African-American) may be more likely to spend time reasoning about the extent to which each answer is correct, and this would adversely affect their scores.

The question of group fairness in intelligence testing was raised when it was found that in the USA and elsewhere, people belonging to several ethnic and racial minorities (e.g. African-Americans, native Americans) tend to score lower on conventional intelligence tests than Caucasian Americans. The disparity appears to have decreased in recent years, but it has not entirely disappeared. Typically children from lower social classes also have lower scores in intelligence tests, and some critics have suggested that this reflects bias in the tests. They argue that test items reflect the Caucasian middle-class cultural heritage of the test creators, so that they are biased against lower-class children and those from other ethnic groups.

Some psychologists have tried to design 'culture fair' tests, i.e. tests that are fair to people from all cultures. This is probably impossible, as scores will always depend to an extent on a person's knowledge and experience, the language spoken and familiarity with a pencil and paper. The Raven's Progressive Matrices Test is one attempt to produce a culture fair test. This test contains no verbal items; a logical sequence of patterns must be completed by choosing the missing item from a set of alternatives. However, it has been found that even with this test people with more education score higher than those with less education.

Exercise 8.2   Answers

1   The correct answer is 'tree'. The community's first experience of
    tobacco was in the form of 'stick' tobacco, so it is classified with tree.
2   Crocodiles, turtles, lizards and birds are all classified as *minh* (animals),
    while snakes together with eels, are classified as *yak* (snake-like
    creatures).
3   'Small female wallaby' is the right answer. Emu is a food that may
    be eaten only by very old people, and everyone knows that if parents
    and children both eat kangaroo the children will get sick.

How well did you do? Do not worry if you got all the answers wrong;
most people in the UK get them wrong. This test, the Original Australian Test of Intelligence, was developed for use with Aboriginal people
in Australia. It is a good illustration of the difficulty of getting the
answers right if you are unfamiliar with the culture for which a test was
designed.

Gender differences and 'gender fairness'

While overall there are no differences in IQ between boys and girls, or between men
and women, some gender differences in specific abilities have been fairly consistently observed (see chapter 11). Could these gender differences reflect gender bias?
It is hardly reasonable to argue that IQ tests in themselves are not 'gender fair'.
Boys and girls are exposed, at least in theory, to the same school curriculum and so
have the same formal preparation for the different components of intelligence measured by IQ scales.

But there may be gender bias of a different sort, based on cultural expectations.
It tends to be assumed, for example, that boys have more mathematical ability than
girls, even when their achievement is comparable. In 1985 Susan Holloway and
Robert Hess found that when girls do well at maths their parents put it down to
hard work, while when they do badly they put it down to lack of ability; but when
boys do well it is attributed to ability, while when they do badly it is thought that
they have not worked hard enough. Further, teachers may pay more attention to
boys than to girls in maths classes and perhaps more attention to girls in reading
classes; one sequel, if not consequence, of this is that more boys than girls tend later
to specialize in maths and physical science, while girls outnumber boys in language-
and literature-based subjects, so that further experience and training maintain and
exaggerate any early sex differences.

It can be very hard to determine whether a given gender difference is chiefly
biological or cultural in nature. Men and boys usually do better than women and

Exercise 8.3

An Extract from a Non-verbal Intelligence Test
(originally produced in 1936)

Can you pick out the correct pattern (from the selection at the bottom) to fit into the gap in the large pattern?

This well-known nonverbal intelligence test was originally produced in 1936, and has been revised several times since then. Test participants (who may be of any age above six years or so) are shown patterns 'with bits taken out', and are asked to identify which of a set of alternatives is the missing bit. Can you solve the two items below? Also try them out with one or two children.

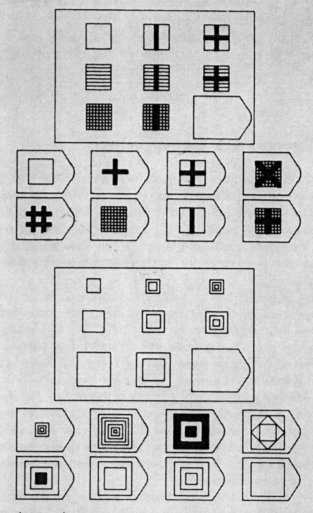

Raven's progressive matrices

See page 138 for the answers.

girls in several tests of spatial ability (though not in all – see the review by Diane Halpern in 1997), but this may be largely due to *underperformance* by women and girls because they lack confidence in tasks which are seen as masculine. For example, in 1998 Mark Brosnan found that men outperformed women when the spatial task they were set was described as 'a test of spatial ability', but that women performed as well as men when the task was described as 'a test of empathy'. It seems that cultural expectations of what boys, and girls, are good at may help to produce gender differences in intelligence-test performance as much as biological factors.

The Development of Intelligence

Does intelligence develop as people grow older? What factors influence its development? Both genetic and environmental factors (individual and cultural experience) are important in determining intellectual achievement. To the extent that intelligence is a matter of given genetic potential, it should be stable over a person's lifespan; but to the extent that it is determined by experience, it could be expected to vary over time, and there might be rather little correlation between a person's performance on, say, IQ tests at one age and her or his performance at another. Also, if a person's intelligence is affected by experience, we might be able to improve it by appropriate training and exposure to situations which could aid development.

Is intelligence stable over time?

From quite early in the history of IQ testing, in the 1930s and 1940s, a number of studies have examined the correlation between measures of intelligence obtained from the same people at different ages. As soon as children are old enough to be given an IQ test (around 2 years), there is evidence of some stability in their scores over time. Early scores are significantly correlated with later scores, and the closer in time the two measurements are the stronger the correlation; see, for example, studies by Helen Bee and her associates in the 1980s. However, some studies have also found considerable individual differences. There seem to be short-term fluctuations in children's performances, often related to life events, and sometimes marked and longer-term ones; for example, the Fels Longitudinal Study of Development conducted in the 1960s by Robert McCall and his associates found that the IQ scores of individual children shifted considerably between the ages of 30 months and 17 years, in either direction and occasionally by enormous amounts.

The role of genetic factors

Much evidence supports the view that heredity has an important role in human intelligence. Some research has examined the relationships between family members and measured IQ. If intelligence is determined, to some extent, by genetic factors, we should expect that the more closely related individuals are the more similar their

Exercise 8.3   Answers

The answers are 8 (i.e. the bottom row, far right) and 7 (bottom row, second from right).

IQs would be. This is generally what has been found. In 1981 Thomas Bouchard and Matt McGue reviewed 111 family studies, and some of their results can be seen in figure 8.2. Correlations of approximately 0.85 have been found for the IQs of identical (monozygotic) twins brought up together, approximately 0.67 for those brought up apart, about 0.5 for ordinary siblings brought up together and 0.24 for siblings brought up apart. (Correlations closer to 1.0 indicate strong relationships between variables while those further from 1.0 indicate weaker relationships.) Identical twins are expected to share 100 per cent of their genes while ordinary brothers and sisters are expected to share 50 per cent so these findings that the more closely related people are the higher their IQ scores correlate supports a role for the influence of genetic factors in intelligence.

Bouchard and his colleagues also found support for a genetic impact on intelligence when they discovered, in 1990, that the IQs of identical twins who were separated early in life and raised in different homes were similar to the IQs of identical twins reared together. These individuals have identical genes but have been exposed to different environments. Consequently, examining their IQs should give us an opportunity to compare the roles of genetic and environmental factors in human intelligence. However, if genetics explained human intelligence completely then correlations of 1.0 would be expected for identical twins. In 1988 Robert Plomin reviewed a large number of twin studies and found that genetics accounted

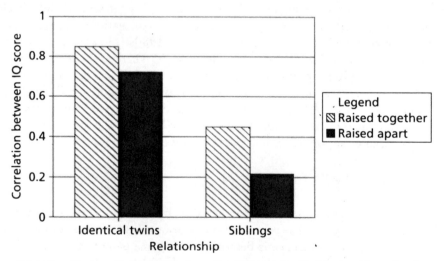

Figure 8.1   *Correlations between IQ scores in different family relationships*

for about 50 per cent of variation in individual IQ. There appears to be little doubt that genetic factors do play an important part in the development of intelligence, but other findings lead to the conclusion that environmental variables are also of great importance.

The role of environment

The role of environmental factors in influencing intelligence is revealed by studies of environmental deprivation and enrichment. Several studies have found that intelligence can be reduced by the absence of certain forms of environmental stimulation early in life. A child who is born with the capacity to become an Olympic athlete will not achieve his or her potential if deprived of the opportunity to run, jump and exercise. Equally a child born with the capacity for great intelligence will not be able to attain it if deprived of stimulation and the opportunity to learn. Several studies have found that removing children from barren, restricted environments and placing them in more favourable situations improves their intellectual development. In 1966 Harold Skeels studied 25 children, of low IQ, who for their first two years were raised in a poor American orphanage with very little social or mental stimulation. Thirteen of the children were transferred to another institution, which provided much more stimulation, with toys to play with and interaction with adults and older children. By the age of 3½ the transferred children had made enormous gains in IQ, while the IQs of the children who remained in the orphanage had fallen.

Skeels followed up the children in adulthood and found that those who had stayed in the orphanage tended to be intellectually subnormal and could not look after themselves. In contrast, many of the children who had been sent to the better institution (a home for the mentally retarded) had normal intelligence and completed school; many were married and in employment.

In the 1980s Arnold Sameroff and Ronald Seifer conducted a longitudinal study that tested the IQs of children, from different backgrounds, at the age of 4 and 13 years. They found a negative correlation between children's IQs and factors such as poor health, poor living conditions, poor diet, poorly educated parents and an absence of books and mental stimulation in their backgrounds. As the number of risk factors increased so a child's IQ decreased. These studies demonstrate the importance of the environment on a person's intellectual development.

It seems then that intelligence is not entirely fixed, but can vary quite substantially over time, presumably according to circumstances and upbringing. The same may be true for some group differences in IQ. In the 1970s and 1980s, for example, Jerome Kagan and his associates compared the IQ scores of Guatemalan village children and children in the USA at different ages. The early living conditions of the Guatemalan children were much poorer than the conditions of those in the USA; the Guatemalan children were less well-nourished, in poorer health and more physically and socially isolated, and had little exposure to human contact or opportunity for exploration and physical activity. They also performed much less well on IQ tests. The contrast between living conditions grew much smaller as the children grew older, and so did the difference in IQ scores: by the time the children reached adolescence the Guatemalans performed almost as well as their counterparts in the USA, the remaining differences being almost certainly because of differences in schooling and culture.

Compensatory education

Further support for the effects of the environment comes from demonstrations of the beneficial effects of special environmental interventions. In the 1960s the US government introduced several programmes of compensatory education intended to improve the disadvantaged backgrounds of many poor children. It was intended to compensate disadvantaged preschool children, so that they could begin their education in the same situation as those from less disadvantaged backgrounds. Two such compensatory education projects, Operation Headstart and the Carolina Abecedarian Project, are described in box 8.4.

In 1989 Ann and Alan Clarke found that when children take part in these enrichment programmes their test scores increase by approximately 10 points. Obviously these massive intervention programmes are expensive, but so are the economic consequences of poverty and unemployment. Programmes like these demonstrate that a cycle of school failure can be broken, and also that intelligence can be increased in a stimulating environment.

Box 8.4   Compensatory Education

How have training programmes set out to improve the intellectual performance of children from disadvantaged backgrounds? An early programme, Operation Headstart, which was part of a presidential War on Poverty campaign, began in 1965 as an eight-week summer programme and developed into an entire year of preschool work. Children were given free health tests and an educational programme intended to improve their chances of success when they began school. Various programmes used different types of enhancement, so that some emphasized basic skills and others encouraged social skills and cooperation. Some programmes took place in children's homes, while others were conducted in nearby centres. Initial assessments showed gains in IQ and improved school performance when the children were compared with those who had not received the programme. However, it appeared at first that these gains were temporary, as a couple of years later they had disappeared. Later assessment though showed that the children who had undergone the programmes were more likely to complete schooling, more likely to have academic success and less likely to get into trouble with the police, to become pregnant or to need state benefits.

Some intervention programmes have typically included an elaborate structured curriculum for both children and parents. One programme, the Carolina Abecedarian Project, used massive and sustained intervention. The study began with 111 disadvantaged children, most of whom had African-American mothers with little education, low IQs and low incomes, and 90 children completed the project. Some children had no intervention, others attended special daycare from 4 months to 5 years of age. The curriculum included mental, linguistic and social development for infants and prereading skills for preschoolers. Some children also had more intervention in their first three years of school, a teacher visiting their homes a few times a month with materials to improve their reading and mathematical skills. The teachers also taught the parents how to use the materials with their children and assisted with communication between their homes and schools. As 12-year-olds the children were tested for written language, mathematics and reading, and it was found that in all three areas their performance reflected the amount of intervention they had received. The children who had experienced the full eight years of intervention had the highest scores, while those with no intervention had the lowest. After intervention children moved from being substantially below average to average grades.

Additional support for the effects of the environment comes from the knowledge that environmental factors such as nutrition can affect intelligence. Prolonged malnutrition has been found to affect IQ adversely, and so has exposure to lead, in the air or in the form of lead-based paint.

So although large-scale studies indicate some stability in IQ scores, measured intelligence can change quite substantially over time, and the change can be largely due to changes in environment and experience. Psychologists have always argued, and continue to argue, about the relative importance of environmental and genetic factors in determining the development of intelligence, but few would deny that both are important. The close relation between intelligence and experience is clear in the development of measured intelligence during childhood and adolescence; it is also very important when we examine the development of intelligence and other aspects of cognition in adulthood and old age.

Cognitive Changes in Adulthood and Old Age

It is a common stereotype that older adulthood is associated with declining cognitive ability – that 'you can't teach an old dog new tricks', that old people are forgetful, and that they are less intelligent. As with most stereotypes, this view is an exaggeration, but there is a little substance behind it. For example, older adults do often fare less well than younger people in tests of attention, learning and memory. They may find it harder to divide attention between two or more tasks or sources of information, and they may be less able to attend selectively and to ignore distractions. They may perform less well at most learning tasks, and, while there is rather little evidence that their short-term memory is impaired, there is plenty of evidence that their long-term memory may be poorer.

Older people also usually perform less well than younger people at standard tests of intelligence. But, as Timothy Salthouse has pointed out, cognitive decline in late adulthood occurs later and is smaller in magnitude than common stereotypes suggest, and even at quite advanced ages there are some people who obtain higher scores than the average 20-year-old. Moreover, when age-related cognitive declines are observed, they may be due to factors other than the ageing process; for example, they may result from older people's tendency to respond more slowly and more cautiously (although it is unclear whether slowing occurs to the same extent in all processing tasks, or whether it is more marked in some tasks than in others).

Age changes or cohort differences?

Studies of cognitive change in adulthood are nearly all *cross-sectional* in design: groups of adults of different ages are tested at one point in time, and their results compared. But people differ not only in age but also in 'birth cohort' (the historical period in which they were born), and people of different birth cohorts grow up in different circumstances. This is particularly relevant to intelligence-test performance:

earlier birth cohorts have on average had appreciably fewer years in formal education, and at any age there is a clear correlation between years in formal education and IQ scores. Of course, it could be argued that the cleverest people spend more time in formal education, hence the relation between education and IQ scores, but this is not the whole story. It is also true that formal education teaches people the skills that are needed for successful IQ test performance, and that those with little formal education are less likely to have acquired such skills. Indeed, when older and younger adults are matched on educational level, their differences in IQ largely disappear. So the age differences observed in cross-sectional studies of intelligence are likely to be partly due to cohort differences, rather than wholly due to age differences.

Some studies of age changes in cognitive abilities have employed *longitudinal* designs, in which the same participants are tested repeatedly over a long period, and *cohort-sequential* designs, which combine features of both cross-sectional and longitudinal designs. In contrast to cross-sectional studies, longitudinal and cohort-sequential studies show little evidence of age-related decline. But, apart from being time-consuming and expensive, longitudinal and cohort-sequential studies face the problem of 'selective participant attrition': when people are retested over periods of several years, they do not all remain available for retesting, for a variety of reasons. Those who do remain available tend to be those who were more able in the first place. This means that such studies may underestimate age differences, while cross-sectional studies overestimate them (for a fuller discussion of research designs, see chapter 16).

Fluid and crystallized intelligence

Some IQ tests show greater age differences than others. Generally speaking, verbal subtests, such as vocabulary or similarities tests, show very little decline with advancing age, while performance tests, such as picture arrangement, certain kinds of pictorial reasoning tests and digit–symbol substitution, show much greater age-related differences. Verbal tests largely reflect what Raymond Cattell has termed 'crystallized intelligence', which is built up over the lifespan through experience and the progressive accumulation of knowledge. Crystallized intelligence is therefore likely to increase with age. In contrast, performance tests largely reflect what Cattell terms 'fluid intelligence', which depends more directly on the capacity to perceive new relations and on abstract reasoning. Fluid intelligence is much less influenced by previous experience than is crystallized intelligence, and has been linked to the efficiency of physiological functioning, which is likely to decline with age.

The problem of 'age-fairness'

Do conventional tests of cognitive ability, such as IQ tests, enable adults of different ages to demonstrate their intelligence? Learning to associate pairs of words, to arrange pictures to tell a story and to suggest the missing item in a display of nonsense symbols may be reasonable tests for people in, or recently out of, school, but they may have little relevance to what most 70-year-olds have been doing with their lives for the past 50 years or so. Tests including such items may not be 'age-fair', and the same may be true of general knowledge and vocabulary items, which may well favour a particular age group (not necessarily the young). Warner Schaie argued in 1978 that we need to devise intelligence tests which have *ecological validity* for older as well as younger people, that is tests which are relevant to the ways in which we cope with everyday problems. Some attempts along these lines have produced smaller age differences than standard tests, and sometimes age increments, rather than 'decrements', in performance. For instance, in 1987 Steven Cornelius and Avshalom Caspi found that, while fluid intelligence reached a peak during the 40s, and declined quite sharply thereafter, both crystallized intelligence and 'everyday problem solving' scores improved with age over the age range from 20 to 70.

Experience: the advantage of being older

Although cognitive ability is usually one of the best predictors of work performance, objective measures of output in a variety of work situations seem to be largely unaffected by the age of the workers. As Roy Davies, Gerald Matthews and Carol Wong concluded in 1991 from a survey of studies of ageing and work, even when age differences in work performance are observed they are relatively small, and it is not unusual to find workers in their late 50s and early 60s outperforming workers in their 20s and 30s. The key factor responsible for an absence of substantial age differences in work performance would seem to be experience. Studies of productivity generally show that when experience (length of service) is controlled for, age differences in work performance disappear; conversely, when workers' age is controlled for, the effects of experience remain. Experience, which is highly age-related, can thus be a stronger predictor of work performance than age itself.

Cognitive performance does not always decline substantially in old age (as in other respects, old people vary enormously in their abilities), and when some age-related impairment appears in the psychological laboratory it does not necessarily relate to any difficulty in carrying out everyday tasks in the real world. Older people are generally very aware of any cognitive difficulties they may have and are well able to compensate for them – by using lists and other reminders, adapting their work methods, trying harder and generally trading off the effects of ageing against the effects of experience – to preserve and increase their independence and competence. As we have seen throughout this chapter, intelligence and experience shape each other and develop, throughout our lives, side by side.

Recommended Reading

Anastasi, A. (1990) *Psychological Testing*, 6th edn. New York: Macmillan. [A standard guide to the field.]

Clarke, A. and Alan, C. (1999) The nature–nurture debate: the essential readings. In S. J. Ceci and W. M. Williams (eds), *Essential Readings in Developmental Psychology*. Malden, MA: Blackwell. [A description of findings that conflict with the traditional view that early life experience sets a child on an immutable path.]

Howe, M. J. A. (1999) *Genius Explained*. New York: Cambridge University Press. [The author suggests that genius is a product of a combination of environment, personality, and sheer hard work. These ideas are developed through a series of case studies of famous figures, including Charles Darwin, George Eliot, the Brontë sisters and Albert Einstein.]

Kail, R. and Pellegrino, J. W. (1985) *Human Intelligence: Perspectives and Prospects*. New York: Freeman. [Includes Piagetian and information-processing approaches as well as psychometric ones.]

Sternberg, R. J. (2000) *Handbook of Intelligence*. New York: Cambridge University Press. [The book deals with different aspects of intelligence, including measurement, development, group differences, biological issues, relation to information processing, testing and teaching, society and culture.]

References

Bee, H. (1994) *Lifespan Development*. New York: HarperCollins. [Includes discussion of her own and others' research on stability of IQ scores.]

Binet, A. and Simon, T. (1905) New methods for diagnosis of the intellectual level of subnormals. *L'Année Psychologique*, 14, 1–90. [One of earliest tests of intelligence.]

Bouchard, T. J. and McGue, M. (1981) Familial studies of intelligence: a review. *Science*, 212, 1055–9. [A review of studies of intelligence in families.]

Bouchard, T. J., Lykken, D. T., McGue, M., Segal, N. L. and Tellegen, A. (1990) Sources of human psychological differences: the Minnesota study of twins reared apart. *Science*, 250, 223–8. [An influential study of twins who have been brought up in differing circumstances.]

Brosnan, M. J. (1998) The implications for academic attainment of perceived gender-appropriateness upon spatial task performance. *British Journal of Educational Psychology*, 68, 203–15. [Evidence that performance of women can depend on whether a task is viewed as related to 'male' or to 'female' abilities.]

Campbell, F. A. and Ramey, C. T. (1994) Effects of intervention on intellectual and academic achievement: a follow-up study of children from low income families. *Child Development*, 65, 684–98. [A follow-up of the Abecedarian Project.]

Cattell, R. B. (1949) The Culture-free Intelligence Test. Champaigne, IL: Institute for Personality and Ability Testing.

Clarke, A. M. and Clarke, A. D. (1989) The later cognitive effects of early intervention. *Intelligence*, 13, 289–97.

Clarke, A. M. and Clarke, A. D. B. (2000) *Early Experience and the Life Path*. London: Jessica Kingsley. [Challenges widely held assumption that early experience has disproportionate effect on later development.]

Connolly, K. and Martlew, M. (eds) (1999) *Psychologically Speaking: A Book of Quotations*. Leicester: BPS Books.

Cornelius, S. W. and Caspi, A. (1987) Everyday problem solving in adulthood and old age. *Psychology & Aging*, 2, 144–53. [A report of research showing maintenance of crystallized intelligence and everyday problem-solving ability into old age.]

Davies, D. R., Matthews, G. and Wong, C. (1991) Ageing and work. In C. L. Cooper and I. T. Robinson (eds), *International Review of Industrial and Organizational Psychology*, vol. 6. London: Wiley. [A survey of studies of workers age and work performance.]

Gardner, H. (1983) *Frames of Mind*. London: Paladin. [Gardner's theory of multiple intelligences.]

Goleman, D. (1995) *Emotional Intelligence*. New York: Bantam. [The importance of emotional intelligence for later success.]

Halpern, D. F. (1997) Sex differences in intelligence – implications for education. *American Psychologist*, 52, 1091–102. [A review of evidence concerning specific 'intellectual' tasks on which men regularly outperform women and vice versa.]

Holloway, S. D. and Hess, R. D. (1987) Mothers' and teachers' attributions about children's mathematics performance. In I. E. Siegel (ed.), *Parental Belief Systems: The Psychological Consequences for Children*. Hillsdale, NJ: Erlbaum. [Includes a survey of parents' preconceptions about mathematical ability in sons and daughters.]

Horn, J. L. and Cattell, R. B. (1972) Age differences in fluid and crystallized intelligence. *Acta Psychologica*, 26, 103–29. [The title is self-explanatory!]

Kagan, J., Kearsley, R. B. and Zelago, P. R. (1980) *Infancy – Its Place in Human Development*, 2nd edn. Cambridge, MA: Harvard University Press. [Includes a report of research comparing IQ scores of Guatemalan and US children at various ages.]

McCall, R. B., Appelbaum, M. I. and Hogarty, P. S. (1973) Developmental changes in mental performance. *Monographs of the Society for Research into Child Development*, 38 (whole no. 150). [A study which found marked fluctuations in IQ scores with increasing age.]

McGue, M. and Bouchard, T. J. (1998) Genetic and environmental influences on human behavioural differences. *Annual Review of Neuroscience*, 21, 1–24. [A review of human behavioural genetic research on individual differences in cognitive and other abilities.]

Neisser, U., Boodoo, G., Bouchard, T. J., Boykin, A. W., Brody, N., Ceci, S. J., Halpern, D. F., Loehlin, J. C., Perloff, R., Sternberg, R. J. and Urbina, S. (1996) Intelligence: knowns and unknowns. *American Psychologist*, 51, 77–101. [Current ideas concerning intelligence.]

Plomin, R. (1988) The nature and nurture of cognitive abilities. In R. J. Sternberg (ed.), *Advance in the Psychology of Human Intelligence*, vol. 4. Hillsdale, NJ: Erlbaum. [A review of studies of twins.]

Salthouse, T. (1991) *Theoretical Perspectives in Cognitive Aging*. Hillsdale, NJ: Erlbaum. [Review and theoretical analysis of cognitive changes in late adulthood.]

Sameroff, A. J., Bartko, W. T., Baldwin, A., Baldwin, C. and Seifer, R. (1998) Family and social influences on the development of child competence. In M. Lewis and C. Feiring (eds), *Families, Risk, and Competence*. Mahwah, NJ: Erlbaum. [An examination of multiple sources of risk as additive contributors to development of competence.]

Sameroff, A. J. and Seifer, R. (1983) Social regulation of developmental communities. Paper presented at the annual meeting of the American Association for the Advancement of Science, San Francisco. [An examination of multiple sources of risk additive contributors to the development of competence.]

Saunders, Pearce and Amato (1983) *The Original Australian Test of Intelligence*. [An intelligence test designed for original Australians.]

Schaie, K. W. (1978) External validity in the assessment of intellectual development in adulthood. *Journal of Gerontology*, 33, 695–701. [A famous appeal for cognitive tests which are age-fair and relevant to everyday functioning.]

Skeels, H. M. (1966) Adult status of children with contrasting early life experiences: a follow up study. *Monographs of the Society for Research in Child Development*, 31(3). [Skeels's final follow-up of his original sample.]

Spearman, C. (1927) *The Abilities of man: Their Nature & Assessment*. London: Macmillan.

Sternberg, R. (1995) For whom the bell curve tolls: a review of The Bell Curve. *Psychological Science*, 6, 257–61. [A review of studies concerning intelligence.]

Sternberg, R. (1997) The concept of intelligence and its role in lifelong learning and success. *American Psychologist*, 52, 1030–7. [A discussion of intelligence and its role in later life.]

Sternberg, R. J., Forsythe, G. B., Hedlund, J., Horvath, J. A., Wagner, R. K., Williams, W. M., Snook, S. A. and Grigorenko, E. L. (2000) *Practical Intelligence in Everyday Life*. New York: Cambridge University Press. [The everyday role of practical intelligence.]

Terman, L. M. and Merrill, M. A. (1960) *Stanford Binet Intelligence Scale, Third Revision Form* L-M. NFER.

Thurstone, L. L. (1938) *Primary Mental Abilities*. Chicago: University of Chicago Press. [A description of seven different primary mental abilities.]

Wechsler, D. (1949) *Wechsler Intelligence Scale for Children*. New York: Psychological Corporation.

Willis, S. L. (1996) Everyday problem solving. In J. E. Birren and K. W. Schaie (eds), *Handbook of the Psychology of Aging*, 4th edn. San Diego, CA: Academic Press. [An analysis of everyday cognitive ability and its relation to increasing adult age.]

9
Creativity and Artistic Development

- What is creativity?
- The nature of artistic development
- Art, music and literature
- The effects of artistic activity

We see children engaged in creative activities from a very young age: drawing and painting, playing with sounds and words in song and rhymes, acting out scenarios in make-believe play, making models in clay and dancing and singing. These open-ended kinds of activity are observed in children of all ages and are seen as an important part of childhood. Yet creativity is not unique to childhood. We can also think of some very creative adults in the visual arts (painting, drawing, photography, sculpture), in literature, in dance and in music: Salvador Dali or Tracey Emin, William Shakespeare or Martin Amis, Isadora Duncan or Merce Cunningham, Ludwig van Beethoven or Philip Glass. (You may not think that all these individuals are great, but they cannot be denied the label 'creative'.)

Creativity is not only to do with the arts. We usually associate creative behaviour with activities like music, drama, literature and the visual arts, but many important advances are made through creative thinking in other fields, such as business, technology, politics and the sciences. The following example from Richard Feynmann, the Nobel Prize winning physicist (National Advisory Committee on Creative and Cultural Education 1999), shows us how creative thinking can have dramatic results.

> I decided I was only going to do things for the fun of it and only that afternoon as I was taking lunch some kid threw up a plate in the cafeteria. There was a blue medallion on the plate – the Cornell sign. As the plate came down it wobbled. It seemed to me that the blue thing went round faster than the wobble and I wondered what the relationship was between the two – I was just playing; no importance at all. So I played around with the equations of motion of rotating things and I found out that if the wobble is small the blue thing goes round twice as fast as the wobble. I tried to figure out why that was, just for the fun of it, and this led me to the similar problems in the spin of an electron and that led me back into quantum

electrodynamics which is the problem I'd been working on. I continued to play with it in this relaxed fashion and it was like letting a cork out of a bottle. Everything just poured out and in very short order I worked the things out for which I later won the Nobel Prize.

Creativity, like play (see chapter 5), is a difficult term to pin down and, as Roy Prentice writes, is 'a complex and slippery concept'. A recent report by the National Advisory Committee on Creative and Cultural Education identifies four features of creativity. *Using imagination* is the first: this is the process of generating something original, providing an alternative to the expected, conventional or routine. This is the kind of insight that Feynmann describes above, seeing new analogies and relations between ideas or objects. *Pursuing purposes* is the second: creativity is defined as resulting from, or being part of, some kind of deliberate activity. Although insights may occur through intuition or by accident, they need to fit into a purposeful scheme of activity in which the insights are used to tackle a problem and provide a solution. *Being original* is the third feature. This can mean different things: being original can be at an individual level, at which the originality relates to what one has done before, at a relative level, in comparison with what other people at the same level (such as children of the same age) are doing, or at a historical level, in comparison with anything that has been achieved before in the particular field. The final feature is *judging value*: depending on the field, different criteria of value will apply, but to be truly creative whatever is being done needs to be supported by some idea of judging its value.

This composite definition tells us what creativity is and what it is not. A chimpanzee given paintbrushes that produces vivid colours and shapes by accident is not considered a creative painter, but a child artist who deliberately chooses similar colours and shapes as part of a considered design to achieve a particular effect is engaging in creative activity. A child who copies a drawing faithfully from a book is not being truly creative, but another child who applies the technique of drawing a three-dimensional cube to produce a drawing of a house is taking a small step along the path of creativity. A group of children who randomly generate sounds on an electronic keyboard and record everything they produce are not truly creating music, but a second group who review their recordings and select sounds they like in a purposeful way are making progress towards a creative musical composition.

Changing attitudes to the arts?

At the start of the twenty-first century, there has been an upsurge of interest and research in children's artistic development. Just as we are beginning to recognize that play is an important aspect of children's development, so the importance of artistic and creative activities is being reaffirmed in both developmental psychology and, to some extent, in education. The National Committee report mentioned above argues very strongly for the place of creative activities within the school curriculum.

The possible 'transfer' effects of the arts on other areas of learning have also been used to bolster the argument for including these kinds of activity in the curriculum. Current government policy seems to recognize the importance of creative industries and the creative aspects of society. Yet there are other important pressures on education, such as the drive to improve literacy and numeracy, which often come at the expense of arts activities. Creativity has a slightly tarnished image in educational circles – as we saw above, it is to do with letting go of tradition and challenging the routine or conventional, and this can be seen as dangerous in the wrong hands.

The Nature of Artistic Development

Howard Gardner, a leading member of the Project Zero team at Harvard University, has carried out a great deal of research into various aspects of children's creativity. He proposes that children develop three different 'systems' in relation to the arts; his proposal is a useful way of getting to grips with the topic of artistic development.

1   The *making* system is to do with producing art works. Children invent their own art works, and in some cases they may perform them (as in music or dance).
2   The *perceiving* system deals with the distinctions that children make between different art works – the role of the art critic.
3   The *feeling* system relates to the emotional side of the response to art. Children gradually develop the role of the audience member.

These three systems are not completely separate, and Gardner suggests that they become more and more interrelated as children grow older. We shall use them as a way of organizing the material relating to children's artistic development.

The Making System

All children engage in the production of art works without requiring any explicit teaching how to do so. The developmental courses of the visual arts, music and story-telling share many features. In each artistic field, the early stages consist of mastering the raw materials – marks on the paper, words or sounds. This is followed by a conventional phase during which children become fascinated with mastering the 'right way' to achieve desired results: drawing an orange in three dimensions, singing a typical song, or telling a formulaic story. This is an important stepping stone along the path towards a more individualistic style of artistic activity, which we might consider closer to true creativity. Let us take a closer look at how development takes place in some different artistic domains.

Figure 9.1   *Scribbling at 2¹/₂ years (picture courtesy of Joy Little Oak Price)*

From scribbles to masterpieces: the development of children's drawing

As soon as children are able to hold a pencil or crayon, they take pleasure in making marks on paper (this may be paper provided specially or other possible drawing spaces like wallpaper tabletops, and any other available surfaces!). Initially children's drawings will take the form of apparently random scribbling (see figure 9.1). But if the crayons leave no trace on the paper, the children quickly lose interest in the activity of scribbling, which suggests that the activity of leaving marks is part of the enjoyment.

As children become more experienced at scribbling, they may notice shapes in their scribbles that resemble real objects. Georges-Henri Luquet describes this as a stage of 'fortuitous realism': although the children do not set out to draw particular shapes, when they notice these shapes in their drawings they are often able to label them and add other features consistent with the label. The next stage is to draw particular shapes intentionally from the outset. This brings with it many problems that children have to learn to solve, for example how to represent real life with a series of lines in two dimensions.

Children's earliest representational drawings are often of other people. Maureen Cox has described the progression of drawings of the human figure in some detail. At about the age of 3, children tend to produce 'tadpole' figures: a circle stands for

Figure 9.2   *Tadpole drawings of the human figure*

the head, with two lines for legs. If arms are drawn, they are usually attached to what seems to be the head (see figure 9.2). Much attention has been devoted to analysing these tadpole figures and trying to establish whether the children have a very schematic idea of what the human body looks like, on the one hand, or whether they are simply unable to represent this through drawing, on the other. In an in-

Exercise 9.1

Assessing Children's Drawings

According to Elizabeth Koppitz's Draw a Person test, children's abilities to draw a detailed human figure relate to their intellectual maturity. Koppitz's list of developmental items is given below. How many points would you give to the drawings shown below? Do you think the drawings are produced by children of the same age? If not, which one is drawn by the older child?

Koppitz's Developmental Items

1	Head	16	Arms correctly attached to shoulders
2	Eyes	17	Elbows
3	Pupils	18	Hands
4	Eyebrows or eyelashes	19	Fingers
5	Nose	20	Correct number of fingers
6	Nostrils	21	Legs
7	Mouth	22	Legs in two dimensions
8	Two lips	23	Knees
9	Ears	24	Feet
10	Hair	25	Feet in two dimensions
11	Neck	26	Profile
12	Body	27	Clothing: one item or none
13	Arms	28	Clothing: two or three items
14	Arms in two dimensions	29	Clothing: four or more items
15	Arms pointing downwards	30	Good proportions

Figure 9.3   *Children's drawings a) Reprinted by permission of Lois Borrelli. b) From the collection of one of the authors*

Answers on page 156.

triguing study carried out by Cox and her colleague Glyn Jarvis, children of 3½–4 years were asked to produce free drawings of a person 'with a tummy' and to draw a tummy on two pre-drawn tadpole figures: one had a longer head and the other had longer legs. Children at this age are able to add a tummy to a conventional drawing of a human figure, and they can also point to their own tummies, so they do understand the concept of a tummy and where it is located. Those children who drew tummies in the head part of the tadpole in their free drawings also positioned the tummy in the head of the pre-drawn figures, regardless of how large the head was; children who drew tummies between the legs did so in both their free drawings and the pre-drawn figures. This shows that the children had a prior idea of where the tummy should go. For the first group of children the head represented the entire torso, whereas for the second group the head refers only to the head and the torso is located between the legs. These seem to reflect two stages in tadpole drawings, the second being the precursor to more realistic drawings of people.

The attempts to draw the human figure are part of G.-H. Luquet's second stage of drawing development, termed 'failed realism', since the drawings look very little like the objects they are supposed to represent. The next stage of drawing is often known as *intellectual realism*. Between the ages of about 4 and 7, children become more interested in drawing what they know to be the case rather than what they actually see. For example, they will draw a picture of a cup with the handle showing, even though their view of the cup has the handle obscured. They also tend to draw 'transparencies': all four legs of a table, or both legs of a man seated on a horse. Luquet suggests that children are drawing according to an internal model at this stage: the internal model of a face, for instance, includes two eyes, a nose and a mouth, and this will typically be drawn even if the face is shown in profile.

From intellectually realistic drawings, children tend to move into a *schematic* phase at about 8 or 9 years of age. At this point their drawings are still visually unrealistic, but children become more interested in how to achieve the desired effects and often use very conventional approaches. The final stage of drawing is characterized by *visual realism*, in which children master the ability to draw objects as they actually look, including perspective and tackling the problems of representing three-dimensional objects on a two-dimensional surface realistically. Leonardo da Vinci suggested that artists imagine they are looking at the scene through a glass window in order to achieve this: by closing one eye, the outline of the object to be drawn can be traced onto the glass. Most of us do not master this stage of drawing, and many great artists are not concerned with true visual realism. Pablo Picasso, for example, often represented a single object from multiple perspectives rather than being concerned with an accurate depiction.

From babbling to opera: the development of children's music making

All children begin to babble from about 9 months, and this takes two main forms. Vocal babbling is a precursor to language, while non-vocal babbling seems to be a

Figure 9.4   *Attempt at visual realism by a 6-year-old*

Exercise 9.1 Answer

The left hand drawing was done by an autistic child aged 5½ years, while the right hand drawing was done by a developmentally normal child of the same age. As the two children are the same age, they should have obtained similar scores. Some children with autism show particular skill in artistic domains, such as drawing or music, yet their development in other fields lags behind the developmental norms.

Note that although these tests can give a rough estimate of a child's intellectual maturity, some good drawers do not perform well intellectually, and some bright children are not good at drawing. The usefulness of this kind of scoring system depends on norms for each age: legs are expected as an item at age 6, for instance; therefore a 6-year-old who omits legs from his or her best effort at a human figure will score −1 on that item.

precursor of singing. Early non-vocal babbling is based on continuous pitches rather than the discrete pitches of adult music – it glides around rather than settling on particular notes. At about 18 months, children begin to produce discrete pitches in their singing. They stick to small pitch intervals, which also happen to be the most common intervals in adult music. Children's songs gradually increase in organization. Two-year-olds tend to produce songs with short phrases of maybe only two or three notes which are repeated over and over again. The phrase length and complexity increases until children reach a stage of 'outline' or schematic songs, at about 3–4 years of age – a little earlier than in drawing, yet showing the same features of conventionality and borrowing familiar features from well-known songs. Later, children begin to fill in more of the details of these outlines and to reproduce their songs more consistently.

Lyle Davidson and colleagues at Project Zero have studied children's early singing abilities extensively, and have also examined their drawings of music. Again the same kind of progression is apparent. At about 4–5 years, children tend to focus on the global aspects of the songs or patterns they are drawing. For example, a pair of hands might be drawn to stand for a clapped musical rhythm, or a drawing of a boat might stand for the song *Row Row Row Your Boat*. Between 5 and 7, children are able to draw single dimensions of the music. A pattern of claps might be drawn as a series of circles, or the pitch contour (ups and downs) of the song might be drawn as a wavy line across the page. At age 7 and above, children are able to combine various features of the music in their drawings, pitch and rhythm being captured in the drawings. These changes are shown in figure 9.5.

As well as singing, children also often take part in musical composition. The current National Curriculum programme of study for music includes composition

a)

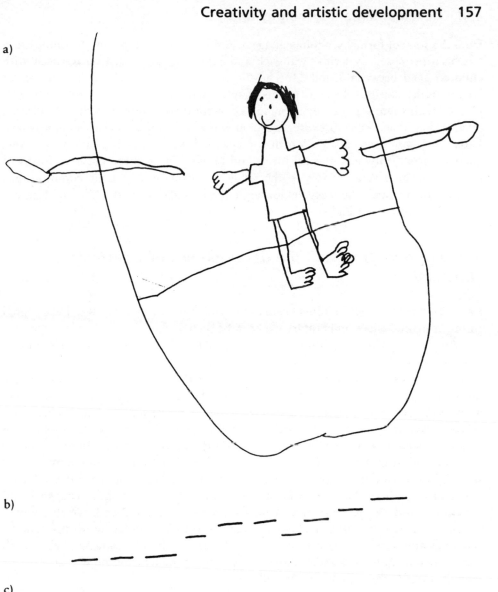

b)

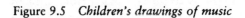

c)

Figure 9.5   *Children's drawings of music*

from the start of formal schooling at age 5. A model of development in composition has been proposed by Keith Swanwick and June Tillman, based on research with children aged between 3 and 11. The stages in this model reflect the features of creativity discussed at the start of this chapter. Children begin by manipulating or playing with sounds, gradually learning to control these sounds to achieve a desired effect. They then begin to express their intentions through musical compositions. Later, they move into a stage which is concerned with form, beginning with 'vernacular' or stereotypical musical forms and moving on to more personal forms of music. The final stage relates to the value or evaluation of their compositions. Progression through the stages is loosely linked to age, in that older children are more likely to be at a higher level.

'Once upon a time . . .': the development of children's story-telling

As we saw in chapter 5, children begin to pretend from a very early age. The scripted forms of make-believe and fantasy play can be seen as the precursors of imaginative story-telling or creative writing, as they involve the creation of a narrative and an awareness of social roles or relationships between the characters in the story.

As soon as children begin to make marks on the page, they are aware of the difference between drawing and writing – even though to the adult eye these marks may look very similar at the outset! Learning to use letters to make words and words to stand for objects or events is a long and complex process. Children often begin by using a single letter to stand for a word, and only later begin to use letters in combination to make recognizable words. They soon move into a conventional stage of mastering the typical format of written language, and also of producing conventional stories. Helen Cowie has suggested that children aged between 2 and 5 tend to produce 'frame stories', with a clear beginning and end, which concern 'stock characters' engaging in all kinds of adventures. The similarities with schematic drawings and outline songs are obvious. With age, children become more able to fill out the details of the story, developing consistent characters and plots that progress from beginning through middle to end.

The Perceiving System

Howard Gardner talks about the perceiving system as the development of children's skills as art critics. There are some necessary steps to go through before we can think of children as able to judge the effectiveness of art works – 'reading' a picture requires all kinds of perceptual and cognitive skills, such as following lines, distinguishing colours and shapes and understanding how marks on a paper or figures in plaster can come to represent objects in the real world. We shall focus here on the specifically artistic aspects of learning to be a critic.

Looking at pictures

In Cox's study of children's drawing, in which children were asked to judge the best and the silliest versions of human figures, their judgements were tied up with their own drawing levels. Tadpole drawers consistently thought that the best was a tadpole drawing and that the silliest was the conventional human figure, while children who were able to produce conventional drawings of people thought these were the best and that the tadpoles were the silliest.

This view has been challenged by some more recent research by Richard Jolley and his colleagues, which suggests that the way the questions are asked may influence the children. Children may well prefer drawings that are closest to their own preferred drawing style, but they may also be aware of the most visually realistic drawing in a set. Jolley and his colleagues asked children aged between 3 and 14 to judge other children's drawings on the basis of realism, preference, and estimation of their own skill: 'Which picture looks most like a real man? Which picture do you like the best? And which picture looks most like how you draw a man?' The children all chose a conventional figure as the most realistic drawing, a more advanced form than their own drawing as their preferred drawing, and overestimated their own drawing skills. This suggests that children have different internal models for comprehending drawings and for producing drawings – again supporting Gardner's distinction between the making and the perceiving systems.

Listening to music

Children's developing abilities to perceive music have been extensively studied, from infancy to adolescence and beyond. Research by Sandra Trehub and her colleagues shows us that infants aged 6 months are able to notice the difference between tunes that go up or down in contour, to detect whether sequences have the same or different rhythms or groupings, and even to notice small changes in pitch. Studies by Michael Lynch and his colleagues have shown a progression in infants' ability to distinguish pitches similar to that which occurs for different languages. At 6 months, infants can notice changes to musical patterns not only of their own culture but also of other cultures. By 12 months, infants have become accustomed to hearing one particular musical system, and they lose the ability to appreciate changes in other musical systems. It seems that the 12-month-old baby is quite a sophisticated music listener!

Children's abilities to perceive different elements of music continue to develop as they grow older and have more experience with various kinds of music. Children's drawings of music can also tell us about the way they understand the music. One of Davidson's colleagues at Project Zero, Jeanne Bamberger, has carried out some interesting research which explores the way children organize familiar music on paper. She asked children of various ages to write down a rhythm which they had been clapping in class: 'something you think would help you remember the rhythm tomorrow or help someone else to clap it who isn't here today'. She classed the

Action drawings

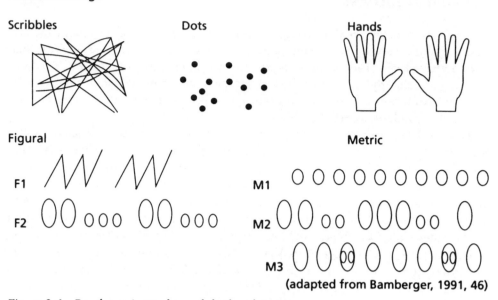

(adapted from Bamberger, 1991, 46)

Figure 9.6 *Bamberger's typology of rhythm drawings*

resulting drawings into three main types. The first she calls '*action* drawings', found in children aged 4 and 5. The children 'performed' the rhythm on the paper with a series of dots or squiggles, or in some cases drew round their hands to represent the activity of clapping. Drawings from older children, aged 6 to 12, capture more features of the rhythms, and these can be divided into two categories. *Figural* drawings give the outline of the shapes and gestures in the pattern, emphasizing groups rather than absolute durational values. *Metric* drawings provide the details of the rhythm itself, giving more emphasis to the durations and less to the phrases. Metric drawings are found by children with more musical experience or with some musical training. Examples of these are shown in figure 9.6.

Children's musical preferences from an early age have also been studied. Marcel Zentner and Jerome Kagan recently found that babies as young as 5 months showed a consistent preference for tonally consonant tunes and chords over dissonant tunes and chords. Ongoing research by one of the authors is beginning to show that the music children hear in the home has a powerful influence on their own musical preferences. Although most babies aged 12 months have a general preference for music with a relatively loud beat and fast pace, they also prefer music which they have heard many times before to different music in a very similar style.

As children grow older and have more experience with listening to music, as well as singing their own songs, their critical abilities with respect to music also become more honed. A study by LeBlanc and colleagues found that young children are relatively 'open-eared' in terms of the range of musical styles they are willing to listen to, while adolescents show strong allegiances to particular popular musical styles. David

Exercise 9.2

Drawing Rhythms

All the children's drawings in figure 9.5 are of the same well-known musical rhythm. See whether you can work out what this rhythm is. When you know what it is, clap it to a 7-year-old child, offer a pencil and paper and ask the child to write down 'something you think would help you remember the rhythm tomorrow or help someone else to clap it who isn't here today'. Try to categorize the drawing as one of Bamberger's types. Repeat this exercise with younger and older children and see how their drawings differ. You could use another familiar rhythm or invent your own.

Answers on p. 162.

Hargreaves has argued that there can be another increase in 'open-earedness' during later adolescence and early adulthood. We sometimes tend to become a little 'stuck' in our musical preferences, which are often formed at critical points in development, such as adolescence, when we have time, energy and emotional investment to devote to particular musical styles of our choosing. As recently shown by Mark Tarrant and his colleagues, the musical preferences of adolescents are an important part of their rites of passage, providing a focus for their forming and evaluating peer groups.

Reading stories

Once children have mastered the complex tasks of learning their alphabet and how to combine letters into phonemes, syllables and words, they still have to learn how to read a story and understand its meaning. As well as understanding the words that go to make up a story, children need to master the meaning that lies behind the words – and indeed, to know that the words are the important part of reading and not the pictures, as some preschool children think. David Wood writes about the need to learn how to interact with texts in order to interpret the writers' intended meaning, emphasizing the fact that reading requires a degree of interpretation.

Children need to work out how to go beyond the words that are given, in order to make inferences. Most written text does not provide all the information necessary to understand its meaning. A study by Jane Oakhill and her colleagues tested 7- and 8-year-olds' understanding of short stories such as the following:

The car crashed into the bus.
The bus was near the crossroads.
The car skidded on the ice.

Exercise 9.2 Answer

The rhythm being drawn by Bamberger's children is 'three, four, shut the door, five, six, pick up sticks'. People who are musically trained find the metric drawings the easiest to read because they are the closest to standard musical notation. Most people without musical training, even adults, will tend to produce drawings more like the figural versions. None of these drawings are better than the others – they simply prioritize and emphasize different aspects of the rhythm. We should expect younger children to produce drawings that fit into the 'action' category and older children to produce drawings that are figural or, if they have extensive musical experience, metric.

The children were asked to say whether either of the following implications or inferences was consistent with the story:

The car was near the crossroads.
The bus skidded on the ice.

The first suggestion is more plausible, since the car crashed into the bus and the bus was near the crossroads; the second suggestion is less plausible, as there is no need for the bus to skid on the ice. There were considerable variations in the children's abilities to draw the correct inference – children with a better reading comprehension level were more able to match the right inference to the story.

Jessie Reid has analysed the forms of written language in relation to speech and thought, which gives us some insight into the difficulty that children have of learning to decode these kinds of structure from a written text. The first example is of what she calls quoted speech with an explicit source: 'I am afraid', said Grimble, 'that after Christmas will be exactly too late.' Although on the face of it it is easy to see that Grimble is speaking, even a simple sentence like this requires a child to store and carry over the syntax and the meaning of the quoted words – to put the two parts of the sentence together as a complete statement which is spoken by Grimble.

The second example is more complex still – an example of quoted speech with an implicit source: 'She stood still, heart hammering. "Is she in there?" Albert's face was contemptuous. "Couldn't hurt you if she was, but she isn't, she is downstairs in her coffin."' This passage signals who is speaking by prefacing the speech with a short description of the speaker (in this case including emotions), but decoding this is far from simple. Although children can read simple stories from a very early age, it is many years before they are able to deal with written text in all its complexity and subtlety. Geoffrey Underwood suggests that reading is an area of expertise and that skilled, or expert, readers use various strategies to solve reading problems – for example, the expert reader does not convert syllables into subvocal speech but goes directly from combinations of syllables to meaning.

The Feeling System

Of Gardner's three artistic systems, the last one – the feeling system – has been the least studied with children. This is partly due to the theories of artistic development discussed above, which suggest that elements relating to emotion tend to be associated with the later stages of development and that young children are thus unable to respond in an emotional way to art works of any kind. Some more recent studies, taking care that they understood the emotion words used by the experimenters, have shown that children from the age of 5 seem able to judge the emotional content of art works.

A recent study by Tara Callaghan in the field of visual art gives us some useful insight into how children might be able to achieve this. Her study explores the emotional reactions of 3- and 5-year-old children to postcards of paintings. She designed a careful explanation of the 'feeling' words used in the study, which involved introducing the children to a collection of teddy bears with various facial expressions (Sad Teddy, Happy Teddy, and so on), and the children were asked to find paintings to suit the houses of each teddy bear. Half the children were helped by the experimenter, who made aesthetic judgements about the paintings and explained why she chose each painting for each teddy; the other half had to choose appropriate paintings without this help. Both the 3- and 5-year-olds were more successful at choosing paintings that matched the emotions of the teddy bears according to adult conventions when they had help from the experimenter. The 3-year-olds were not able to do this without help, but the 5-year-olds could make consistent emotional judgements about paintings on their own.

This intriguing study suggests that very young children can judge the emotional content of paintings in a way that is consistent with adult expectations, but, more importantly, that social interaction with an adult who is making judgements about art seems to help the children make these kinds of aesthetic judgement. This leads back to the importance of art education as a way of helping children tackle the emotional as well as the formal or intellectual aspects of art works.

The Effects of Artistic Activity

Howard Gardner has argued that there are at least seven different kinds of intelligence: linguistic, mathematical, spatial, kinaesthetic, musical, interpersonal and intrapersonal. From this list, he suggests that individuals have a certain amount of each kind of intelligence and, at a neurological level, that the kinds are separate from one another. Being good at mathematics does not mean that you are necessarily talented at music, for instance; having a keen sense of kinaesthetic (bodily) appreciation need not be related to abilities in the linguistic field. Some more recent research suggests that there *may* in fact be some cross-overs between different fields and, in particular, that expertise gained in artistic domains can have an effect on other intellectual and social areas of children's development.

An interesting *intervention study* by Moore and Caldwell in the United States found some short-term effects of arts activity on children's narrative writing. Children aged 7–9 participated in either a drama session or a drawing session, a control group having no extra session, before they wrote a narrative story. After both the drama and the drawing activities the children wrote stories whose organization, ideas, context and style were assessed, by independent judges, to be better than those of the stories written by children who had not experienced either art or drama. This suggests that there may be some transfer between various kinds of arts activity, or between some of Gardner's types of intelligence.

Frances Rauscher and her colleagues have carried out intervention studies with children aged from 3 to 7 years, giving some a programme of formal musical training and others various kinds of extra activities, such as computer lessons. The children's performance on one specific cognitive ability – spatial–temporal skills – was found to improve after at least six months of music training, but this was not found for the control groups, who received other kinds of activity. It was only spatial–temporal skills – the skills we use when following a map or carrying out mathematical tasks such as fractions and ratios – that were improved by the music lessons. These findings have been used by Gordon Shaw to suggest that music training in young children acts as a kind of brain exercise which helps strengthen the spatial–temporal part of the brain.

There is some evidence that music training has transfer effects on other cognitive abilities, particularly those that involve a temporal dimension. For example, Katie Overy has shown that music training can help children with dyslexia in their reading. In a recent review of these and other studies, Caroline Sharp concludes that the jury is still out on the case of transfer effects from the arts to other areas of children's development. As suggested at the start of this chapter, although these arguments may be useful for arts advocacy in education if they are proven, they can be damaging for the place of the arts in education should they be disproven. Time will tell whether there is a robust transfer effect from artistic endeavours to cognitive development or academic achievement. But it is important to note the findings of studies such as those by Madeleine Zulauf, that engaging in arts activities does improve children's social skills, and particularly their self-esteem.

General Summary

We have considered how creativity applies to children, and traced the development of artistic abilities in drawing, music and story-telling. Each skill follows a similar pattern, beginning with a stage of mastering the material, moving through a stereotypical or conventional stage to reach a more personal or individual means of expression. In most cases, children are able to understand art works at a level more sophisticated than that which they show in their own creations, as they are hindered by a lack of technical skill and expertise. However, developmental psychology can offer insights into the creative understanding of children by analysing their creative products. Although this is a complex and difficult area to study, it is also one of the most rewarding.

Recommended Reading

Cox, M. (1992) *Children's Drawings*. London: Penguin. [A detailed but accessible examination of the process of drawing development, with many visual illustrations.]

Hargreaves, D. J. (ed.) (1989) *Children and the Arts*. Milton Keynes: Open University Press. [An interesting collection of articles relating to various aspects of children's artistic development.]

Winner, E. (1982) *Invented Worlds: The Psychology of the Arts*. London: Harvard University Press. [A very readable textbook with plenty of visual examples.]

References

Bamberger, J. (1991) *The Mind Behind the Musical Ear: How Children Develop Musical Intelligence*, Cambridge, MA: Harvard University Press. [In-depth studies of children's musical drawings and musical understanding, presented in an entertaining style.]

Callaghan, T. C. (2000) The role of context in preschoolers' judgments of emotion in art. *British Journal of Developmental Psychology*, 18, 465–74. [A study of how adults can help young children make emotional judgements about paintings.]

Cowie, H. (1989) Children as writers. In: D. J. Hargreaves (ed.), *Children and the Arts*. Milton Keynes: Open University Press. [A review of research into children's writing.]

Cox, M. (1992) *Children's Drawings*. London: Penguin. [A detailed but accessible examination of the process of drawing development, with many visual illustrations.]

Davidson, L. and Scripp, L. (1988) Young children's musical representations: windows on music cognition. In: J. A. Sloboda (ed.), *Generative Processes in Music: The Psychology of Performance, Improvisation, and Composition*. Oxford: Clarendon Press. [Research into children's drawings of music.]

Eisenberger, R., Haskins, F. and Gambleton, P. (1999) Promised reward and creativity: effects of prior experience. *Journal of Experimental Social Psychology*, 35, 308–25.

Gardner, H. (1973) *The Arts and Human Development*. New York: Wiley. [Gardner's original theory of artistic development, including three artistic systems.]

Gardner, H. (1993) *Multiple Intelligences*. New York: Basic Books. [Gardner's more recent theory of seven different kinds of intelligence.]

Hargreaves, D. J. (1986) *The Developmental Psychology of Music*. Cambridge: Cambridge University Press. [A comprehensive review of children's musical development and aesthetic appreciation of music.]

Jolley, R. P., Knox, E. L. and Foster, S. G. (2000) The relationship between children's production and comprehension of realism in drawing. *British Journal of Developmental*

Psychology, 18, 557–82. [Evidence of differences in the making and the perceiving systems for drawing.]

Koppitz, E. (1968) *Psychological Evaluation of Children's Human Figure Drawings*. London: Grune and Stratton. [The Draw a Person test.]

Lamont, A. (2001) Musical preferences in infancy. Paper presented at the annual conference of the Society for Music Perception and Cognition, Toronto, August. [Research by one of the authors: study showing preference for different styles of music in 12-month-old infants.]

LeBlanc, A., Sims, W., Siivola, C. and Obert, M. (1993) Musical style preferences of different age listeners. Paper presented at the 10th National Symposium on Research in Musical Behavior, Tuscaloosa, AL. [Study showing varying tolerances for musical styles.]

Luquet, G.-H. (1927) *Le Dessin enfantin*. Paris: Alcan. [Luquet's theory of drawing development.]

Lynch, M. P. and Eilers, R. E. (1992) A study of perceptual development for musical tuning. *Perception & Psychophysics*, 52(6), 599–608. [Sophisticated music listening in 12-month-old infants].

Moore, B. H. and Caldwell, H. (1993) Drama and drawing for narrative writing in primary grades. *Journal of Educational Research*, 87(2), 100–10. [Study showing improvements in children's writing after art or drama activities.]

Oakhill, J., Yuill, N. and Parkin, A. (1986) On the nature of the difference between skilled and less-skilled comprehenders. *Journal of Research in Reading*, 9, 80–91. [A study of children's comprehension abilities and abilities to draw inferences.]

Overy, K. (2000) Dyslexia, temporal processing and music: the potential of music as an early learning aid for dyslexic children. *Psychology of Music*, 28(2), 218–29. [Evidence for improvements in reading in children with dyslexia after music training.]

National Advisory Committee on Creative and Cultural Education (1999) *All Our Futures: Creativity, Culture & Education*. Sudbury: DfEE Publications. [A report and review of research commissioned by DfEE.]

Prentice, R. (2000) Creativity: a reaffirmation of its place in early childhood education. *Curriculum Journal*, 11(2), 145–58. [A powerful argument for inclusion of arts and creative activities in early years classrooms, together with some important analysis of government policy and educational practice.]

Rauscher, F. H., Shaw, G. L., Levine, L. J., Wright, E. L., Dennis, W. R. and Newcomb, R. L. (1997) Music training causes long-term enhancement of preschool children's spatial-temporal reasoning. *Neurological Research*, 19, 2–8. [A study showing transfer effects of musical training on spatial-temporal reasoning in 3–5-year-olds.]

Reid, J. (1990) Children's reading. In: R. Grieve and M. Hughes (eds), *Understanding Children*. Oxford: Blackwell. [A thorough investigation of skills required for reading, with interesting analysis of the complexity of written language from child's point of view.]

Sharp, C. (1998) *The Effects of Teaching and Learning in the Arts: A Review of Research*. London: QCA/NFER. [A review of many studies of possible transfer effects of the arts.]

Shaw, G. L. (2000) *Keeping Mozart in Mind*. San Diego, CA: Academic Press. [A controversial book describing some very complex research in a simple manner, outlining theory of music training as brain exercise.]

Swanwick, K. and Franca, C. C. (1999) Composing, performing and audience-listening as indicators of musical understanding. *British Journal of Music Education*, 16(1), 5–19.

Swanwick, K. and Tillman, J. (1986) The sequence of musical development: a study of children's composition. *British Journal of Music Education*, 6, 305–39.

Tarrant, M., North, A. C. and Hargreaves, D. J. (2002) Youth identity and music. In: R. A. R. MacDonald, D. J. Hargreaves and D. Miell (eds), *Musical Identities*. Oxford: Oxford University Press. [A study of adolescents' uses of musical preference.]

Trehub, S. E., Schellenberg, E. G. and Hill, D. (1997) The origins of music perception and cognition: a developmental perspective. In: I. Deliège and J. Sloboda (eds), *Perception and Cognition of Music*. Hove: Psychology Press. [A review of recent studies into infants' perception of musical patterns.]

Underwood, G. and Batt, V. (1996) *Reading and Understanding*. Oxford: Blackwell. [Includes studies of expert and novice readers.]

Wood, D. J. (1998) *How Children Think and Learn: The Social Contexts of Cognitive Development*. Oxford: Blackwell. [Chapter 7, The Literate Mind, outlines the progression of children's reading from decoding letters to making sense of texts.]

Zentner, M. R. and Kagan, J. (1998) Infants' perception of consonance and dissonance in music. *Infant Behavior & Development*, 21(3), 483–92. [Preference for consonant tunes and chords from 5-month-old infants.]

Zulauf, M. (1993) Three-year experiment in extended music teaching in Switzerland. *Bulletin of the Council for Research in Music Education*, 119, 111–21. [Evidence for beneficial effects on children's social skills after a programme of extended music teaching.]

10

Moral and Social Development

- What is moral behaviour?
- The voice of conscience
- Do we learn our moral values?
- The importance of reasoning
- Caring or justice?
- Are there gender differences?
- Are there cultural differences?

> Everything's got a moral if you can only find it.
> Lewis Carroll (1832–1898), *Alice's Adventures in Wonderland.*

We have all seen headlines in our newspapers about children who have behaved with either deliberate cruelty or great bravery and kindness. Some articles describe those who have helped others, while risking harm to themselves, and other reports concern children who have robbed or injured weak and vulnerable people. Headlines like this make many of us wonder what leads some people to act in ways that earn widespread admiration, while the actions of others can attract such disapproval. Psychologists have been interested for a long time in why some individuals become responsible members of society but others do not.

What is moral behaviour?

Morality concerns our ideas about right and· wrong. Moral decisions are everywhere, as Lewis Carroll said, and none of us can avoid them in our lives. There have been various opinions about the nature of morality (see box 10.1), and people will have various opinions about precisely what is right and what is wrong. The accepted ideas of different cultures may also vary, and even within one culture views of morality may change over time (for example, in the past slavery was not considered immoral in several countries). We all live in communities, and the only way we can exist relatively peacefully together is if we share certain ideas of what is right and what is wrong.

Box 10.1   Ideas about Morality

What is moral is what you feel good after, and what is immoral is what you feel bad after.

Ernest Hemingway (1899–1961), *Death in the Afternoon*

Half, at least, of all morality is negative and consists in keeping out of mischief.

Aldous Huxley (1894–1963), *The Doors of Perception*

Morality is the custom of one's country and the current feeling of one's peers. Cannibalism is moral in a cannibal country.

Samuel Butler (1835–1902), *The Notebooks of Samuel Butler*

So how can we define moral behaviour? A reasonable answer seems to be that moral behaviour is concerned with the distinction between right and wrong taking into consideration the current feeling of the society in which one lives.

Why study moral behaviour?

Psychologists who study the development of moral behaviour are not judging the particular moral values of a person or a society; they are interested in *how* people acquire moral values and standards and what contributes to this process. Why do psychologists study moral development? One reason is that increasing our understanding of the development of moral behaviour may help us to improve our child rearing methods. We may also learn about the limits of moral responsibility, so that we know whether children are capable of understanding the difference between right and wrong. It is more than useless to blame a child for doing something wrong when he or she is too young to understand that it is wrong. A crawling baby who crumples up her older sister's homework will be unaware of the damage she is doing. Issues of moral development take on a crucial importance when children who have committed criminal actions have to be dealt with by the legal system (as in recent well-publicized cases in the USA and the UK).

The Voice of Conscience

Moral rules and moral values

Some psychologists distinguish between moral rules and social values (or conventions). Moral rules can be thought of as being designed to protect people, so the forbidding of theft and murder are moral rules. Social conventions, in contrast, are

standards of behaviour that are fairly arbitrary and are agreed to by cultural groups to ease interactions. So social conventions dictate that we use cutlery to eat our dinner while seated at a dining table, and that we thank people if they have given us a present. Recent research has considered the age when children begin to make this distinction between moral rules and social conventions. In 1990 Judith Smetana and Judith Braeges asked children to decide whether hurting people or taking their belongings were more serious misbehaviours than eating ice cream with their fingers or not listening to a story. By the age of 3 years most children in the study could distinguish the two types of rule.

Self-control

One of the first steps towards moral behaviour is the development of self-control: a child has to learn not to constantly do whatever is tempting at the moment. There is evidence that a child as young as 3 years can make plans to regulate his or her behaviour, and self-control will improve during school years. As children grow older parents are not always present to help them decide what to do. Gradually the voices of parents, teachers and other respected people are absorbed within a child, who can then listen to his or her own guiding voice (the conscience), or choose to ignore it. When a child has internalized rules and values in this way, and goes on to ignore the voice and give way to temptation then guilty feelings are likely to follow. By this stage a child will usually have the self-restraint to avoid wrongdoing,

Exercise 10.1

Children's Behaviour at Home

Try the following questionnaire. Maybe you could ask your friends to try it and then compare your answers. Do you find a difference between the reactions of males and females? If you have friends of different nationalities, or religions, do their answers vary?

1   Are there certain behaviours (e.g. not being rude to others, being kind to animals, being tidy, working hard at school, having good table manners, respecting older people etc.) that you believe your child should concentrate on?
2   What are they?
3   What do you think are the three most important behaviours?
4   Are these three important to other adults in your family when they are looking after the child?
5   What do you do when the child shows one of the behaviours you disapprove of?
6   Do you expect all children in the family to show these behaviours? If not, why not?

even if no one would discover the bad behaviour. An adult's presence is no longer necessary for a child to behave according to the rules.

Moral development is affected by three influences, first our feelings about a behaviour, secondly our behaviour, and thirdly whether we think something is good or bad. Each of these aspects of moral development has been focused on by various psychologists, working in different fields of psychology, but we need to bear in mind that the three aspects are likely to interact. Our thoughts about a particular behaviour will influence our feelings about it, and both will affect our actions. In addition, our behaviour will affect our thoughts and feelings, while our feelings will affect our thoughts and actions. Much recent work concerns the role of moral emotions in moral behaviour, and evidence has been found to show that embarrassment, guilt and shame are all related to moral conduct. A review of the literature by Nancy Eisenberg, in 2000, concluded that emotion and its regulation are important in moral development.

We all know that people have consciences of different strengths (or 'loudness' as 13-year-old Christopher described it), and that from very early on some children will obey their caregivers more easily and reliably than others. Recent research indicates that children have different levels of self-control, but individuals are fairly consistent across tasks and over time. However, many children who had little resistance to temptation at preschool age later became adolescents with good self-control. Parents and other caregivers will also communicate guidance to their children with varying effectiveness. Correlational studies have demonstrated a link between parental behaviour and children's self-control. In 1990 Shirley Feldman and Kathryn Wentzel found evidence that self-control was lower in children who had very strict parents, while greater self-control was found in children whose parents encouraged them to be independent and make their own decisions. It appears that by giving children more chances to regulate their own behaviour and to see the effects of their own decisions parents can nurture self-control.

A 'learning theory' viewpoint

Learning theorists suggest that a child learns moral judgment just as he or she learns other things. Classical conditioning and instrumental conditioning are thought to be important influences in teaching a developing child to resist temptation. Behaviours, such as confession, self-criticism and apology, that indicate guilt are thought to be learned responses that reduce anxiety when rules have been disobeyed. Other psychologists observe that this theory overlooks the person (e.g. parent or teacher) who is dispensing punishment and reward, which is not just an impersonal result of a child's actions. A child's relationship to the person who is handing out punishment is vital when we consider moral development. A child who wishes to please and follow his or her mother, father or teacher will take more notice of his or her advice than the advice of someone for whom there is no affection or respect.

Identification and imitation

Some theorists have suggested that imitation and identification are both important in the development of moral awareness. In the psychoanalytical tradition the child 'incorporates' parental values in an 'ego ideal', which forms the basis of his or her moral standards. In the early part of the twentieth century it was suggested by Sigmund Freud that this happens when the Oedipus complex is resolved, at approximately 5 years of age (see recommended reading and chapter 11 for further details).

A social learning perspective: the role of modelling

Social learning theorists, such as Albert Bandura, reason that moral and other behaviours are acquired through learning (which can involve classical and operant conditioning), but modelling also has a very important influence. Children (and adults) observe the behaviour of people around them and witness the consequences of those actions. In this way we are all continually observing models of behaviour and their subsequent results. Someone who is seen being punished for bad behaviour is unlikely to be imitated. However, we are likely to imitate people we consider similar to ourselves, and this imitation is of great importance in the moral development of a child. This, together with our tendency to imitate those who are thought to be warm, supportive or powerful is crucial when we consider the actions of parents, teachers and other influential people surrounding the child. Strong bonds of affection and respect between parents and children are of particular importance, as a child's identification with his or her parents will put both child and parents on the same side. This will make it more likely that the child will adopt the parents' point of view and value system and use this to judge his or her own actions.

Conformity and non-conformity

In ideal circumstances parents will encourage their child to act with a sensible level of conformity, acquiring 'prosocial', not antisocial, patterns of behaviour. This will help the child to become socially accepted, and avoid the dangers of too much or too little conformity. If a child persistently refuses to conform to the standards of the group, he or she is likely to become a social outcast, while constant slavish conformity will prevent independence of mind. A socially excluded child will lose both the learning experiences and the feelings of friendship which result from belonging to groups. Achieving this balance between conformity and non-conformity is not easy for a child, or an adult. Solomon Asch and other psychologists have shown that adults, under fairly minor levels of social pressure, will often conform and give answers that, although obviously incorrect, agree with their group's. Asch's subjects reported considerable anxiety when people tried to resist social pressures, and children also experience these feelings.

A variety of models

Many real models for imitation surround children, and other powerful models are provided by the various forms of media, TV, films, magazines etc. A growing child is exposed to numerous models in an increasing variety of circumstances, and as this happens his or her understanding of moral issues becomes more complex, and many more responses, together with their likely consequences, are learned. Normally children grow to internalize the standards that have surrounded them and to accept particular ways of behaving as correct. When children act according to the moral values of those close to them this leads to rewarding feelings.

The actions of people close to a child are as important, maybe more so, than what they are saying. A child who is physically punished by an adult after some aggressive behaviour will be observing an aggressive model to be imitated later. Parents who tell their child not to smoke, while smoking themselves, increase the likelihood that the child will become a smoker later. A famous television personality and author of cookery books has spoken on radio of her father's excessive drinking.

Despite strongly disliking and disapproving of his behaviour she described a feeling of 'coming home' when she began to drink excessively herself.

Inconsistent behaviour

Moral choices in life are rarely simple; usually they are very complex. So a child's models (parents, teachers, peers) are unlikely to be consistently good or consistently bad. In the real world poor behaviour can often lead to benefits, while good behaviour can frequently go unnoticed and unrewarded. As a result a child's behaviour will also be inconsistent and will depend upon a combination of past experiences, the child's thoughts about what will result from acting in a particular way and internalized standards. Social learning theory explains why we all behave well sometimes and badly at other times, as our extremely varied learning experiences underlie the individual character of each person's moral standards.

Parents offer guidance to their children for many years. It seems likely that during this period the praise and punishment that a child receives for various behaviours will have at least some influence. Social learning theory accounts for this and also explains why we have so many moral codes varying both between individuals and between different cultures. Support for the effect of models on our behaviour has come from research which indicates that children can develop an understanding of moral ideas (e.g. sharing and cooperating) from watching television programmes that encourage these concepts (e.g. *Sesame Street*).

Unfortunately the great variation in people's learning histories makes social learning theory very difficult to test. Two people who appear to have very similar backgrounds can often behave surprisingly differently, and this makes it hard to demonstrate exactly how a child's upbringing contributes to her or his later moral development. This theory takes little account of the effects on moral development of changes that are purely maturational in nature. Social learning theory is also discussed in relation to gender identity development in chapter 11.

Reasoning and Moral Development

It seems likely that biological factors, such as the development of the brain and changes in cognition (thinking), which take place as children mature can be expected to influence their attitudes to moral issues. Patterns in moral development which are related to age have been identified by two very influential researchers, Jean Piaget and Lawrence Kohlberg. Their cognitive approaches to the development of morality are primarily concerned with how people think about moral issues and how they come to decide when behaviour is morally wrong. Both Piaget's and Kohlberg's theories of moral development have the basic idea, that there is a direct relationship between moral reasoning and moral action. The maturing moral awareness of a growing child leads to judgements of right and wrong and an obligation to behave appropriately.

Jean Piaget

If you watch a group of 6-year-olds playing a game you may be surprised at how strictly they keep the rules, as they understand them. This inflexibility is typical of Jean Piaget's first stage of moral development. In 1932 he proposed one of the first theories of moral development. Much of his work on both moral and cognitive development was based on a technique of clinical interview. He discussed games and stories with children, gaining an important insight into their understanding of rules, wrongdoing, justice and punishment.

The game of marbles played an important role in forming Piaget's theory of moral development; because no written rules exist, any group of children can create their own version. This in many ways echoes real life, as moral behaviour is often rule-governed, but some choice is possible and groups of people choose different conventions of behaviour. Consequently Piaget investigated children's understanding of the rules of marbles, where they came from and whether they could be changed.

Considering intentions

Piaget also used a technique of telling children pairs of stories followed by questions about them. He used the children's answers to explore their understanding of rules and people's intentions when they broke rules. A pair of stories would describe a similar misbehaviour, but each with different causes and intentions behind the actions. One story involved a boy accidentally breaking 15 cups and saucers when he opened the kitchen door, while the accompanying story told of another boy who broke one cup and saucer when taking some jam from a cupboard (without permission and while his mother was out). Piaget would ask the children if one boy had been naughtier than the other. He found that young children thought the boy breaking most cups was the naughtiest, but older children thought it was the one trying to take the jam without permission. After extensive work Piaget proposed several stages in the development of morality.

Piaget's stages of moral development

Table 10.1 describes Piaget's stages of moral development. He suggested a progression of three levels, from preschool children (stage 1, with no understanding of rules) to children of approximately 11 years (who understand rules and use new abstract reasoning abilities to judge actions by intentions).

Around 4–5 years (stage 2), Piaget suggested that a child begins to understand rules but believes that something bad happens to you because you deserve it. Piaget proposed that at approximately 11–12 years a child begins a new stage of moral development, and that advanced cognitive reasoning allows the understanding of the reasons behind rules. A child's interactions with friends give her or him the experience to understand the need for rules and how they are created. Children in this third stage know that rules are made by agreement and can be changed by

Table 10.1   *A summary of Piaget's stages of moral development*

Age	Stage	Description
Below 4–5 years	Premoral judgement	Rules are not understood, so judgements cannot be made about the people who break them.
4–5 to 9–10 years	Moral realism (heteronomous morality of constraint)	Rules are thought to come from an external higher authority (e.g. parents, teachers), and they cannot be altered. Actions are judged by their outcomes (amount of damage or punishment). Punishment is seen as inevitable retribution.
From about 10 years	Moral subjectivism (autonomous morality of cooperation)	It is understood that people create rules and that consequently the rules can be altered by agreement. Actions are judged by their intentions. Punishment is not inevitable but serves a purpose and should fit the crime.

Based on Piaget, 1932.

agreement (the children in the photograph know they can use any form of rules they choose for their game, and that half-way through, if everyone agrees, they can change to a different rule).

12-years-old and beyond

Piaget argued that by approximately 12 years of age a child can reason in an adult way, using abstract concepts, so in his view such a child was capable of adult moral reasoning. This was not explored further though, and he did not investigate whether

12-year-olds reasoned differently from 25-year-old adults, or 18-year-olds differently from 40- or 50-year-olds. This has an important bearing on cases of criminal behaviour involving children of about 12 years. Recent tragic cases in which children have killed others have required a careful consideration of the stage of moral development of the accused children.

Criticisms of Piaget

There have been many criticisms of Piaget's work. It relied heavily on clinical interviews involving a small number of children, sometimes his own, and many of the children's replies could be interpreted differently. We now have evidence that even children of 2 years do not consider all rules in the same way, so that breaking a moral rule (e.g. hitting or robbing someone) is thought more serious than breaking a social rule (e.g. not saying please or thank you). Piaget's stories do not always make intentions clear, and other researchers (e.g. Sharon Nelson) have found that even 3-year-old children consider the intentions behind deeds when making judgements about simple stories. Research has also shown that young children believe adults' authority to be limited, and that preschool children believe that pushing another child or damaging his or her toys is wrong even when an adult sanctions it.

Piaget's work has, however, been supported by many cross-cultural studies and continues to supply a useful framework for a substantial body of research. Several psychologists have continued with the technique of presenting stories about moral dilemmas to children and young people. However, as can be seen from examples in this chapter, they have often also continued to use moral dilemma stories, with males as the main characters.

Adolescent Moral Reasoning

Lawrence Kohlberg

Lawrence Kohlberg worked on extending Piaget's ideas that moral awareness relies on cognitive development and matures in stages. However, whereas Piaget described children's moral development until about 10 years of age, Kohlberg began by investigating moral development in adolescents and spent 20 years developing a theory of continued progression in adulthood. This theory has been an important influence on such varied fields as psychology, education and criminology.

Kohlberg devised a number of dilemmas about difficult moral issues. His most famous dilemma involves a man (Heinz) who steals an expensive drug, which he cannot afford to buy, but which might save the life of his dying wife. After telling the story to a young person Kohlberg asked whether Heinz was right to steal the drug and for what reasons. (You may like to stop and read the story about Heinz. See exercise 10.2. What do you think? Should Heinz have stolen the drug? Why?) Kohlberg made the decision difficult, as each alternative involved some undesirable consequences, and there were no 'correct' answers. Different moral dilemmas were

Exercise 10.2

A Moral Judgement Interview

Try this exercise for yourself and then on children you know well. Relate the answers to Kohlberg's stages of moral reasoning outlined in table 10.2.

A woman was near death from a kind of cancer. There was one drug that the doctors thought might save her. It was a form of radium that a chemist in the same town had recently discovered. The drug was expensive to make, but the chemist was charging ten times what the drug cost him to make – he paid £200 for the radium and charged £2,000 for a small dose of the drug.

The sick woman's husband Heinz went to everyone he knew to borrow the money, but he could only get together about £1,000, which is half what the drug cost. He told the chemist that his wife was dying and asked him to sell it cheaper or let him pay later. But the chemist said, 'No, I discovered the drug and I'm going to make money from it.' So Heinz became desperate and considered breaking into the chemist's store to steal the drug for his wife.

1   Should Heinz steal the drug? Why or why not?
2   If Heinz does not love his wife, should he steal the drug for her? Why or why not?
3   Suppose the person dying were not his wife but a stranger. Should Heinz steal the drug for the stranger? Why or why not?
4   If you could consider stealing a drug for a friend, how would you feel in the following situation? Suppose it is a pet animal he loves; should Heinz steal to save the pet? Why or why not?
5   Why should people do everything they can to save another's life?
6   It is against the law for Heinz to steal. Does that make it morally wrong? Why or why not?
7a Why should people generally do everything they can to avoid breaking the law?
7b How does this relate to Heinz's case?

Heinz did break into the store. He stole the drug and gave it to his wife. In the newspapers the next day there was an account of the robbery. Brown, a police officer who knew Heinz, read the account. He remembered seeing Heinz running away from the store and realized that it was Heinz who had stolen the drug. Brown wonders whether he should report that Heinz was the robber.

1   Should Officer Brown report Heinz for stealing? Why or why not?

2   Officer Brown finds and arrests Heinz. Heinz is brought to court, and a jury is selected. The jury's job is to find whether a person is innocent or guilty of committing a crime. The jury finds Heinz guilty. It is up to the judge to determine the sentence. Should the judge give Heinz some sentence, or should he suspend the sentence and let Heinz go free? Why?

3a Thinking in terms of society, why should people who break the law be punished?

3b How does this relate to Heinz's case?

4   Heinz was acting out of conscience when he stole the drug. What reasons are there for not punishing a lawbreaker if he or she is acting out of conscience?

5   What does the word conscience mean to you? If you were Heinz would your conscience enter into the decision?

6   Heinz has to make a moral decision. Should a moral decision be based on one's feelings or on one's thinking and reasoning about right and wrong?

7   Is Heinz's problem a moral problem? Why or why not? In general, what makes something a moral problem? What does the word morality mean to you?

8   If Heinz is going to decide what to do by thinking about what is right, there must be some answer, some right solution. Is there some correct solution to moral problems like Heinz's, or, when people disagree, is everybody's opinion equally right? Why?

9   How do you know when you have come up with a good moral decision? Is there a way of thinking or method by which one can reach a good or adequate decision?

10 Most people believe that thinking and reasoning in science can lead to a correct answer. Is the same thing true in moral decisions, or are they different?

presented to children, adolescents and adults, and from their answers Kohlberg formulated his theory of moral development.

Kohlberg's stages

Kohlberg proposed that moral development progressed through three levels, with two subdivisions at each stage (six stages altogether). Across these six stages there is a clear shift in the basis for children's moral reasoning. In the early stages external forces (for example promises of reward or threats of punishment) govern moral

Table 10.2 *A summary of Kohlberg's stages of moral judgement*

Level	Stage	Behaviour	Typical response
Preconventional	Heteronomous morality	A child acts to avoid punishment. Obedience is for its own sake, and physical damage is avoided.	Heinz should not steal, as stealing is against the law.
	Individualism, instrumental purpose and exchange	Rules are followed only to gain reward. Behaviour should be fair and agreements should be honoured.	It is fine to steal, as his wife will reward him later.
Conventional	Mutual interpersonal expectations, relationships and interpersonal conformity	Families become important, as do motives, concern for others, trust, loyalty, respect and gratitude. A child tries to please others and live up to expectations.	He should not steal, so that he is seen to be an honest man who obeys the law.
	Social system and conscience	The focus shifts from family and close groups to society, which should be contributed to. Agreed duties must be fulfilled, social rules upheld and laws obeyed, unless they conflict with other social duties.	He should steal, to do all he can to save his wife. *or* He should not steal as it is against the law that benefits all people.
Postconventional (principled)	Social contract or utility and individual rights	It is realized that people have different values and that most rules are relative, that some values (life, liberty) must be defended despite majority opinion.	He should steal, as the law against theft is not benefiting the individual in this case.
	Universal ethical principles (removed from recent versions as only a minority ever achieve them)	Individual chosen ethical principles are developed, and life is conducted according to them. Principles usually agree with laws, but if there is conflict conscience dominates.	He should steal, as life is of prime importance.

Based on Kohlberg, 1976.

reasoning. At the highest levels the basis of moral reasoning depends upon a personal, internal moral code, which does not depend on other people's expectations but instead involves abstract ideas of justice and rights with a much more social orientation. You can see this gradual shift in reasoning in Kohlberg's three levels, described in table 10.2.

Reasoning and moral behaviour

As our thinking becomes more complex we apply this complexity to moral issues, so stage 1 reflects the egocentric thinking of children, and level 3 depends on an ability to reason abstractly (Piaget's formal operational thinking). Kohlberg argued that when we can reason about morality in more advanced ways, we can also understand the lower stages of reasoning without agreeing with them. Association with others whose moral reasoning is a stage higher than ours will also help us understand the problems with our present stage of reasoning, and encourage us to reach the next stage. Kohlberg argued that children's behaviour is motivated by an inborn need to master their environment, and that adult approval for their actions should be seen as recognition of a suitable level of competence. A child seeks the reward of adult approval to confirm that a task has been performed well, but the task is not performed well with the prime purpose of gaining praise. This is in contrast to learning theory, which considers that a child performs a task with the express intention of gaining reward and approval.

Both Kohlberg and Piaget considered that all children develop moral reasoning in the same way, moving through the stages in the same order but that the *order* was more important than the age at which each stage appears. Research has indicated that Kohlberg's level 1 reasoning is normally found up to approximately 11 years, level 2 from approximately 12 to 15 years, while level 3 may develop later. The majority of adults are expected to be in stages 3 and 4 (level 2). Only about 10 per cent of adults are thought ever to achieve level 3 reasoning, and very few are expected to reach the final stage (6). However, Kohlberg's predictions of a simple correlation between moral reasoning and delinquency have not been confirmed by research. Any existing association appears to be complex and affected by many variables of circumstances and personality.

Criticisms of Kohlberg

Some criticisms of Kohlberg's work have involved the construction and interpretation of the moral dilemmas which are artificial and concern situations (e.g. caring for a dying wife) unfamiliar to children. Subjective interpretations are also made about children's responses to the stories, and different researchers do not always rate the responses identically. Some psychologists object to the idea of stages in moral development that cannot account for the changeable aspects of everyone's moral behaviour.

Other criticisms concentrate on Kohlberg's dependence on what people say, not their actions. People who behave differently can still be at the same level of development according to how they justify their behaviour (as in stage 4: see table 10.2). One difficulty with this is that a person could be morally advanced but not articulate enough to justify a judgement. Another problem is that someone's actions could be interpreted as a better guide to moral development than any verbal justifications (actions speak louder than words). Moral reasoning may determine what we say we shall do, but we do not always do it when we are actually faced with a moral dilemma, especially when strong social pressures are involved.

Cultural influences

Many critics object to the idea that Kohlberg's stages apply to all, and Carol Gilligan's concerns about bias towards male moral development will be discussed later. Several critics have commented that Kohlberg's concentration on individual rights and justice reflects only Western, Judaeo-Christian culture. Not all cultures share this emphasis, and moral reasoning may be based on different values in various cultures. Cultural differences can be found in moral behaviour, and respect for the family and elders is more important in some cultures than in others. Kohlberg scores respect for the family at a low level of moral development, but in some cultures it would be seen as the highest level. Few, if any, individuals in cultures that emphasize the importance of collective responsibility reach stage 5 or 6.

The main component of morality in African and Asian cultures is interdependence and community, so duties, not rights, are of primary importance. Taoist tradition views individualism and competition as a manifestation of evil which must be opposed; the ego must be eliminated as a person develops an awareness of her or his dependence on others. Studies which compare African, Indian, Chinese and Japanese mothers with American mothers have indicated that African and Asian mothers prepare their children for a cultural environment in which psychological interdependence plays an important role in social interactions. In Israel too, kibbutz communities were specifically organized on the principles of sharing, and research using Kohlberg's moral judgement interview in these communities has found that subjects refused to accept that the chemist has the right to decide who gets the drug. The Hindu religion also emphasizes duty and responsibility to others, not individual rights and justice. Children brought up with traditional Hindu beliefs would emphasize caring for others in their moral reasoning more than children brought up in the Western tradition.

Caring or Justice-based Solutions?

Joan Miller, David Bersoff and cultural differences

In 1992 two psychologists, Joan Miller and David Bersoff, examined cultural differences in moral reasoning by using dilemmas with care-based and justice-based solutions. One story concerned a young man who had his wallet stolen while taking the rings to his best friend's wedding in San Francisco. It was vital that he was punctual, but no one would lend him the money for a train ticket. Suddenly he noticed an unattended coat together with a ticket to San Francisco (and money for a replacement ticket). What should he do? One solution (not stealing) stressed individual rights and justice above caring for friends, while the other (stealing to get the rings to the wedding in time) stressed caring for others. A small majority of children and adults in the USA chose the justice-based response, whereas Hindu children and adults living in India overwhelmingly chose the care-based solution. (You could try exercise 10.3. Should the young man steal or ruin his best friend's wedding? Why?)

Exercise 10.3

Joan Miller and David Bersoff's 'Justice' or 'Caring' Response Dilemma

This is an example of a conflict situation dilemma, which Joan Miller and David Bersoff presented to various cultural groups when comparing 'justice' and 'caring' responses. The fulfilment of one behavioural expectation entails the violation of another. Carol Gilligan draws a similar contrast when distinguishing between a justice response in which a subject 'worries about other people interfering with each other's rights' and a caring response in which a subject 'worries about the possibility of omission, of not helping others when you could help them' (Gilligan, 1982, 21).

Try it out yourself. After reading the dilemma, which of the two alternative actions do you think Ben should take? Why do you feel he should take the suggested action?

Now, ask for the opinions of any obliging children, adolescents or adults that you know well. Do you find a difference between the responses of males and females? If you have friends of different nationalities, or religions, do they have differing responses?

Ben was in Los Angeles on business. When his meetings were over, he went to the train station. Ben planned to travel to San Francisco in order to attend the wedding of his best friend. He needed to catch the very next train if he was to be on time for the ceremony, as he had to deliver the wedding rings.

However, Ben's wallet was stolen in the train station. He lost all of his money as well as his ticket to San Francisco. Ben approached several officials as well as passengers at the train station and asked them to loan him money to buy a new ticket. But, because he was a stranger, no one was willing to lend him the money he needed.

While Ben was sitting on a bench trying to decide what to do next, a well-dressed man sitting next to him walked away for a minute. Looking over at where the man had been sitting, Ben noticed that the man had left his coat unattended. Sticking out of the man's coat pocket was a train ticket to San Francisco. Ben knew that he could take the ticket and use it to travel to San Francisco on the next train. He also saw that the man had more than enough money in his coat pocket to buy another train ticket.

In the case of the conflict described above, ask subjects to select which of the following two alternatives Ben should undertake:

1   BEN SHOULD NOT TAKE THE TICKET FROM THE MAN'S COAT POCKET – even though it means not getting to San Francisco in time to deliver the wedding rings to his best friend;
2   BEN SHOULD GO TO SAN FRANCISCO TO DELIVER THE WEDDING RINGS TO HIS BEST FRIEND – even though it means taking the train ticket from the other man's coat pocket.

In this example, the first alternative is scored as the justice choice, and the second alternative is scored as the interpersonal choice.

Moral reasoning does seem to reflect the emphasis of the culture in which we are reared. American children are reared in a culture that emphasizes individual rights and justice, while Indian children are brought up in a culture that places a priority on caring for friends and family. Kohlberg's stages in moral reasoning do not seem to be universal, as he suggested; instead, moral reasoning appears to reflect cultural values. Individuals' will reason about what is right and what is wrong, but the moral rules may vary in different societies. However, the means of transmitting these rules is likely to be similar. Arthur Mones and Erinn Haswell, reviewing stage theories of moral development in 1998, concluded that the family (not necessarily an American Western view of the family) is the crucial factor directly and indirectly translating cultural values to children.

Nancy Eisenberg and prosocial behaviour

Nancy Eisenberg has suggested that in real life children's moral dilemmas do not involve law-breaking or disobeying authority; they are usually choices between self-interest and helping others. Eisenberg and her colleagues used stories that allowed children to choose between helping another person and self-interest. One story

asked if a child should go to get the parents of an injured child or abandon her to avoid being late for a birthday party tea. Eisenberg classified various levels of prosocial behaviour according to how children and adolescents justified their choices.

A progression was found for prosocial behaviour, from children at the first level acting from self-interest to those at the final level making decisions with regard to the rights and dignity of others. Eisenberg and her colleagues conducted longitudinal studies in many countries and found that children move through the different stages in sequence. In 1996, Paul Miller and his colleagues demonstrated that children who have attained the higher stages are more likely to help others in real situations than those who are at lower levels.

Eisenberg's and Kohlberg's theories both emphasize a developmental shift from self-centred thinking to social standards and moral principles. However, Eisenberg stresses the importance of caring for others in normal moral reasoning. This allows

Exercise 10.4

An Example of a Story Designed to Tap Prosocial Moral Reasoning
(from Eisenberg-Berg, 1979)

Try it for yourself and then on children you know well. How do children of different ages vary in their answers?

A poor farming village named Circleville had a harvest that was just enough to feed the villagers with no extra food left over. Just at that time a nearby town named Larksdale was flooded and all this town's food was ruined, so that they had nothing to eat. People in the flooded town of Larksdale asked the poor farmers of Circleville to give them some food. If the farmers did give the food to the people of Larksdale, they would go hungry after working so hard all summer for their crops. It would take too long to bring in food from other villages further away, because the roads were bad and they had no airplanes. What should the poor farming village do? Why? What kind of things do you feel are important in making this decision?

a wider view, with, as Kohlberg argued, moral reasoning becoming more sophisticated as children develop, but, unlike in Kohlberg's theory, justice and rights do not always underlie the reasoning. Sometimes concern for others underpins moral reasoning.

Carol Gilligan and gender differences

Carol Gilligan (one of Kohlberg's research assistants) and her colleagues also considered caring for others to be important in normal moral reasoning. In 1982 she suggested that Kohlberg's theory is biased towards a male view of the world. Kohlberg's research indicated that the higher stages of moral development tend to be achieved more by males than by females. Gilligan argued that women's reasoning of moral issues is often underpinned by concern for others, and that Kohlberg's emphasis on justice is more relevant for men than for women. While interviewing women about the difficult decisions concerning abortions, Gilligan found they constantly spoke of a duty to care and an obligation to reduce distress and showed a great concern about relationships. They were much more concerned about people and feelings than the principles proposed in Kohlberg's model.

Like Kohlberg, Gilligan proposed a developmental progression, but one with individuals acquiring a better understanding of caring and responsibility. At first

Box 10.2   A 25-year-old man (in Kolhberg's study) responding to the question: 'What does the word morality mean to you?'

Nobody in the world knows the answer. I think it is recognizing the right of the individual, the rights of other individuals, not interfering with those rights. Act as fairly you would have them treat you. I think it is basically to preserve the human being's right to existence. I think that is the most important thing. Secondly, the human being's right to do as he pleases, again without interfering with somebody else's rights.

A response from a 25-year-old woman to the question: 'Is there really some correct solution to moral problems, or is everybody's opinion equally right?'

No, I don't think everybody's opinion is equally right. I think that in some situations there may be opinions that are equally valid and one could conscientiously adopt one of several courses of action. But there are other situations in which I think there are right and wrong answers, that sort of inhere in the nature of existence, of all individuals here who need to live with each other to live. We need to depend on each other, and hopefully it is not only a physical need but a need of fulfilment in ourselves, that a person's life is enriched by co-operating with other people and striving to live in harmony with everybody else, and to that end, there are right and wrong, there are things which promote that end and that move away from it, and in that way it is possible to choose in certain cases among different courses of action that obviously promote or harm that goal.

children are concerned with their own needs and wants. In the second stage they care for others, especially those who, like infants or the elderly, cannot care for themselves. The third stage combines the two into caring in all human relationships. At what stage would you put the boy in the photograph on page 191 who is helping his younger brother to learn how to ride a bike?

Gilligan argued that both Piaget and Kohlberg paid little attention to the moral development of women (Piaget assumed 'the child' was male, and Kohlberg included no girls in his original sample). Gilligan suggests that differences in upbringing (boys being encouraged to be concerned with independence and justice, girls to think about the welfare of others) affect moral reasoning. She believes men and women have different ideas about what constitutes morality, men basing morality on abstract laws and justice and women basing it on principles of compassion and care. As a result women are at Kohlberg's conventional level, while men are at the post-conventional level. Gilligan writes 'herein lies a paradox, for the very traits that traditionally have defined the "goodness" of women, their care for and sensitivity to the needs of others, are those that mark them as deficient in moral development'

Box 10.3   Extracts from Carol Gilligan's Interviews with Women in 'In a Different Voice: Psychological Theory and Women's Development'

Jenny: Jenny speaks of a morality of selfless-ness and self-sacrificing behaviour, typified by her mother who represents the ideal. She describes herself as 'much more selfish in a lot of ways'.

If I could grow up to be like anyone in the world, it would be my mother, because I've just never met such a selfless person. She would do anything for anybody, up to a point that she has hurt herself a lot because she just gives so much to other people and asks nothing in return. So! Ideally that's what you'd like to be, a person who is selfless and giving. (page 136)

Sarah: Sarah's parents' divorce had left a legacy of issues that entwined with the themes of adolescence, raising questions of identity and morality. Having 'tried a lot of different ways of living', she tried to discover what was of value in life:

I wanted just literally to throw away all the moral values that I'd been taught and decide for myself which ones were important to me. And I figured that I'd know which ones were important if I missed it! If I pitched it out the window and said 'To hell with that', and then came up a few months later really feeling the pinch because that wasn't there in my life. Then I'd know that was important. So just throwing everything out and then just picking selectively what I wanted. And I've sort of surprised myself because I've come back around, not to the way of life that my mother would have liked me have, but a lot more like it than I thought. And it's so interesting when I look back and I think, 'Hmm, I never thought I'd turn out that way'.

Source: reprinted by permission of the publisher from *In a Different Voice: Psychological Theory and Women's Development*, Carol Gilligan, pp. 136, 140, Cambridge, Mass.: Harvard University Press, Copyright © 1982, 1993 by Carol Gilligan

(Gilligan, 1982, 18). She argues that instead of one type of reasoning being better than the other they are simply different and complement each other.

Males care too

Lawrence Walker challenged Gilligan's view in 1995, finding that differences between the sexes in moral reasoning rarely appear and are small when they do. He proposed that both sexes are capable of displaying orientations towards care and

relationships. The Ethics of Care Interview (ECI), which uses hierarchical levels of development of the care ethic, was designed to test the developmental aspects of Gilligan's theory. In 1998 Eva Skoe reviewed the studies of children, adolescents and adults that had used this measure and concluded that care-based morality is important for general human development, especially personality development.

The development of conscience

Studies of moral development suggest that all the occasions of discipline that influence social awareness and behaviour have certain things in common. Whatever technique of discipline is involved, there appear to be three components, the assertion of power, the withdrawal of approval and explanation. In different incidents these three are used in varying proportions, any one dominating at a particular time.

Probably the most dependable finding concerning components of discipline is an inverted relationship between the assertion of power (an authoritarian, harsh, domineering manner) and several measures of moral behaviour, which is found for both sexes and all ages in childhood. Severe punishment (e.g. harsh physical punishment) alienates a child from the person who is applying it. Trying to instil 'moral' behaviour in this way will ensure the child learns not to get caught next time, but does not encourage identification with the adult or internalization of disapproval of the action.

Fear of the withdrawal of parental love and approval does not appear to contribute greatly to the internalization of parental values, but some evidence exists that the threat may help to inhibit anger. Threatening 'Mummy doesn't love you when you do that' causes anxiety, which may inhibit angry responses. It may make the child more amenable to adult control, giving the impression that the threat has had the intended effect, but without necessarily affecting internal moral development. The child may learn not to give in to an impulse to hit another child who gets more sweets but lack any feeling that it is wrong to use violence when protesting.

Induction (or reasoning) has been found to be the type of discipline most favourable to moral development. The effects of a child's behaviour are pointed out, together with reasons and explanations. A child could be shown her brother's wounds after she has pushed him off his bike, together with reminders of how hurt she was when she fell off her bike. This would help a child to understand the reasons behind actions and the consequences which follow.

Moral and social training

Some factors that help the development of moral and social awareness could be of value to caregivers. They include:

- a loving relationship between parents and child;
- parents making firm moral demands of their child;
- the consistent application of rules;
- using psychological punishments (e.g. withdrawing approval) rather than physical punishments, causing apprehension instead of anger;

- using reasoning (induction), giving explanations rather than 'because I say so';
- giving appropriate responsibilities to the child;
- helping the child to consider other people's roles;
- encouraging the child to show empathy;
- increasing the child's level of moral reasoning by discussion.

This list of guidelines represents an ideal, but it is clear to most of us that we cannot always achieve the standards set out. However, we can try to work towards those standards even while recognizing our fallibility.

Recommended Reading

Bee, H. (1997) *The Developing Child*. New York: Harper & Row. [Clear account of facts and theories of child development.]

Berry, J. and Dasen, P. R. (1997) *Handbook of Cross-cultural Psychology*, vol. 2: *Basic Processes and Human Development*, 2nd edn. Boston: Allyn and Bacon [A summary of cross-cultural research on moral judgement.]

Goodnow, J. J. and Collins, W. A. (1990) *Development According to Parents: The Nature, Sources, and Consequences of Parents' Ideas*. London: Erlbaum. [A superb account of children's moral, social and other aspects of development as seen by parents.]

Grusec, J. E. and Kuczynski, L. (1997) *Parenting and Children's Internalization of Values: A Handbook of Contemporary Theory*. New York: Wiley. [A discussion of parent/child developmental interactions and the development of conscience.]

Herbert, M. (1998) *Clinical Child Psychology: Social Learning, Development and Behaviour*. Chichester: Wiley. [An account of moral and other aspects of children's behaviour and their clinical implications.]

Miller, J. and Bersoff, D. M. (1999) Development in the context of everyday family relationships: culture, interpersonal morality and adaption. In M. Killen and D. Hart (eds), *Morality in Everyday Life: Developmental Perspectives*. New York: Cambridge University Press. [Explores development of interpersonal morality and influence of context.]

References

Asch, S. E. (1956) Studies of independence and conformity: I. A minority of one against a unanimous majority. *Psychological Monographs,* 70(9), no. 416. [Classic studies of the pressures to conform.]

Bandura, A. (1977) *Social Learning Theory*. Englewood Cliffs, NJ: Prentice-Hall. [An account of social learning theory.]

Eisenberg, N. (1982) The development of reasoning regarding prosocial behavior. In N. Eisenberg (ed.), *The development of prosocial behaviour*. New York: Academic Press. [A developmental account of prosocial behaviour.]

Eisenberg, N. (2000) Emotion, regulation and moral development. *Annual Review of Psychology,* 51, 665–97. [The important role of emotions in moral development.]

Eisenberg, N., Fabes, R. A., Murphy, B., Carbon, M., Smith, M. and Maszk, P. (1996) The relationship of children's dispositional empathy-related responding to their emotionality, regulation, and social functioning. *Developmental Psychology*, 32, 195–209. [A study of empathy, emotion, regulation and social functioning in children.]

Eisenberg-Berg, N. (1979) Prosocial moral reasoning. *Developmental Psychology*, 15(2), 128–37. [An investigation of prosocial moral reasoning.]

Feldman, S. S. and Wentzel, K. R. (1990) The relationship between parental styles, sons' self restraint, and peer relations in early adolescence. *Journal of Early Adolescence*, 10, 439–54. [Parenting styles and later self-restraint and peer relations in adolescent boys.]

Freud, S. (1933) *New Introductory Lectures on Psychoanalysis*. New York: Norton. [An early account of psychoanalysis.]

Gilligan, C. (1982) *In a Different Voice: Psychological Theory and Women's Development*. Cambridge, MA: Harvard University Press. [An account of differing development of moral behaviour in men and women.]

Kohlberg, L. (1976) Moral stages and moralization. In T. Lickona (ed.), *Moral Development and Behaviour: Theory, Research and Social Issues*. New York: Holt, Rinehart and Winston. [A synoptic account of a major theory of moral development.]

Miller, J. G. (1999) Cultural psychology: implications for basic psychological theory. *Psychological Science*, 62, 1393–408. [The importance of culture in psychological explanation.]

Miller, J. G. and Bersoff, D. M. (1992) Culture and moral judgement: how are conflicts between justice and interpersonal responsibilities resolved? *Journal of Personality and Social Psychology*, 62, 541–54. [The importance of culture in moral development.]

Miller, J. and Bersoff, D. M. (1999) Development in the context of everyday family relationships: culture, interpersonal morality and adaption. In M. Killen and D. Hart (eds), *Morality in Everyday Life: Developmental Perspectives*. New York: Cambridge University Press. [Explores contextual influences on development of interpersonal morality.]

Miller, P. A., Eisenberg, N., Fabes, R. A. and Shell, R. (1996) Relations of moral reasoning and vicarious emotion to young children's prosocial behaviour towards peers and adults. *Developmental Psychology*, 32, 210–19. [Moral reasoning and emotions in children.]

Mones, A. G. and Haswell, E. L. (1998) The process of moral development within the 'family culture'. *Journal of Social Distress and the Homeless*, 7(2), 91–105. [Various theories of moral development considered in the context of the role of the family.]

Nelson, S. A. (1980) Factors influencing young children's use of motives and outcomes as moral criteria. *Child Development*, 51, 823–9. [Young children's use of motives and outcomes in moral behaviour.]

Piaget, J. (1932) *The Moral Judgement of the Child*. New York: Harcourt and Brace. [An early classic study of moral behaviour in childhood.]

Skoe, E. E. A. (1998) The ethic of care: issues in moral development. In E. E. A. Skoe and A. L. von der Lippe (eds), *Personality Development in Adolescence: A Cross National and Life Span Perspective. Adolescence and Society*. New York: Routledge. [A review of studies of children, adolescents and adults that used the Ethics of Care Interview (ECI) to test the developmental aspects of Gilligan's theory.]

Smetana, J. G. and Braeges, J. L. (1990) The development of toddlers' moral and conventional judgements. *Merrill-Palmer Quarterly*, 36, 329–46. [A study of the age when most children can distinguish between different types of rule.]

Walker, L. J., Pitts, R. C., Henning, K. H. and Matsuba, M. K. (1995) Reasoning about morality and real life moral problems. In M. Kellen and D. Hart (eds), *Morality in Everyday Life: Developmental Perspectives*. Cambridge: Cambridge University Press. [A discussion of reasoning in moral development.]

11

Gender Development and Gender Differences

- Sex and gender
- Gender differences in ability
- The development of gender identity
- Theories of gender identity development
- Gender typing in adult life
- Greater androgyny with age

All of us have ideas about the ways in which males and females differ. We may hear parents say of their child that 'He's a real boy' or 'She's so feminine.' Consider for a moment what being a real boy or being feminine means to you or within your culture. Could you list the characteristics that such a child would or would not have? For example, you may think of football as a boy's game, and ballet as a suitably feminine pastime. Do interests in these two areas tell us anything about sex differences? Before we answer this, let us digress for a moment. You will notice that this chapter is not about sex but about gender. Why do psychologists make this distinction?

Sex and gender

These terms are controversial. Sex refers to biological differences: inborn characteristics relating to sex chromosomes, sex organs and reproduction. Thus sex is a narrow term, but gender is a broad one. Gender refers to psychological characteristics and social categories created by human culture (see Margaret Matlin for a further discussion). To return to our earlier examples, an interest in football or ballet is not necessarily confined to one sex or the other, so they are not sex differences, but gender differences. The relation between sex and gender is not clear cut. Gender differences may have their origins in biological differences but the exact part, if any, played by biology is far from clear.

In this chapter we shall explore some well-known gender differences – in the field of intelligence and abilities – and we shall consider how research has influenced the extent to which we believe that observed differences are determined by biology. We shall then explore the development of gender identity – in particular focusing on the development of the sense of ourselves as females or males, and how this influences our behaviour in adult life.

Gender Differences in Ability

It has been widely accepted for centuries that men are 'the superior sex', more intelligent and more able than women in almost any sphere of life. Charles Darwin, for example, was certainly of this opinion. School education has been widely available for males for centuries, whereas education for women up to university level is a relatively recent occurrence. In general, in the world of work men have more wealth, power and prominence, while women are found in the lower echelons of many occupations; ironically, when women come to predominate in a particular sphere its status declines. Power and status have been considered inherently inappropriate for females.

However, as Stephanie Shields pointed out in 1978, research into early sex difference was tremendously biased and lacked objectivity.

Today it is generally accepted that the intelligence of the sexes as measured by intelligence tests does not differ (see chapter 8). However, Eleanor Maccoby and Carol Jacklin, reviewing the literature in 1974, concluded that the sexes do differ in visual spatial abilities, verbal abilities and mathematical abilities. Their review was the stimulus for much research designed to explain why such differences might arise, and whether biological sex differences were a significant factor in explaining them. For example Hugh Fairweather in 1976 was very cautious in his review of this topic in attributing such differences to biology.

One problem with this topic is the mass of contradictory findings. For example, in the area of gender differences in verbal ability some papers report that girls are better than boys, some report no differences, others that boys are better than girls. The use of the statistical technique called meta-analysis can help us overcome this problem. It calculates the findings for a series of studies, all investigating a single issue, in effect statistically summarizing the effect of gender across a number of studies. This technique has, in recent years, been used extensively in gender difference research.

Boys and visual spatial abilities

In general boys are thought to be more able in this area, but in what way are these skills revealed? In everyday terms they include playing electronic games, map making, doing jigsaws, arranging furniture and making up garments from two-dimensional patterns. Figure 11.1 illustrates three different types of visual spatial task. Task A is a spatial perception task: in this task participants are asked to draw a line to indicate the water level on the tilted bottle. Task B is a spatial visualization task:

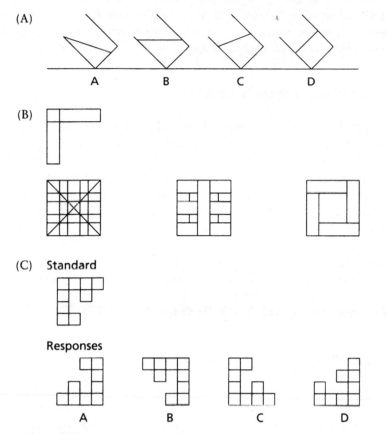

Figure 11.1   *Three different types of visual spatial task*
Tests of visual–spatial skills typically assess spatial perception (A), spatial visualization (B), or mental rotation ability (C). In task A, participants are asked to indicate which bottle has a horizontal water line. In task B, participants are asked to identify the simple geometric figure in the complex figures underneath. In task C, participants must identify one response that depicts a rotated vision of the standard. Generally males perform better than females on spatial perception and mental rotation tasks.
Source: Based on Linn and Petersen, 1985

participants are asked to identify the simple geometric figure on top in the more complex figures below. Task C is a mental rotation task: participants are asked to identify the one response that depicts a rotated version of the standard.

In 1985 Marcia Linn and Anne Petersen reported a meta-analysis of 38 studies published between 1974 and 1982. They found no gender differences in the visualization task (task B in figure 11.1), but males did outperform females on mental rotation (task C) and to a lesser extent on spatial perception tasks (task A). A much larger meta-analysis conducted by Daniel Voyer and his colleagues in 1995 found results similar to those of Linn and Petersen. So males perform much better than females on mental rotation, on spatial perception there was a large but less consistent difference, and on spatial visualization the results were highly variable, often with no differences evident. No gender differences were found below the age of 10, and the size of differences increased with age.

Verbal abilities: are girls better?

Maccoby and Jacklin reported clear evidence of gender differences in verbal abilities, emerging at about 11 years of age (although girls also acquired early vocabulary more quickly than boys, up to about 2 years of age). But more recent studies suggest that the difference is very small. For example, Janet Hyde and Marcia Linn, in a meta-analysis of 165 studies, found differences favouring girls in most aspects of verbal ability, but the difference was substantial only in speech production. They also found that the slight superiority of girls was evident at all ages, not just after the age of 11.

However, large gender differences are found in the incidence of language *disabilities*. Mild developmental dyslexia is five times more likely to occur in boys than in girls, and severe developmental dyslexia is ten times more likely in boys. There are also four times as many male stutterers as female stutterers.

Are boys better at mathematics?

According to Maccoby and Jacklin boys excel in mathematical ability, and gender differences first emerge about the age of 12–13. Janet Hyde and her colleagues in their meta-analysis (1990) of over 100 studies of mathematical ability involving over 3 million participants found that males were slightly better than females.

They then examined three different areas of mathematical ability: computation (involving simple memorized facts), concepts (involving the comprehension of mathematical ideas) and problem solving (involving applying mathematical knowledge in novel situations, such as in story problems). Females were found to be better than males at computation and understanding mathematical concepts, but males were better than females at problem solving. Hyde and her colleagues also examined the studies for possible age trends. They found that between the ages of 5 and 14, girls were slightly better than boys at computation, but there were no differences in problem solving. Over the age of 14, males began to perform better than females in complex problem solving. The gender differences increased with selectivity, males outperforming females in populations whose participants were mathematically precocious.

What is the cause of these ability differences?

As we saw at the start of this section, differences between females and males were in the past attributed to basic biological differences. One of the most frequently cited explanations is concerned with the lateralization of brain function. The most favoured explanation is that initially proposed by Jerre Levy in 1972. The two hemispheres of the brain specialize in different functions to some extent. In most people the left hemisphere deals with language and the right hemisphere with spatial material. It is suggested that the male brain is more lateralized than the female, so task specialization is greater. However, clear evidence in support of this is far from established, nor is it clear that more lateralized brains give rise to observed gender differences in cognitive abilities. Others have suggested explanations of gender differences in spatial ability in terms of genetics, for example Richard Stafford, or of male hormone effects, such as Anne Petersen, but these explanations too have lacked supporting evidence.

We know that a variety of social factors can influence the performance of males and females. Relevant experience may differ between the sexes. Michael Lewis showed that mothers comfort girls using language more than they do boys, and other research suggests that boys are permitted greater freedom in play than girls, which may benefit the development of visual spatial skills. In schools, boys and girls may have different levels of opportunities available to them in tasks relevant to these particular abilities. Of particular concern has been the use of computers by boys – we discuss this in box 11.1.

In addition to different exposures to or opportunities within particular areas, we also know that people's expectations about gender differences influence children and adults' perception of their capabilities (this was discussed in chapter 8). For example, boys see themselves as more competent in maths than girls do, even though they may receive lower grades. Females are also less likely than males to attribute their success to their own ability (attributing it more often to outside factors such as luck); hence they may have a more negative perception of their abilities than males, which will influence their expectations about their own performances.

Box 11.1 Computers Are for Boys?

At kindergarten children consider computers more appropriate for boys than for girls. Overwhelmingly the heavy users of computers at primary school are boys. Secondary schoolboys are three times more likely to use a computer at home, participate in computer activities at school or attend a computer camp. In the United States, for example, only 5 per cent of girls at high school enrol in computer science courses, as compared with 60 per cent of boys. The proportion of female students enrolling for computing courses at secondary and higher levels has recently decreased.

What possible reasons could there be for this gender difference in the use of computers? One explanation is that teachers and parents may encourage boys to use computers because of their own stereotypical beliefs about appropriate activities for each gender. Parents may believe computer skills are linked to promising careers for their sons and therefore invest in computers and software. There is some evidence to support this explanation, a number of studies reporting that parents are more likely to buy computers for their sons than for their daughters. Another possible explanation for these gender differences is that girls may be less attracted to the aggressive and competitive themes that frequently characterize computer games and educational software. Studies have reported that over 92 per cent of arcade games contained no female characters; educational software is designed for boys, and 70 per cent of the characters in educational software used in the United States are male. This software bias is thought to be demotivating for girls and to have a detrimental effect on their performance.

Karen Littleton and her colleagues carried out a very interesting study that supports this explanation. They compared girls' and boys' performances on two pieces of software: 'The King and Crown' and 'The Honeybears'. 'The King and Crown' is a computer adventure game. The king has lost his crown and the children have to find it. To do this they have three male characters: a driver, a captain and a pilot. These characters can travel around their little world in either a car, two ships or a plane. Once the children have found the crown they have to return it to the king for a feast, while avoiding the pirates. Littleton and her colleagues found that with this task there was a substantial gender difference. Boys performed a lot better than girls. However, the picture is very different with 'The Honeybears', which presents essentially the same task as that in 'The King and Crown', but with a different setting and different characters. The honeybears would like a picnic, but have no honey. The children have to find the honey and return for a picnic, while avoiding the 'honeymonster', who will eat the honey if the children are not careful. To do this they have three honeybears: Airbear, Ponybear and Waterbear, and a pony, a balloon and two boats. Littleton and her colleagues found that there was no gender difference in performance with this software. Girls and boys performed equally well, and the boys did not perform any worse than when they were playing 'The King and Crown'.

Discussions with the children after playing with the games supported the idea that this difference in the girls' performance was caused by a difference in their engagement with the software. Some girls spontaneously talked about which bear was their favourite. More than one talked about taking particular bears on their journey to get the honey, because they would not like them to be left behind. This sort of discussion was not apparent after the girls had played 'The King and Crown'.

Whereas once boys were generally thought to be the more able sex, outperforming girls, today girls' excellent school performance is the cause of popular concern. GCSE and A level results in the UK in the year 2000 showed girls outperforming boys. The change in performance suggests that the abilities of boys and girls do not differ very greatly, but that changes in the way school subjects are taught, or in attitudes towards gender differences, may markedly alter their performance. If biological differences were crucial in the explanation for such differences, then we should not expect social and cultural influences to have such a major impact.

Gender Identity Development

How do we come to know ourselves as male or female? Perhaps this question seems unnecessary; most of us probably feel that being male or female has always been part of our knowledge of ourselves, and determined by nature rather than nurture. But a moment's thought will remind us that there are people who say that they feel 'trapped in the wrong body'. These people are *transsexuals*; they appear to be wholly male or female in physical attributes but feel that their real sex in not their biological sex. The journalist and travel writer Jan Morris is an example. She started life as James Morris but, after marrying and having a family, 'changed' in middle age, with surgery and hormone treatment, into a woman. How could this happen if our nature – biology – determines our gender identity? See box 11.2 for a case of a boy whose sex was reassigned in infancy.

Psychologists have used several theories or approaches in their attempts to explain the development of gender identity. They are:

- the biological approach
- psychoanalytic theory
- cognitive developmental theory
- social learning theory
- gender schema theory.

We shall now consider these.

The biological approach

When researching the biological approach to gender identity development we have a fundamental problem, which is discussed in the methods section of this book. How can we carry out experiments to show the role of biology in shaping gender identity? We cannot use sex as an independent variable in an experiment, because people are either male or female – we cannot assign sex to them. To compare the experiences of males and females we can only undertake correlational studies (discussed in chapter 16), which, of course, cannot tell us about causal effects.

Box 11.2   Can a Boy be Made Into a Girl?

This may sound like a ridiculous question, but consider the following true case.

In 1972 John Money reported a case of identical boy twins one of whom had, as a result of an accident during circumcision, suffered severe burning to his penis, which damaged it so badly that reconstruction was not possible (at that time). After agonizing over his state the parents, on the advice of Money, decided to allow their child to have surgery to reassign his sex to female and to alter his genitals as far as was possible. His testes were removed, and his genitals were altered so that they resembled a female's. The surgery was carried out when the boy was aged 22 months, and subsequently he was reared as a girl. Money's advice was based on the view that babies are psychosexually neutral and that gender identity is learned.

In his book *Man and Woman, Boy and Girl* (1972) Money reported on the success of the reassignment, and as a result of this similar reassignments were carried out elsewhere. However, the twins' case has an unsettling ending. In 1999 reports appeared in the press about the twin who had received the reassignment surgery. Apparently 'she' behaved very much like her brother and resisted attempts to feminize her. During puberty she was given female hormones, but she refused to wear dresses and gave up attempting to urinate in the seated position. At 15 years of age 'she' was told the truth about the reassignment, immediately decided to undergo a sex change and by 16 had had surgery to amend this problem. Eventually he married and is father to three stepchildren.

Clearly Money's view that reassignment could be successfully achieved is undermined by this later evidence. Indeed, it is claimed that much of the truth was overlooked in the earlier reports. Nevertheless, what does it tell us about gender identity development? Does it show that biology cannot be overruled? It is hard to say. The 'girl' twin was reared as a boy for nearly two years before reassignment. This early experience must also be considered in the debate. But this case is unlike all those described elsewhere in this chapter, because the boy in question was a normal male exposed to inappropriate rearing.

(See Colapinto, 1997, for more information on this case.)

How can we resolve this difficulty? There is no ideal solution, but one approach that has been used to grapple with this problem is to compare 'normal' males and females with those who are known to have some anomaly of chromosomes or hormones to see if these influence the development of gender identity.

Some studies of this kind suggest that rearing and social learning are more important than chromosomal and hormonal factors in determining gender identity. For example, girls with Turner's syndrome have only one X-chromosome instead of two. They experience abnormally low levels of female hormones early in life, do not develop secondary sexual characteristics and are infertile; but because they look like females at birth and are reared as girls they develop a normal feminine gender identity; indeed some studies find them more feminine than controls. So in the absence of normal chromosomes and hormones they still feel like girls.

John Hampson studied over 100 pseudohermaphrodites, people with an inconsistency between their external genitals and various internal structures (such as gonads, hormones and chromosomes). All had been reared as the sex that later medical investigation showed to be the less appropriate of the two. Yet the Hampsons reported that nearly all the sample were adjusted to their sex of rearing, and concluded that gender identity is learned.

But other studies challenge this view. In 1979 Julienne Imperato-McGinley and her colleagues studied individuals with a rare genetic disorder (5 alpha reductase deficiency) found in Santa Domingo in the Dominican Republic. These individuals are male, but owing to their disorder they may have genitals that are not properly formed. As a result some look like girls at birth and are reared as girls, some look like boys and are reared as boys. At puberty the children's hormonal activity causes a dramatic masculinization of the genitals, and those reared as girls subsequently change their behaviour and gender identity. Imperato-McGinley argues that male hormones at puberty give rise to psychological changes which cause this late shift in gender identity.

This study, in contrast to that of the Hampsons, seems to show that hormones can override the influence of rearing. However, in a society in which the boys grew up the condition was widely known, so there was some acknowledgement that certain girls may really be or become boys. This would make it easier, if not straightforward, to make the change at puberty. We should also remember that the development of gender identity in people who are chromosomally or hormonally different from the norm may not be the same as that for 'normal' boys and girls.

Finally, we shall consider transsexuals. They are biologically one sex but feel themselves to be the other. No physical cause has been established for this condition, but tentative biological theories have been put forward, and there is also some evidence to implicate early rearing in the cause. In the latter case, researchers report that children have shown definite opposite sexed styles in childhood and that parents have permitted or even encouraged cross-dressing in childhood. So early learning experiences may play a role in this condition, although this is not fully understood.

The biological evidence does not fully explain the development of gender identity, and it leads us to doubt whether biology is the sole cause of the determination of psychological sex.

Psychoanalytic theory

Freud's theory of psychosexual development centres on the small child's feelings about his or her mother and father. Freud considered the traditional nuclear family the norm and assumed that the mother was the primary love object for her infant. However, during the phallic stage of psychosexual development, between the ages of 3 and 5 years, children focus on their genitals as a source of pleasure. For a boy, the penis becomes the source of interest and he develops a desire to replace his father in his mother's affections. This gives rise to intense feelings of rivalry with the father and a fear that the father will castrate him for his illicit feelings. The resolution of the *Oedipus complex*, as this is called, occurs through his identification with the father (incorporationg many features of the father's personality into his own) and thus establishing his male gender identity.

For girls the situation is less clear cut, and Freud himself admitted this. Girls observe that boys have penises and that they do not; so, Freud argued, they feel castrated (Freud considered the male body the norm and the female body a deviation from it), hold their mothers responsible for their lack of a penis and so turn away from their mothers and towards their fathers – this is called the *Electra complex*. Ultimately Freud believed that girls turn their backs on their mothers, but this may not occur until they becomes mothers themselves.

Freud's theory may be seen to have its roots in biology, because its starting point is the genital differences between the sexes. Although Freud's views have been highly influential in the past, from the standpoint of psychology they are not considered to be especially useful because they cannot be demonstrated empirically.

Cognitive developmental theory

Lawrence Kohlberg took a rather different approach. He was unhappy with Freud's theory but impressed with the work of the Hampsons referred to above. He took an interactionist approach, believing that both biology and the environment have roles in shaping gender identity. Kohlberg was also influenced by Piaget's stages in cognitive development (outlined in chapter 7).

Kohlberg's theory considered the child's thinking about gender differences. Initially children's views on the differences centre on superficial differences. A change in these superficial features (e.g. dress) can, children believe, enable a girl to become a boy, and vice versa.

Kohlberg suggested that once a child has achieved 'gender constancy' she or he can understand that she is female or he is male, then want to do things consistent with this category. He believed that it is natural to want to do things consistent with, or like, the self, so that it is natural for boys and girls to model themselves on the same sex parent and siblings. In addition to this, Kohlberg also said that children will want to imitate those who have prestige or power, and that, because males are seen to have more of these qualities, girls are likely to want to imitate both females and males. Kohlberg suggested that girls, unlike boys, will show complementary modelling, that is their femininity is defined in terms of their acceptance and approval by males.

Gender constancy is believed to be achieved at around the age of 6 or 7 years, at about the time when Piaget claimed that other constancies (such as conservation of quantity) are achieved. This age is later than is predicted for boys in psychoanalytic theory, and there is some evidence to support Kohlberg.

Social learning theory

According to this theory the aquisition of gender identity occurs as a result of the internalization of the characteristics of a person or role through observation, imitation and reinforcement. Advocates of this theory in the 1960s were Walter Mischel and David Lynn. Although this theory recognizes that both boys and girls are likely to identify with their mothers initially, the acquisition of appropriate behaviour by boys is reinforced, and boys model themselves on males such as their fathers. The model for girls is more likely to be available, since most children are raised primarily by females, and this theory predicts that the whole process is easier for girls. The starting point in this theory is the importance of rewards and reinforcement, and gender identity is acquired through the process illustrated for a boy as 'I want rewards, I am rewarded for doing boy things, therefore I want to be a boy.'

There is plenty of evidence to support the idea that rewards are powerful in shaping behaviour, but can observation, imitation and reinforcement be enough to create gender identity? This theory considers children to be relatively passive, unlike the children in Kohlberg's theory, and some psychologists feel that this is a weakness.

Gender schema theory

Another theory that places emphasis on the role of the child's thinking in its understanding of gender is Bem's (1981) gender schema theory. This theory is based on the idea that people naturally tend to categorize information: they develop schemas based on their experience. Schemas are cognitive structures that we use to impose structure and meaning on stimuli. A gender schema could contain any information about males or females. Anything, behaviour, attitudes, emotions, physical attributes and so on, could be part of a gender schema. As a result we can see that a female or male gender schema in different cultures might vary a lot.

The first gender schema will be concerned with the things a child associates with one or other sex, and this will only arise once the child has some idea of his or her own gender. Gender schemas are important in influencing the child's sense of himself or herself, but they do not explain fully the initial reason why children form the kinds of schema that they have. Bem devised a well-known measure to assess the extent to which a person is gender typed, the Bem Sex Role Inventory (BSRI) (see

Psychology and You, by Julia Berryman et al. 1997, chapter 3). The inventory has been used to measure how masculine, feminine, androgynous (having both masculine and feminine characteristics) or undifferentiated a person is. The BSRI was devised in the USA and thus reflected one particular view of masculinity and femininity. It is culturally specific and does not, in any sense, represent what females and males should be, or indeed make any distinction between attributes which may be primarily shaped by biological differences and those that are partially or wholly learned. Nevertheless, gender schema theory adds an important contribution to our understanding of the importance played by gender in a person's way of looking at the world.

Which theory is right?

We have seen some very different approaches to the understanding of gender identity development, and as yet we do not have any clear cut answers. Psychologists are not unanimous in their views of this topic, but most take an interactionist perspective; neither biology nor learning alone fully explains the development of gender identity – both play a role. But how they work together is not yet understood.

Gender Differences in Adult Life

In developing a sense of oneself as male or female we have seen that there are a variety of influences that shape this process. These include our reactions to our bodies and the possession of particular genitals, our observation of others who are like us (girls observing girls and women, boys observing boys and men) and our wish to be like them, the likelihood of our being reinforced for showing behaviours appropriate to our sex, and our thinking about gender and the extent to which this influences our behaviours, feelings and attitudes. Gender typing is the extent to which we organize our perceptions of ourselves and others, as male or female, masculine or feminine.

As we have seen, there are various views about the age at which gender identity becomes fixed: by adolescence our sense of ourselves as male or female crystallizes, because this is the stage at while identity issues become particularly salient. But what happens in adult life?

It is generally agreed that gender typing is strongest in the young adult years, but becomes less strong as people grow older: elderly people are thought to be less gender-typed and more androgynous than they were – or at any rate than they appeared to be – when they were younger. Why should this be?

Young adulthood: the 'parental imperative'

David Gutmann argued in the 1970s that gender typing in younger adult years is largely due to the traditional division of labour in the family and, above all, to the demands of parenting. The husband is the breadwinner, and success in that role requires that he should be active and, to some extent, aggressive, competitive, dominant; the wife is the homemaker, and the qualities needed in that role are sensitivity, the nurturance of others rather than competition with them and a readiness to accept dependence and to provide emotional support. So traditional gender typing is useful and adaptive; it helps parents to cope more smoothly with what Gutmann called the *parental imperative*, a stage of life which he described as a state of 'chronic emergency' (most parents will know what he means!).

Other theorists generally agree that gender typing is strongest in young adulthood, but many have disagreed with the claim that it is adaptive. For example, Sandra Bem argued that androgyny, rather than gender typing, is related to efficient coping and psychological well-being. Yet others have argued that it pays to be masculine, that traditional gender roles are advantageous for men but not for women, and that evidence shows that psychological well-being is positively related, for both men and women, to a high score on measures of masculinity (see the review in 1982 by Marylee Taylor and Judith Hall).

Older adulthood: greater androgyny?

As people grow older their lives are likely to change in ways that blur the distinction between breadwinner and homemaker. Children grow up and leave home, so that active parenting ceases or at any rate diminishes; paid employment comes to an end with retirement; and bereavement – or separation, or divorce – creates a single-person household in which all the necessary tasks, whether 'women's work' or 'men's work', have to be done by the same person. Under these circumstances women and men may be more free to express aspects of themselves which have been suppressed before. Women may become more independent, less sentimental, more dominant in their relationships; men may become more passive and dependent and may be more likely to express their caring impulses and their emotions. Gutmann described this change as 'the normal unisex of later life' – not a wholesale role reversal, but increased androgyny and less rigid gender typing. At this stage in life, he argued, androgyny is adaptive, both because it allows a fuller expression of those aspects of one's personality that do not conform to stereotypes and also because it helps people to carry out the life tasks which come with greater age.

Other theorists have emphasized other life events, such as retirement, as being at least as important as the end of parenting in triggering diminished gender typing. There are also arguments about whether gender typing is adaptive in earlier adulthood or whether it is better to be androgynous at all ages, not just in later life: see, for example, discussions by Jan Sinnott and Ann Taylor. It is also possible that diminished gender typing is best seen simply as one example of the flexibility and openness to complexity in ourselves and other people, which Fredda Blanchard-Fields and Yiwei Chen suggested may increase in late adulthood.

Is Gutmann's view 'old-fashioned'?

Gutmann's account of changes in gender typing rests on a narrow view of how women and men live and relate to one another. It assumes marriage, or at any rate a stable and long-term relationship between one man and one woman, with dependent children and a single, male breadwinner. In fact only a minority of families now take this form (see chapter 14). How useful is Gutmann's description for one-parent families, for the childless and the never-married, for dual-career families, for people whose relationships end early by divorce or separation, for people in subsequent relationships?

But perhaps Gutmann's views are not as out of date as they appear. Even in families in which both the parents work full-time, women usually take responsibility for housework and childcare, and do substantially more of it than their husbands or partners. Women are still at a disadvantage in traditionally male-dominated professions and are predominantly employed in work of less prestige, lower pay and less power, with an effective limitation – the so-called 'glass ceiling' – on their advancement prospects; the man's job is usually considered more important than the woman's, even if they are equivalent in prestige and salary (see, for example, the reviews of findings and trends by Margaret Huyck in 1990 and Phyllis Moen in 1996). So gender typing in modern family life is still a reality, and Gutmann's account of its course may not be completely inappropriate.

Studies of gender typing in older age

Is there firm evidence to support the claim that gender typing diminishes as adults grow older? Studies vary widely in their approaches and, sometimes, in their findings. This is not perhaps surprising, since the meaning of gender typing is not always clear. Does it refer to behaviour? Or to attitudes and beliefs about gender-appropriate behaviour? Or to the importance of 'man' or 'woman' in the way we define ourselves? Or to the possession of masculine or feminine personality traits? Different meanings may suggest different answers to our question.

Projective tests, ratings and attitude scales

Some studies have used 'projective tests' to examine people's perceptions of the roles of older and younger men and women; one famous example is the study by Bernice Neugarten and David Gutmann, which is described in exercise 11.1 and box 11.3. Some have used questionnaires, such as the BSRI, to compare the masculinity and femininity scores of younger and older adults – for example Jan Sinnott, Ravinna Helson, and Shirley Feldman and her associates. Others have carried out *longitudinal studies*, testing the same people when younger and when older, looking at attitudes to marital equality or at self-ratings on 'masculine' or 'feminine' traits; see, for example, the work of Carole Holahan and of Ravinna Helson and Paul

Exercise 11.1

The Perceptions of People: Gender and Age

Show the picture in figure 11.2 to a number of people, one by one, and ask them to make up a story about the characters in the picture. They should describe what the situation is, what each character is doing and/or saying, how each character is feeling and what the outcome will be.

(continued next page)

Figure 11.2   *Picture used by Neugarten and Gutmann for an adapted version of the Thematic Apperception Test*

Try to ask people of both sexes and of a wide range of ages (and make up your own story first, if you like).

When you have collected your stories, make a list of the descriptions given for each of the characters: the young man, the young woman, the elderly man, the elderly woman. Then read box 11.3 to see how this test was used by previous researchers, and what their findings were.

Box 11.3   Notes on Exercise 11.1

The picture shown in figure 11.2 was used in a classic study of gender-role changes in ageing carried out by Bernice Neugarten and David Gutmann in the 1950s. It formed part of an adapted version of the Thematic Apperception Test (TAT), in which participants are shown pictures and asked to describe the people portrayed and to make up a story about their situation and its likely resolution.

Neugarten and Gutmann were particularly interested in the roles which their participants assigned to the four people in this picture: the young man, the young woman, the old man and the old woman. They found that most participants saw the young man as being dominant and active in the suggested scenario, while the young woman was seen as more passive and dependent. But roles were reversed for the older couple: the old man was seen as passive and submissive, and the old woman as dominant and authoritarian (sometimes benignly, sometimes malignly). The reversal in interpretation was most marked for the older participants in the study (ages ranged from about 40 to about 70).

Do your findings match those of Neugarten and Gutmann?

In the drawing they used, the elderly man is bent and pipe-smoking, the elderly woman large and powerfully built. Might the storytellers assign different roles if the elderly woman were shown as frail, the elderly man as large and powerful? If you can find (or draw for yourself) a picture which represents people in this way, try the experiment again using it, and see if the results are different. What might this suggest about the validity and interpretation of projective tests?

Wink. Studies of these various kinds all suggest that gender typing, or a traditional gender-role orientation, does diminish as people get older, although whether men or women show the effect more strongly depends on the measure used. There have also been reports, for example from Sinnott and from Neugarten and Gutmann, that androgyny (or, perhaps, according to Sinnott, high masculinity) is positively related to good physical and mental health for both men and women; this offers further support for Gutmann's proposal that sex-role blurring is adaptive in late adulthood.

Measures of behaviour: who does the housework?

A few studies have looked at measures of behaviour, such as sharing household tasks. We have already seen that when heterosexual partners both work, in the overwhelming majority of cases the woman takes broad responsibility for the domestic arrangements and spends more time working in the home (and see also chapter 14). It has been argued that when husbands retire they share housework more, so that the division of labour in the home is less gender-typed. But not all studies have found that housework is more equally shared after retirement, and even when it is the allocation of jobs still seems organized along gender lines. Husbands frequently take over, or do the lion's share of, grocery shopping and putting out the rubbish; they are much less likely to make the beds or do the washing. They are more likely to put away clean clothes than to hang them out to dry. So observations of behaviour do not lend very powerful support to the notion of diminished gender typing in late adulthood.

Conclusion: does gender typing diminish in late adulthood?

Overall, there is evidence for some reduction in gender typing in late adulthood, principally from studies using projective tests and attitude surveys, and rather less clearly from studies using questionnaires such as the BSRI. Some of these studies also suggest that diminished gender typing is serviceable, and associated with enhanced morale and physical health in later life, whether or not it is so earlier. But the findings vary in their detail: for example, sometimes change is more marked in men (as in Sinnott's study) and sometimes in women (as in Holahan's). We have also seen that gender typing, if not the course it takes during adulthood, may vary for different birth *cohorts* (that is people born in different historical times). And do different cultures and subcultures show different patterns of gender-role development? There is evidence that they may: for example, some studies have found that young Afro-American women and Asian American students of both sexes show stronger gender typing in their attitudes than their white American counterparts, although Afro-American women were also found to be more androgynous in self-reported personal attributes (see the studies reported by Victoria Binion and by Kenneth Dion and Paul Yee).

Finally, we have to remember that we are studying changes in gender typing during a period in which social roles and expectations for both men and women have changed enormously, and that the impact of social change may be greater than any purely age-related change over the same period. Will innate predisposition and the parental imperative maintain the pattern, no matter how society changes in the future? Or will gender-role development be radically altered by demographic and cultural changes, such as women's increasing participation in the workforce, high unemployment and early retirement, and the ever-decreasing popularity of conventional marriage? Questions about gender identity and sex roles may have different answers in different generations.

Recommended Reading

Berryman, J. C. (1989) *Differences Between the Sexes: Their Relevance for Adult Educators.* Nottingham: University of Nottingham. [A useful review of this area, which discusses how teachers may, or may not, need to take account of reported gender differences in ability in their teaching.]

Caplan, P. J., Crawford, M., Shibley Hyde, J. and Richardson, J. T. E. (1997) *Gender Differences in Human Cognition.* Oxford: Oxford University Press. [A good review of the topic.]

Hyde, J. S. (1991) Meta-analysis and the psychology of gender differences. *Signs,* 16(1), 55–73. [A review of research using meta-analysis to investigate wide range of gender differences.]

Matlin, M. W. (2000) *The Psychology of Women.* London: Harcourt College Publishers. [A very readable text focusing on women.]

Nicholson, J. (1995) *Men and Women: How Different Are They?* Oxford: Oxford University Press. [A good introductory text.]

Richardson, J. T. E. (1997) *Gender Differences in Human Cognition.* Oxford: Oxford University Press. [An edited collection of papers from key researchers into gender differences in cognition.]

References

Ballweg, J. A. (1967) Resolution of conjugal role adjustment after retirement. *Journal of Marriage and the Family,* 29, 277–81. [A study of housework sharing among retired couples.]

Bem, S. L. (1981) Gender schema theory: a cognitive account of sex typing. *Psychological Review,* 88, 354–64. [Sandra Bem's gender schema theory.]

Berryman, J. C., Hargreaves, D., Howells, K. and Ockleford, E. M. (1997) *Psychology and You: An Informal Introduction.* Leicester: B.P.S. Books (see ch. 3 on 'Your sex' for discussion of Bem Sex Role Inventory.)

Binion, V. J. (1990) Psychological androgyny: a black female perspective. *Sex Roles,* 22, 487–507. [Androgyny and gender typing in African-American women.]

Biramah, K. (1993) The non-neutrality of educational computer software. *Computers and Education,* 20(4), 283–90. [A study which showed that 70 per cent of characters in educational software were males.]

Blanchard-Fields, F. and Chen, Y. (1996) Adaptive cognition and aging. *American Behavioral Scientist,* 39(3), 231–48. [A discussion of flexibility of outlook and personality in older people.]

Camp, T. (1997) The incredible shrinking pipeline. *Communications of the ACM,* 40(10), 103–11. [A paper which reports that gender difference in number of women taking computer courses is growing larger.]

Colapinto, J. (1997) *As Nature Made Him*. London: Quartet Books. [A story of male twin damaged in surgical accident and reared as girl.]

Collaer, M. L. and Hines, M. (1995) Human behavioural sex differences: a role for gonadal hormones during early development. *Psychological Bulletin*, 118, 55–107. [A useful review relevant to biological influences on gender identity.]

Davison, G. C. and Neale, M. N. (1996) *Abnormal Psychology*. New York: Wiley. [See chapter on sexual disorders.]

Dion, K. L. and Yee, P. H. (1987) Ethnicity and personality in a Canadian context. *Journal of Social Psychology*, 127(2), 175–82. [Examines gender typing in Asian-American men and women.]

Fairweather, H. (1976) Sex differences in cognition. *Cognition*, 4(3), 231–80.

Feldman, S. S., Biringen, Z. C. and Nash, S. C. (1981) Fluctuations of sex-related self-attributions as a function of stage of family life cycle. *Developmental Psychology*, 17, 24–35.

Freud, S. (1933) 'Femininity' (lecture 33), in *New Introductory Lectures on Psychoanalysis* (1973). Harmondsworth: Penguin. [Freud's views on psychosexual development.]

Gutmann, D. (1975) Parenthood: key to the comparative psychology of the life cycle? In N. Datan and L. Ginsburg (eds), *Life Span Developmental Psychology*. New York: Academic Press. [The classic statement of Gutmann's views on gender typing in young and older adulthood.]

Gutmann, D. (1987) *Reclaimed Powers: Men and Women in Later Life*. Evanston, IL.: N.U.P. [A more recent statement, and revision, of Gutmann's position.]

Hampson, J. L. (1965) Determinants of psychosexual orientation. In F. A. Beach (ed.), *Sex and Behaviour*. New York: Wiley. [Research on hermaphrodites.]

Hedges, L. V. and Nowell, A. (1995) Sex differences in mental test scores, variability and numbers of high scoring individuals. *Science*, 269, 41–5. [A study of sex differences on mental test scores collected over 32 years. Authors found that females perform better on tests of reading comprehension, perceptual speed and associative memory, while males perform better on tests of mathematics and social studies.]

Helson, R. and Wink, P. (1992) Personality change in women from the early 40s to the early 50s. *Psychology and Aging*, 7, 16–55. [A longitudinal study of gender typing in college women.]

Holahan, C. K. (1984) Marital attitudes over 40 years: a longitudinal and cohort analysis. *Journal of Gerontology*, 39, 49–57. [A study of attitudes to marriage, combining cross-sectional and longitudinal comparisons.]

Huff, C. and Cooper, J. (1987) Sex bias in educational software: the effect of designers' stereotypes on the software they design. *Journal of Applied Social Psychology*, 17(6), 519–32. [A study which shows that educational software is designed for boys.]

Huyck, M. H. (1990) Gender differences in aging. In J. E. Birren and K. W. Schaie (eds), *Handbook of the Psychology of Aging*, 3rd edn. San Diego, CA: Academic Press. [A review of findings concerning gender differences and gender typing in old age.]

Hyde, J. S. (1984) How large are gender differences in aggression? A meta-analysis. *Developmental Psychology*, 20(4), 722–36. [A meta-analysis of 143 studies which showed that there were small but reliable differences in aggression.]

Hyde, J. S., Fennema, E. and Lamon, S. J. (1990) Gender differences in mathematics performance: a meta-analysis. *Psychological Bulletin*, 107(2), 139–55. [A meta-analysis of 100 studies, which showed that females outperformed males by only a negligible amount.]

Hyde, J. S. and Linn, M. (1988) Gender differences in verbal ability: a meta-analysis. *Psychological Bulletin*, 104(1), 53–69. [A meta-analysis of 165 studies, which found slight female superiority in verbal skills.]

Imperato-McGinley, J., Peterson, R. E., Gautier, T. and Sturla, E. (1979) Androgens and the evolution of male-gender identity among male pseudohermaphrodites with 5 α-reductase deficiencies. *The New England Journal of Medicine*, 300(22), 1233–7. [Studies of 'girls' who change to boys, quotes on pages 1236 and 1234 respectively.]

Janssen Reinen, A. M. and Plomp Tj. (1997) Information technology and gender equality: a contradiction in terminus. *Computers & Education*, 28(2), 65–78. [A recent review of gender differences in attitudes across 10 countries.]

Keating, N. C. and Cole, P. (1980) What do I do with him 24 hours a day? Changes in the housewife role after retirement. *Gerontologist*, 20, 84–9. [A study of impact of men's retirement on their wives.]

Kohlberg, L. (1966) A cognitive developmental analysis of children's sex-role concepts and attitudes. In E. E. Maccoby (ed.), *The Development of Sex Differences*. London: Tavistock. [Cognitive developmental theory.]

Levy, J. (1972) Lateral specialization of the human brain: behavioral manifestations and possible evolutionary basis. In J. A. Kiger (ed.), *The Biology of Behaviour*. Corvalis, OR: Oregon University Press. [A theory concerned with greater brain lateralization in males.]

Lewis, M. (1972) State as an infant – environment interaction: an analysis of mother–infant interaction as a function of sex. *Merril-Palmer Quarterly*, 18, 95–121. [A study suggesting women comfort girls using language more than they do boys.]

Linn, M. C. and Petersen, A. C. (1985) Emergence and characterisation of gender differences in spatial ability: a meta-analysis. *Child Development*, 56, 1479–98. [A meta-analysis which showed sex differences in spatial ability and reported evidence that they emerged around 10.]

Littleton, K., Light, P. H., Joiner, R., Messer, D. and Barnes, P. (1998) Gender, task scenarios and children's computer based problem solving. *Educational Psychology*, 18(3), 327–40. [The study described in text which shows that if girls are engaged by software they can perform as well as boys.]

Lynn, D. B. (1966) The problem of learning parental and sex-role identification. In E. E. Maccoby and C. N. Jacklin (eds) (1974), *The Psychology of Sex Differences*. Stanford, CA: Stanford University Press. [The authoritative review of 1970s.]

Maccoby, E. E. and Jacklin, C. N. (1974) *The Psychology of Sex Differences*. Stanford, CA: Stanford University Press. [The seminal book on children's sex differences.]

Mischel, W. (1966) A social learning view of sex differences in behaviour. In E. E. Maccoby (ed.), *The Development of Sex Differences*. London: Tavistock. [Social learning theory.]

Moen, P. (1996) Gender, age and the life course. In R. H. Binstock and L. K. George (eds), *Handbook of Aging and the Social Sciences*, 4th edn. San Diego, CA: Academic Press. [A review of gender differences in late adulthood.]

Morris, J. (1974) *Conundrum*. New York: Harcourt Brace Jovanovich. [A transsexual's story.]

Moss, H. A. (1967) Sex, age and state as determinants of mother–infant interaction. *Merrill-Palmer Quarterly*, 13, 19–36. [Mothers' contact with infant boys and girls.]

Neugarten B. L. and Gutmann, D. (1977) In J. E. Birren and K. W. Schaie (eds), *Handbook of the Psychology of Aging*. New York: Academic Press. [The classic study, using projective tests and interview material, of perceived changes in gender roles with age.]

Petersen, A. C. (1976) Physical androgyny and cognitive functioning in adolescence. *Developmental Psychology*, 12(6), 524–33.

Shields, S. (1978) Sex and the biased scientist. *New Scientist*, 80(11321), 752–4. [Early research into sex differences and Darwin's ideas.]

Sinnott, J. D. (1982) Correlates of sex roles of older adults. *Journal of Gerontology*, 37, 587–94. [A study of masculinity and femininity, using BSRI, in older and younger adults.]

Stafford, R. E. (1961) Sex differences in spatial visualization as evidence of sex-linked inheritance. *Perceptual and Motor Skills*, 13, 428. [A genetic explanation of male superiority in spatial ability.]

Steele, C. M. (1997) A threat in the air: how stereotypes shape intellectual identity and performance. *American Psychologist*, 52, 613–29. [Boys' perceptions of their abilities.]

Taylor, A. (1986) Sex roles and aging. In D. J. Hargreaves and A. M. Colley (eds), *The Psychology of Sex Roles*. London: Harper, Row. [A discussion of theories and evidence concerning gender roles and gender typing in older adulthood.]

Taylor, M. M. and Hall, J. A. (1982) Psychological androgyny: theories, methods and conclusions. *Psychological Bulletin*, 92, 347–66.

Voyer, D., Voyer, S. and Bryden, M. P. (1995) Magnitude of sex differences in spatial abilities: a meta-analysis and consideration of critical variables. *Psychology Bulletin*, 117(2), 250–70. [A meta-analysis of gender differences in computer attitudes and behaviour.]

Whitley, B. E. (1997) Gender differences in computer-related attitudes and behaviour: a meta-analysis. *Computers in Human Behaviour*, 13(1), 1–22. [A meta-analysis of gender differences in computer attitudes and behaviour.]

12

Childhood Problems

- What is a problem?
- What is normality?
- Family therapy
- Self-image
- Conduct and emotional disorders
- Do childhood problems persist?
- The vulnerable child

> Children 'fall apart' repeatedly, and unlike Humpty Dumpty, grow together again.
> Erik Erikson, in M. J. E. Senn, *Symposium on Healthy Personality*, 1950.

What do we mean when we talk of childhood problems? What kind of actions of children should make us suspect the presence of behaviour that deserves serious concern? Can little signs point to a psychological problem needing professional advice? Before we can answers these questions we need to know what the word problem means when it is applied to children's behaviour.

What is a Problem?

There are no easy answers to this question. The word problem is often used in a loosely defined way, which can make it indistinct and difficult to pin down. Children are described as problems for many reasons, and sometimes for no good reason. Parents and teachers are obviously going to become concerned when a child in their care is persistently difficult and acts in a way that does not seem normal. But what do we mean by normal? Children can often be troubled, and also troublesome, but when does their behaviour stop being normal? Throughout this chapter we shall return to two simplified case studies of children who have been referred to a child and family guidance clinic; see box 12.1.

> **Box 12.1   The Case Histories of Two Children**
>
> Carl is an 11-year-old boy whose older brothers have both been arrested for aggressive behaviour and whose violent father has now left the family home. When he fails to get his own way at home he has violent tantrums, and his mother feels that she has lost control. The school referred him to a child and family guidance clinic because of his aggression towards other children, poor concentration and poor progress in academic work.
>
> Manjit is a 12-year-old girl who has recently become more argumentative at home. She is also getting thinner, and her mother is very worried by this. The teachers at her school are not concerned by Manjit's behaviour; they describe her as helpful, polite and hard-working, but inclined to be shy.

Perceptions of problems

Problem behaviour can be annoying, but that does not mean that all the annoying behaviour that makes problems for parents should be associated with maladjustment. Parents' tolerance for their children's 'problem' behaviour will vary. Many early breath-holders, nail-biters, face-twitchers and casual masturbators grow, without professional help, into normal, happy and well-adjusted adults because of the high level of tolerance of many loving and practical parents.

There is evidence that some parents may be reflecting problems in themselves (e.g. over anxiety), not their children, when they go to clinics with their 'problem' children. The disobedient and uncontrollable behaviour of a son or daughter can be very threatening to adult self-esteem, and research has indicated that parental satisfaction is low under these circumstances. We may learn from experience, to have lower expectations of both the children we care for and of ourselves. Less experienced teachers tend to take a more serious view of many undesirable acts than that of those who have taught for some years.

Popular views

A child whose actions are puzzling and difficult to understand is often termed a 'problem child' ('She's completely out of control' or 'I just can't understand him'). It is often thought that normal behaviour should be understandable, reliable and controlled and that it is abnormal if behaviour does not conform to particular limits of meaning, predictability and restraint. Parents and teachers will often become anxious if a child behaves in a way that is difficult to understand, unreliable or uninhibited.

There is a popular view that terms such as normality and abnormality are clear cut and easy to define. Sometimes they are thought to be mutually exclusive, representing opposites, like up and down, new and old. This implies that allegedly abnormal children will be easy to distinguish because they will be generally different from normal children. However, the reality is that children with emotional and behavioural difficulties are not all 'problems'; they are simply children with some problems.

Different situations

All of us (children and adults) alter our actions according to the different circumstances in which we find ourselves and our understanding of those circumstances. The term 'situation specificity' has been used to describe how behaviour is not usually random but is tailored to fit a situation. The likelihood that a particular behaviour will occur varies according to circumstances and the environment. So a troublesome child may be difficult in the home, or the classroom, or the playground, or the shopping centre, but not necessarily in all of them. The circumstances in which a problem behaviour occurs may also be further refined to specific situations within a particular environment. A child who has severe temper tantrums only at home may have them specifically at bedtime or mealtimes and be quite cooperative at other times when at home.

Michael Rutter and other researchers have found only slight agreement between mothers' and teachers' accounts of children's behaviour. This could be explained by the influence of situational factors. Mothers and teachers see children in different circumstances that are governed by different rules and restrictions, so it is predictable that their opinions would differ. Sometimes parents are surprised at this and find a teacher's description of their child's behaviour in school quite unrecognizable. A child who is difficult and troublesome at home can be well behaved in the classroom and vice versa.

Despite the low correlation between mothers' and teachers' ratings of children's behaviour, they do tend to be stable over time; although differing they tend to remain consistent. There is evidence that a rating may be influenced by factors that apply to the person who is evaluating and also by issues connected to the situation being rated (for example, a parent's mood, especially depression, seems to influence that parent's rating of a child's behaviour).

A spectrum of emotions and behaviours

Most well-adjusted children will demonstrate minor variations in their emotions and behaviours of the type that would become a problem if they were extreme. Many children are shy at times, and most of them occasionally find it difficult to sit still and pay attention, but some are constantly anxious and avoid social situations, while others rarely sit still or concentrate. Normality and abnormality are therefore two extremes of a continuum, merging together almost imperceptibly somewhere in the middle.

This means that there is no clear distinction between the characteristics of 'problem children' and others. Psychological maladjustment is not a disease with clear symptoms that can be diagnosed with a laboratory test. The emotional or behavioural problems that are a sign of psychological maladjustment tend to be an exaggeration of, or combinations of, patterns of behaviour that are common to all children (e.g. aggression, social ineptitude).

There are, broadly speaking, three classes of problematic behaviour:

1   excessive behaviour, e.g. screaming, hitting ('behavioural excesses');
2   behaviour that is normal or appropriate in itself, but happens in restricted contexts, e.g. following the norms of a gang instead of the family;
3   absent or very weakly demonstrated behaviour, e.g. incontinence, poor social skills, low self-esteem ('behavioural deficits').

Acknowledging that abnormal conduct is an exaggeration of behaviour that is common to all children means that we should expect it and normal behaviour to develop in a similar way. This simplifies the treatment of children with behavioural difficulties, since if abnormal behaviour develops in the same way as normal behaviour (following the same laws and principles) then it can be changed in the same way. This means that we need to know how all behaviour develops and cannot confine ourselves to problem behaviour.

Returning to Carl and Manjit (box 12.1) the clinicians reached different conclusions about them. Manjit's new assertiveness in arguments was considered to be normal for a girl of her age who is beginning the transition into young adulthood. She was thought to be developing normally. Although she was becoming slimmer this was not thought to result from an eating disorder but to be because she had recently grown considerably in height (as is normal for a girl of her age). However, it was agreed that she should see the family doctor in a few weeks time to ensure that she was not losing weight. In contrast, Carl *was* thought to have a problem, which could well persist and which suggested treatment for himself, help for his family and consultations with the school. The clinic staff decided that his difficulties denoted a deep-rooted problem of maladjustment.

Normality

What do we mean by normal? This question, too, is more complex than it sounds. A child's progress and behaviour is compared with a set of expectations so that if it does not conform (intellectually, socially or morally) he or she is considered a 'problem'.

Norms

As our children grow we expect them to adjust to norms of behaviour that are based on personal, cultural and theoretical judgements. However, biases and prejudices may affect these norms, and this can cause difficulties. If we scrutinize standards of normality and abnormality we can see they are social standards (rules, expectations, conventions). Children not conforming to the norms of the majority (because they will not or cannot) are then thought to be disturbed. It is important to bear in mind that judgements about problem behaviour are value judgements and are not universal.

Behaviour that is found to be a problem in one society may not be considered a problem in another. Societies' views vary about the ages at which aggression, crying, bedwetting, masturbation and sexual activity are considered normal. Social anthropologists have demonstrated large variations in what are considered to be desirable attributes and attitudes. Subcultures are also found within societies, so that a neighbourhood with norms different from those of our wider community may consider shoplifting or truancy acceptable. Ideas of normality can also change with time, as we can see when we consider the standards of behaviour for a normal child a century ago (in 1910 most 14-year-olds in the UK would have left school and would be contributing to the family income).

Schools, parents and peers usually decide what behaviour is unacceptable using the criteria of conventional social behaviours (e.g. sympathy, respect for others, honesty). However, as much behaviour that is considered a problem is often found in the general population, a certain level of aggression or disobedience must be 'normal'. Even delinquency is difficult to define; research has found that many non-delinquent groups commit a wide variety of illegal acts. This excerpt from the case history of another boy illustrates the difficulty.

> He [Tom] . . . proceeded to his seat and started a quarrel with the first boy who came handy. . . . [the teacher] turned his back a moment and Tom pulled a boy's hair in the next bench, and was absorbed in his book when the boy turned around; [Tom] stuck a pin in another boy, presently, in order [to] hear him say 'Ouch!' and got a new reprimand from his teacher.

What can we deduce from Tom's behaviour? He seems aggressive, disobedient and disruptive, but this extract is from *The Adventures of Tom Sawyer* by Mark Twain (1876, 454), and Tom Sawyer has traditionally been thought of as the prototype all-American boy. As another character, Aunt Polly, said, *'he warn't bad, so to say – only mischievous. Only, just giddy, and harum-scarum'*(503).

Rare behaviours

Society generally considers only relatively rare behaviours abnormal, and a child conforming to what is usually done is considered to be normal. This idea can conjure up dispiriting thoughts of a world where everyone must be average and no child should be individual or stand out in any way. The line between normality and conformity must be carefully considered; society often claims to support individualism while becoming alarmed at expressions of individuality. The idea that problem behaviour is rare, however, should not be inverted so that children with rare qualities are considered to be disturbed (for example, child prodigies have qualities that are generally considered desirable, but they are rare).

Developmental norms refer to how often particular behaviours and other characteristics are found in children of various ages. Jean McFarlane and her colleagues reported evidence, from an early long-term longitudinal study, that problematic behaviours are fairly common in children and tend to change with age. In most children problems were found briefly at certain periods and then declined, before disappearing or becoming negligible. It is likely that this reduction was achieved mainly by sensitive and sensible parental supervision. McFarlane found that difficulties such as moodiness, over dependence, sombreness and irritability persisted, but that problems of speech and toilet training, fears and thumb sucking were most likely to decline with age. Also declining, but later and more slowly, were overactivity, destructiveness and explosions of temper, one-third of boys still having outbursts of temper at 13 years. Poor appetite and lying peaked early before declining, while several personality problems (e.g. restless sleep, disturbing dreams, physical timidity, irritability, attention demanding, over dependence, sombreness, jealousy and, in boys, fussiness with food) were common around or just before school age, then declined, but increased again in puberty. The only problem that increased steadily with age was nail biting, which peaked (and then began to reduce) around the end of adolescence. Some problems (e.g. oversensitivity) showed little or no relationship to age.

Parents, teachers and psychologists find it useful to know about these norms when they are trying to assess whether or not a child has a problem. Our two examples earlier in the chapter involved Manjit, whose behaviour was not unusual for her age group and situation, and Carl, whose behaviour was unusual.

Working criteria

A psychological disorder is seen as having undesirable social and personal consequences for the child involved (e.g. social withdrawal), for the family (e.g. school refusal) and often for the community at large (e.g. vandalism). Professionals decide about a child's psychological well-being by considering his or her unique personality together with any particular circumstances, opportunities and stresses. A psychologist, when asked to make an assessment, will establish a child's position on the developmental scale determining whether physical and mental progress are appropriate for his or her age. Several questions may be asked when deciding if a child needs help, and these are likely to include the following:

1   Is the child's adaptive (coping) behaviour appropriate to his or her age, intelligence and social situation?

2   Is the environment making reasonable demands of the child?
3   Is the environment satisfying the crucial needs of the child – i.e. needs that are vital at his or her stage of development?

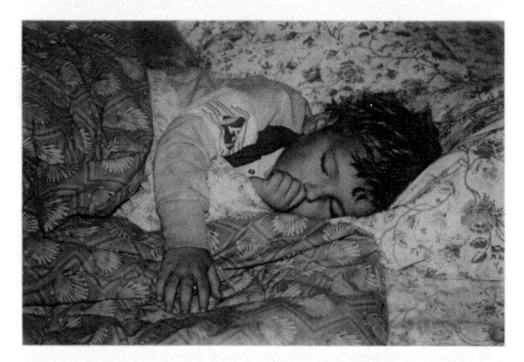

Let us consider our examples again; Carl's environment was aggressive – he had witnessed the aggressive behaviour of his father, and his older brothers had been arrested for aggressive behaviour. In addition, his mother had felt she had lost control, so his environment was neither making reasonable demands of him nor satisfying his needs. Manjit's environment appeared, in contrast, to be both satisfying her needs and making reasonable demands of her.

Sometimes parents and teachers can make conflicting or excessive demands of the children in their care (for example, unhappy parents can make children an emotional battleground for their marital disputes, and depressed parents can make excessive emotional demands of their children). The family is usually the chief means of socializing a child, but this is also where he or she is most vulnerable. Usually the socializing process goes well, producing independent, constructive members of the community, but occasionally the family, the basic unit of society, is itself psychologically disturbed (to varying degrees). If a child's behaviour is abnormal (unusual) or troublesome, and answers to questions 2 and 3 above are no, then there is still a problem, but it is a problem situation instead of a problem child. Carl's situation is the difficulty. Another situation in which the environment, not the child, was a problem is reported in box 12.2, which describes a different type of harmful environment.

Box 12.2   A Case of Successful Recovery from Extreme Isolation

Alison Soutter has reported a case of recovery in adolescence from an extremely isolated early environment. Tom's parents intended to keep him safe (their first child had died in an accident, for which a neighbour was blamed), so they kept him, from birth, in a room resembling a padded cell. He was clean and well fed but had very little interaction with others. Tom's mother was agoraphobic, and both parents avoided any social contact, trusting no one and seeing the world as a very dangerous place; they found safety in rigid rules. Tom stayed in his room with no stimulation until he was 6, when he had to attend the village school, but his parents arranged that he could go home for lunch, all games lessons and any outdoor activities. In the 1980s, 10-year-old Tom was sent to a small local independent school. Soutter described her first impressions when he arrived:

> . . . very neatly dressed . . . not a hair out of place . . . a completely expressionless face . . . this image was contradicted by his frightened, darting eyes. Their fear was so contagious that it was difficult not to glance over one's shoulder to see what the terrible danger was. . . . His hands hung loosely down with the palms going backwards and he walked with an awkward gait as if his knees were stuck together. . . . receptive language seemed normal but it was difficult to judge the expressive language of such an inhibited child. Despite all this the overall impression was not of brain damage or autism but of an injured, normal child. Many remarked that despite his darting eyes, he had a certain dignity.

Tom sat in a back corner of the classroom next to a very gentle girl, but he could not speak to her at all. As he was afraid when the class emptied he stayed behind until everyone had left. Tom enjoyed learning and was very hard-working, but his writing was untidy as he had little muscle control. At lunchtimes he walked round the edge of the playground like a 'caged animal', so he was allowed to help in the library. *'The classroom was probably his only source of stimulation, in a life of sensory deprivation. . . . Despite many obvious difficulties he was not thought to be autistic. He had normal intelligence and no pathological need for sameness, or odd, repetitive play patterns. Tom certainly realized that people had different points of view but he thought they were hostile.'*

BREAKTHROUGHS

After a year Tom so enjoyed a class play that he spoke spontaneously for the first time. A programme of therapeutic drama was begun; he learned facial expressions, and his performances increased his status. When he was 14 Tom's parents agreed to a school camping trip with Soutter accompanying him. Although very frightened, he agreed to go and for the first time he went into shops, to MacDonald's, walked in woods, visited other homes, ate new foods and laughed; *'he had ventured into the outside world, which he believed to be so dangerous and it had proved to be safe and enjoyable. He had also proved his courage to himself'*. The experience affected him deeply, and he now felt able to talk to his classmates, so social skills training began. Tom began to be interested in dance and did surprisingly well. Finally before taking his A-levels, he went, without Soutter, on an exchange trip to France. Being with other adolescents on a foreign trip was a bonding experience. He joined in their activities and loved discos as he danced very well. This enhanced his status. *'He was no longer seen as odd.'*

After arriving home he negotiated new rules with his parents, finished his A-levels and went to a local university. Soutter believes that Tom will always be rather shy, but this no longer interferes with his ability to lead a full life. Soutter noted that Tom arrived at this point as a result of many factors, one being his great courage, as he came to school every day despite being so afraid of other children.

Source: from A. Soutter (1995). 'Case report: successful treatment of a case of extreme isolation'. *European Journal of Child and Adolescent Psychiatry*, 41(1), 39–45

The child in the family

The development and dynamics of family life are of major importance. Since the 1970s an approach that has proved useful is one that views family life as a system in which all its individuals are affected by the activities of other family members, while they themselves influence the actions of the others. The behaviour of any family member is a response and a stimulus to others. Ideas such as these have influenced the thinking of many clinicians who focus on an individual and on the system of relationships in which she or he lives. Therefore *family therapy* not only focuses help on the child referred to the clinic, but extends it to the family as a whole.

Self-image

However, besides the importance of the family, and a child's other social contexts, we need to bear in mind 'the person' and the basic core of personality known as 'the self'. A child's positive or negative self-perceptions (i.e. self-image) and awareness of his or her relationships with others are important factors in psychological difficulties. Many of children's problems are social; they can have difficulties in getting along with siblings, peers, teachers, parents – even themselves. We all need to view ourselves reasonably realistically, so a child must get to know who he or she is, understanding any limitations and capitalizing on strengths.

In 2000, Ian Hay examined the self-concepts of adolescents in Australia (107 male, 21 female) whose persistent behaviour problems led to their being excluded from school. Using self-description questionnaires he formed profiles of each student, finding that the boys' antisocial behaviour was associated with striving for a masculine self-image, while the girls' was associated with social marginalization. Girls were less likely to be involved in antisocial behaviour but appeared to be more emotionally damaged and socially marginalized when they were. Hay suggests that programmes for girls at risk should help them to establish positive female peer relationships, while those for boys should emphasize the fostering of positive prosocial masculine role models in their lives, the learning of aggression management strategies and social skills. Returning to the case of Carl, a relationship with a male who did not use aggression to solve his problems (but modelled alternative strategies for coping with anger) would be expected to help.

The classification of problems

Unsurprisingly professionals have tried to bring order to the enormous variety of behaviours that are thought of as childhood problems. Statistical analyses have been applied to quantities of data, from clinical records and epidemiological surveys, to identify patterns, or syndromes, of problems. Herbert Quay and his colleagues analysed many studies, identifying two main categories (conduct disorders and emotional disorders).

Conduct and Emotional Disorders

Conduct disorders

Conduct disorders include many different behaviours that are expressed frequently and intensely. Typically they include physical and verbal aggressiveness, disruptive behaviour, destructive behaviour, irresponsibility, non-compliance and poor personal relationships. While telling the odd lie does not indicate an underlying conduct disorder, persistently telling large and malicious lies may do so. Young people with conduct disorders exhibit a basic inability or unwillingness to keep many of society's rules and codes of conduct. The rules may not have been learned through not being absorbed in the first place or because a child has learned different standards to those of mainstream society which enforces them.

In 1998 John O'Keefe and his colleagues compared the psychological profiles of girls and boys with conduct disorders, finding that they displayed different behaviour patterns. Female behaviours included membership of deviant peer groups, lying and running away, while males showed higher levels of cruelty, bullying, destructiveness, carrying weapons and initiating fights.

Young people with these disorders act confrontationally and provocatively, and this has often been found to be a result of harsh life experiences. In 'A 70-year history of conduct disorder', Lee Robins concluded that levels of conduct disorder change over time and probably vary from culture to culture, but that all cultures in which they have been investigated seem to provide recognizable examples of the disorder, the predictors and outcomes seeming remarkably similar across time and place.

There is some evidence that some conduct disorders may be genetically influenced, but there is a large body of evidence that abnormal family circumstances and the effects of parental conflict also have an impact on their development. Many twin and adoption studies (e.g. Michael Rutter and colleagues, 1997) have suggested that children's and adolescent antisocial behaviour is influenced by both genetic and environmental factors. Several studies have found that it is frequently found in children who are physically abused by their parents or other caregivers. In industrialized countries the rates of conduct disorder appear to have been increasing during the past 50 years, with much higher levels in males than in females, and in families that are stressed by conflict, poverty and parental psychiatric disorder (e.g. antisocial personality and alcoholism).

Are children with conduct disorders delinquent?

Although it is clear that many children commit delinquent acts at some time or another, some, especially those from privileged homes and schools, are more likely than others to avoid detection. The concept of a delinquent is basically an administrative and legal definition rather than a clinical one. Not all children with conduct disorders become delinquent, and not all delinquents exhibit the clinical features of conduct disorder.

There is substantial evidence that a clear line cannot be drawn between delinquents and non-delinquents. Surveys have shown that children and young people known to the police are not the only ones to have broken the law. When a large number of English grammar school boys were asked about delinquencies approximately half of them admitted committing some kind of antisocial act. More than half had stolen money, two-thirds had shop-lifted and 90 per cent had stolen from the school. In a survey of one thousand 9–14-year-old school children in Norway and Sweden, 89 per cent admitted petty illegal offences, 39 per cent theft, 17 per cent burglary and 14 per cent wilful damage to property. A recent survey of young people's attitudes to burglary, robbery and sexual offences found no differences between the attitudes of teenage inmates of a juvenile offenders unit and 'ordinary' adolescents of the same age.

Emotional disorders

The second main category of childhood problems is emotional disorders. These disorders include childhood fears and phobias, depression and social inhibition (shyness), and they tend (with some exceptions) to be more benign and short-lived than the conduct disorders. The following case study illustrates a mild temporary phobia, which was dealt with by the child's mother. Three-year-old Clare was so frightened by a loud, low-flying aeroplane while she was playing outside one day that she ran screaming into the house, refusing to venture out again. During the following weeks she was very frightened of leaving the house and terrified by any aeroplanes that appeared in the sky, however distant. Clare's mother began a gradual campaign to dispel her daughter's fear by slowly increasing her familiarity with aeroplanes. Together with her mother, Clare

1   gradually ventured outside when no aeroplanes were about;
2   looked at picture-story books about aeroplanes while safely at home on her mother's lap;
3   watched through the window as aeroplanes flew by;
4   visited a small local aeroplane museum;
5   enjoyed a family visit to a small air display, which included demonstrations of skywriting etc.

The pleasant experiences of the gradual exposure to aeroplanes contributed to the temporary nature of the phobia.

However, despite these two main categories of childhood problem, many children have behavioural difficulties that to a large degree are a combination of emotional and conduct disorders.

Continuity and Change

Do patterns of behaviour remain stable over time? Are children who are seriously antisocial when young (e.g. 6 or 7 years) still likely to be antisocial when they are adolescent or adult? Several studies have investigated this question, but there are considerable problems concerning methodology and interpretation. A number of longitudinal studies show that many children who demonstrate antisocial behaviours in childhood continue to do so, at least during adolescence. However, by no means all antisocial behaviour continues into adolescence. Several longitudinal studies reveal a sizeable group of children who have high levels of conduct problems during childhood which decline in adolescence. Terrie Moffitt and colleagues in the 1996 large-scale, Dunedin longitudinal study identified three groups of boys according to their antisocial behaviour during childhood and adolescence. Two groups had persistently high ratings (from parents and teachers) for conduct problems between 5 and 11 years. One ('life-course persistent') had high levels of self reported delinquency during adolescence, but the other ('recoveries') showed not only a steep decline in their parents' and teachers' ratings of their conduct problems after 11 years of age but also low levels of self-reported delinquency in adolescence. The third group ('adolescence limited') received near-normal ratings from their parents and teachers during childhood, but showed increased levels of self-reported delinquency during adolescence.

Long-term, longitudinal studies indicate that many people have a great capacity for change; later experience has frequently been found to mediate the effects of events in early childhood. The course of human development appears to be much less fixed than many earlier theorists have believed, and there are many reports of case studies that illustrate the degree of recovery possible during adolescence and adulthood (for example the case of recovery from isolation described in box 12.2).

In 2000, researchers (e.g. Paul Thompson, Jay Giedd and others) found evidence that could explain the mechanisms allowing adolescents to recover from childhood adversity. Using *magnetic resonance imaging* scans to reveal detailed pictures of body tissues, they demonstrated a spurt of growth, and then loss, in areas of the brain, which happen around puberty and adolescence. This has been interpreted as an opportunity for change when the brain is open to novelty. Even following a bad start in life these mechanisms could allow compensation at adolescence, a chance to make good earlier damage.

There is also evidence that the emotional problems, fears, phobias and inhibitions of childhood tend to be fairly transient, often only lasting for months or a year (but with some exceptions). Adults who, as children, attended clinics for these types of disorder are indistinguishable from those who as children did not do so. It is generally agreed that those disorders involving disruption, aggression or antisocial behaviour are the most persistent into adolescence and even adulthood. This is likely to be because adverse environmental influences tend to be reinforced time and time again, year after year. Most notable are cases of sexual abuse, in which the abuser is often a member of the family.

A large number of young people commit crimes, but few develop into adult offenders. The frequency of delinquent acts rises during childhood and early adolescence, peaking around 18 years and then declining. After this temporary phase most 'delinquents' gradually merge with the general population of essentially law-abiding people. Leaving school (which some children find irrelevant and the source of unhappiness), together with the rewards and responsibilities of a job, marriage and family, may well encourage this settling down process.

The Vulnerable Child

Almost all of us know someone who as a child had to cope with many problems but fortunately appears to have no serious difficulties as a result. In contrast we usually know of others who seem to have had enormous trouble coping with similar problems. Why do some children, but not others, develop serious emotional problems when faced with difficulties? Why are some children emotionally vulnerable? It would be very convenient if we had a list of factors (1, 2 and 3) that would always result in specific consequences (a, b and c) for a child (for example if we could say that inconsistent discipline, maternal rejection, being an only child or having a parent die would always cause disobedience, juvenile delinquency, shyness or depression).

However, life is rarely simple, and various combinations of influences with rather unpredictable results produce human actions. A particular environmental background, or style of child rearing, can produce one emotional problem in one child but a different emotional problem in another – and no difficulty at all in a third. There appear to be individual differences in coping.

Cultural differences in coping

There is some evidence for cultural differences in the coping strategies that children use when they are under stress. Carolyn McCarty and her colleagues asked American and Thai children about their coping strategies when they were feeling stressed by adult authority figures (for example in the presence of adult anger). Many cross-cultural similarities were identified, but the Thai children reported using more than twice as many concealed coping strategies as those used by the American children. For example, a Thai child would say 'I didn't talk back to them', whereas an American child would say 'I believed I was right so I argued.' Thai children are taught to minimize displays of feeling (e.g. to conceal anger etc.); they are taught from an early age to maintain smooth interactions with respected people by adjusting to situations they would not choose, or by deferring to the wishes of others. American children in contrast are taught to express their emotional states, thoughts and feelings openly.

Learning

Most children's behaviours, including abnormal behaviours, are learned. Psychologists have studied the laws of learning and behaviour, and the knowledge they have obtained is useful when we need to know how a child becomes a problem and what can be done to help. Each case requires a detailed analysis based on the idea that changes in a person's behaviour produce changes in her or his environment and vice versa. So parents who make a fuss and attend to their daughter's tantrums will ensure that the tantrums continue and even increase in strength, because they result in a pay-off for her (positive reinforcement).

All types of learning are generally useful to a child, as they help him or her adapt to life's demands. However, under certain circumstances they can also contribute to maladjustment; then the learning is dysfunctional. A young person who learns to avoid dangerous situations by being reinforced for doing so can also learn in the same way (but maladaptively) to avoid school and social gatherings. Simply attending to immature behaviour can unwittingly reinforce it.

It is all too easy for parents to unintentionally reinforce the very behaviours they want to discourage. When Anna was told to stop watching television her response was to argue, complain and whine for a long period, until her father gave in and allowed her to continue, just to stop the unpleasant behaviour. She learned that arguing, complaining and whining worked; her father withdrew his request and so

> **Box 12.3   A Rule of Thumb for Learning Behaviours**
>
> Acceptable behaviour + reinforcement = more acceptable behaviour
>
> Acceptable behaviour + no reinforcement = less acceptable behaviour
>
> Unacceptable behaviour + reinforcement = more unacceptable behaviour
>
> Unacceptable behaviour + no reinforcement = less unacceptable behaviour

rewarded her behaviour. We usually expect a behaviour to be strengthened if we follow it by presenting something desirable, but it is also strengthened if we follow it by removing something unpleasant. Box 12.3 contains a quick guide to the learning of behaviours. You may want to stop here and work out some of the examples in exercise 12.1.

Punishment

Research has shown that punishment is not very effective in changing a child's behaviour. Why? Punishment is mainly suppressive. A punished response tends to stop, but if a child does not learn a new behaviour to substitute then the old undesirable behaviour tends to return. Banning brothers from watching television as a punishment for fighting may well stop the fighting in the short term, but it is likely to return if they do not find new ways of resolving their differences.

Punishment can also have undesirable side-effects. Children get upset when they are punished, and this makes it unlikely that they will take in the reasons for the punishment. The brothers being denied television as a punishment for fighting may become angry about the punishment itself but ignore the reason why they were punished. If children are punished physically, research has found that they often imitate this behaviour with others (including peers and younger siblings), and children who are beaten often use aggression to resolve their disputes with others.

One form of punishment that has been found to work relatively well is a system called *time out*. In this system a child who misbehaves must briefly sit alone in a quiet, unstimulating place. Sometimes this can be sitting in the corner of a room, but it is punishing because it interrupts the child's activities, isolating him or her from all rewarding stimulation (friends, toys, etc.). The child remains there briefly (usually a few minutes), so this method can be used consistently. Both parent and child have the opportunity to calm down during this time, and when it is over the parent can explain what was wrong about the punished behaviour and what the child should do instead. This type of 'reasoning' is effective even with preschool children, because it emphasizes why a parent has punished and how to avoid the punishment in the future.

Exercise 12.1

Predicting the Consequences of Parental Behaviour

Can you predict the long-term consequences, following the child's behaviour, for each of the parental behaviours described below? Use the equations described in box 12.3 to help you.

Antecedents (A)	Behaviour (B)	Immediate consequences (C)
1 Harish was asked to hang his coat up when he came in from outside.	He hung his coat up as he was asked.	His mother said thank you and praised him.
2 Liam was asked to get dressed ready for school.	He continued to bounce his ball.	Nothing; his father was preoccupied with reading his newspaper.
3 Alice was supposed to be getting ready for school.	She did not even try.	Her mother dressed her to save time.
4 William wanted a new toy that had been advertised on the television, but his mother said she was not going to buy it.	He screamed and cried and lay on the floor kicking.	His mother ignored the tantrum. Eventually he grew tired of protesting and started to play.
5 Karla was outside playing with her friends when she was asked to come in to have her dinner.	She argued and complained but did not come in.	Her father said she could play outside for another hour.
6 Lucy was eating a meal with her family.	She kept getting up and starting to play.	Her father followed her with a spoon and the food, feeding her when possible.
7 David asked his sister Joanne if he could have a piece of her chocolate bar.	Joanne broke off two pieces and gave them to David.	Nothing; David ate the chocolate without saying thank you, and his parents said nothing.

See page 232 for the answers.

Exercise 12.1   Answers

1   Harish is more likely to hang his coat up when he comes in.
2   In the future Liam is more likely to disobey instructions when they are given to him.
3   Alice is less likely to dress herself next time.
4   William is more likely to comply with his mother's wishes next time.
5   Karla is more likely to argue and complain next time she does not want to do what she is asked.
6   In the future Lucy is unlikely to sit properly at the table to eat her meals.
7   Joanne is less likely to share a chocolate bar in the future.

Behaviour therapy

Behaviour therapy (or behaviour modification) has been found to be a useful theoretical and practical approach to the treatment of a wide range of childhood and adolescent disorders. The traditional view tended to expect that only highly trained professionals should be involved in the treatment of 'psychopathologies', but this excluded others in a child's immediate environment. In contrast a family-orientated behavioural approach involves the child's natural environment and uses the goodwill and strong influence of those in close everyday contact with her or him.

There is growing evidence that the effective assessment and treatment of many childhood disorders (especially conduct disorders) requires an observation of and an intervention into the child's natural environment. Charlotte Waddell and her colleagues have summarized the research evidence about conduct disorder in children and young people. They recommend that assessment should include various methods and multiple informants in many settings, while treatment should involve the young person, his or her parents or family, and community agencies. Most authors suggest using multiple long-term interventions with continuing care approaches.

A case illustration

The following is a simplified version of a case history and treatment programme for a difficult 7-year-old child.

Andrew's behaviour was very difficult and disruptive at home. At 7 he was defiant, refusing to obey or accept correction and flying into a violent temper, screaming, shouting and even destroying furniture if he was thwarted in any way. He frequently teased his 6-year-old brother until fights began. Observations in Andrew's home revealed that getting attention from his parents was reinforcing his defiance and refusal

Exercise 12.2

Predicting More Consequences of Behaviour

Charlotte was very bored by her maths class, so she threw a scrunched up piece of paper across the room. The teacher sent her outside the room to a busy corridor, where she could see other classes using the school hall. How do you think this will affect Charlotte's behaviour in future? See page 236 for the answer.

Think of your own children's behaviour: have there been times when inappropriate or antisocial behaviour has been rewarded by attention?

to obey. When on rare occasions he behaved well his parents took no notice, taking advantage of the peace to attend to other things.

The family was put under considerable stress by this situation, so they agreed to get help from a psychologist. Together, the parents and the psychologist began a programme to deal with the situation. It was agreed that as soon as Andrew began to scream and shout he should be removed from the room to avoid the possibility that he would gain attention for his antisocial behaviour (time out from positive reinforcement). Alongside this, Andrew was also to be rewarded for prosocial behaviours. Rewards took the form of tokens, which could be exchanged for a privilege (such as staying up late) or a treat (such as a favourite activity with his parents).

This simplified programme was designed to improve Andrew's relationship with his parents by setting limits to his behaviour and creating opportunities for mutually enjoyable (reinforcing) activities. Various aspects of their attitudes to child rearing were also discussed with Andrew's parents. At the end of the programme Andrew was much happier and calmer and got on much better with his family, showing much more prosocial behaviour.

Alternative approaches

The account of children's problems discussed in this chapter has been short and restricted. The main approaches discussed have been chosen because they are reasonably strongly supported by empirical evidence. However, this does not imply that there is no value in other approaches to child development and to dealing with the difficulties of growing up.

Recommended Reading

Herbert, M. (1996) *ABC of Behavioural Methods.* Leicester: British Psychological Society. [A guide to skills training for parents, adolescents and children.]

Herbert, M. (1996) *Coping with Children's Feeding Problems and Bedtime Battles*. Leicester: British Psychological Society. [Advice on coping with specific behaviour disorders.]

Kazdin, A. (1995) *Conduct Disorders in Childhood and Adolescence*. Thousand Oaks, CA: Sage. [A discussion of conduct disorders with much to offer the beginner.]

Nathan, P. E. and Gorman, J. M. (eds) (1998) *A Guide to Treatments that Work*. New York: Oxford University Press. [Reviews research into treatments that have shown promise in treatment of conduct disorders in children and adolescents.]

Quay, H. and Hogan, A. (1999) *Handbook of Disruptive Behaviour Disorders*. New York: Kluwer Academic / Plenum Publishers. [A handbook of disruptive disorders.]

Rutter, M., Giller, H. and Hagell, A. (1998) *Antisocial Behaviour by Young People*. New York: Cambridge University Press. [A review of research on antisocial behaviour of young people, analysing what has been learned over past 30 years.]

References

Coleman, J. (1999) *Key Data on Adolescence*. Brighton: TSA Publishing. [A clear collection of recent data concerning adolescents in UK.]

Hay, I. (2000) Gender self-concept profiles of adolescents suspended from high school. *Journal of Child Psychology and Psychiatry*, 41(3), 345–52. [An examination of the self-concepts of adolescents.]

Kunitz, S. J., Gabriel, K. R., Levy, J. E., Henderson, E., Lampert, K., McCloskey, J., Quintero, G., Russell, S. and Vince, A. (1999) Risk factors for conduct disorder in Navajo Indian men and women. *Social Psychiatry and Psychiatric Epidemiology*, 34(4), 180–9. [Risk factors for conduct disorders in Navajo Indians.]

McCarty, C. A., Weisz, J. R., Wanitromanee, K., Eastman, K. L., Suwanlert, S., Chaiyasit, W. and Band, E. B. (1999) Culture, coping, and context: primary and secondary control among Thai and American youth. *Journal of Child Psychology and Psychiatry*, 40(5), 809–18. [A study of different cultural coping strategies in American and Thai children.]

McFarlane, J. W., Allen, L. and Honzik, M. P. A. (1954) *A Developmental Study of the Behaviour Problems of Normal Children Between Twenty-one Months and Fourteen Years*. Berkeley, CA: University of California Press. [Classic longitudinal study of children and their normal problems.]

Moffitt, T. E., Caspi, A., Dickson, N., Silva, P. and Stanton, W. (1996) Childhood-onset versus adolescent-onset antisocial conduct problems in males: natural history from ages 3–18 years. *Development and Psychopathology*, 8, 399–424. [A study of antisocial problems in males which begin in childhood or adolescence.]

O'Keefe, J. J., Carr, A. and McQuaid, P. (1998) Conduct disorder in girls and boys: the identification of distinct psychological profiles. *Irish Journal of Psychology*, 19(2–3), 368–85. [A comparison of psychological profiles of girls and boys with conduct disorders.]

Quay, H. C., Routh, D. K. and Shapiro, S. K. (1987) Psychopathology of childhood: from description to validation. *Annual Review of Psychology*, 38, 491–532. [A useful account of emotional and behavioural disorders of childhood.]

Robins, L. N. (1999) A 70-year history of conduct disorder: variations in definition, prevalence, and correlates. In P. Cohen and C. Slomkowski (eds), *Historical and Geographical Influences on Psychopathology*. Mahwah, NJ: L.E.A. [A history of conduct disorders.]

Rutter, M. (1997) Nature–nurture integration: the example of antisocial behaviour. *American Psychologist*, 52, 390–8. [The role of genetics and environment in antisocial behaviour.]

Rutter, M., Dunn, J., Plomin, R., Simonoff, E., Pickles, A., Maughan, B., Ormel, J., Meyer, J. and Eaves, L. (1997) Integrating nature and nurture: implications of person–environment correlations and interaction for developmental psychopathology. *Development and Psychopathology*, 9, 335–64. [The role of genetics and environment in developmental psychopathology.]

Rutter, M., Tizard, J. and Whitmore, Y. (eds) (1987) *Education, Health and Behaviour*. London: Longman. [A survey of health and behaviour of a cohort of Isle of Wight children.]

Soutter, A. (1995) Case report: successful treatment of a case of extreme isolation. *European Child and Adolescent Psychiatry*, 4(1), 39–45. [A contemporary case history of recovery from severe isolation in childhood.]

Thompson, P. M., Giedd, J. N., Woods, R. P., MacDonald, D., Evans, A. C. and Toga, A. W. (2000) Growth patterns in the developing brain detected by using continuum mechanical tensor maps. *Nature*, 404, 190–3. [Growth patterns in the developing brain, identified by magnetic resonance imaging.]

Tolan, P. H. and Thomas, P. (1995) The implications of age of onset for delinquency risk, II: Longitudinal data. *Journal of Abnormal Child Psychology*, 23, 157–81. [Longitudinal data about age of onset of delinquency.]

Waddell, C., Lipman, E. and Offord, D. (1999) Conduct disorder: practice parameters for assessment, treatment, and prevention. *Canadian Journal of Psychiatry*, 44 (suppl. 2), 35S–40S. [A summary of research evidence about conduct disorder in children and young people.]

Exercise 12.2   Answer

Charlotte will know that next time she is bored in class, causing trouble will enable her to escape to a much more interesting place outside.

13

Puberty and Adolescence

- Are adolescents children or adults?
- Dependent or independent?
- Changing bodies
- Early and late development
- Changing views of the self
- Pressures on adolescents
- Different experiences of adolescence

Treasure's age is variable. It varies from three to thirty. She is sixteen to thirty while shopping, three to five getting ready for school and when poorly, ten to fifteen for homework and five to eighteen when visiting relatives. It is sometimes difficult to adjust to these sudden transformations.
Gina Davidson, *Treasure: the Trials of a Teenage Terror*. London: Virago, 1994

There is always one moment in childhood when the door opens
and lets the future in.
Graham Greene (1904–1991), *The Power and the Glory*,
quoted in Connolly and Martlew, 1999

Children or adults?

Are adolescents children or adults? Are they dependent or independent? Adolescence is a time of change, and this uncertainty causes much of the puzzling behaviour that can exasperate parents. We all pass through this period of transition as we move from the immaturity of childhood towards adopting a full adult role in life. Gina Davidson, above, describes the ambiguity and uncertainty that is an aspect of adolescence which affects both teenagers and parents. At times adolescents will behave like adults, while at others seeming more like children. Parents and teachers may treat them as immature, while their peers are likely to act as though they are grown up. To add to the confusion they do not always know themselves whether they want to be treated as children or as near-adults, and, like Treasure's mother, the parents of teenagers can find the sudden changes bewildering.

Timing

It has been said that 'adolescence begins in biology and ends in culture'. However, neither the beginning nor the end of adolescence is clearly defined, and feeling unsure whether one is grown up or not can be difficult. It is generally assumed that adolescence begins at puberty, but although some girls will begin menstruation as early as 9 years old we do not usually consider primary school pupils to be adolescents. Equally some boys may not begin puberty until they are 16, but they are still adolescents in other respects.

Society adds to the confusion by giving many mixed messages about the timing of adolescence and about its expectations of teenagers. Even legally the situation is unclear. In the UK 15-year-olds can fly an aeroplane, 16-year-olds can leave school and marry with parental consent, but cannot drive a car until their 17th birthday and cannot vote, watch certain films or buy alcohol until they are 18. Further education students can be financially dependent on their parents until their early twenties or later, but their thoughts and views will have become far more adult. As a result of this uncertainty we can only guess when adolescence begins and ends, our decisions based on each individual and the stages that have been begun, lived through or left behind.

Duties and privileges

Adolescents are neither adults nor children; they are a mixture of both. A young person may feel torn between the excitement and lack of restrictions of adulthood and a fear of leaving childhood. In addition, parents may fear that their child cannot cope yet with independence. Parents and children often have different views about the roles, status, duties and privileges that are suitable at various ages, and this can lead to disagreements. (You could try exercise 13.1 or 13.2.)

Disputes between adolescents and parents often concern rights and responsibilities. Adolescents frequently complain that they are expected to have adult responsibilities without the corresponding freedoms (for example to be responsible enough to baby-sit but unable to decide when to have sex). Adults often feel the reverse, that adolescents expect freedoms without the corresponding adult responsibilities (for example to choose what time to come in at night but not to help with housework). However, surprisingly and in spite of this, most adolescents get on well with their parents and have a fairly trouble-free time: a recent survey found that most say they have a good relationship with their parents.

Culture

Psychological developments, which are loosely related to the physical growth spurt of puberty, are strongly influenced by a person's culture. In the West, since the 1950s, there has been a growing view that youth has a character separate from childhood and adulthood. This, for the most part, is a Western cultural, not a biological, phenomenon. Other cultures often mark the transition from childhood to adulthood differently, and in several societies the beginning of adolescence is frequently indicated by a ceremony. Some authors suggest that the onset of puberty is handled better in these societies, where formal rituals are a public signal that a child has changed into an adult. Others have expressed the view that these ceremonies are used to reinforce the authority of the elders of the society. It has also been suggested that the strong links which boys have with their mothers are deliberately broken by male rites of passage.

In Western culture the stage of transition from child to adult used to be rapid following puberty (sometimes involving rites of initiation). Recently, this stage has become prolonged, and some psychologists suggest that while childhood ends earlier in Western society, adults are extending their adolescence and not acknowledging maturity until their 20s and 30s. Peter Beaumont wrote of a nation of Peter Pans perpetually stuck in adolescence: 'You see them in Hyde Park – 30- and 40-somethings on roller blades and skateboards.' Many people in their mid-twenties have still not taken on all their adult responsibilities, while children and adolescents must cope with adult concepts bombarding them from many sources (e.g. television, magazines, computer games, the internet).

Exercise 13.1

How Strict Should Parents Be?

What rights should 15-year-olds be allowed? Circle the number of the answer you most agree with. When you have finished count up the numbers in the circles to reveal how strict you think parents should be. If you know any adolescents, ask them for their answers. What do you think your parents' answers would be? Compare the answers. Are they very different?

Bedtime should be
1   a set time during term;
2   open to discussion;
3   any time they like.

Appearance (clothes, hair etc.) should be
1   totally decided by their parents;
2   largely decided by the adolescents with some boundaries set by their parents;
3   totally decided by the adolescents.

Personal money should be
1   fixed weekly pocket money;
2   a few larger sums at regular intervals (e.g. a monthly clothing allowance);
3   unlimited, supplied when wanted.

Concerning personal freedom (telling their parents where they are and what they are doing)
1   they should always say;
2   they should sometimes say;
3   there is no need to say at all.

Schoolwork should
1   be under the strict supervision of their parents;
2   involve some parental supervision;
3   involve no parental supervision.

Relationships with the opposite sex should
1   be controlled by their parents;
2   be subject to some parental control;
3   be subject to no parental control.

Exercise 13.2

Acceptable Behaviours by Age

What age do you feel would be acceptable for the listed activities? At what age would they be considered to be normal behaviours?

Do you think the responses of different generations would vary? If you know any adolescents, ask them for their answers. What do you think your parents' answers would be? Do the responses vary?

1 Leaving school
2 Having a steady relationship with someone of the opposite sex
3 Having sexual intercourse
4 Getting married
5 Drinking alcohol
6 Leaving the parental home
7 Going to university
8 Starting work
9 Having children

Puberty

The changes of puberty

The beginning of adolescence for many young people, however, does correspond with the start of puberty. The body, which a child has taken for granted, suddenly begins to change dramatically. 'Mirror gazing' becomes common as a young person carefully scrutinizes and analyses 'good' and 'bad' points. In boys an increase in the size of their testes, scrotum and penis marks the end of childhood, while for girls there is an enlargement of their breasts, ovaries and the uterus (or womb). These physical changes are a result of the actions of hormones, and, on average in the UK, they begin at about 10 years in girls and 12 years in boys; but considerable variation between individuals is normal.

The average age at which puberty begins varies between cultures. In some cultures (e.g. the UK, the USA) the age of entering puberty declined during the twentieth century, and this seems to have occurred together with improvements in nourishment and health care. It seems likely that these improvements are at least partially responsible for the downward trend. However, most research indicating this decline was conducted around the 1970s, so it is not clear whether the age of entering puberty is still declining. One recent piece of evidence indicating that it could still be declining comes from a team of British researchers headed by Jean Golding. This ongoing, large-scale study, which has been widely reported in the media, has tracked the development of 14,000 children from birth. The interesting, but as yet inconclusive, early findings are that one in six girls of 8 years are showing early signs of puberty (i.e. breast budding or early pubic hair).

The growth spurt

At adolescence rates of growth for almost all parts of the body begin to increase, so that sometimes teenagers seem to shoot up and become 'all hands and feet'. A short period of relative clumsiness can occur, while adolescents adjust to new dimensions, but quite soon they are back 'in proportion'. At this time of increased social awareness some teenagers can find the feeling of being out of balance very distressing. We all become uncomfortable if we feel that events are out of our control; teenagers are no different.

Other changes

In addition to changes in the shape and size of his or her body, an adolescent's glands also begin to secrete different levels of hormones. Before puberty boys and girls differ only slightly in the levels of the male and female hormones that are circulating in their blood streams. After puberty begins, this changes dramatically, and levels of the appropriate sex-related hormones increase significantly. These alterations in hormonal levels also cause psychological changes; so adolescents must begin to cope with sexual arousal, while their parents must handle the teenager's new, hormone-driven assertiveness.

In 2000, Paul Thompson and others demonstrated interesting changes occurring in the brain during adolescence. Using magnetic resonance imaging (which gives detailed pictures of body tissues) they showed that areas of brain growth, and loss, occurred around puberty. These could be mechanisms that allow adolescents to adapt to adulthood before acquiring responsibilities (a chance for shaping by social culture). In this view adolescence is a useful time during which even following a poor start in life there is room for recovery.

Early and late development

There is considerable variation in the age at which puberty is reached, but by the age of 16 the average boy is sexually fully developed and could become a father. The start of puberty is marked in boys by the beginning of ejaculation or emission of semen and in girls when breast growth starts. Menstruation generally indicates that a girl is producing ova and could become a mother. The growth in height, strength and sexual attractiveness, which accompanies these changes, is usually

welcome in both sexes, but recent evidence indicates that the timing of these physical changes is important.

Boys

Early maturing boys have been found to be generally more socially relaxed and more popular than other boys. This is probably a result of their greater strength and size, which are useful in both sports and social situations. While early maturing boys benefit, late maturing boys can suffer (more so than late maturing girls). Boys who develop late can become self-conscious about their small size, and this can lead to reduced self-confidence, which may continue into adulthood. Generally boys begin puberty about two years later than girls, so a boy who matures late is behind most of his peers, both male and female. Male adolescents who are overweight may also be distressed by their size and occasional awkwardness.

Girls

In contrast to boys, a girl who matures late is still at a stage similar to that of most boys of the same age, and this may help her. However, both late maturing girls and boys are likely to be teased by their peers: they still look childlike at a time when their friends are beginning to appear adult.

The situation is different for early maturing girls. Whereas boys gain advantages from early maturity, girls do not always find it welcome. Some are worried by the sudden accumulation of fat and increased hip width, which is normal in adolescent girls but occurs at a time when they have stopped growing taller. Teasing from others can increase any worries about body weight, as can media that stress the importance of being slim. There is evidence that the girls who are most content with their body weight at this stage are those who are underweight. Some psychologists have suggested that this could explain why so many adolescent girls experiment with dieting. In 1997, John Turtle and his colleagues found that approximately 50 per cent of 13–16-year-old girls in the UK either think that they should lose weight or are actively dieting to do so. (You could try exercise 13.3 now.) There is some evidence that there is a relationship in girls between perceived early development and low self-esteem, which may be explained by early developing girls being heavier than others girls of the same age. Ballet dancers and gymnasts have also been found to be negative about early development.

Some girls who mature early will also have difficulties due to self-consciousness about their sexual development, which others may see as provocative. Early maturity can lead girls to associate with older adolescents, and there is evidence that this can encourage them to act in ways inappropriate for their age (e.g. drinking, smoking or sexual behaviour). Fortunately, by adulthood most of these effects associated with early or late adolescence will have disappeared, so although the rate of maturation is important during adolescence the effects do not necessarily continue.

Also the difficulties experienced by early maturing girls are not helped by the negative image of menstruation, but attitudes are progressively changing and only a minority of girls are still likely to see menstruation as 'the curse'. Advice and support often comes from their mothers at this time, and this usually has the positive result of strengthening bonds between mothers and daughters. Nevertheless, there are some girls who do not have this help. The Revd Chad Varah founded the Samaritans Association after, as a young minister, he had to bury a young girl who was so frightened by her first menstrual period that she committed suicide; no one had explained menstruation to her.

Exercise 13.3

Pervasive Influences Concerning Body Image

1   Write a list of as many words as you can think of that mean fat and a second list of words that mean thin. How many of the words are either slightly or very insulting (even if used as a joke)? What does this tell children, as they grow, about our opinions of people of various sizes?

2   Look through five magazines or newspapers. How many advertisements and articles feature positive images of underweight people? Now count again; how many feature positive images of overweight people? Finally, how many have positive images of average people. What do our children learn from this as they grow? Try the exercise again using teenage magazines. How do they compare with adult magazines?

3   This is a chance to sit down and watch children's television programmes one Saturday morning. Draw three columns on a piece of paper and write Thin at the top of one, Average at the top of the second and Large at the top of the third. Now put a tick in the appropriate column for each new television presenter or other positive role model who appears on the television screen. After ten minutes turn to another channel and continue making ticks in the appropriate columns. Watch each channel for ten minutes, ticking the appropriate columns. When you have gone through all the main channels that children watch regularly go through them again for another 10 minutes, adding to your ticks. (You may not have followed the programmes very well, but you will have a small cross sample.) Now, count the number of ticks in each list and compare them. You have a sample of the numbers of thin, average and large positive role models that appear on children's television. How do they compare? What does this tell our children?

Body image

As they develop sexually adolescents become increasingly concerned with how they look and how attractive they are to the opposite sex. Hormonal changes can stimulate the sebaceous glands, so acne often appears at this stage. Most adolescents, especially boys, suffer for a while, but in some this stage is extended and can cause considerable distress. The experiences of an adolescent who is seen as attractive are often easier than one who is not, as they have more positive reactions from others. However, most adolescents manage with support from their families and friends,

and only a few become seriously depressed owing to anxiety about their physical appearance. The attitude taken by their families towards their physical changes and sexuality has an important effect on how adolescents feel about their own physical development. This can sometimes be a problem if it results in feelings of shame about normal development.

Body image is very important in Western culture, and this can be seen in the amount of time and effort that we all spend on our appearance. At any age we all want to dress either fashionably or to fit in with our particular group of friends and acquaintances. Teenagers are particularly preoccupied with this, as they are developing a set of feelings and attitudes towards their bodies that add considerably to their growing sense of their individual identities. Our impressions of our body image are largely made up of our idea of other people's attitudes to our bodies, and this makes than very subjective. The resulting body image can be pleasing and will boost an adolescent's self-esteem; or it can be worrying and will reduce a teenager's confidence.

A Sense of Identity

The changes of adolescence mean that family and society begin to react differently to individuals, more being expected from them than is expected from children. This is a stage when emotional, sexual and moral issues become increasingly important.

The psychoanalyst Eric Erikson suggested that central to adolescence is the task of forming an adult identity. Adolescents are in a stage of choosing, and adjusting to, a new adult role, and many will try out a variety of roles and behaviours before they settle for one. This experimentation can often include conduct which seems extreme to adults (for example fashions that upset older people).

Parents can sometimes be puzzled or shocked by the way their teenagers dress or decorate themselves. One mother observed that her teenage daughter 'gets up in the morning as a beautiful young woman and then spends an hour turning herself into a monster before going out'. There are many reasons why adolescents dress in ways that adults find strange. They could simply be trying to fit in with their friends, they may just want to shock, or they may be finding a way of saying 'Look at me, I am different, this is a new identity.'

Much of the self-absorption of adolescence originates in this search for an identity. Sometimes there will be rapid and extreme mood swings, even from total self-satisfaction and conceit to complete dislike for oneself and self-hatred. A teenager who experiences a large difference between a self-concept 'myself as I am' and his or her idealized self 'myself as I would like to be' can become anxious and oversensitive.

Identity crisis

It has become a popular belief that adolescence must be accompanied by a personal identity crisis that causes at least some anxiety, depression, conflict etc. Erikson described adolescence as one of eight stages in the life cycle (also discussed in chapter 16), each with a particular developmental task, or challenge, to be resolved before the move to the next. These stages are built upon each other like a pile of bricks, the early ones of childhood and adolescence being the foundations. Unresolved conflicts in these early stages are expected to cause shaky foundations that are vulnerable to stress later in life. The adolescent is leaving childhood behind and a major preoccupation is thought to be answering the question 'Who am I?' For Erikson the teenager has a conflict between 'identity' and 'identity diffusion'. Before developing a firm sense of who they are and what they stand for adolescents will often try out different identities, experimenting with various roles and relationships.

Identity confusion or diffusion can take any of the following forms:

- Directionless drifting through many roles may accompany abnormal or delinquent behaviour (e.g. drug taking, suicide) if it is severe. Unable to resolve the identity crisis an adolescent may assume an extreme position (separate from the crowd, in preference to uncertainty).
- An adolescent may fear a commitment to close relationships, so that anxiety about losing his or her identity leads to stereotyped relationships or isolation.
- Anxieties about change, and becoming an adult, may lead to an inability to plan for the future or keep any sense of time.
- Concentration may prove impossible; or frantic work on one activity may prevent all other activities (resources are not channelled realistically).

Identity formation

James Marcia extended Erikson's work, identifying four statuses of identity formation. He suggested that an adolescent achieves a mature identity by experiencing several crises and exploring life's alternatives before finally arriving at a commitment. Marcia's four statuses are:

- *identity diffusion*   an inability to adopt some type of adult identity;
- *identity foreclosure*   settling too soon for an immature identity without exploring the many available options;
- *identity moratorium*   postponing decisions about identity while alternatives are investigated;
- *identity achievement*   crises having been experienced, emerging with firm commitments, goals and ideology.

Obviously many of us continue altering our identities for much of our lives, but we are usually quite sure of a core personality, which is always central to our idea of ourselves as a person.

It must be kept in mind that Erikson's theories were not formed from large-scale research; they were based on observations of his patients and the literature. The adolescents who attended his clinic would, by definition, have had problems, and some psychologists have proposed that Erikson does not explain why most adolescents have no severe difficulties. Further problems with Erikson's proposals stem from his suggestion that the stages and conflicts were universal and applied to all.

Gender differences

Researcher Carol Gilligan has suggested that Erikson's stages applied only to males. She criticized Erikson (and Kohlberg – see chapter 10) for proposing stages that apply to all despite the absence of supportive data concerning women. She argued that females are more interested in developing warm and nurturing relationships and less interested than males in forging separate identities (see box 13.1 for quotations). Gilligan proposed that girls and boys are brought up differently and that in the process they are encouraged to be concerned about different things. Boys are encouraged to consider independence and justice, girls to think about the welfare of others. Gilligan proposed that as a result of this different emphasis, males and females are likely to have different experiences of adolescence. (You could try exercise 13.4.)

Cultural differences

Other researchers have suggested that self-concept varies between cultures. Self-image develops within a social or community context (referring to how people see

Exercise 13.4

Decision Making

Try this questionnaire yourself, then ask friends of both sexes to do it. Compare their responses.

1   You are a teenager about to go to university for the first time. The course you would like to take is at an institution that is miles away from home, but you know that your parents desperately want you to stay fairly close. What should you do?

    (a)   Enrol on the course of your choice despite your parents.
    (b)   Find a similar course close by.

2   The company you work for has been taken over by a foreign multi-national company, and now your job will involve a long period abroad. You have elderly parents who are ill and need considerable attention; they could even die while you are abroad. What should you do?

    (a)   Take the risk and go abroad for the sake of your career.
    (b)   Give up your job or take a demotion, to be near to your parents.

3   Your child is to be awarded a prize at school, and it is very important to him/her that you should be present at the ceremony. There is an important meeting at work that you know you should attend, and your absence will not look good. What should you do?

    (a)   Go to the prize giving and worry about work later.
    (b)   Miss the prize giving to attend the meeting.

4   You have been offered a wonderful promotion, but it will mean that you and your family must move to another city. Your partner has retired and does not mind moving, but your children are at a crucial stage in their education and do not want to leave. It is the chance of your life. What should you do?

    (a)   Move and take the family with you (the schools are good in that city too).
    (b)   Move, but leave the family and travel back at weekends.
    (c)   Turn down the promotion.

5   Your partner has retired early and wants you to retire too so that you can spend more time together. You do not want to. What should you do?

    (a)   Retire reluctantly.
    (b)   Wait until you are ready, then retire.

Now see page 252 for comment.

Exercise 13.5

Describing Yourself

Describe yourself in five words.
I am . . .
I am . . .
I am . . .
I am . . .
I am . . .

See comments on page 252.

Box 13.1   Extracts from Carol Gilligan's Interviews with Women (1982)

Emily: Emily describes the conflict with her parents over where she will go to medical school. Her parents want her to stay close by but she would like to go further away. She describes a contrast between moral and selfish justifications. Explaining the main reason for her decision to stay she describes constructing the dilemma as a balance of selfishness concluding that 'the greater selfishness' was hers. She dismissed her own hurt 'not having a new experience is not a hurt in the absolute sense', and compared it with the responsibility she would experience for being the cause of 'a fairly great loss' to her parents.

> They were really, really hurt by the whole situation, and I didn't feel the loss so greatly, not going. So I guess I began to view my selfishness as more than their selfishness. Both selfishnesses started out being equal, but somehow or other they appeared to be suffering more. (p. 140)

Alison: Alison has difficulty telling her parents that she wants to take a year off school, because she knows it is important to them that she should stay at college. She sees college as a ' " 'selfish' institution where competition over-rides co-operation so that working for yourself, you don't help other people". She wants to be "caring, sensitive and giving", occupied in cooperative, not competitive, relationships.' (p. 140)

Source: reprinted by permission of the publisher from *In a Different Voice: Psychological Theory and Women's Development,* Carol Gilligan, pp. 136, 140, Cambridge, Mass.: Harvard University Press, Copyright © 1982, 1993 by Carol Gilligan

Comment for Exercise 13.4

Do you think the answers of male subjects reflect more individualistic ideas than those of females?

Comments on Exercise 13.5

Now ask friends of both sexes to do the exercise. Compare the descriptive words that males and females use. Do the males use more individualistic words than the females when describing themselves? Do the females refer to themselves in terms of relationships? Do the males use more individualistic descriptions?

themselves and how they think others see them). Kwame Osuwu Bempah suggests that cultures outside the Western world have varying views of the self-image, some considering not only 'Who am I?' but also 'What was I?', sometimes including the dead as well as the living. Self-concepts then develop from different sources and are expressed in varyious ways in different cultures. Western cultures consider individualism more important than collectivism, but they too vary in the degree to which this is applied, and self-preoccupation is found more in some Western cultures than in others. Outside the Western world a clear emphasis on the self may be regarded with distrust. Chinese people have been found to prefer self-effacement and support group-orientated self-concepts to individualistic ones. Indigenous Dutch children have been found to use many more individualistic statements than Moroccan and Turkish children of the same age, who referred more to group aspects of the self. This variation in self-concept between cultures is likely to lead to different experiences in adolescence. It seems that the search for individual identity is not a universal concept.

Other research has indicated that during adolescence various ethnic minority groups (e.g. African-Americans) develop an ethnic identity. Jean Phinney identified three stages in this development; an adolescent moves from disinterest, through curiosity, to the achievement of a distinct ethnic self-concept, integrated with a mainstream self-concept (for example, Chinese-Americans would consider themselves to be Chinese *and* American). Visiting festivals, cultural events and learning cultural traditions (for example cooking traditional foods) help this process. Large cultural differences between ethnic groups 'and their mainstream cultures will mean that the experience of adolescence will be very different for individuals in varying cultural groups.

A crisis for all?

So do most adolescents experience a crisis? Ever since Stanley Hall suggested, in 1904, that adolescence is a time of 'storm and stress' this period has been seen as inherently full of problems. Clinicians who treated extreme cases and journalists who delighted in sensational stories have added to this view, until it became firmly established in the public imagination. By 1958 Anna Freud was writing that it was abnormal if a child kept a 'steady equilibrium during the adolescent period'. However, although it used to be thought that experiencing so many changes over a few years had to cause difficulties, the evidence suggests that this is not necessarily true. While not wanting to underestimate the difficulties of adolescence we believe the evidence does not support the idea that most teenagers suffer severe 'storm and stress'.

The development of identity is not always easy for adolescents, but there is considerable evidence against Erikson's claim that they *usually* endure a crisis of identity. Many studies show that most teenagers have a positive but fairly realistic self-image. However, everyone's journey through adolescence is an individual matter, which may be understood only by examining their emotional, cultural and social circumstances and the effects these have on their experience of the changes that are occurring.

The normal majority

Two researchers, John Coleman and Leo Hendry, have suggested that other theories of adolescence concentrated on the difficulties experienced by a minority of teenagers but ignored approximately 80 per cent of them, the normal majority who maintain a reasonable level of stability. Adolescence is a difficult time for some, but most adolescents seem to experience a period of relative calm and seem able to cope without undue distress. Coleman and Hendry's focal theory (based on a study of 800 male and female adolescents) explains this. They found that, in both sexes, concerns about various issues reached a peak at different ages. They argue that particular types of relationship patterns are most important at different ages. For example, some adolescents will be dealing with conflicts with parents but not yet be dealing with anxiety about heterosexual relationships. Others, however, could be dealing with two or three issues at the same time. Coleman and Hendry do not suggest that these are the only concerns adolescents have to deal with, or that there is a specific age when they arise: adolescents' concerns about issues vary widely. However, they do suggest that most teenagers cope with stressful changes by trying to spread the issues out and to deal with them one at a time. In Coleman and Hendry's view those adolescents who experience more than one problem at a time are the ones in whom difficulties are most likely to occur. These findings have been replicated in large North American and New Zealand samples.

The Problems of Adolescence

Adolescence is a period of major transition, so it would be a surprise if no teenagers experienced some serious problems. Contrary to popular opinion, adolescents do not seem to be more vulnerable to problems than people at other stages of development, but about 20 per cent of them do experience significant psychological problems, which may involve some of the following:

1 *depression* (and sometimes self-harm, which is more common in females, and occasionally even suicide, which is more frequent in males);
2 *anxieties*, especially about school and social situations;
3 *conduct problems and delinquency*, statistics for 1997 in England and Wales (Stationery Office, 1998) showing that crime rises between 12 and 18 years, then falls dramatically;
4 *eating disorders (anorexia nervosa and bulimia nervosa)*, with considerably higher rates in females than in males;
5 *substance misuse.*

Adolescents are experimenting with and rehearsing adult roles, so any mistakes in judgement at this time can have far-reaching effects (for example the use of drugs by adolescents).

Substance use and misuse

Firstly, what are drugs? The term includes many things, from alcohol and tobacco to cannabis and heroin. Most parents have some experience of the first two, while few have knowledge of the last two; but all can have fearsome consequences.

Naturally parents are upset and often desperate after discovering that their child has taken or is taking drugs. However, teenagers today have no experience of a world without cannabis and ecstasy, so the temptation to experiment is bound to be strong. Brief experimentation does not make them addicts, just as getting drunk when they were young did not make their parents alcoholics.

Many adolescents do not take drugs, but it appears that drug culture is part of the lives of the majority of young people. John Balding has surveyed many thousands of 14–15-year-olds in Exeter and found substantial increases between 1990 and 1996 in those knowing someone who uses drugs (45–50 per cent to 70 per cent), but this appears to have levelled off or even declined since then (58 per cent in 2000). However, in 2000, another researcher, Eilish Gilvarry, reviewed the evidence on substance abuse by young people, finding an upward trend in the UK (with large regional and cultural variations). Cannabis was the dominant drug for young people, then 'dance' drugs (e.g. ecstasy), a minority using heroin or crack cocaine. There is some evidence, for boys but not for girls, that an association exists between parental support and less cannabis use, and between teachers' support and less tobacco, cannabis and alcohol use. Classmate support seemed to be associated with substance use in girls.

Most young people are fairly sensible and are probably more informed about the risks of drugs than their parents. They are probably more knowledgeable about drugs than they are about the risks of excessive drinking, and levels of alcohol consumption have been found to be rising dramatically in young people. A UK health survey of adolescents has shown that males drink more than females at all ages, and that the amount of alcohol consumed increased surprisingly between 1993 and 1997 (an average weekly increase of approximately 5 units for males and 3 units for females).

Adolescents who are under pressure at school, having conflicts with their parents, on bad terms with their peers or bored can be more vulnerable to temptation. Something exciting which 'everyone takes' is likely to appeal, and, although some will not waver, increasing numbers are giving in to curiosity or social pressure. Not everyone who uses alcohol or other drugs is unhappy, emotionally disturbed or psychiatrically vulnerable, and most young people will outgrow drugs and the drug scene. However, the risks of adolescent substance use are not equal for everyone, and the homeless, truants, school drop-outs and those with mental health problems and/or learning difficulties often experience the most complex and lasting problems. Many of these young people come from backgrounds of risk and lack protective influences. In her recent review Gilvarry concluded that problems of substance abuse do not occur in isolation, but are part of a cluster of previous and existing developmental and environmental difficulties added to the risks and opportunities of the transition period of adolescence.

The dangers of sliding accidentally into addiction have not been fully assessed, so education about drugs seems essential if people are to avoid this risk. Harmless experimentation in the beginning may lead to dependency if the drug is addictive. John Coleman's book (1996, see recommended reading) offers useful advice for parents and some addresses of specialist agencies.

Sexual behaviour

Sometimes it is not easy for parents to come to terms with their child's developing sexuality. It is a normal part of adolescence, but it can be difficult for parents when they see their child becoming an adult. In recent years there have been many changes in sexual behaviour in Western society, and the effects of these changes can be seen in adolescents' behaviour, just as it can in that of other groups. This is often worrying for the parents of teenagers. There has been great concern about the rates of teenage pregnancy, and the national figures for England and Wales in 1997 (Office for National Statistics Monitor) reported 8,400 conceptions among 13–15-year-olds. However, these rates have not changed considerably during the three decades from 1969 to 1997.

Adolescents, like other members of society, have become less rigid in their attitudes to pre-marital sex, but this does not necessarily mean that there is a massive rise in casual sexual relationships. Young people, especially girls, continue to emphasize the importance of love and stable emotional attachment in premarital sex, although marriage or its prospect is no longer seen as necessary. Most still appear to consider that a stable relationship is a crucial requirement for the raising of children, girls continuing to display more conservative attitudes to these issues than boys.

Intellectual changes

Intellectual changes mean that adolescents become aware of more than one way of looking at things, and this can lead to the questioning of adults', attitudes on various topics. If this is seen as a challenge to authority then it can lead to arguments. However, there is evidence that with major issues, such as moral or political beliefs, most adolescents tend to agree more with their parents than with their friends. In the UK there appeared to be more disagreement over important issues between present-day parents and *their* parents than they now have with their own adolescent children. This could be because there were dramatic shifts in people's attitudes to society, religion, marriage and personal morality during the 1960s and 1970s. There have been smaller changes since then, so it seems probable that the

Exercise 13.6

Family Life Map

This is an example of a family system at work (a family life map). Draw a similar outline for a family you know well (or an imaginary family) and work out the number of life tasks and life events. How do these affect the family members as they interact to facilitate relationships or create potential tension?

Tim: 22 months	Anne: 10 years	Peter: 14 years
Life tasks	Life tasks	Life tasks
• develop motor skills • develop self-control • elaborate vocabulary • explore his world – make 'discoveries'	• cope with academic demands at school (underachieving) • developing her sense of self • learn to be part of a team	• adjust to physical changes of puberty • and to sexual awareness • cope with the opposite sex • deepen friendships (intimacy)

Continued on page 258

Tim: 22 months

Life events

- parents insist on obedience now
- adjust to temporary separations when mother works
- not the centre of attention and 'uncritical' deference

Anne: 10 years

Life events

- afraid to go to school (cannot manage maths)
- bullied by a girl in her class
- jealous of the attention Tim gets (calls him a spoilt brat)
- worried about her father's health

Peter: 14 years

Life events

- worried about his skin (acne) and the size of his penis
- has a girlfriend – his first
- upset by his parents' quarrels
- complains that his mother is always watching him

Mother: 38 years

Life tasks

- review her life and commitments
- adjust to the loss of youth and (in her perception) 'looks'
- cope with an adolescent, as a patient and caring parent

Father: 45 years

Life tasks

- review commitments in mid-life
- develop new phase in relationship with wife
- face physical changes – some limitation on athletic/sexual activity

Granny: 66 years

Life tasks

- deal with increasing dependence on others
- come to terms with old age/ death
- cope with the loss of peers

Life events

- coping with late child – an active toddler
- has taken part-time job to relieve feeling trapped
- feels guilty
- bouts of depression
- no longer enjoys sex

Life events

- threat of redundancy
- high blood pressure
- worried about drifting apart from his wife
- had a brief affair
- feels unattractive

Life events

- poor health
- gave up home when bereaved (may have made a mistake!)
- enjoys 'the little one', but
- feels 'claustrophobic' with all the activity/squabbles

generations would disagree more then than now. Adolescents need to test the boundaries of authority as they grow into adults, and they need to push against other beliefs to establish their own. However, there seems little evidence to support the extreme view of a wide generation gap between adolescents and their parents.

Environment

The environment in which the physical, emotional and intellectual growth of adolescents takes place also has a large effect. Open discussion will help adolescents to explore their new abilities to think and argue, but if families, schools, social groups or cultures are suspicious of debate it can restrict bright adolescents. In some social settings girls are not expected to speak up for themselves, and in these situations schools can help by treating boys and girls impartially; equal expectations can help all pupils realize their full capabilities.

Adoption

Children who have been adopted and their adoptive parents can find adolescence a critical time. Who are my biological parents? Where are they? What are they like? Am I like them? These questions can seem vitally important at a time when a child is trying to sort out an identity. Adoptive parents, too, may worry whether they have done the right thing.

Adoption has often been regarded negatively, and this has been discussed in chapter 3. However, research indicates that adoptees do not necessarily suffer crises of identity. A study of 50 white, mainly middle class adoptees (adopted before the age of two) found no evidence of more identity problems than in a carefully matched control group (Humphrey 1988). A large-scale American study, in 1999, by Ann Brand and Paul Brinich also concluded that the great majority of adopted children and adolescents show patterns of behaviour problems similar to those of non-adopted children.

Transracial adoption has also been discussed earlier (see chapter 3). As we saw, research has shown that it does not necessarily give rise to problems. In Sweden in 1999 Marianne Cederblad and her colleagues interviewed 211 adolescents who were adopted, from other countries, during the 1970s. Most were transracially adopted and so looked different to their adopting parents. The adoptees were found to have as good mental health as non-adopted Swedish young people of the same age, and they also reported good self-esteem. In a 1997 review of studies of transracial family placements in the UK and the USA, Alan Rushton and Helen Minnis concluded that over 70 per cent had satisfactory outcomes, which compared well with same-race samples.

Parental Prejudice

So why is the worst often expected of teenage children? There are many reasons, but the family framework in which teenagers are growing cannot be ignored. Parents too are facing changes in their own personal development, usually moving from youthful maturity to early middle age. When we consider adolescents and their problems we must also think of the ways in which they are interacting with their parents, who have problems and anxieties of their own. Parents of teenagers are usually over 30 years old, and often in their 40s or 50s. They, too, may be feeling vulnerable as their bodies are changing and their identities and purpose in life are being reassessed, and they may be viewing the future with trepidation. Parental worries about body image and the changing directions that their lives are taking can in many ways mirror those of their adolescent children. These converging preoccupations, the adolescents on the brink of vastly expanding opportunities and their parents reviewing their lives and commitments, may contribute to the ambivalence of parent–teenager relationships. (See exercise 13.6.)

Many parents will view the approach of their children's adolescence with mixed feelings. They may experience regret that their childhood is ending, pride as they grow into healthy, independent young adults and worry for the problems that they will be facing in their independence. None of us is trained to be a parent, and releasing the 'reins' can be one of the most difficult parts of parenting. The teenage years can sometimes seem puzzling and difficult, but they can also be a rewarding and enjoyable time, and parents are just as necessary to teenagers as they are to children.

Recommended Reading

Attie, I., Brooks-Gunn, J. and Petersen, A. C. (1990) A developmental perspective on eating disorders and eating problems. In M. Lewis and S. M. Miller (eds), *Handbook of Developmental Psychopathology*. New York: Plenum Press. [The development of eating disorders.]

Coleman, J. C. (1995) Adolescence. In P. E. Bryant and A. M. Colman (eds), *Developmental Psychology*. London: Longman. [Part of 12-volume series, chiefly aimed at students of psychology and other subjects with psychology components.]

Coleman, J. (1996) *Teenagers: A Survival Guide for Parents*. London: Community Programmes Unit for Carlton Television. [A booklet and/or video of the same name, with helpful advice for parents and some addresses of specialist agencies.]

Learner, R. M., Petersen, A. C. and Brookes-Gunn, J. (1991) *Encyclopaedia of Adolescence*. New York: Garland. [A useful reference book.]

Netherton, D. H. and Walker, C. E. (1999) *Child and Adolescent Psychological Disorders: A Comprehensive Textbook*. Oxford: Oxford University Press. [A wide-ranging view of disorders.]

Nicholson, D. and Ayers, H. (1997) *Adolescent Problems: A Practical Guide for Parents and Teachers*. London: David Fulton. [Practical help and advice for parents and teachers.]

Rutter, M. and Smith, D. (1995) *Psychosocial Disorders in Young People*. Chichester: Wiley. [Psychosocial disorders in children and adolescents.]

Santrock, J. W. (1996) *Adolescence: An Introduction*. London: Brown & Benchmark. [An introductory text.]
Scott, R. and Scott, W. A. (1998) *Adjustments of Adolescents: Cross-cultural Similarities and Differences*. London: Routledge. [Research with adolescents in several countries, including Canberra, Winnipeg, Phoenix, Berlin, Hong Kong, Osaka and Taipei.]

References

Balding, J. (1998) *Young People in 1997*. Exeter: Schools Health Education Unit, University of Exeter. [A report of survey of thousands of 14–15-year-olds in Exeter.]
Beaumont, P. (1996) Thirtysomethings who won't grow up. *The Observer*, 19 May. [An article discussing the reluctance of many young adults to take on adult responsibilities.]
Brand, A. E. and Brinich, P. M. (1999) Behavior problems and mental health contacts in adopted, foster, and nonadopted children. *Journal of Child Psychology and Psychiatry*, 40(8), 1221–9. [A large-scale American study of adopted children and adolescents.]
Cederblad, M., Höök, B., Irhammar, M. and Mercke, A. (1999) Mental health in international adoptees as teenagers and young adults: an epidemiological study. *Journal of Child Psychology and Psychiatry*, 40(8), 1239–48. [A Swedish study of transracial adoption.]
Coleman, J. C. (1999) *Key Data on Adolescence*. Brighton: T. S. A. Publishing. [A clear presentation of data concerning adolescents.]
Coleman, J. C. and Hendry, L. (1990) *The Nature of Adolescence*, 2nd edn. London: Routledge. [An overview of research on normal adolescent development.]
Connolly, K. and Martlew, M. (eds) (1999) *Psychologically Speaking: A Book of Quotations*. Leicester: BPS Books.
Erikson, E. H. (1968) *Youth, Identity and Crisis*. New York: Norton. [Adolescent crises of self-image and identity.]
Freud, A. (1958) *Adolescence: Its Psychology and its Relationship to Physiology, Anthropology, Sociology, Sex, Crime, Religion and Education*. New York: Appleton. [Adolescents' lack of equilibrium.]
Gilligan, C. (1982) *In a Different Voice: Psychological Theory and Women's Development*. Cambridge, MA: Harvard University Press. [The different identities, moralities and relationships of males and females.]
Gilvarry, E. (2000) Substance abuse in young people. *Journal of Child Psychology and Psychiatry*, 41(1), 55–80. [A review of evidence on substance abuse in young people.]
Golding, J. (2000) Personal communication.
Hall, G. S. (1904) *Adolescence: Its Psychology and its Relationship to Physiology, Anthropology, Sociology, Sex, Crime, Religion and Education*. New York: Appleton, 2 vols. [An early classic.]
Humphrey, M. and Humphrey, H. (1988). *Families with a Difference: Varieties of Surrogate Parenthood*. London: Routledge. [Identity problems and adoption.]
Marcia, J. E. (1980) Identity in adolescence. In J. Adelson (ed.), *Handbook of Adolescent Psychology*. New York: Wiley. [A discussion of identity in adolescence.]
Minty, B. (1999) Annotation: outcomes in long-term foster family care. *Journal of Child Psychology and Psychiatry*, 40(7), 991–9. [A review of outcomes of long-term foster care in the UK, the USA, Canada and France.]

Observer Review (2000) Too much too young, 18 June. [A press article proposing a continuing decline in puberty.]

Office for National Statistics Monitor (1997) *FM1 Conceptions in England and Wales.*

Phinney, J. S. (1996) When we talk about American ethnic groups, what do we mean? *American Psychologist*, 51, 918–27. [Ethnic identity in American ethnic minority groups.]

Rushton, A. and Minnis, H. (1997) Annotation: transracial family placements. *Journal of Child Psychology and Psychiatry*, 38(2), 147–59. [A review of studies of transracial family placements in UK and USA.]

Rutter, M. et al. (1979) *Fifteen Thousand Hours*. London: Open Books. [A study of London schools, their attributes and influence on pupils.]

Rutter, M., Giller, H. and Hagell, A. (1998) *Antisocial Behaviour by Young People*. Cambridge: Cambridge University Press. [A review of research into the antisocial behaviour of young people, analysing what has been learned over last thirty years.]

Stationery Office (1998) *Criminal Statistics, England and Wales. 199.*

Thompson, P. M., Giedd, J. N., Woods, R. P., MacDonald, D., Evans, A. C. and Toga, A. W. (2000) Growth patterns in the developing brain detected by using continuum mechanical tensor maps. *Nature*, 404, 190–3. [An MRI study demonstrating interesting changes in the brain that occur during adolescence.]

Turtle, J., Jones, A. and Hickman, M. (1997) *Young People and Health: The Health Behaviour of School-aged Children*. London: Health Education Authority. [A study of health behaviour in school children.]

14

Growing Older: Young and Middle Adulthood

- Work and leisure
- Job satisfaction
- Working women and older workers
- Unemployment
- Romantic love and selecting a mate
- Happiness in marriage and parenting
- Maternal employment
- Is the family declining?

Growing older, like growing up, is both a biological and a social matter. It is biological in that humans, like members of other species, inherit a genetically fixed *lifespan*. Although improvements in health care and in occupational safety mean that life expectancy at birth is now much greater than it was 100 or even 50 years ago, the biblical account of the years of man as 'three score and ten' is still a reasonable approximation of our lifespan, barring accidents, today. Few of us will live beyond 80 and very few past 90. There are family differences and sex differences in lifespan, even when differences in life circumstances between the sexes and among families are allowed for.

But growing older is also socially defined and determined. Any society has a 'social clock' – conventions and expectations about appropriate behaviour at given ages and about the 'proper' age at which different life stages should be attained, although the clock's setting is different for different societies and for a society at different times. In our own society, for example, it tends to be seen as 'age-appropriate' to hike cheaply round the world when you are 21, but not when you are 35, or 55, or 65, to live an independent life in your twenties, but to settle down with a steady job (at least if you are a man) and children when you reach the late twenties or thirties, for a woman of 20 to wear a miniskirt and sunbathe in a bikini, but less so for a woman of 50 – and certainly not appropriate for a woman of 70.

As we shall see in chapter 16, a number of writers have attempted to describe the life stages which help to define our development not only throughout childhood but also throughout adulthood and into old age. Daniel Levinson, for example, proposed that people's lives can be seen as an orderly progression through alternating periods of stability and transition. Major transitions, requiring reorganization, adjustment and growth, occur on entry into early adulthood, in mid-life, and in late adulthood; other, less chaotic transitions occur within the generally stable periods of early and middle adulthood. Levinson's best evidence was related to the mid-life transition period, since his primary data, published in 1978, were interviews with 35–45-year-old men, and with a similar sample of women in a second study published in 1996. For both men and women, Levinson argued, mid-life is a time of appraisal – of the extent to which early aspirations have or have not been fulfilled within work, marriage and relationships, and of the need to reassess dreams and cut them down to size. The conflicts at this time are common also to the crisis points of young and older adulthood: the change from being young to growing older, reconciling masculine and feminine aspects of one's character, balancing attachment to and detachment from others, balancing destructiveness and constructiveness. In mid-life people also begin to develop *generativity*, an interest in generations after their own and a preparedness to take on a mentoring role to younger people, to contribute to future generations, to 'leave something behind'.

In chapter 15 we shall return to the notion of life stages and adaptation, and also to the question of stereotypes and age discrimination, with particular reference to stereotypes of old age. In *this* chapter we shall consider some life events typical of young and middle adulthood, concentrating on aspects of work and leisure, marriage and parenting.

Work and Leisure

For most people work means earning money, whether on an employed or on a self-employed basis. Work, by this definition, is different from leisure activity, which is carried out for enjoyment rather than for economic reward. But the distinction is not as clear cut as it seems. For one thing, are housework and childcare in your own home and for your own family regarded as work? Most people, if not all, would class housework as work, while childcare may be harder to classify and may be seen to have elements of both work and leisure (or at any rate pleasure). One frequent complaint about fathers who are 'good with the children' is that they share the enjoyable aspects of childcare, such as playing with the children or taking them out, but are less likely to take their turn at changing dirty nappies or the sheets after a child has wet the bed.

Paid employment often means more to the employee than simply a way of earning a living. Robert Havighurst, for example, pointed out that work, for many workers, provides new experiences and a variety of activity. It may offer the opportunity for creativity and the use of a person's skills; it may be a source of self-respect, prestige and status. It is also a way of making, and maintaining, contact with friends. Of course these are characteristics of leisure activity too, and satisfaction with both work and leisure, and with life in general, depends partly on how well activity fulfils these conditions. For more discussion of Havighurst's views, and those of others, see the review by Boris Kabanoff.

Work and leisure may not have the same characteristics or fulfil the same needs in every person's life. As Kabanoff pointed out, the relation between work and leisure can take several forms. Leisure activity may be a spillover from work, having similar characteristics and functions; or it may be complementary, meeting the needs work does not fulfil and providing a change from it; or it may be quite different and 'segregated' from work activity. Some factors important for job satisfaction, such as the variety of work and the chance to use one's skills, are not reliable indicators of life satisfaction in retirement, during which the most important ingredient of non-work activity seems to be social interaction. The relation between work and leisure varies for different people and also, of course, for different types of work and leisure activity. (See exercise 14.1.)

Job satisfaction

Satisfaction or dissatisfaction with one's work is not simple or all-or-none. There are a number of contributors to job satisfaction, for example the nature of the work itself, the degree of commitment to one's organization, pay, promotion prospects, the kind of supervision received, one's access to training, relations with the boss or supervisor and with fellow workers. Very generally speaking, job satisfaction is greater for people in professional or business employment than for manual workers; it tends to be greater for older workers than for younger, in spite of the problems which older workers sometimes encounter; and it is as high for women as it is for men, even though women at work typically enjoy lower financial rewards and lower status (see, for example, the reviews by Randy Hodson, Brian Loher and his associates, and Susan Rhodes in the 1980s).

A distinction is often made between extrinsic and intrinsic sources of satisfaction. Extrinsic factors are the objective, practical aspects of the work, such as pay and hours. Intrinsic factors are inherent to the work, such as the variety of skills required and the extent to which they are fully used, the degree of autonomy or independence of a worker in organizing his or her work, the feedback available about the performance of a task, and whether the work results in an identifiable end product which has some significance for the lives of others. All these factors have been found to relate to employees' ratings of their job satisfaction. The quality of interpersonal contact at work is also likely to be important, and has been found to be related to physical and psychological well-being, particularly for women. Other aspects of work may be more two-edged: for example, both a highly demanding task and an undemanding task may be associated with low job satisfaction. Adrian Furnham and Marion Zacherl found that, as one might expect, *person-job fit* is important for

Exercise 14.1

Meanings of Work and Leisure

What do people's work and their leisure activities mean to them? Talk to people who are, or who have been, in paid employment. Ask each person to tell you his or her job (or previous job) and to list three leisure activities in which he or she is engaged on a regular basis (just about anything is acceptable – hang-gliding, stamp collecting, watching television, sex).

Then ask him or her to rate each of the four activities on the check list below, giving:

- 5 to a statement that is *very true* for that activity;
- 4 to a statement that is *quite true*;
- 3 to a statement that is *so-so*;
- 2 to a statement that is *fairly untrue*;
- 1 to a statement that is *very untrue*.

Activity (job or leisure)   [*Rating*]

                                    Job   Leisure 1   Leisure 2   Leisure 3

A source of income
Intellectually stimulating
Earns me recognition and
   respect from others
Allows me to relax or let
   off steam
Makes a change from other
   activities
A chance to meet other people
A chance to be useful to others
A chance to express myself
A chance to use my skills
A way of passing time

What are the meanings that people most often, and most strongly, associate with their work and with their leisure activities? How far are the meanings of work and of leisure alike or different?

If the people in your study have described a wide range of jobs and leisure activities, do there seem to be differences between the meanings of different occupations and interests?

Compare your conclusions with the discussion in this chapter and in the references given.

job satisfaction: the match between a worker's skills and his or her job, and the extent to which the job provides opportunities to meet his or her needs, are both important. The evidence is not very strong, at least partly because the range of match and mismatch is not very high: people tend to choose jobs that suit them, or to leave them if they do not. This of course assumes choice and opportunity to change employment, which may be one reason why job satisfaction is greater for people in jobs which require higher qualifications (bringing with them, on the whole, greater occupational choice).

Working women

One of the most striking changes in the nature of the labour force in industrialized countries during recent years has been the increasing number of women in paid employment. It is now the norm for women to have a paid job, whether or not they are married or in a long-term partnership, at least until the first child is expected; and the number of employed mothers has increased dramatically in recent years, although many of them, particularly those with preschool children, work part-time. There are many possible reasons for these trends. For one thing, technological advances and economic recessions in industrialized societies have led to a decline in some traditionally male industrial jobs and an increase in some traditionally female jobs, such as health care and other service occupations. Rising costs of living have more or less obliged some women to become second earners to keep their families going, and unemployment rates among men and rising divorce and separation rates have turned others into primary breadwinners.

However, women's earnings are consistently lower than those of men. Traditionally female-dominated jobs are generally worse paid than male-dominated jobs, and women working in male-dominated jobs tend not to advance as rapidly, or at all, to higher pay levels. They are more likely to have an interrupted career pattern; and family commitments, if they have partners and children, may make it impossible for them to accept promotion, which may mean greater mobility and longer hours away from home. It is also frequently assumed that women have less commitment to their work than men, and this can affect their access to further training and promotion. In fact the evidence is mixed; studies suggest that women's commitment is often as great as men's, but that they may see commitment rather differently from men – more in terms of involvement, concern for others and availability, and less in terms of completing tasks, challenge and innovation (see, for example, the findings reported by Diane Dodd-McCue and Gail Wright and by Val Singh and Susan Vinnicombe).

Yet in spite of their comparative lack of extrinsic and intrinsic work rewards, women's job satisfaction is, on the whole, as great as men's. Hodson has suggested that this is because of the greater emphasis which women place on relations with fellow workers as a source of satisfaction, and that this is mirrored in their attitudes to leisure. Where men tend to stress competition and 'a change from work' as sources of leisure satisfaction, women are more likely to stress the importance of social interaction. This partly reflects a degree of gender typing in leisure activity: for example, women participate less than men in sporting activity, in which competition is more likely to be a factor than in some other spheres. In fact women spend less time than men on most kinds of leisure activity, mainly, they report, because of lack of time. For more discussion of gender differences in leisure activity, see the review by Ann Colley.

Older workers

In virtually all Western industrialized societies the percentage of older men in the labour force has declined, over perhaps the past 100 years in the case of men aged 65 or more and the past 50 in the case of 55–65-year-olds. The decline is partly due to the fairly recent phenomenon of retirement, and to the provision of state occupational pensions; but it is also due to age-related problems of employment for the older worker. These problems are particularly acute in industrialized societies, and much less evident in developing, primarily agricultural societies. In industrialized societies workers typically have to adjust quickly to new methods and techniques and, perhaps, to work at a fast pace. Middle-aged and older employees may be less well equipped to work in this way, and their skills and training are more likely to be obsolete than those of younger workers. And even if they are not in fact at any significant disadvantage, employers, other employees and they themselves may believe that they are. They may be seen as out-of-date, untrainable and less productive than younger workers. They are less likely to be offered places on retraining programmes, and if they become unemployed they are less likely to be re-employed than younger people.

Are these negative views of the older worker justified? It is difficult to answer this question, since quality of work may be defined in various ways, age affects different types of work productivity differently and a number of methodological problems make studies difficult to interpret. To take one example, if a study finds no difference in performance between older and younger workers, this may simply be because the older workers who could no longer cope well with their work have either left voluntarily or been eased into other work or out of the workforce, leaving only the most able of the older workers to be compared with a cross-section of younger ones. On the whole, however, the empirical evidence does not convincingly support the stereotype: see, for example, the reviews by Roy Davies, Gerald Matthews and Carol Wong and by Timothy Salthouse and Todd Maurer. There is very little evidence that older workers are less competent than younger ones, except in jobs requiring considerable physical strength, fast reactions or close attention to visual detail. Older workers are not noticeably more prone to accidents at work, although when they suffer injury they are likely to need more time off work to recover than younger workers do; and their job satisfaction and commitment to work may be higher.

Given these problems, it is quite surprising that older workers report job satisfaction as high as that of younger workers (although they are not necessarily satisfied with specific elements, such as their pay, prospects, supervisors and colleagues). Various explanations have been suggested. Perhaps *cohort* effects are at work: older people may be more easily satisfied because they have always expected less satisfaction from their work. Perhaps older workers represent a biased sample, because those who were dissatisfied with their work have had more time than younger people to change their jobs, retrain, or retire early; those who remain may have found employment which fits their skills and needs. And perhaps as people grow older they have different goals in employment, becoming less interested in career advancement and skill development than when they were younger, and more interested in security, support and feedback on their performance (although these factors are by no means guaranteed for them). Again there is some correlation with changes in leisure interests as people get older: naturally enough, they are less involved in sport and other taxing physical activity (such as DIY) and show more (or at least continued) participation in cultural, community, social and family concerns.

Unemployment

The risk of being unemployed varies according to education, skills and qualifications, and, perhaps largely because of this, according to age. Unemployment is greater for men in unskilled and semi-skilled manual occupations, least for those in managerial and professional work, and both older and younger men are more at risk of unemployment than men of, say, 25 to 50. Similar patterns appear for both women and men, but women's unemployment has been much less intensively studied; since most research has been concerned with male unemployment, this is the area we propose to consider.

The most obvious consequence of unemployment is loss of income, and often poverty, for the unemployed and their families. There are also psychological costs, related and unrelated to loss of income, which have been investigated in a number of studies from the 1930s onwards; see the review by Julia Berryman. They have found that unemployed men are less happy and less satisfied with life than men in employment, have lower self-esteem and are more likely to experience physical and psychiatric health problems; in particular, they are at greater risk of depression and even suicide. Obvious reasons for poorer morale and health are low income and financial worry. Insecurity and uncertainty about the future constitute a major problem for the unemployed at all occupational levels. Another is that, partly because of low income, the amount and variety of activities and social contacts are restricted. Unemployed men take on more childcare and meal preparation, but they also spend more time sitting about, sleeping and watching television.

Perhaps the worst aspect of unemployment is lowered self-esteem. An unemployed man is apt to feel that he has failed as a breadwinner and even disgraced his family; and low self-esteem is encouraged and aggravated by unfavourable, and even hostile, social attitudes towards him. Unemployed men are often regarded as being to blame for their unemployment, and even if they are not considered guilty it is often, apparently, felt that unemployment benefits should be kept punitively low to encourage them to look for work rather than to remain idle.

Studies of long-term unemployment and adaptation suggest that difficulties of adjustment arise fairly early in unemployment, after an initial feeling, sometimes, of being on holiday. With time people do seem to adjust to unemployment, although they may not return to the psychological well-being of their employed days, and there is some evidence that men who cope best with unemployment are those who stay active and maintain their membership of religious, political or community groups.

Marriage and Parenting

Marriage and parenting are still the norm in our society, but they take many forms and their nature is changing. The traditional view, that a family consists of a male breadwinner, a dependent wife and children describes a pattern that now applies to only a minority of Western families, although it is still typical of many Pakistani and Bangladeshi families, for example, in the UK. Some social changes affecting family structure are described in box 14.1.

Box 14.1   Changing Patterns of Family Life

How is the nature of the family changing? There have been remarkable changes in developed Western societies during recent decades, reflecting changes in legislation (for example relating to divorce, abortion and the legal status of women) and in health and medical knowledge (for example in infant and maternal mortality, longevity and women's control over their own fertility).

Declining rates of marriage   The number of 'first marriages' in the UK in 1996 was about half that in 1966 and about two-thirds that in 1976, although the number of remarriages (for either or both partners) almost doubled between 1966 and 1976, but has not increased substantially since. Marriage rates in the UK are lowest for members of the Caribbean ethnic group, and highest for members of Pakistani and Bangladeshi communities. The average age at first marriage has also increased in the UK, and in every EU country except Portugal and the Irish Republic; in the UK the change is greater for men than for women, increasing from 25 in 1961 to 28 in 1996.

Increasing divorce rates   The number of divorces in the UK more than doubled between 1970 and 1996 (the greatest increase was for marriages which had lasted less than two years, reflecting the changes in divorce law which came into effect in 1984). Large numbers of children were involved in divorce – approximately 150,000 in 1997; and it has been estimated that almost 25 per cent of children born in 1979 have been affected by divorce by the time they reach 16.

Working women and mothers   Most couples are now dual-earner couples, and most mothers, including almost half of mothers with pre-school children, also work, though many of them work part-time.

Lone parenthood   Growing numbers of families with children are now headed by a single parent, most often the mother (in 1998 about 20 per cent of dependent children in the UK were living in single-parent households).

Cohabiting parents   Over a third of children in the UK in 1997 were born outside marriage, but about 80 per cent of those births were jointly registered by both parents, and about 75 per cent of those parents were living at the same address. In the UK in 1998 about 80 per cent of dependent children were living in two-parent families, 10 per cent of those in families in which the parents were not married to each other. These families vary considerably, but in many cases are virtually indistinguishable from those of the conventionally married, and cohabitation may lead to the marriage of the partners (the British Household Panel Survey recently reported that 15 per cent of women in their survey who were cohabiting in 1991 had married their partners by 1997).

Stepfamilies   About 10 per cent of children live in 'reconstituted' families in which divorce (or, less often, bereavement) has been followed by remarriage and step-parenting.

Opting out of parenthood   There is a growing tendency in the UK for women to delay or avoid motherhood. Over the past 20 years or so the fertility rates for women aged 20–24 have fallen, while those for 30–34-year-olds have increased. Of women born in 1952 in England and Wales, 44 per cent were childless at 25, 14 per cent at 35 and 12 per cent at 45 (after this age the likelihood of having a first child is very small); but of women born in 1972 62 per cent were childless at 25, and it is projected that 29 per cent and 22 per cent respectively will still be childless at 35 and 45. While obviously not all childless women are so by choice, medical advances make it almost certain that the increase in childlessness largely reflects changing decisions and attitudes.

Romantic love and mate selection

People seem to have a universal need for emotional relationships with others, although the need is affected by age and by sex. It is stronger in women than in men, in younger than in older women, and in older than in younger men (a finding which is interesting in relation to gender-role changes in later adulthood, discussed in chapter 11). A common way of satisfying the need is through intimate relations with a mate, in a marital or other stable partnership, and the usual assumption is that marriage is beneficial for physical and mental health (an assumption we shall return to later in this chapter).

The decision to marry in contemporary Western societies is usually related to romantic love. Robert Sternberg, in his so-called 'triangular theory', suggested that romantic love has three components: intimacy, passion and commitment. In any relationship between two people all, some or none of these factors can be present, ranging from 'non-love', in which all are absent, to 'consummate love', in which all are present; and not only different relationships, but also the same relationship at different times, will vary in the comparative strength of the components present. But marriage based on romantic love is a fairly recent and a culture-dependent phenomenon. In previous centuries, and in non-Western cultures, marriage has been essentially a business arrangement, aimed at preserving an ancestral line, transmitting and safeguarding property or cementing political and commercial alliances. Even in contemporary Western societies, where romantic love is 'officially' the basis for marriage, love is not blind: in practice there are important social factors governing mate selection. Marital partners tend to be similar in religion, race, socioeconomic status and occupational background, and some studies have found that they are also alike in intelligence, attitudes and values, and in physical attractiveness: see the review by David Buss.

The stages of marriage

All marriages follow their own patterns, but in most there are clearly identifiable stages or milestones, not only in the marriage but also in the lives of its partners. In most cases the early months or years of marriage end at the birth of the first child, when parenting begins and marital roles and priorities have to be renegotiated. After the birth of the last child the pattern of the marriage may again change, as the emphasis shifts from child bearing to child rearing, and may change again when the children go to school and when they reach adolescence. Active parenting is concluded with what is colourfully called a 'launching' period, in which the children, one by one, leave home; and then couples reach the post-parental stage, which can involve both preretirement and postretirement phases, and, at some stage, grandparenting. All these stages involve enjoyment, but also transition, stress and adaptation.

Happiness in marriage

How does happiness, or marital satisfaction, vary over the stages of marriage and parenting? Our answers are not very reliable, because they involve introspective reports from marriage partners in which the various elements of satisfaction – with the spouse, with children, with work, income, living arrangements – are difficult to disentangle. But a number of studies have reported that marital satisfaction declines steadily throughout the early and middle years of marriage (see the review by Norval Glenn). The behaviour most closely correlated with dissatisfaction is the expression of negative feelings – confrontation, aggression, anger, 'whining'. Women are more likely than men to express negative feelings about marital interaction, and they also report greater dissatisfaction with some aspects, at least, of their marriages. Women also generally report poorer morale and sense of well-being than men, at most adult ages; but this finding is considerably clearer in the case of married than of unmarried people. This has led to the suggestion that marriage is 'good for men but bad for women', clearly an overstatement, but with some interesting truth in it. ·

Do children make parents happy or unhappy?

Parenthood is at best a mixed blessing. It results in a heavy workload, a renegotiation of relationships, a problematic division of labour between spouses, extra expenditure and a loss of income if one partner stops earning or reduces the extent of paid work. Some studies have found that the marital satisfaction of couples with children is lower than that of childless couples, but the couples compared have tended to differ with respect to age and time married. Other studies report that both childless and parenting couples are decreasingly satisfied with their relationships over time, and that childless couples are neither more nor less satisfied than those with children. For parenting couples the sources of dissatisfaction are generally concerned with sharing household and childcare tasks, which both partners often report is burdensome and unfair, and also with decreased opportunities for companionship and shared activities. Many women also find that parenthood brings a loss of autonomy and status. But most parents, when asked, say that children are 'worth it', a positive source of joy, fun, self-fulfilment and pride. Parenthood can then reduce marital satisfaction, but can also increase it or have no impact on it, when viewed against a general decline during the early and middle years of marriage; see the review by Ted Huston and Anita Vangelisti. ·

Most studies of later-life marriages have found that satisfaction increases after the children have left home. Rosalie Gilford and Vern Bengtson and Laura Carstensen and her colleagues, for example, found that older couples appear to enjoy their relationships more, experience less conflict and express fewer negative feelings and more positive affection than younger ones. Of course, one possible explanation for the upswing when it occurs is that when the divorce rate is high and divorce comparatively easy it is the most happily married couples who stay married after the children have gone and are still around to complete satisfaction ratings. Another likelihood, as Lynn White and John Edwards have suggested, is that the loss of children from the home, which is often referred to as the 'empty nest' stage, is generally a positive experience, representing increased disposable income and greatly increased freedom. Although many mothers and fathers have mixed feelings when the last child is launched, it is principally the so-called 'supermothers', who have devoted their lives to their children and seem to have no other interest and activities to fall back on, who find themselves living in an empty nest rather than in a child-free home.

Maternal employment

How does the paid employment of wives and mothers affect their families? The most obvious effect, and in most cases the motive for maternal employment in the first place, is that family income goes up, and the material standard of living is improved; but the improvement is usually achieved at a cost. As Darlene Pina and Vern Bengtson have pointed out, the cost is greater for women than for men, because in addition to their paid work, most employed mothers, even if they are not lone parents, also shoulder most of the responsibility for housework and childcare (including making child-minding arrangements). They are also likely to experience 'overload' and stress and a conflict between the demands of their paid work and the domestic burden. Yet most studies find that employed mothers report higher morale than unemployed mothers, particularly where there is a more egalitarian relationship between the partners and, not surprisingly, when employment, and the nature of the paid work, are the woman's choice and are not forced upon her by economic necessity (see the discussions by Ronald Kessler and James MacRae and by Linda Tiedje and her associates).

The effect of wives' employment on their husbands' morale, by contrast, seems often to be unfavourable, in spite of the increased income the employment brings. This may be partly because of greater domestic responsibilities and less emotional support from busy wives, but the explanations most clearly supported by the evidence are that husbands of employed wives feel less adequate as breadwinners and that they may resent the greater domestic burden which they are obliged to accept. Their dissatisfaction is greater than that of fathers in single-earner families, who, when they share childcare, share from choice rather than from necessity and are more likely to feel comfortable and competent in the role.

There has been a great deal of concern about the effects of maternal employment on children, partly prompted by the common assumption that the children of employed mothers are likely to be emotionally deprived and ill-cared for. Obviously the quality of substitute care is important (see the discussion of daycare in chapter 3), but on the whole research, for example by Lois Hoffman between the 1970s and the 1990s, suggests that the children of employed mothers may be advantaged rather than disadvantaged. Although working mothers spend less time with their children, the quality of their mother–child interactions is not poorer than those of mothers who stay at home, and may be better. Children of mothers in paid work are generally more independent, both practically and emotionally, and often do better in school, although, as many researchers have pointed out, any relation between maternal employment and a child's academic achievement is likely to be due at least partly to other factors, such as family income, the mother's educational level, the child's IQ and its birth order. John Horwood and David Fergusson, for example, have reported a longitudinal study of 8–14-year-old children in New Zealand, which found that when such factors were parcelled out there was no significant relation between maternal employment and children's achievement in school. Finally, dual-earner families provide for their children a model of higher female status and independence, and of a more equal economic and domestic partnership between the sexes, which is appropriate for the roles which the children themselves will almost certainly take on in adult life. Maternal employment is now the rule rather than the exception, and is likely to remain so.

Is 'the family' declining?

Look again at the changes in family structure outlined in box 14.1. Clearly, the nature of the family has radically altered in recent years, and the changes bring problems of adjustment for the people (which means most of us) who are caught up in them, other problems for politicians and social scientists seeking to understand them, and anxiety for the many theologians and moralists who see them as indicating a dangerous decline in moral values and in emotional security, most of all for children. Lone parenthood is often associated with low income and stress, at least for the parent. Divorce is often traumatic, involving both emotional and financial problems for the divorcing partners and if there are children for them too.

But divorce, like other problematic life events, is not the end of the world. It can have positive effects when an unsatisfying relationship ends, and in a sense less negative effects when, as we have seen already, it is increasingly common and when the social stigma attached to being divorced has largely disappeared. Diversity in partnering and parenting patterns is here to stay, is increasingly accepted, and does not necessarily mean a decline in the human values which bring people to form and foster relationships.

Recommended Reading

Fitzpatrick, M. A. and Vangelisti, A. L. (eds) (1995) *Explaining Family Interactions*. Thousand Oaks, CA: Sage. [A wide-ranging review of research into family relationships, largely but not entirely from North American perspective.]

Kabanoff, B. (1980) Work and non-work: a review of models, methods, and findings. *Psychological Bulletin*, 88, 60–77. [A classic review of relations between work and leisure.]

Social Trends Produced annually by the Office of National Statistics and published by HM Stationery Office. [A valuable source for survey data and other statistics quoted in this chapter.]

References

Berryman, J. C. (1985) *The Psychological Effects of Unemployment*. Leicester: University of Leicester, Department of Adult Education. [Reviews effects of unemployment, including its links with higher rates of anxiety, depression and attempted suicide.]

Buss, D. (1985) Human mate selection. *American Scientist*, 73, 47–51. [A discussion of non-randomness in mate selection and of ways in which partners resemble one another.]

Carstensen, L. L., Gottman, J. M. and Levenson, R. W. (1995) Emotional behavior in long-term marriage. *Psychology and Aging*, 10, 140–9. [Reports that older couples interact and feel more positively towards each other than do younger couples.]

Colley, A. M. (1986) Sex roles in leisure and sport. In D. J. Hargreaves and A. M. Colley (eds), *The Psychology of Sex Roles*. London: Harper and Row. [Examines gender differences in leisure participation.]

Davies, D. R., Matthews G. and Wong, C. (1991) Ageing and work. In C. L. Cooper and I. T. Robinson (eds), *International Review of Industrial and Organizational Psychology*, vol. 6. London: Wiley. [A comprehensive review of research concerned with the older worker.]

Dodd-McCue, D. and Wright, G. B. (1996) Men, women and attitudinal commitment: the effects of workplace experience and socialization. *Human Relations*, 49, 1065–91 [A study comparing work commitment and job satisfaction of men and women.]

Furnham, A. and Zacherl, M. (1986) Personality and job satisfaction. *Personality and Individual Differences*, 7, 453–9. [A review of studies in this area, concluding that the important factor for job satisfaction is 'person–job fit'.]

Gilford, R. and Bengtson, V. (1979) Measuring marital satisfaction in three generations: positive and negative dimensions. *Journal of Marriage and the Family*, 41, 15–50. [A detailed analysis of differences among young, middle-aged and old marriages in positive and negative feelings of spouses towards each other.]

Glenn, N. D. (1990) Quantitative research on marital quality in the 1980s: a critical review. *Journal of Marriage and the Family*, 52, 818–31. [Discusses evidence relating to trends in marital satisfaction over time.]

Hodson, R. (1989) Gender differences in job satisfaction: why aren't women more dissatisfied? *Sociological Quarterly*, 30, 385–99. [Suggests some explanations for women's high job satisfaction in spite of objectively inferior working conditions.]

Hoffman, L. W. (2000) Maternal employment: effects of social context. In R. D. Taylor and M. C. Wang (eds), *Resilience Across Contexts: Family, Work, Culture and Community*. Mahwah, NJ: Erlbaum. [Reviews her own and others' work on effects of maternal employment.]

Horwood, L. J. and Fergusson, D. M. (1999) A longitudinal study of labour force participation and child academic achievement. *Journal of Child Psychology and Psychiatry*, 40, 1013–24. [Finds that apparent relation between maternal employment and children's school achievement is due to other factors, such as birth order, family income and mother's education.]

Huston, T. L. and Vangelisti, A. L. (1995) How parenthood affects marriage. In M. A. Fitzpatrick and A. L. Vangelisti (eds), *Explaining Family Interactions*. Thousand Oaks, CA: Sage. [Review of studies examining impact of parenthood on marital happiness.]

Kessler, R. C. and MacRae, J. A. (1982) The effect of wives' employment on the mental health of married men and women. *American Sociological Review*, 47, 216–27. [Report on large-scale study, which found that wives' employment was positively related to their mental health but negatively related to mental health of their husbands.]

Levinson, D. (1978) *The Seasons of a Man's Life.* New York: Knopf. [Discussion of life stages based chiefly on in-depth study of men aged 35–45.]

Levinson, D. (1996) *The Seasons of a Woman's Life.* New York: Knopf. [Extends his earlier studies of life stages in men to consideration of women's life trajectory.]

Loher, B. T., Noe, R. A., Moeller, N. L. and Fitzgerald, M. P. (1985) A meta-analysis of the relation of job characteristics to job satisfaction. *Journal of Applied Psychology,* 70, 280–9. [Examines relations between job characteristics and job satisfaction, compiling evidence from 28 studies.]

O'Brien, G. E. (1981) Leisure attributes and retirement satisfaction. *Journal of Applied Psychology,* 66, 371–84. [Examines the contribution of different types of leisure activity to life satisfaction in retirement.]

Pina, D. L. and Bengtson, V. L. (1993) The division of household labor and wives' happiness: ideology, employment, and perceptions of support. *Journal of Marriage and the Family,* 55, 901–12. [Explores relations among household task sharing, full-time employment, egalitarian attitude and wives' happiness.]

Rhodes, S. R. (1983) Age-related differences in work attitudes and behavior: a review and conceptual analysis. *Psychological Bulletin,* 93, 328–67. [Review of large number of studies of age and work.]

Salthouse, T. A. and Maurer, T. J. (1996) Aging, job performance, and career development. In J. E. Birren and K. W. Schaie (eds), *Handbook of the Psychology of Aging,* 4th edn. New York: Academic Press. [A recent chapter reviewing studies of age and work.]

Singh, V. and Vinnicombe, S. (2000) Gendered meanings of commitment from high technology engineering managers in the United Kingdom and Sweden. *Gender, Work and Organization,* 7, 1–19. [Concludes from interviews with men and women managers and senior technologists that women are not less committed to work than men but may express and interpret commitment differently, and that differences in expression may harm their access to career development.]

Staines, G. L., Pottick, K. J. and Fudge, D. A. (1986) Wives' employment and husbands' attitudes toward work and life. *Journal of Applied Psychology,* 71, 118–28. [Reports that wives' employment is negatively related to their husbands' mental health, and discusses possible reasons.]

Sternberg, R. and Barnes, M. L. (1988) *The Psychology of Love.* New Haven, CT: Yale University Press. [Discusses adult love, including Sternberg's own 'triangular theory'.]

Tiedje, L., Wortman, C., Downey, G., Emmons, C., Biernat, M. and Lang, E. (1990) Women with multiple roles: role-compatibility perceptions, satisfaction, and mental health. *Journal of Marriage and the Family,* 52, 63–72. [Examines employed mothers' perceptions of combining work with parenting, and relates their experiences of conflict and of positive effects to happiness and mental health.]

White, L. and Edwards, J. N. (1990) Emptying the nest and parental well-being: an analysis of national panel data. *American Sociological Review,* 55, 235–42. [Argues that departure of last child from parental home increases satisfaction of parents.]

15
Growing Old

- Personality and ageing
- Retirement and leisure
- Families in later life
- Becoming a grandparent
- The never married
- Coping with bereavement
- Coming to terms with dying

What happens to us as we grow old? When we are young and old age seems a long way off, we tend to think of it as a rather depressing time of declining health and capacity with only death to look forward to. (Try doing exercise 15.1) Certainly late adulthood – from, say, the 60s onwards – brings some disadvantages and difficulties. Energy levels may be reduced, and older people are generally less capable of strenuous physical exertion. Sensory capacities, especially vision and hearing, but also taste and smell, are likely to show signs of impairment. In many tasks older people work more slowly and respond more cautiously, especially if the tasks are difficult or complex, and they also tend to obtain lower scores on standard intelligence tests and, often, tests of learning and memory, which to some extent can be

Exercise 15.1

Beliefs about Different Ages

Ask as many people as possible to rate typical members of three adult age groups, by filling in three rating sheets. Each sheet lists a number of characteristics; ask your volunteers to place a tick in one of the five columns alongside each statement, to show how true he or she believes it to be. The first rating sheet is shown below.

People aged 20–29 are likely to be	Very true	Quite true	Don't know	Quite untrue	Very untrue
1 Creative					
2 Serene					
3 Lonely and isolated					
4 Forgetful					
5 Cranky					
6 Good at learning new things					
7 Happy					
8 Opinionated					
9 Independent					
10 Boring					
11 Selfish					
12 Competent					

The second and third sheets are identical, except that the second is headed *People aged 45–55 are likely to be*, and the third *People aged 70 and over are likely to be*.

A tick in column 1 scores 5; column 2 scores 4, column 3 scores 3, column 4 scores 2, column 5 scores 1. Work out the average score for each characteristic and for each age group separately. Are the scores different for the age groups? What do they suggest about our beliefs about and expectations of people of different ages?

Most people would probably agree that items 1, 2, 6, 7, 9 and 12 are desirable characteristics and the rest undesirable. Try reversing the scores for the undesirable items, so that strong agreement gains a score of 1 rather than 5, strong disagreement a score of 5 rather than 1, and so on. Totalling the scores over all 12 items will now give you a 'desirability' rating overall. Are people in any one of the three age ranges seen to possess more 'desirable' characteristics than people in another?

If your participants are themselves of different ages, does the age of the rater make any difference to the way he or she rates people of different ages? And do the ratings of people who have plenty of contact with members of other age groups differ from those of people who have little present contact with people in age groups other than their own?

related to reduced *fluid intelligence* associated with an ageing brain: see the discussion of cognitive changes with age in chapter 8.

But impairments are not necessarily extreme, even in old age, and common stereotypes of old age often exaggerate its problems. In preliterate societies old people have often been valued, respected and even feared as sources of knowledge and wisdom. In contemporary industrialized societies such as our own, in contrast, they often seem to be negatively valued, regarded as senile, past it and a worthless drain on the nations' economic and social resources. Our society is to some extent ageist, just as it is, sometimes, sexist and racist, but with the bizarre distinction that while men are unlikely to become women, or whites to become blacks, we are all – barring accidents – likely to become old.

Compensating for decline

Although there is some decline in capacities as we age, this does not mean that everyday functioning has to suffer. To a considerable extent we can cope with minor difficulties and find ways of living as efficiently as we have always done. Paul Baltes has described adaptation to growing older as 'selective optimization with compensation'. We select the most important concerns and priorities for attention; we focus our energies and work to optimize our achievements in these areas; and we use compensation by accepting external supports in areas where we cannot perform well without help. Compensation includes seeking help from other people, but it also includes such obvious external aids as glasses, hearing aids, and shopping lists if we do not trust our memories.

Old age – the last developmental stage

What have life-stage theorists such as those mentioned in chapters 14 and 16 had to say about the 'developmental tasks' of late life? The theorist who has paid most attention to old age is Erik Erikson. Like Daniel Levinson, whose ideas were described in chapter 14, he proposed that the major task of middle life was to achieve generativity – a sense of our own worth in terms of the contribution we make to others, and in particular later generations. For many people generativity may continue into old age, via work, social involvement and family roles such as grandparenting. But eventually, Erikson argued, we face a final developmental task: to achieve *ego integrity* rather than despair. It requires that we become more inward-looking than before, and spend more time in contemplation and reminiscence. We have to review what we have made of our lives, accept what has passed and what has been achieved, and see meaning and fulfilment in it.

As we shall see in chapter 16, life-stage accounts such as Erikson's and Levinson's need careful assessment because of the interesting but often subjective nature of the evidence on which they are based. For example, are older people in fact more introspective, less socially engaged than younger people? Is such 'disengagement' positively related to happiness or satisfaction with life? The following section includes some discussion of these issues.

Personality in Later Life

People often assume that our personalities change as we grow older. William Fleeson, Jutta Heckhausen and Joachim Krueger, for example, have found that young and old adults generally agree that 'undesirable' personality traits increase in strength, and 'desirable' ones decrease, after about 30–40 years of age, and 'old people' are often considered stubborn and rigid, irritable and complaining, withdrawn, passive and dependent. However, late life is not seen just as a time of decline. Some 'desirable' traits, such as serenity and contentment, are perceived to increase with age, and each age is seen to have its own advantages.

Most studies find that personality does not change substantially in adulthood, particularly when cohort differences arising from different socialization experiences can be allowed for. Probably the most influential work in this area has been that of Robert McCrae and Paul Costa, who examined the evidence concerning five general traits or dispositions: neuroticism, extraversion, openness to experience, conscientiousness and agreeableness. They found virtually no age-related change in these dimensions between the ages of 35 and 85. When marked personality change does occur it is likely to be evidence of ill health or pathological senility. Indeed, Bernice Neugarten suggested that with advancing age people become more like themselves: essential characteristics become more salient, and, perhaps because social pressures and expectations ease after retirement and the end of active parenting, underlying features, needs and wishes that have been muted in earlier life are more fully expressed (as an example, see the discussion of gender typing in late life in chapter 11).

However, there may be some modification of personality with age. Dan McAdams, for example, argued that, while underlying traits and dispositions of the kind measured by McCrae and Costa show stability throughout adult life, change may occur in measures of personality which are more directly related to our current concerns and priorities and to the way we integrate and organize them into our plans and activities. McAdams described these as level 2 and 3 personality traits, in contrast to level 1 traits, as he termed them, researched by McCrae and Costa. Laura Carstensen suggested in her 'socioemotional selectivity' theory that as we grow older our goals become less expansive and future-oriented, and more concerned with the present, with current needs and sources of satisfaction, and with people to whom we are close. Finally, some studies examining dispositional traits such as those studied by McCrae and Costa report what seem to be genuinely age-related changes; it is quite often, though not always, found that old people become less active and more passive in their attitudes and adaptation to events, and that they become more introverted and less sociable. Changes of these kinds have led to the theory of disengagement, which was proposed in the early 1960s by Elaine Cumming and William Henry.

Activity and disengagement

Cumming and Henry defined disengagement as a mutual withdrawal of the individual from social interaction, and of society from the individual. It can come about for various reasons. Changes in work and family roles, illness, reduced fitness and energy, communication difficulties and forgetfulness may all encourage withdrawal from social interaction and make it more difficult. It may also be that detachment and 'inner-directedness' arise as part of a general tendency for at least some old people to spend time looking back, reviewing and making sense of their lives – in Erikson's terms, striving to achieve *ego integrity*.

Cumming and Henry argued that disengagement is a natural and inevitable feature of late life. They also argued that it helps people to adjust to old age, and leads to greater life satisfaction and higher morale. But research by Neugarten, Robert Atchley and others has found that on the whole the relation between disengagement and life satisfaction is negative rather than positive. This has led to an opposing argument, so-called activity theory, that the maintenance of activity and social interaction is desirable and necessary to preserve our self-esteem and morale in later life.

There is rather more evidence in favour of activity as a predictor of happiness than in favour of disengagement. But this is at least partly because factors making for happiness, such as good health and adequate income, also make social interaction and leisure activities possible. There is no guarantee that being active will make you happy; if anything it is more likely that being happy will make you more active. And we shall see in the following section that only certain kinds of activity, particularly social interaction, are reliably related to life satisfaction in retirement.

Retirement and Leisure

In theory, retirement should have both good and bad sides: good because it is a stage of life free from the demands of work and of parenting, but bad because it may mean loss of income, social role and identity. Yet people often assume that retirement is only a negative experience, causally associated with lowered morale, life satisfaction and health and perhaps with increased mortality.

There is some evidence for poorer morale and health in retired people than in still-working people, and for greater death rates; but retired people are generally poorer and older than those still in work. Atchley, for example, found that about 50 per cent of retired people interviewed in the USA found adjustment to retirement difficult, but very few said that this was because they missed the work; rather, they quoted money, health problems and bereavement. When retirement is associated with poor health, it is often because poor health leads to retirement, rather than the other way round. As Terry Gall and her associates have pointed out, the impact of retirement is more likely to be adverse when the retirement is involuntary rather than a matter of choice, and when it is associated with poor health and limited

income. When these conditions do not obtain, retirement may be associated with improved health rather than the reverse (see, for example, the work of David Ekerdt and his colleagues).

It has also been suggested that the effect of retirement depends on a person's occupation and attitude to work – the nastier the job, the more favourable one's attitude to retirement, while the more we enjoy our work the less we wish to give it up. In fact studies of our attitudes to work and retirement find little or no relation between the two, and when some relation is found it is as likely to be positive as negative. This may be because, as Carstensen has argued, as we grow older and approach retirement our emotional investment in work becomes less, and other aspects of life such as family, friends, leisure and community activity are more central to our satisfaction and well-being; we referred to this finding in the context of job satisfaction in chapter 14.

Women's retirement

Most studies of retirement have been concerned with men, while a few have dealt with wives' adjustment to their husbands' retirement. It has often been assumed that retirement has less impact on women than on men, because women's domestic role continues after retirement from work and because they are more used to 'role inconstancy' throughout adult life. But studies of retired women tend to find that retirement can be just as traumatic for women as it is for men, more problematic in some cases, in fact, since women's lower rates of pay and often interrupted work history may result in appreciably lower retirement income. A husband's retirement can also cause problems for his wife, since it can create more housework and limit her daytime freedom; Norah Keating and Priscilla Cole titled their research paper on the subject 'What do I do with him 24 hours a day?' Miriam Bernard and Chris Phillipson, in their review, pointed out that emphasis is now shifting, and needs to shift further, towards research into 'dual-retirement' families rather than into the classic but obsolescent case of the retiring husband and his unwaged wife.

Stages of retirement

People may adjust to retirement via a number of stages. Atchley, for example, suggested that there is typically a honeymoon phase, followed, six to 12 months after retirement, by disenchantment. This in its turn is followed by a period of reorientation and stability. There is some empirical evidence for stages of retirement, and adjustment to it, along roughly these lines, although the findings are not very consistent, and the timing of the stages appears to vary widely even when they are consistently reported; see the studies by Gall and Ekerdt and their associates.

Most women and men adjust satisfactorily to retirement, at least in the short term, and very many actively look forward to and enjoy it. The psychological impact of retirement, good or bad or a bit of both, is principally related to income and health. It is also likely to be related, as Donald Reitzes and his associates found, to personality: people who are well adjusted when working are likely to adjust happily to retirement. Adjustment may also be related to the existence of substitute activity – social, leisure and familial – both during working life and after retirement.

The importance of leisure activity

We saw in chapter 14 that patterns of leisure activity change somewhat after retirement. We also saw that leisure may bear varying relations, or no relation, to work – serving the same needs, compensating the needs that work does not satisfy, or entirely segregated from work in its characteristics and rewards. Does leisure activity play a different role after retirement? Some studies, although not all, suggest that it may. Alan Roadburg, for example, found that working and retired people have different perceptions of leisure activity: for those still in work, freedom and choice are important features of leisure activity, while retired people are more likely to stress the enjoyment and fulfilment it provides. Also, activities such as charity work and other volunteer activity which are classed as leisure activity before retirement tend to be classed as work after it. This suggests that to some extent leisure may take over from work after retirement, providing the sources of satisfaction that work used to provide.

However, Gordon O'Brien and others have found that the features seeming to make for satisfaction with work do not always appear to make for satisfaction with retirement. Variety of occupation and the opportunity to utilize one's skills were important predictors of job satisfaction, but were not particularly relevant to satisfaction with retirement, for which the most important predictor was social participation (which, as we saw in chapter 14, is important for job satisfaction for women, but not noticeably for men). This underlines the comment already made, that the nature of satisfaction and well-being may change in emphasis as we grow older. For more discussion of leisure activity in retirement, see the review chapter by Miriam Bernard and Chris Phillipson.

Families in Later Life

Psychologists who study family relationships in late life have to face the enormous problem that the nature of 'the family' varies considerably between different societies and, within the same society, between different birth cohorts (some recent changes in family structure were discussed in chapter 14). So our discussion can really apply only to the present, and can not predict what older families will look like in 20 or 30 years' time; it also means that most studies comparing younger and older marriages, which are cross-sectional, are so contaminated by differences in birth date and cultural experience that they are very hard to interpret. Most studies have taken place in Britain and the USA, and many of them have taken little or no account of ethnic groups within those cultures, which of course limits our knowledge even more.

Parents and adult children

When active parenting ceases, the parent–child relationship goes on. Although very few parents live with their adult children (fewer than 10 per cent in the USA and Britain, according to surveys), most of them live fairly close, see them often and talk to them over the telephone. It has been suggested that the strongest link is between mother and daughter, showing both the most frequent contact and the strongest emotional attachment. As Karen Fingerman has pointed out, the link is strong, but it is often lopsided: mothers may be more emotionally involved with their adult daughters than the daughters with them, and daughters are more likely to criticize their mothers and report differences of opinion.

Generally studies have found that the quality of parent–child relationships contributes to well-being in old age, and that parents and adult children offer each other mutual help: for example, mothers help with their daughters' children, daughters help their mothers in illness or after bereavement. Mutual help is associated with attachment, but it can also be associated with resentment and misunderstanding; both sides may find the burden of care oppressive, and if parents, particularly mothers, become more frail and dependent upon their child or children it can be difficult for both sides to come to terms with a reversal of the caring relationship that existed when the family was younger.

Grandparenting

Grandparenting takes many different forms. As Peter Smith pointed out in a recent review, early studies often reported conflict, particularly between mothers and grandmothers, over the way children should be brought up, grandmothers' views being more strict and inflexible. Later studies, from the 1960s onwards, recorded much more diversity in the line that grandparents were likely to take. They found a shift towards a more formal or detached style, and also towards a fun-loving role, in which grandparents were the source of treats and gifts; see, for example, the description by Andrew Cherlin and Frank Furstenberg of 'the new American grandparent'. Grandparents may also be reservoirs of family wisdom, preserving and passing on family history and traditions, a role which has been stronger in agrarian and developing societies than in developed urban ones. They may take an active part in family outings and share their grandchildren's activities; they may be 'someone to talk to' or a source of sympathy and advice when a child feels unable, for one reason or another, to talk freely to parents.

The form grandparenting takes depends, of course, on individual personality and preference, and also on such factors as geographical proximity (not much chance of shared activities if you live 100 miles apart). Grandparenting style also changes with the age both of grandparents and of grandchildren. Finally, the involvement of grandparents with their grandchildren depends partly on gender – grandmothers are generally more involved than grandfathers – and also on lineage, the mother's parents, particularly her mother, tending to be most involved with their grandchildren and considered closest by them.

Is grandparenting enjoyable?

Many people report that grandparenting is a source of pleasure and satisfaction, but the role can be problematic. If people become grandparents comparatively young (or even not so young), they may feel too young and 'not ready yet' for the label and public image of an elderly person which their status may bring. If they become grandparents comparatively late, say in their 70s, they may regret that they will probably not have enough time left to enjoy their grandchildren and watch them grow up. Grandmothers, in particular, may resent a loss of freedom if they find themselves frequently or regularly called on to help with the children, by babysitting or taking over childcare from working parents; a survey carried out by ICM and the *Guardian* newspaper in December 2000 found that more than one-third of grandparents interviewed reported spending more than 21 hours a week looking after their grandchildren.

Margaret Jendrek talked to grandparents who for one reason or another had become primary caregivers for their grandchildren, and found that most reported physical and financial stress, and also worry. But they also reported positive aspects of their experience: new friendships, changes in activity, the companionship and love of their grandchildren and the feeling of helping and caring for others in a difficult situation.

More evidence of the positive value people place on their grandparenting comes from the distress they can feel if they lose contact with their grandchildren. If parents divorce or separate, or if one dies, grandparents often step in to help, and their contact with the grandchildren can increase; but it may decrease drastically if the parents form new partnerships. Preserving such a relationship can require care, tact, patience and effort; and the additional relationship of step-grandparenting may enter the equation. Grandparenting, like parenting, involves both pain and gain.

The never married

We saw in chapter 14 that marriage and parenting bring problems as well as pleasure, and in this chapter that relations with adult children and grandchildren can be difficult in later life; and long-term partnerships such as marriage end, if not in divorce, almost inevitably in bereavement. What of people who have never married? Do comparisons suggest that the benefits of having been married outweigh the costs in older age, or vice versa? We speak of marriage rather than of other partnerships because, at the present time, older people have grown up in a culture in which marriage has been the norm. At present few people aged over 65 have never been married (less than 10 per cent of the 65+ population in the UK, perhaps only 5 per cent or even less in the USA).

It has sometimes been argued that never-married people may be at risk in late life because of social isolation and the absence of children as potential caregivers; they may also suffer from negative images of 'singlehood' as well as from ageism. Women may be particularly vulnerable: in popular culture (for example in humour) spinsters have often been objects of derision, while bachelors are seen as having escaped marriage (although they may also be assumed to be gay, not always with approval or tolerance). But it has also been suggested that the never-married are protected from certain stresses, most notably bereavement, and that their old age may therefore be easier in terms of intimacy and isolation. Jaber Gubrium found that never-married people in old age were a 'special type' in terms of personality: they were socially fairly isolated, but not lonely, and their isolation seemed to have been something of a life-long pattern. He also found, as others have found, that their satisfaction with life was no lower than that of married individuals and considerably higher than that of the divorced or widowed. However, Robert Rubinstein, in a series of studies conducted throughout the 1980s and 1990s, found that never-married older people were not necessarily isolated, often had close friends and did not appear to have been 'lifelong isolates'; *some* were lonely, *some* reported suffering from the stereotypes described above, and they were as likely as others to suffer bereavement and loss. Rubinstein concluded that it is unwise to generalize either about the miseries or about the benefits of being single in old age.

Death and Dying

Death is the last life event we shall experience, and it differs, of course, from other life events in that there is no post-adaptation stage from which we can view it. However, in recent years there has been a great deal of interest in the study of death – on the one hand in attitudes to death as a concept, and on the other hand in how people come to terms with dying.

Death anxiety

Most people, not surprisingly, have experienced some anxiety about, or fear of, dying: they are worried about the prospect of pain, about the loss of independence, and sometimes about the 'nothingness' that death brings. There is quite a sharp distinction between attitudes to death and attitudes to dying. Nobody likes the idea of dying, but many people are in favour of euthanasia, at least in principle, and feel that death can be preferable to life when life means irremediable pain or discomfort, mental deterioration, loss of independence and usefulness or 'being a burden'. But approval of euthanasia is easier in theory than in practice; and Victor Cicirelli, for example, found that over half of the elderly people he interviewed said they would wish to go on living even if they were terminally ill, or suffering from senile dementia or some other distressing and irreversible condition. Generally older and younger adults have similar views about 'good' and 'bad' deaths. 'Good' deaths are 'easy' and 'tranquil'; they may be very quick, or they may involve a 'proper leave taking' in the setting of a united (or reunited) family. 'Bad' deaths are those that are 'off-time', either too early or too late, or 'protracted', involving a loss of dignity and control for the dying person and an intolerable emotional (and often physical) burden for family and carers. There is also a general agreement that death is more tragic when it happens to the young than to the old, who have 'lived their lives'.

Most studies report that elderly people think and talk about death more, and also more calmly, than younger adults. Robert Kalish suggested that this is because old people have had more exposure to death in the past, and also because they see their own deaths as being 'on-time' rather than 'off-time', since they have fewer life plans still to achieve. Another suggestion has been that *disengagement*, which we discussed earlier in the context of personality, prepares us for our own deaths by beginning the process of detachment from things and even people, which can be the hardest thing to bear in the prospect of dying. Other factors related to death anxiety include religious belief. Not surprisingly, people with a strong religious belief are least fearful of death; but confused or tepid believers are more anxious than atheists or agnostics.

Coping with bereavement

Bereavement in the context of studies of ageing is usually the death of a spouse or long-term partner, but other bereavements are important too: the death of parents, brothers, sisters and other family members, and the death of friends and confidants. All such bereavements are likely to bring grief and a sense of loss. Bereavement is also often associated with a greater than average incidence of physical and mental health problems, particularly during the first few months (see the discussion of 'stages of bereavement' by Colin Murray Parkes). But these findings can be difficult to interpret; for example, widowed people are likely to be older and in poorer health (even before their bereavement) than the still-married groups with whom they are often compared.

Some bereavements may be particularly problematic – for example the death of a child (including an adult child), or a death which involves hidden grief, such as the death of a gay partner the nature of whose relationship has not been openly acknowledged. Bereavement is also more distressing when the death occurs 'off-time', for example in youth or middle age, or when it is sudden and unexpected. Some researchers (for example Parkes) have found that adjustment is harder for widows than for widowers, some (for example Margaret and Wolfgang Stroebe) the reverse, others (for example Marjorie Feinson) that there is no reliable difference between the two.

Most counsellors of bereaved people agree that they need to accept the reality of the death, to mourn openly, to adjust to a new life, to learn to care again about living and to develop or renew attachments to others; see the discussion of counselling and stages of grief by Janet Belsky. But too firm prior expectations and ideas about 'acceptable' responses to bereavement and 'appropriate' time limits to grief are unlikely to be useful when adapting, or helping others to adapt, to loss.

Coming to terms with dying

How do people cope with the knowledge that they are terminally ill? One important consideration is that people are not always told that their illness is terminal; and
if you do not know, you can not adapt. But awareness is not all-or-none. Barney
Glaser and Anselm Strauss were among the first to point out that there are stages of
awareness, which range from 'closed awareness', in which the ill person is unaware
although the medical staff and the immediate family know the diagnosis, through
'suspected awareness' and 'mutual pretence', to 'open awareness', in which the
reality is acknowledged by all. Open awareness means that the dying person can
plan his or her remaining time and can be counselled and supported; but it can also
be emotionally exhausting, and sometimes family members and friends find it hard
to cope even if the dying person does not; they may withdraw from contact, leaving
him or her isolated. Being labelled dying can be disabling in itself, ending employment
and social life, for example, before it is medically necessary.

The stages of adaptation

Assuming that people are aware that their death is close, how do they adapt?
Elizabeth Kubler-Ross produced what remains the best-known account of the stages
of adaptation to dying. They range from denial, through anger, bargaining and
depression, to final acceptance, which is a stage largely empty of feeling. Any description of stages tends to imply both that people *have* to work through the stages
in order, and that they *should* progress through them to achieve successful adaptation: in this case, for instance, that the dying person should work his or her way
through various reactions to a state of acceptance, calm and absence of feeling.
Kubler-Ross's account has been criticized on both counts. The stages she describes
are not always present; they do not necessarily follow a set order, and they are
not exclusive to the experience of dying, having a lot in common with reactions
to bereavement and to other losses – loss of limbs, imprisonment. And we must
remember that 'successful dying', like 'successful ageing', may take many forms.
For some people peaceful acceptance is the right attitude to achieve; others may
find more integrity if they 'rage against the dying of the light', to take the poet
Dylan Thomas's famous words to his dying father.

Most people are agreed that the best support we can offer a dying person is to
tackle the various causes of distress which she or he may experience – pain and
other symptoms, which can be relieved by medical care, worries about those who
are about to be left behind, which can be reduced by financial and other kinds of
planning, and depression, helplessness and hopelessness, which may be reduced by
counselling. Initiatives such as the hospice movement in recent years have helped to
show that although dying may be a bitter experience it can also, strangely, be one of
fulfilment and even growth.

Recommended Reading

Belsky, J. (1999) *The Psychology of Aging*, 3rd edn. Pacific Grove, CA: Brooks/Cole. [An excellent, broad and up-to-date review, primarily North American in context.]

Bond, J., Coleman, P. and Peace, S. (eds) (1993) *Ageing in Society*. London: Sage. [Good reviews of areas covered in this chapter, with emphasis on British as well as American evidence.]

References

Atchley, R. (1976) *The Sociology of Retirement*. New York: Halstead. [A classic study of impact of retirement.]

Baltes, P. B. and Baltes, M. M. (eds) (1990) *Successful Aging: Perspectives from the Behavioral Sciences*. Cambridge: Cambridge University Press. [Contains chapter, by editors, on Baltes's theory of selective optimization with compensation.]

Bernard, M. and Phillipson, C. (1995) Retirement and leisure. In J. F. Nussbaum and J. Coupland (eds), *Handbook of Communication and Aging Research*. Mahwah, NJ: Erlbaum. [Reviews impact of retirement on retirees and their spouses and role of leisure activities in retirement satisfaction.]

Carstensen, L. L. (1995) Evidence for a life-span theory of socioemotional selectivity. *Current Directions in Psychological Science*, 4, 151–6. [Discusses how emotional investment and priorities change as people grow old.]

Cherlin, A. and Furstenberg, F. F. (1986) *The New American Grandparent*. New York: Basic Books. [An account of grandparenting styles in USA in 1970s and 1980s.]

Cicirelli, V. G. (1997) Relationship of psychosocial and background variables to older adults' end-of-life decisions. *Psychology and Aging*, 12, 72–83. [Examines old people's views about euthanasia.]

Cumming, E. and Henry, W. (1961) *Growing Old*. New York: Basic Books. [The classic statement of theory of 'disengagement' in late adulthood.]

Ekerdt, D. J., Bosse, R. and Levkoff, S. (1985) An empirical test for phases of retirement: findings from the Normative Aging Study. *Journal of Gerontology*, 40, 95–101. [Reports evidence for 'honeymoon' and 'disenchantment' phases in retirement, and less secure evidence for 'recovery' phase.]

Ekerdt, D. J., Bosse, R. and LoCastro, J. S. (1983) Claims that retirement improves health. *Journal of Gerontology*, 38, 231–6. [Reports that retirees often feel that their health has improved as result of retiring, although there is little objective evidence for either improvement or deterioration.]

Erikson, E. H. (1986) *The Life Cycle Completed*. New York: Norton. [A discussion of 'developmental tasks' of late adulthood.]

Feinson, M. C. (1986) Aging widows and widowers: are there mental health differences? *International Journal of Aging and Human Development*, 23, 241–55. [Concludes that overall there are no differences between men and women in adjustment to bereavement.]

Fingerman, K. L. (1996) Sources of tension in the aging mothers and adult daughters relationship. *Psychology and Aging*, 11, 591–606. [The title speaks for itself.]

Fleeson, W. and Heckhausen, J. (1997) More or less 'me' in past, present and future: perceived lifetime personality during adulthood. *Psychology and Aging*, 12, 125–36. [Asked young, middle-aged and old adults to describe themselves now, in the past and in the future, and found that people felt positively about themselves at all stages and saw special strengths and advantages in every life stage.]

Gall, T. L., Evans, D. R. and Howard, J. (1997) The retirement-adjustment process: changes in the well-being of male retirees across time. *Journal of Gerontology*, 52B, P110–P117. [Examines stages of adjustment to retirement, and factors which help or hinder it.]

Glaser, B. and Strauss, A. L. (1968) *A Time for Dying*. Chicago: Aldine. [Includes discussion of levels of awareness and their implications for adjustment to terminal illness.]

Gubrium, J. (1975) Being single in old age. *Aging and Human Development*, 6, 29–41. [A discussion of characteristics of never-married.]

Jendrek, M. (1993) Grandparents who parent their grandchildren: effects on life style. *Journal of Marriage and the Family*, 55, 609–21. [A review of costs and payoffs for grandparents who are primary caregivers for their grandchildren.]

Kalish, R. A. (1985) The social context of death and dying. In R. E. Binstock and E. Shanas (eds), *Handbook of Aging and the Social Sciences*, 2nd edn. New York: Van Nostrand. [Discusses attitudes to death and dying.]

Keating, N. and Cole, P. (1980) What do I do with him 24 hours a day? Changes in the housewife role after retirement. *Gerontologist*, 20, 84–9. [Looks at impact on their wives – not aways favourable – of husbands' retirement.]

Krueger J. and Heckhausen J. (1993) Personality development across the adult life span: subjective conceptions versus cross-sectional contrasts. *Journal of Gerontology*, 48B, P100–P108. [A study of old and young adults' opinions on how 'desirable' and 'undesirable' personality traits change with age.]

Kubler-Ross, E. (1969) *On Death and Dying*. New York: Macmillan.

McAdams, D. P. (1994) *The Person: An Introduction to Personality Psychology*, 2nd edn. San Diego, CA: Harcourt Brace Jovanovitch. [An examination of effects of ageing on various levels of personality.]

McCrae, R. R. and Costa, P. T. (1990) *Personality in Adulthood*. New York: Guilford Press. [A review of relevant studies, which concludes that personality in most respects remains stable rather than changing as people age.]

Neugarten, B. (1977) Personality and aging. In J. E. Birren and K. W. Schaie (eds), *Handbook of the Psychology of Aging*. New York: Van Nostrand. [Proposes that there is some change, but more stability, in personality with age, and that pre-existing personality traits become more marked in late life.]

O'Brien, G. E. (1981) Leisure attributes and retirement satisfaction. *Journal of Applied Psychology*, 66, 371–84. [Compares factors which make for job satisfaction with characteristics of leisure activity.]

Parkes, C. M. (1986) *Bereavement*, 2nd edn. London: Tavistock. [A general review.]

Reitzes, D. C., Mutran, E. J. and Jernandez, M. E. (1996) Does retirement hurt well-being? Factors influencing self-esteem and depression among retirees and workers. *Gerontologist*, 36, 649–56.

Roadburg, A. (1981) Perceptions of work and leisure among the elderly. *Gerontologist*, 21, 142–5. [Examines different meanings of leisure for retired and still-employed people.]

Rubinstein, R. L. (1987) Never married elderly as a social type: re-evaluating some images. *Gerontologist*, 27, 108–13. [A review of psychological characteristics of the never-married, coming to conclusions rather different from Gubrium's.]

Smith, P. K. (1995) Grandparenthood. In M. H. Bornstein (ed.), *Handbook of Parenting*, vol. 3: *Status and Social Conditions of Parenting*. Mahwah, NJ: Erlbaum. [A good review of recent research as well as of 'old-fashioned' stereotypes.]

Stroebe, M. and Stroebe, W. (1980) Who suffers more? Sex differences in health risks of the widowed. *Psychological Bulletin*, 93, 279–301. [A careful analysis of evidence, concluding that elderly men are more at risk than elderly women and discussing possible reasons.]

Thomas, D. Do not go gentle into that good night. In *Collected Poems 1934–1953*. London: Phoenix. [A poem to poet's dying father, urging him to 'rage against the dying of the light'.]

16

Studying Development

- The hypothesis
- Methods in developmental psychology
- Correlational studies
- The experimental method
- Longitudinal and cross-sectional studies
- Studying life-span development
- Reliability and validity

- *How does the baby perceive the world* in utero?
- *What is the role of love in human development?*
- *How does personality develop?*
- *Why do children play?*
- *How do children learn language?*
- *Is children's thinking different from that of adults?*
- *Can we measure intelligence successfully?*
- *How do children acquire aesthetic appreciation?*
- *Do children have a sense of right and wrong?*
- *Is adolescence always a time of problems and stress?*
- *In what ways does ageing change a person?*

Psychologists have tried to answer all these questions, and of course many more. Just a few of the methods they have used have been outlined in chapter 1, and you, the reader, will have gleaned something about methodology as each study was described. Let us look at the current state of this developing 'science'.

John Watson was a highly influential figure in the early years of research in developmental psychology. Watsonian behaviourism emphasized that experience influenced the shaping of a person. There was an emphasis on learning. What do children learn? When? How? In recent years the methods of the *ethologists* (those who emphasize the importance of research on animals in their natural habitat) have begun to have considerable impact on developmental psychology. Ethologists have traditionally emphasized the innate qualities of an organism. In studying animal behaviour they looked for 'species-specific' patterns. Behaviour just as much as structure (morphology) was seen as something that evolved and behaviour patterns could be considered just as characteristic of a particular species as its shape, size or colour. The notion that many animals were programmed to behave in quite specific ways may seem highly inappropriate when applied to humans. We see ourselves as infinitely flexible creatures. Instinctive patterns are for the birds and bees; human responses are more subtle, highly tuned by experience to fit each situation. It is easy to get into this nature–nurture debate and assume that one or the other is more influential, but as we shall see this dichotomy is, in itself, a valueless one, for each depends on the other and the interaction between them is crucial in shaping an organism.

Although the methods used by the ethologists grew out of a concern with the 'innateness' of behaviour patterns, it is their techniques of observation that have been important in psychological methodology. Modern ethology places its emphasis on careful observation of a species before any form of experimentation, and this has added an important dimension to methodology in developmental psychology.

Niko Tinbergen argues that when we ask questions about behaviour we are actually looking at four different levels of question:

1　Why does the animal behave in this way now? [Immediate causation.]
2　How did this particular individual grow up to respond this way? [Development and learning.]
3　What use is this response to the animal? [Survival value.]
4　Why does this kind of animal solve this problem in this particular way? [Evolutionary origins.]

Thus we can see that learning has a place, but it is only one possible facet in a range of answers to the questions which we can ask of behaviour. Take the example of the behaviour called rooting (searching for the nipple) in babies. The immediate causation may be the touch of the mother's nipple on her baby's cheek. In terms of development we know that this is a reflex – an unlearned response, but it is not an enduring feature of humans. If you touch your own cheek you will not find yourself turning towards that finger, for the reflex is lost early in development. Its use in survival would seem to be to facilitate feeding, enabling the baby to locate its source of food more efficiently. Finally, in evolutionary terms these questions concern the nature of mammalian infant feeding systems and their evolution.

The rooting reflex is an innate response, but to a new parent this is not necessarily evident. A mother may try to help her newborn locate her nipple by nudging its cheek towards her breast. In so doing she impedes the infant's progress to her nipple, for it will move towards her fingers and away from her breast. Thus our everyday understanding of behaviour may not reveal the true cause of a given behaviour pattern.

As we mentioned earlier, the ethological approach emphasizes careful *naturalistic* observations before any form of controlled experimentation. Prolonged observation leads to the generation of more realistic hypotheses. Armchair speculation, or even speculation in the laboratory, can lead to ludicrous questions which have no bearing on what children or adults do in real life.

Sit and watch

This first phase of research is to do just that. Observe your participants unobtrusively and see what they do. Make notes but avoid using major categories (categories that are too broad) in classifying behaviour. 'The girl showed frequent bouts of aggression' tells us nothing for the observer has already classified the behaviour. Ethologists distrust major categories and prefer simple description of movements, facial expressions and so on. The advantage of using a method originally developed for non-human animals is that with humans it is difficult not to be emotionally involved, and hence lacking in objectivity.

Events that we consider insignificant may be important in explaining subsequent behaviour. Yawning in higher primates (including us) is an example. This pattern is not just something to do with being tired – it also reveals a lot about the dynamics of the social situation and the status of the individuals (their level of anxiety for instance) within it. Only careful analysis of sequences of behaviour in primates led to this conclusion. The same applies to humans – we must avoid making assumptions about which types of behaviour are important and which are not.

Nick Blurton Jones warns against the idea that if we want to study aggression or attachment we must look for a 'good' measure of it. Counting movements of all kinds may be difficult, but if we decide what is meaningful before embarking on research then why bother with the research?

Because humans can talk, we have a tendency to short-circuit the time-consuming observation phase by asking questions. Indeed introspection was a major source of data for early psychologists, but it is only one facet of reality. Sigmund Freud relied heavily on what his patients said, or dreamt, or indeed left unsaid, but when formulating his ideas about psychosexual development he was not out in the field observing babies and children. He constructed a view of the 'normal' child's psychosexual development (see chapter 11 for details) via the preoccupations of his adult patients and the concerns of childhood elicited during psychoanalysis, but his view of normality was also generated through his observation of those who might be considered abnormal. Had Freud been an ethologist today it is unlikely that the notion of the Oedipus complex would have emerged.

The hypothesis

After the observation phase comes the posing of questions and the generation of a testable hypothesis. While questions may be broad and general, hypotheses must be quite specific. For example, 'What factors foster the development of love in human babies?' is an important and interesting question, but the psychologist needs to be precise about his or her choice of factors, the definitions of babies (the age range) and the expression of love by babies. The hypothesis can only take on one minute element of this question. It may be necessary to limit the study to infants aged 3 months and to explore the impact of the amount of physical contact they receive from specific caregivers. Now, the hypothesis, which is a statement of prediction, could be 'Increased physical contact between the mother (or main caregiver) and the baby facilitates the development of attachment by the baby.' This statement is now testable, and a study can be planned to verify or refute it.

Methods in Developmental Psychology

It is likely that the hypothesis generated above has been derived from the observational phase of research. The psychologist starts out with a hunch of some sort and then carries out some observations of babies and their caregivers before deciding how to proceed. In the example linking physical contact and more rapid attachment formation in infants, one of the most obvious methods of proceeding might be the *correlational study*.

Correlational studies

In this we might select a group of babies and mothers and record the frequency of all forms of physical contact in a given period, then assess the development of the babies' attachment to their mothers during that same period. We should have to assess that development, and chapter 3 describes some widely used measures of attachment behaviour.

Suppose we find that the babies whose mothers classed as high on physical contact are also those babies who score high on measures of attachment behaviour, and that those scoring low on physical contact also score low on the latter measure – does this show clear support for our hypothesis?

It does not. Undoubtedly we have found a positive correlation between the frequency of physical contact and our measures of attachment, but we cannot conclude that one causes the other. Why not? Perhaps mothers who hold their babies more often also show other forms of maternal responsiveness more frequently than mothers who do not. Or perhaps Rudolph Schaffer's cuddliness factor influences the babies' behaviour. Perhaps non-cuddler babies prefer talking to touching, and hence we may need to take into account the infants' temperamental characteristics. It may be true that there is a causal relation between these two factors – but this correlational study cannot reveal it. A carefully controlled experiment may bring us closer to the answer. Nevertheless, absolute proof is an entirely different matter.

The experimental method

As we saw in the first chapter, the experimental method is designed so that the psychologist ideally controls all but one variable – the independent variable – and varies the amount of this variable in two or more groups or conditions. In reality it is impossible to control all but one variable. All our participants are individual and unique and thus introduce variability into the study. Following the design as described in chapter 1 we should select the participants from a particular population and randomly assign them to either the *experimental group* or the *control group*. Since in our study the independent variable is the amount of physical contact between mother and baby, one way of testing the effect of this variable might be to ask the mothers in the experimental group to adopt their normal daily regime with their babies but also to pick them up and hold them for an additional 60 minutes a day in not more than three separate sessions.

An adequate control group would not simply be given no instructions – mothers might be asked to spend at least 60 minutes close to their children but not physically touching them. Alternatively there could be two controls, one to whom no instructions were given and one like that described above.

In each group, attachment behaviour (the dependent variable) would have to be recorded throughout the study period. Let us say that the duration of the study was to be six months, from 3 to 9 months; since we know the time when attachments are typically formed we might expect to observe differences between the groups, should they occur, within this period.

The problems of experimental design

As you read this experiment it is probable that you are thinking: 'But what if . . . ?' Let us look at some problems.

- *How do we find participants?*
- *Do volunteers differ from non-volunteers?*
- *What do the participants think the experiment is about?*
- *How do the participants interpret the instructions?*
- *Do they try to please the experimenter?*
- *Do they behave differently because they are being studied?*
- *If participants drop out do they differ in some systematic way from those who do not?*
- *If they cannot or will not carry out the instructions do they say so?*
- *How ethical is it to interfere with something as important as how often mothers cuddle their babies?*
- *Can the experimenter really be objective when recording the dependent variable?*
- *Can the experimenter be consistent in the methods of recording over the period of the study?*

. . . and lots more.

Each of the questions above has to be considered carefully. It is unlikely that our participants will be a random sample of the population, so if volunteers are used the psychologist must be very cautious in the generalizations he or she may wish to make about the findings. The view the participants take of the study is important because it will undoubtedly influence their performances in the experiment.

If the participants know too much about the experimenter's hypothesis they are likely to be biased. Sometimes experimenters have to try a little subterfuge. But in our hypothetical study the experimenter is requiring a lot of the participants: to ask for 60 minutes contact a day is a tall order, even for willing participants. Eager-to-please mothers may go beyond the call of duty, and do more than the average mother might. Less eager mothers may drop out during the test period, or simply pretend that they have carried out the instructions rather than disappoint the researcher. The ethics of this study are tricky. Would you be prepared to do it? Even if an ethical committee accepted this proposal, the people invited to participate may feel differently.

Experimenters are just as human as their participants. Quite often it is said that the area psychologists choose to research reveals a lot about their personal concerns. Is physical contact a particular problem area for the psychologist planning this study? Has he or she a bit of a 'touch taboo' and wants to understand more about the role of physical contact in child development? Has he or she a vested interest in showing that touch is not so important as people believe? If so, will it bias his or her attitude in running the study? One way round this is to use an additional researcher blind to each participant's diagnostic category to assess the dependent variable. Thus in this example the researcher would not know which of the babies being assessed were in the 'extra contact' experimental group or either of the control groups.

Experiments play an important role in helping us understand causal relationships, but in exploring the whole of human psychological development we need to look at studies over a much longer period, as we outlined in chapter 1. This is where cross-sectional and longitudinal studies have a role.

Longitudinal and cross-sectional studies

As we saw in chapters 1 and 14, the main problem with these two methods is that they appear to give two different answers to the same question (see Figure 16.1).

Cross-sectional studies confound historical (or generational) changes with individual (or ontogenetic) changes. The generational differences may be so great that they account for most of the variation between different age groups studied at one point in time. Thus to attribute the observed differences to age *per se* is quite inappropriate. Longitudinal studies suffer from a loss of participants, problems associated with repeated testing and – a very practical problem for researchers – that funding for research rarely enables the psychologist to plan more than a few years ahead and hence undertake a long study. The loss of participants is important because in a longitudinal study those who drop out may be very different from those who stay. Thus the sample we end up with may be quite unlike the original participant population.

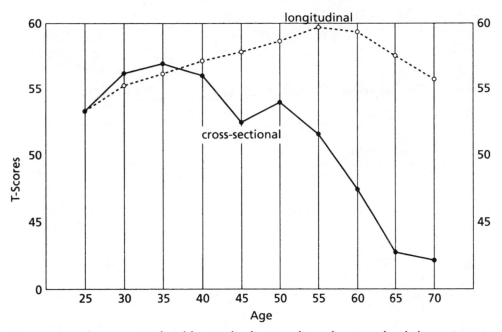

Figure 16.1   *Cross-sectional and longitudinal age gradients for tests of verbal meaning*

Schaie's 'most efficient design'

Warner Schaie and his colleagues were interested in exploring age-related changes in cognitive abilities and devised a 'most efficient design' for investigating both the impact of the cohort effect and the problem of the loss of participants in these two methods of study.

Schaie decided he would convert a cross-sectional study into a longitudinal one (to give what has been called a cohort sequential design – see chapter 8). In 1956 he carried out a cross-sectional study of cognitive abilities; seven years later in 1963 a follow-up was conducted, and he was able to re-test 60 per cent of the 1956 group. To deal with the loss of participants a new sample of participants was taken from the same population and age range in 1963, seven years after the first study, and this group was tested just as the 1956 group had been. This gave one longitudinal study over seven years and three cross-sectional studies, one in 1956 and two in 1963.

Seven years later Schaie was able to re-test the same population for a third time. This time he had data from some people for 14 years and data for many people for two distinct seven-year periods. Figure 16.2 shows comparative cross-sectional and longitudinal data for the space test (which is concerned with spatial visualization and is used as part of an intelligence test).

The particularly interesting result of these studies was, as we might have predicted, that later-born cohorts performed at a higher level than earlier-born ones.

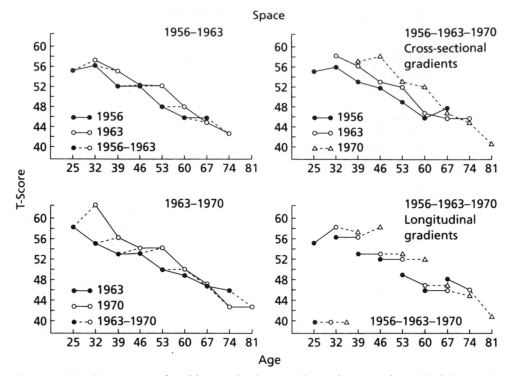

Figure 16.2   *Cross-sectional and longitudinal age gradients for tests of spatial ability*

Each generation appeared to be getting cleverer. Could this be true? Schaie's conclusion was rather different. He argued that in the areas of intellectual skills and abilities older people in general (and if they are reasonably healthy) are not showing a decline, but the skills and abilities they developed in their youth have become obsolete (see the discussion in chapter 8). Thus the further they are from their youth and from their experience of full-time education, the more decline they appear to show in a cross-sectional study. However, the longitudinal studies, which examine change within the individual, produce quite different results. Here the 14-year period revealed little decline until quite late in life: participants showed either an improvement or little change; only the oldest cohort showed a significant drop.

In summary, these findings appear to show that environmental change and ontogenetic change are interdependent. Age differences are not a guide to psychological change within a person; what we need to look at is the interlinkage between people and their life events.

Baltes's approach

Paul Baltes and his colleagues have developed this sort of idea further by identifying three major systems of influence on development. For each person the basic determinants of the influences which Baltes proposes are biology, the environment and the interaction between them. The extent to which any one of these may have an impact on a person varies. For instance, it is not possible to say that, at the level of the individual, intelligence is determined, say, 80 per cent by biological factors. The balance varies, and at present we cannot specify what that balance is.

The influences that shape development are in Paul Baltes's view 'normative age graded', 'normative history graded' and 'non-normative life events'. Age-graded events are said to be normative if they tend to occur in highly similar ways (their timing and duration) for all individuals in a culture (or subculture). They may have been determined by biological, or environmental factors or an interaction between them. Examples include education and schooling, puberty, marriage, having children, the menopause, retirement and so on; each of these is not set at one specific age but biological clocks and 'social clocks' play a greater or lesser part in determining when they occur. Thus the menopause is influenced more by the former and the age of retirement or marriage more by the latter. Normative history-graded influences again have the same biological and/or environmental determinants, but these are influences to which most members of a generation or cohort are exposed. Wars, major epidemics and economic depression would be examples. 'Non-normative life events' are events that do not occur in either of the above ways for most people. They are highly individual. Before proceeding further, look at exercise 16.1, which enables you to explore your own course of development.

Baltes suggests that examples of non-normative life events might be an accident, illness, career change, death of a loved one and so on. If we consider the impact of these three types of influence it is easy to see, particularly in cross-sectional research, why age *per se* may be a totally inadequate concept to explain differences or similarities between people. A child who has lived through a famine in Ethiopia, or the Ceauşescu regime in Romania, compared with one reared in an aristocratic family in the UK, and one who lives in the black ghettos of New York, has so little in common that age tells us nothing about her or his physical growth or psychological development.

Attempts to look at the lifespan in terms of developments beyond the purely biological time clock have produced some interesting findings.

Studying Lifespan Development

Most people recognize that throughout the course of human life there are important stages or milestones. Shakespeare reflected this view in his cynical and poetical description of the 'seven stages' in human life. Recently there have been more systematic attempts to identify stages in life common to individuals in a given culture.

Charlotte Buhler and others studied 400 biographies and autobiographies and from them discovered that certain phases repeatedly appeared in the lives which they analysed. They identified five biological phases that could be linked to five stages in psychosocial development (see table 16.1). Essentially, psychosocial development

Exercise 16.1

Looking at Your Own Life

Draw a horizontal line across a page and write birth at one end and death at the other. Now write all the main events and turning points in your psychological development along this 'life line', marking them at the appropriate places. Do not stop at the present; add all the main events that you anticipate are ahead of you. Think about your personal development rather than the more public events such as leaving school, marriage etc. Complete this task before reading further.

When you have completed your life line consider the following points.

1 Do you see your life in terms of stages or milestones? If so, how many events are influenced by biological change (e.g. puberty) and how many are not? What does this tell you about the relation between biological and psychological development?
2 At what time(s) in your life do you think that most learning occurs?
3 Are there things in your life which are important to you but for which you are aware that you are now too old?
4 Are there things in your life which are important to you but for which you feel you are still too young?
5 Are there times in your life when you have consciously assessed yourself and your life?
6 At what age do you expect to feel old and be aware of the constraints that age places on you?

Comment: There is no correct way to complete this task – it is a personal summing up of your psychological development. Compare your answers to those of your family and/or friends. You may be surprised to see how differently others view their lives.

was viewed in terms of goal setting. The theory considers the peak period of life to be the 20s, 30s and 40s, and the phase after 45 as one of contraction.

Life's problems and crises

Another approach to the life cycle has emerged from the clinical setting. Carl Jung, Alfred Adler and later Erik Erikson all formulated their views as a result of helping people with various types of psychological disorder. For Jung, life stages were

Table 16.1   *Buhler's biological and psychological phases of life*

Approximate age	Biological phase	Psychological phase
0–15	Progressive growth	At home, before self-determination of goals
16–25	Continued growth and ability to reproduce sexually	Preparatory expansion, experimental determination of goals
26–45	Stability of growth	Culmination
46–65	Loss of reproductive ability	Self-assessment after striving for goals
Over 65	Progressive growth and biological decline	Experience of fulfilment or failure

Adapted from Buhler, 1968

concerned with how a person dealt with problems of the psyche. In 'Youth', a period which he identified as from puberty to the middle years (around the age of 40), the concerns are focused on overcoming inferiority and coping with sexual drive. After this phase there are gradual changes which often involve an increase in rigidity and intolerance. Jung observed that in old age there may be a shift in psychological terms, so that an older woman may become more masculine and an older man more feminine.

Adler saw three great problems in life: social interest, occupation, and love and marriage. While these problems are not specifically associated with ages in life it is obvious that they are the almost universal concerns of the adult years.

Erikson identified eight 'ages of man' and saw the boundaries of each as a crucial turning point or crisis. As has already been noted (see chapter 4), he, like many others, saw most change occurring in the first part of life (see table 16.2) – five of his turning points occur under the age of 20, only three during the rest of life. In

Table 16.2   *Erikson's eight ages of man*

The ages (approximate)	Psychological crises of issues
1 Oral Up to 2 years	Basic trust versus mistrust
2 Anal 2–4 years	Autonomy versus shame, doubt
3 Genital 5–7 years	Initiative versus guilt
4 Latency 6–12 years	Industry versus inferiority
5 Adolescence 13–19 years	Identity versus role confusion
6 Young adult 20–30 years	Intimacy versus isolation
7 Middle adult 31–65 years	Generativity versus stagnation
8 Late adult	Integrity versus despair

Erikson's view how we cope with each stage influences our subsequent coping. Each age can be seen as a building block. If we cope successfully each block sits neatly on the one below; if not, then we may have a rocky tower, one that is easily knocked down by the slightest turbulence in life. Clearly the main foundations are laid in childhood, and it is on them that later coping depends. However, Erikson's intriguing theory has been criticized on several grounds. It is hard to prove empirically; it recognizes little in the way of coping or change during the major part of adult life; and it seems sex-biased very much in the direction of male rather than female adult development.

These approaches towards studying life show very clearly that, in psychological terms, age *per se* is not a crucial factor in shaping us. It is what happens to a person and the expectations of his or her particular society and culture in a given historical time that can have an overriding influence.

Other Research Methods

Studying twins

The influence of environmental factors was stressed in the preceding section, yet all of us are aware that biology must play a key role too. At the start of this chapter, it was noted that the ethologists emphasize this view, and these two approaches have sometimes given rise to the nature–nurture debate. Which is more important – biology or environment?

One way of examining the biological components of behaviour is to study twins. Identical twins are monozygotic (MZ): they come from a single egg and thus share *all* their genetic material. Fraternal twins are dizygotic (DZ): they come from the fertilization of two separate eggs, and thus genetically they are no more similar than ordinary siblings. Of course they share the uterus and are born at the same time, so if experience is to be more influential than biology we might predict that they should be just as similar as MZ twins at birth (on average). Sharing a uterus does not necessarily mean having identical environments: one twin may have a better position than the other. We are often particularly aware of this in the young of animals that have large litters. In a litter of piglets there is often a runt, one very small piglet that had the least advantageous part of the uterus.

If samples of MZ twins are compared with samples of DZ twins on any characteristic, we know that while the former share 100 per cent of their genes the latter share only 50 per cent on average. By correlating our measure with the twin type we may well find that the concordance rates (agreement between the correlations) of MZ twins and DZ twins differ. Hill Goldsmith and Irving Cottesman looked in this way at the heritability of activity level in babies and found a concordance rate of 0.57 for MZ twins compared with 0.35 for DZ twins (a significant difference), where 1.00 would be a perfect correlation. From this study we might conclude that biology plays a greater role in babies' activity levels than environment. But there are problems with this argument. Most babies are not twins, so using twin babies to help us explain behaviour in general may be misleading.

Another way of examining *heritability* is to use MZ twins reared together and compare them with those who, through force of circumstance, have been reared apart. This is quite an appealing method initially, because while holding the genetic component constant we can manipulate the environmental component to a greater or lesser degree. Studies of the incidence of various psychological disorders, such as schizophrenia, have used these methods to try to assess the influence of these two components on the likelihood that a person will suffer this disorder. The results of this work are not clear cut. Some studies find much higher concordance rates than others, thus suggesting that the influence of biology and environment is variable. Again there are problems with such research; the first problem, identified above – that most babies are not twins – still applies. Second, the families chosen to rear the separated twins are often fairly similar in terms of education, socioeconomic status and other characteristics, so that they do not represent the range of possible environments in which children can be reared.

Heritability is often misunderstood because some people believe that it reveals the degree to which a characteristic is determined by the genetic component in an *individual*. However, it can only ever be applied to populations. It is the extent to which a characteristic is determined by inherited components within a population, so at the level of the individual it tells us nothing. It is important to remember that genes and the environment are not separate components. Exactly how a given gene works, how it shows itself in the individual, depends on the type of environment it is in. The genes and the environment interact. Good examples are the Himalayan rabbit, the guinea pig and the Siamese cat.

In their infancy the young of these animals require a certain ambient temperature if they are to develop the light body with dark extremities (ears, nose, feet and tail) with which we are familiar. The expression of this genetic predisposition depends on the temperature of the skin during a critical period of postnatal development. Normally the extremities are cooler than the rest of the body, and at normal rearing temperatures they turn browny-black. If our kittens or guinea pigs are raised in a very warm atmosphere they remain light in colour, and if placed in an ice box they become uniformly dark.

So two individuals who are genetically identical may have different phenotypes as a result of very different environments, while two who are genetically very different may, because they share an environment, emerge very similarly.

Measures of heritability can give us a rough guide to the influence of genetic factors for a given sample, but for individuals it is an entirely inappropriate concept. It is also a rather dangerous concept, for if we mistakenly attribute a given characteristic to our genetic programming then this prevents us from considering the possibility that anything can be done to alter that characteristic. For example 'Boys are aggressive, it's in their nature' implies that we cannot change them so it is not worth trying. There may be genetic influences on aggression, but these undoubtedly interact with environmental influences. Since we can influence someone's environment but do very little about her or his genes (although this now is beginning to change) then it is surely to the former that we should direct our attention.

Case studies

In relation to the nature–nuture debate it was noted that heritability refers to populations and not individuals. Many psychological methods deal with fairly large samples of people, so that we can look for general rules governing behaviour, thought and emotion. Yet individually we all feel unique, and often when we read about psychological studies our reaction may be 'That doesn't apply to me, I behaved quite differently in those circumstances.' Exceptions to rules usually arise because generalizations do not allow for individual variation. One way of capturing the uniqueness of a person is to use a case study.

This method, which has often been used in the clinical setting, enables us to record a person's life in detail. It may involve interviews with the participant about his or her experiences, plus interviews with people who are close, family and friends for example. Memories of past events may be verified through historical records, so it is possible to reconstruct the participant's life as he or she and others see it. Case studies mentioned in this book include those of baby biographers such as Charles Darwin (in chapter 1), Isabelle, who was described by Kingsley Davis and was the little girl who made astonishing progress after many years of deprivation, and the 'wild boy of Aveyron' (in chapter 3). Case studies are usually of one person, but they may involve small groups.

While generalizations about people cannot be made from case studies, they may often provide interesting hypotheses. Jean Piaget's detailed records, or case studies, of his children referred to in chapter 7 led to his research on cognitive development. In his book *Living Through the Blitz* Tom Harrison shows that a person's memories of historical events differ quite dramatically from accounts documented at the time. Such work shows us that each of us interprets or construes the world in unique ways, depending on our own particular experiences. The truth, as each of us sees it, is only one facet of reality, yet trying to account for each person's way of viewing events is an important area in psychology and one, as we shall see in the next section, with which the discipline is now trying to grapple.

Qualitative methods

The case study is one method of examining a single individual in depth. It has always had a place in psychology, particularly in a clinical setting, as we noted in chapter 12, in which several childhood problems were considered. However, in general psychologists have tended to emphasize objectivity and a scientific approach. Today however things are changing, and during the past decade or so there has been a recognition that psychology needs also to take account of subjective experience.

See Karen Henwood and Nick Pidgeon's discussion of this topic: these authors point out that 'over-reliance upon theory testing and verification can lead to a neglect of strategies for the systematic generation of new theory'.

Qualitative research is research where the findings are not arrived at by means of statistical procedures or other methods of quatification. Data come from interviews, observations and various other sources, which could include personal accounts and other documentary evidence. Findings are arrived at by means of various different analytic or interpretative procedures, including techniques for conceptualizing data by means of 'coding'.

This approach has given rise to 'grounded theory' or theory grounded in experiences: unlike the traditional approach in psychology, one does not begin with a theory, but with an area of study, then what is relevant to that area is allowed to emerge. Or, as Anslem Strauss and Juliet Corbin note, 'Data collection, analysis and theory stand in reciprocal relationship to each other.'

Carol Gilligan (see chapter 10) and others have pointed out that a disregard for the subjective experiences of participants in psychological research may lead to research that lacks real meaning. Experiments have an important place in psychology, but this should not be at the expense of individual's accounts of their own experiences. Both have a place, and qualitative methods seek to be sensitive to people's own understanding within their own particular frames of reference.

Qualitative methods are widely used in disciplines such as sociology and anthropology, and we need to learn from these disciplines if we are to develop qualitative approaches within psychology. Even today there is still resistance from some quarters to the integration of these methods in psychology, but the need for change is gathering a momentum which will be hard to resist.

Surveys

When they want to make broad generalizations about people, researchers often use the survey method. Surveys have been carried out on everything from opinions about tomato ketchup to sexual behaviour, or the way people are likely to vote at an election. You will probably have been stopped in the street and asked your opinion of products.

Surveys often use very large samples of people who are selected so that they represent a given population. Audience research carried out for television and radio often involves samples of a thousand or more people who are chosen to represent the viewing or listening public. Thus the age, sex, educational background, socioeconomic status and many other variables have to be accurately identified in the whole of the population being researched and faithfully represented in the sample to be surveyed. If the sample is not representative, then the results will be biased. Surveys are typically *correlational studies*. They tell us much about the associations between types of people and behaviour patterns, but nothing about causes.

Reliability and Validity

If one psychologist carries out an experiment and finds some exciting results, these findings are not accepted until the research can be replicated by another researcher. Reliability in research is confirmed by the repeatability of the research. If the method is followed by another investigator, it should produce the same results if it is reliable. If it does not, then we may question the objectivity of the researcher and the care with which he or she has reported what was investigated. Research studies must always be reported in such a way that others can repeat the work. If the methodology is glossed over, then we are justified in questioning the findings. Cyril Burt is probably one of the most well-known psychologists whose unreliable methodology eventually emerged.

Research is *valid* when the test or assessment we are using measures what we think it measures. Early studies of intelligence in non-human animals involved setting many different species tasks such as maze learning. Some animals such as rats were found to be intelligent and others (many fish species) to be unintelligent. If by intelligence we mean the ability to solve certain problems, the difficulty was that the task set for a species was often highly inappropriate for it. Deep-sea fish are unused to mazes, and they rarely encounter walls in their environments, whereas rats are used to living in holes and are well suited to solving maze learning tasks. To conclude that certain fish are unintelligent on the basis of this sort of test is invalid. Such research merely tells us that these fish cannot learn mazes.

Laboratory work has often been criticized when researchers claim that their findings represent what people or other animals do in real life. If you took part in a psychology experiment in a laboratory it is unlikely that you would be your natural self in it. You might be shy or awkward, for instance. If the researcher were studying social skills and concluded that you were a shy and awkward person with others, the conclusion would probably be invalid. You might be exactly the opposite in real life; the psychologist and the laboratory may have produced a change in your behaviour. The essence of validity is this: does the test or experiment measure what the psychologist thinks it does? The method employed may be reliable – it can be replicated by other researchers – but are the results meaningful in the way that is claimed?

In Conclusion

Psychologists have developed a variety of methods to enable them to investigate many facets of human behaviour. If the questions asked are generated from careful observation of people in natural settings, then the hypotheses formed are likely to illuminate our understanding of people. However, even if the research methods are both reliable and valid there are many areas of human life that cannot be researched directly. Ethical issues may prevent us from being able to investigate experimentally, as we saw in chapter 1. In other areas of life we are restricted to correlational studies, which can never uncover the causes of human behaviour. However sophisticated the methodology, we shall never find all the answers. Each person is unique and mysterious, so developmental psychology faces a continual challenge in its attempts to explain the development of behaviour, emotion and thought. One of the exciting, and sometimes maddening, features of this subject is that there are no simple answers. We cannot explain a person's behaviour without reference to his or her unique biology and environment. The answers must always be prefaced by 'it depends' – because in psychological terms we are complex beings, and the causes of our behaviour are generally complex too. The answers we come up with today may be inappropriate for future decades.

Nevertheless psychological research has provided guidelines to help us deal with a host of human concerns: in the widest sense it has been used to shape social policy, and it has also had impact on us all at a most personal level.

Recommended reading

Coolican, H. (1999) *Research Methods and Statistics*. London: Hodder & Stoughton Educational. [An excellent general text book.]

Lisney, M. (1989) *Psychology: Experiments, Investigations and Practicals*. Oxford: Blackwell. [A useful guide on how to run psychological experiments.]

Schaie, K. W. and Willis, S. L. (1996) *Adult Development and Aging*. London: HarperCollins. [Chapter 5 is an excellent account of methods in developmental psychology.]

Strauss, A. and Corbin, J. (1990) *Basics of Qualitative Research: Grounded Theory Procedures and Techniques*. London: Sage. [An excellent text book on qualitative research; quote is on page 23.]

References

Baltes, P. B., Reese, H. W. and Lipsitt, L. P. (1938) Life-span developmental psychology. *Annual Review of Psychology*, 31, 65–110. [Baltes's approach to lifespan development.]

Blurton Jones, N. (1972) Characteristics of ethological studies of human behaviour. In N. Blurton Jones (ed.), *Ethological Studies of Child Behaviour*. Cambridge: Cambridge University Press. [Discusses ethological research and Tinbergen's four questions about behaviour.]

Buhler, C. (1968) The developmental structure of goal setting in group and individual studies. In C. Buhler and F. Massarik (eds), *The Course of Human Life*. New York: Springer. [Buhler's view of life cycle.]

Goldsmith, H. H. and Cottesman, I. I. (1981) Origin of variation in behavioural style: a longitudinal study of temperament in young twins. *Child Development*, 52, 91–103. [Activity levels in twins.]

Harrison, T. (1976) *Living Through the Blitz*. London: Collins. [Memories of historical events.]

Henwood, K. and Pidgeon, N. (1995) Grounded theory and psychological research. *The Psychologist*, 8(3), 115–18. [The discussion of grounded theory; quote is on page 116.]

Hofer, M. A. (1981) *The Roots of Human Behaviour: An Introduction to the Psychology of Early Development*. San Francisco, CA: W. H. Freeman. [Coat colour in kittens as a function of ambient temperature.]

Jung, C. G. (1971) The stages of life. In J. Campbell (ed.), *The Portable Jung*. New York: Viking. (Originally published in 1933.) [Jung's views of life.]

Kuhlen, P. G. and Johnson, G. H. (1952) Change in goals with increasing adult age. *Journal of Consulting Psychology*, 16, 1–4. [Support for Buhler's view of life from study of teachers.]

Maier, H. W. (1978) *Three Theories of Child Development*. London: Harper & Row. [Erik Erikson's theory.]

Orgler, H. (1973) *Alfred Adler: The Man and His Work*. London: Sidgwick & Jackson. [Alfred Adler's 'three problems of life'.]

Peck, R. C. (1968) Psychological developments in the second half of life. In B. L. Neugarten (ed.), *Middle Age and Ageing: A Reader in Social Psychology*. London: University of Chicago Press. [Peck's refinement of Erikson's life stages.]

Schaffer, H. R. (1982) *Mothering*. Glasgow: Fontana.

Schaie, K. (1975) Age changes in adult intelligence. In D. S. Woodruff and J. E. Birren (eds), *Aging: Scientific Perspectives and Social Issues*. New York: Van Nostrand. [Longitudinal studies of ageing and intelligence discussed.]

Schaie, K. W. and Labouvie-Vief, G. (1974) Generational versus ontogenetic components of change in adult cognitive behaviour: a fourteen-year cross-sequential study. *Developmental Psychology*, 10, 305–20. [Details of 14-year longitudinal study of ageing and intelligence.]

Schaie, K. W. and Stromer, C. R. (1988) A cross-sequential study of age changes in cognitive behaviour. *Psychological Bulletin*, 70, 671–80.

Stafford-Clark, D. (1965) *What Freud Really Said*. Harmondsworth: Penguin. [Freud's ideas and methods.]

Watson, J. B. (1913) Psychology as the behaviourist views it. *Psychological Review*, 20, 158–77. [Watson's views on learning.]

Glossary

Accommodation   a Piagetian term describing the changes which occur in thinking when new objects or experiences are encountered. When an infant discovers that some objects can be sucked but that others cannot, for example, his or her sucking scheme is said to be accommodated to those new objects. Accommodation refers to processes of adapting thinking to new experiences (see also **assimilation; equilibration; schemes**).

Activity theory   a theory that activity and social participation are positively related to well-being in later life.

Adolescence   the stage in development which begins at puberty and ends when physiological or psychological maturity is reached. However, the attainment of maturity is impossible to specify precisely.

Adult–child register   a form of speech, characterized by simplicity, clarity and repetition, typically used by adults when talking to children; also called baby talk or 'motherese'.

Ageism   the existence of unfavourable stereotypes of elderly people expressed by attitudes, beliefs and discriminatory behaviour.

Age norms   the average scores obtained on psychological tests by people at given age levels.

Agoraphobic   a person who is afraid of open spaces. It is the phobic disorder most commonly cited by those seeking psychological or psychiatric treatment. The most common manifestation is a deep fear of being caught alone in a public place. When in threatening situations agoraphobics may experience panic attacks.

Androgens   a collective term for the hormones produced chiefly by the testes, the chief one of which is testosterone. It is responsible for the maintenance and development of many male sexual characteristics.

Androgyny   the combination of masculine and feminine characteristics within an individual.

Assimilation   a Piagetian term describing the changes which occur in thinking when new objects or experiences are encountered. Assimilation refers to the process of altering incoming information to fit a person's existing ways of thinking (see also **accommodation** and **equilibration**).

Attachment   a binding affection, an emotional tie between individuals.

Attachment behaviour   behaviour which promotes proximity and physical contact with the object of the attachment.

Attachment figure   based on Bowlby's theory of infant attachment. Infants are first shown to be attached to their mothers or primary caregivers when they become aware of different people and their roles, at around 9 months. As children get older they may transfer their attachment to an object like a teddy bear or a comfort blanket.

Autistic   a serious disorder of childhood, characterized by a withdrawn state, a lack of social responsiveness or interest in others, serious communicative and linguistic impairments and a failure to develop normal attachments. Autistic children are generally fascinated by inanimate objects and insist on routine, order and sameness.

Autonomic nervous system (ANS)   a major division of the nervous system. It is called autonomic because many functions under its control are self-regulating (or autonomous).

Autonomous morality   Piaget's second stage of moral reasoning, characterized by judgement of intent and an emphasis on reciprocity.

Biological clock   an internal (physiological) mechanism that keeps time or rhythm so that the organism shows by its behaviour that many biological processes are timed. The cycles of such rhythms may vary widely: especially common are daily, tidal, monthly and annual rhythms.

Circular reaction   a Piagetian term describing an infant's repetition of an action after it has produced some observable effect on the environment.

Classical (respondent) conditioning   the process whereby new stimuli gain the power to evoke responses. In the language of learning theorists, if a stimulus, originally neutral with respect to a particular (and natural) response, is paired a number of times with a stimulus eliciting that response, the previously neutral stimulus will itself also come to elicit that response.

Cognition   a person's thoughts, knowledge and ideas about him- or herself and the environment.

Cognitive processes   mental activities involving evaluation and appraisal. They can sometimes be used as equivalent to thought.

Cohort a group of persons born at approximately the same time.

Cohort-sequential study   a complex research design involving two or more longitudinal studies of people of the same age but of different cohorts.

Compensation   a Freudian term describing the process by which unconscious problems can be overcome by acting them out in a stress-free medium, such as play.

Cones   elements of the retina concerned with colour vision.

Conservation   a cognitive advance which Piaget proposed as a central feature of concrete operational thinking acquired at around the age of 7.

Constancy   the fact that an object perceived from different points of view still looks like that object.

Control group   a group in an experiment that is not given the treatment whose effect is being studied (see also **experimental group**).

Conventional morality   the second level of moral judgement proposed by Kohlberg, in which a person's judgements are dominated by considerations of group values and laws.

Correlational study   a study designed to find out the degree of correspondence or association between two sets of measures.

Cross-sectional study   a study in which groups of people differing in age (and thus birth cohort) are tested, and their performance compared, at a single point in time.

Cross-sequential study   a complex research study in which people of different ages are measured at different intervals. It involves a series of longitudinal studies with a cross-sectional twist.

Crystallized intelligence   an intellectual ability which builds upon experience and knowledge.

Cybernetics   the study of systems of control and communication applied by psychologists to animal and human behaviour, and notably to the ways family systems function.

Dependent variable   the behaviour or response, measured in a psychological experiment, which is believed to be changed by the independent variable.

Disengagement theory   a theory which states that withdrawal from social participation is a natural concomitant of old age, and that the withdrawal is positively associated with well-being.

Dyadic model   one-to-one, face-to-face therapy.

Ecological validity   the appropriateness of a given test as an indicator of people's performance, or competence, in everyday situations.

Egocentrism   the tendency to see the world only from one's point of view, which Piaget believed to be a central feature of early childhood, although it is still apparent throughout childhood.

Ego integrity   according to Eriksen, the last developmental stage of life: reviewing our achievements, coming to terms with ourselves and finding meaning and fulfilment in our lives.

Elaborated code   a mode of speaking which is sufficiently rich and varied as to be meaningful without reference to the immediate context (see also **restricted code**).

Electra complex   the Freudian notion that at a certain stage a girl becomes aware that she lacks a penis. She is said to feel 'penis envy' and blame her mother for her feelings of castration. A girl then rejects her mother and turns to her father. The complex is named after the Greek myth in which Electra connived at the death of her mother, who had murdered her father.

Elementary mental functions   a number of basic mental functions, such as perception and attention that Vygotsky proposed children are born with (see also **higher mental functions**).

Empiricists   those who base their views on the fundamental assumption that all knowledge comes from experience (see also **nativists**).

Equilibration   a Piagetian term for describing the process of trying to maintain a state of equilibrium between assimilation and accommodation. In Piaget's theory, the driving force behind development (see also **assimilation** and **accommodation**).

Ethnocentric   a tendency to see things from one's own ethnic or cultural perspective only.

Ethologist   one who researches the behaviour of animals and who works primarily in their natural habitats rather than in a laboratory.

Experimental group   a group in an experiment that is given the treatment whose effect is being studied (see also **control group**).

Figural strategy   an approach to drawing which captures the brond shape of a subject rather than its precise details (see also **metric strategy**).

Fluid intelligence   an intellectual ability not dependent on experience but on the capacity to reason and to perceive relations in novel tasks.

Gender identity   the concept of oneself as either masculine or feminine.

Gender schema   a mental structure that organizes a person's perceptual and conceptual world into gender categories (male–female, masculine–feminine).

Gender typing   people's perception of themselves, and others' perception of them, as being male or female and therefore possessing the characteristics which are thought typical of their biological sex.

Gene   the biological unit of inheritance for all living organisms. Genes are located on the chromosomes, which are inside the cell nucleus. A gene, or a combination of many genes, is responsible for inherited characteristics, e.g. eye colour, personality, components of intellectual ability.

Generativity   according to some theorists, a major concern of people in midlife who recognize the task of encouraging and educating younger generations to take their place and to equal or exceed their achievements.

Genetic epistemology   the study of the origins of knowledge, which Piaget used as a description of his work with children.

Grammar   a model of language use, including the study of speech sounds, words and sentences, and sometimes meaning.

Habituation   the reduction in the strength of a response to a repeated stimulus.

Heritability   the proportion of the variation of a trait within a population that is attributable to the genetic differences between the individuals in that population.

Hermaphrodite   an individual who has both male and female reproductive organs, also applied to individuals in whom there is a contradiction between their external genitals and/ or secondary sexual characteristics and various internal structures, for example gonads.

Heteronomous morality   Piaget's first stage of moral reasoning, ending at 6 or 7 years of age and characterized by moral absolutism and a belief in imminent justice. Judgements are based on consequences rather than on intent.

Higher mental functions   those functions that, according to Vygotsky are developed through social interaction. Examples include mnemonic strategies and number systems (see also **elementary mental functions**).

Holophrase   a single word which serves as, and may have the implicit grammar of, a complete sentence.

Hysteria   a form of neurosis, often involving emotional outbursts and physical symptomatology (e.g. imaginary illnesses, paralysis, etc.).

Ideational fluency   the ability to generate a number of different ideas from a given open-ended problem.

Identification   a process of personality development involving taking on the characteristics of other people.

Imitation   a technical term used by Piaget to describe children's adaptation of their thinking to copy the world around them.

Imprinting   the learning that occurs within a limited period early in life (usually in relation to the mother and likened by Lorenz to a pathological fixation), and which is relatively unmodifiable.

Independent variable   the variable in a psychological experiment which is under the control of the psychologist, and is varied by him or her.

Inflections   endings (such as -ing, -s, -d) added to the stem of a word to modify its meaning, but not its grammatical class.

Intellectual realism   a characteristic of young children's drawing according to which they draw 'what they know, and not what they see'.

Intelligence quotient (IQ)   a person's age-referenced score on an intelligence test.

Intervention study   an experimental approach in which participants are exposed to a particular kind of intervention, something that would not normally happen, and in which the responses are studied after the intervention. Normally the group that receive the intervention need to be compared with a control group that do not receive the intervention. This is often used in educational settings – an example would be a reading intervention programme given to one class whose reading scores are compared after the intervention with another class who did not have the intervention programme.

Lifespan   the genetically fixed life expectancy of members of a given species, barring accidents or major illness before old age.

Longitudinal study   a study in which a group of people of the same birth cohort are tested more than once over a period to measure age-related changes.

Long-term memory   the third phase of the three store model human information processing. Information is transferred to long-term memory from short-term memory. There is no limit to the amount of information that can be stored in long-term memory or to the length of time it can be stored there (see also **sensory registers, short-term memory**).

Magnetic resonance imaging (MRI)   a non-invasive procedure that provides a detailed picture of body tissue. An MRI resembles a CAT (computerized axial tomography) scan but uses a strong magnetic field instead of X-rays. Strong magnetic fields cause the nuclei of some molecules in the body to spin. When a radio wave is passed through the body the nuclei emit energy at various frequencies that are picked up by the MRI scanner; a computer then interprets the pattern of the emissions and assembles a picture of the slice of tissue MRI scans have several advantages over CAT scans and PET (positron emission tomography) scans. They present fine detail more clearly, they do not use potentially damaging X-rays, and they make scans in the sagittal or frontal planes as well as the horizontal planes.

Mean length of utterance (MLU)   a measure of sentence length, either in words or in morphemes (word stems plus inflections), averaged over a number of sentences.

Melodic contour   the 'shape', i.e. the pattern of ups and downs, of a melody.

Metric strategy   an approach to drawing which incorporates the precise details of a subject (see also **figural strategy**).

Monotropism   the innate tendency of an infant to become attached to one individual, with the implication that this attachment is different in kind from any subsequent attachments formed.

Morpheme   the smallest linguistic unit of meaning. It may be a word capable of standing alone (a free morpheme) or a part of a word, such as an inflection (a bound morpheme).

Motherese   a popular term for an adult–child register.

Nativists   those who base their views on the assumption that genetic, inherited influences on behaviour, thought and emotion are of overriding importance (see also **empiricists**).

Non-sequential design   a complex research design in which individuals of various ages are measured at different intervals. It involves a series of longitudinal studies with a Gross-sectional twist.

Object permanence   the concept that objects still exist when they are out of sight, which Piaget proposed was acquired in infancy.

Oedipus complex   the Freudian notion that at a certain stage a boy experiences a conflict between a sexual desire for his mother and punishment (castration) by his father, and which derives from a famous Greek myth.

Ontogenetic   pertaining to the development of an individual organism.

Operant (instrumental) conditioning   the strengthening of a response by presenting a reinforcer if, and only if, the response occurs.

Paradigm   a theoretical model or perspective; a very general conception of the nature of a scientific endeavour within which a given enquiry or psychological intervention is being undertaken.

Parental imperative   the importance, and the demands, of child rearing at the active parenting stage of family life.

Personal Construct Theory a theory of the mind put forward by George Kelly.

Person–job fit the degree to which a person's skills and abilities match the demands of his or her job, and to which the job matches the skills, abilities and needs of the worker.

Phonology the study of recognizably different speech sounds and their patterning.

Polygenic inheritance the action of several genes, the basic units of inheritance (applies to the genetic basis, *inter alia*, of personality and intelligence).

Preconventional morality Kohlberg's first level of morality, in which moral judgements are dominated by a consideration of what will be punished and what feels good.

Principled morality the third level of morality proposed by Kohlberg, in which considerations of justice, individual rights and contracts dominate moral judgement

Privation a lacking of satisfaction, or the means to achieve satisfaction of one's needs (as opposed to deprivation, which is the removal of such means).

Psychoanalysis a method developed by Freud and his followers to treat mental and nervous disorders, in which the role of the unconscious is emphasized.

Psychology the systematic study of cognition (thoughts), emotion (feelings) and behaviour.

Psychometrics the theory and practice of psychological testing.

Psychotic suffering from a mental illness, involving symptoms such as hallucinations, thought disorders, delusions.

Puberty the age at which the sex organs become reproductively functional. It is marked by the menarche in girls, but in boys it is less easy to specify; the growth and pigmentation of underarm hair is often taken as criterial.

Qualitative research research methods that contrast with the quantitative approach and are concerned with subjective data. This research may include verbal or written reports, the use of open-ended questions that have not been converted into points on numerical scales, and case studies.

Quantitative research analysing data as numerical values. This approach is used in traditional psychology, with an emphasis on objectivity and 'the scientific method'.

Reciprocal tutoring a teaching technique based on Vygotskian ideas (see also **scaffolding**).

Reflex a physiological reaction, such as an eye-blink in response to a bright light, over which we have no control.

Regression a return to immature activities and behaviours.

Reliability a statistical index of the degree to which a test provides consistent measurements.

Repertory grid a technique devised by George Kelly to assess personal constructs.

Restricted code a mode of speaking which is not meaningful without reference to the immediate context (see also **elaborated code**).

Rods elements of the retina concerned with black and white vision.

Role theory the explanation of people's behaviour in terms of their acting out social roles.

Scaffolding a method of teaching by which the level of tutorial support is adjusted in response to the child. More tutorial support is given when the child is having difficulties and less support when he or she is successful (see also **reciprocal tutoring**).

Schemes cognitive structures which are abstract representations of events, people and relationships in the outside world.

Semantics the study of meaning.

Sensory registers the first phase of the three store model of human information processing. Information enters the cognitive system from the sensory registers. They hold a large amount of information for a brief period (see also **short-term memory; long-term memory**).

Short-term memory the second phase of the three store model of human information processing. The short-term memory (or working memory) is where all the active thinking occurs.

It has a limited capacity and can store between 3 and 7 units or chunks of information for around 15–20 seconds (see also **sensory registers; long-term memory**).

Sign language   in this book, a natural human language equal in complexity and expressiveness to verbal languages, but in which the 'building blocks' are not verbal but gestural.

Social clock   a particular society's sense of the appropriate ages for achieving life stages, such as finishing education, becoming a parent, entering and leaving employment.

Social learning theory   a theory proposed by Albert Bandura, suggesting that children learn through the observation and imitation of adults' actions. A famous study in which an adult performed violent acts on a large inflatable doll showed that young children imitated the adult's aggressive actions as long as the adult did not appear to be punished.

Sociometric approach   the study of children's friendships using a peer nomination system. Children are given a list or photographs of classmates and asked whom they would most like to play with, how much they like to be with each individual, and so forth. The degree of each child's popularity can then be derived from these peer nominations of liking and disliking.

Somatic   to do with the body; somatic (i.e. physical) symptoms.

Stereotypes   generalized sets of beliefs or attitudes, often inaccurate, about identifiable groups of people.

Symbolic play   play in which children use their own bodies or objects as symbols for other people or objects, and in which they create make-believe or fantasy.

Syntax   the lawful patterning of words and parts of speech into sentences.

Temperament   the constitutional (inherited) aspects of personality.

Theory of mind   a term used to describe the ability to understand that other people have beliefs different from one's own.

Time out   behavioural techniques removing a child temporarily from a situation in which he or she is being reinforced for undesirable behaviour.

Transsexual   a person with a disorder of sexual identity. For example, a transsexual man typically feels himself to be a female trapped in a male body and may want to live as a woman and to have surgery to feminize his body.

Triadic model   working therapeutically through a third person (mediator) to help a child. This may involve training a caregiver to work therapeutically.

Triangular theory   Sternberg's description of the three components of romantic love: intimacy, passion, commitment

Validity   a statistical index of the degree to which a test measures what it is supposed to measure.

Visual realism   a characteristic of children's drawings after the age of 10 or so, whereby objects are represented as they actually appear.

Working memory   the same as short-term memory.

Zone of proximal development   a Vygotskian concept for understanding how learning arises through social interaction. It is the distance between what children can do on their own compared with what they can do with the help of a more able member of their community.

Author Index

Subject Index